READING RACE

Theory, Culture & Society

Theory, Culture & Society caters for the resurgence of interest in culture within contemporary social science and the humanities. Building on the heritage of classical social theory, the book series examines ways in which this tradition has been reshaped by a new generation of theorists. It also publishes theoretically informed analyses of everyday life, popular culture, and new intellectual movements.

EDITOR: Mike Featherstone, *Nottingham Trent University*

SERIES EDITORIAL BOARD
Roy Boyne, *University of Durham*
Mike Hepworth, *University of Aberdeen*
Scott Lash, *Goldsmiths College, University of London*
Roland Robertson, *University of Pittsburgh*
Bryan S. Turner, *University of Cambridge*

THE TCS CENTRE
The Theory, Culture & Society book series, the journals *Theory, Culture & Society* and *Body & Society*, and related conference, seminar and postgraduate programmes operate from the TCS Centre at Nottingham Trent University. For further details of the TCS Centre's activities please contact:

Centre Administrator
The TCS Centre, Room 175
Faculty of Humanities
Nottingham Trent University
Clifton Lane, Nottingham, NG11 8NS, UK
e-mail: tcs@ntu.ac.uk
web: http://tcs.ntu.ac.uk

Recent volumes include:

Occidentalism
Modernity and Subjectivity
Couze Venn

Simulation and Social Theory
Sean Cubitt

The Contradictions of Culture
Cities, Culture, Women
Elizabeth Wilson

The Tarantinian Ethics
Fred Botting and Scott Wilson

Society and Culture
Principles of Scarcity and Solidity
Bryan S. Turner and Chris Rojek

Modernity and Exculsion
Joel S. Kahn

READING RACE

Hollywood and the Cinema
of Racial Violence

Norman K. Denzin

SAGE Publications
London • Thousand Oaks • New Delhi

First published 2002

Published in association with *Theory, Culture & Society*,
Nottingham Trent University

SAGE Publications Ltd
6 Bonhill Street
London EC2A 4PU

SAGE Publications Inc
2455 Teller Road
Thousand Oaks, California 91320

SAGE Publications India Pvt Ltd
32, M-Block Market
Greater Kailash - I
New Delhi 110 048

British Library Cataloguing in Publication data

A catalogue record for this book is available from
the British Library

ISBN 0 8039 7544 9
ISBN 0 8039 7545 7 (pbk)

Library of Congress Control Number available

What Did I Do to Be so Black and Blue? (Ellison, 1952, p. 8)

A marginalized group needs to be wary of the seductive power of realism, of accepting all that a realistic representation implies. (Lubiano, 1997, p. 106)

Hollywood does not represent ethnic and minorities; it creates them and provides an audience with an experience of them. (López, 1991, pp. 404–405)

Contents

Acknowledgments

I would like to thank Stephen Barr and Mike Featherstone for their support of this project. Interactions in the Program in Cultural Values and Ethics, and in the Unit for Criticism and Interpretive Theory at the University of Illinois, and conversations with Joseph Vandiver, Mitch Allen, Peter Labella, Patricia Clough, Laurel Richardson, Yvonna S. Lincoln, James Carey, Clifford Christians, Kim Rotzoll, Walt Harrington, Bill Berry, David Desser, Katherine Ryan, Nate Summers, Johanna Bradley, Richard Bradley, Rachel Denzin, Michael Maehr, Henry Giroux, and Stanford M. Lyman helped to clarify my arguments. I have been teaching portions of this book since 1997. I thank all of the students who joined in the conversation about this project. I especially thank Sylvia Allegretto, Shawn Miklaucic, Michael Elavsky, Jack Bratich, and Mark Nimkoff for their outstanding assistance in the construction of the filmography in the Appendix.

I wish to thank Justin Dyer for his careful copy editing, Mark Nimkoff, Michael Elavsky and Jeremy Toynbee for their meticulous reading of the page proofs, Patricia Hymans for the production of the index, and Rosemary Campbell for her patience and assistance throughout the production process.

Portions of the materials in Chapter 1 appeared in Norman K. Denzin, 'Reading the Cinema of Racial Violence,' *Current Perspectives on Social Problems*, 10 (1998): 30–61; portions of the materials in Chapter 2 appeared in Norman K. Denzin, 'Race and the Grand Canyon,' *Current Perspectives on Social Problems*, 11 (1999): 3–23; portions of the materials in Chapter 4 appeared in Norman K. Denzin, 'Lethal Weapons in the Hood,' *Current Perspectives on Social Problems*, 12 (2000): 149–178; portions of the materials in Chapter 6 appeared in Norman K. Denzin, 'Zoot Suits and Homeboys (and Girls),' *Review of Education/Pedagogy/Cultural Studies*, 2001.

Norman K. Denzin
Champaign, Illinois

Introduction

there is no escape from the politics of [racial] representation. (Hall, 1996b, p. 473)

Films are not necessarily good because black people make them.... Once you enter the politics of the end of the essential black subject you are plunged head-long into the maelstrom of a continuously contingent, unguaranteed, political argument and debate: a critical politics, a politics of criticism. (Hall, 1996a, pp. 443–444)

The contemporary history of race relations in America is, in large part, a history of the representation of violent, youthful minority group members in mainstream Hollywood cinema and in commercial television (Watkins, 1998, pp. 6–7; Gray, 1995, p. 8; Bogle, 1994, p. xviii; Lyman, 1990a, p. 51; Guerrero, 1993a, p. 3).[1] This is a study of one slice of this history, what I call Hollywood's cinema of racial violence; the so-called 'ghetto action film cycle' (Watkins, 1998, p. 8), the 'hood' and barrio movies of the 1990s, those films associated with the new black[2] (and Chicano) realism (Diawara, 1993a, p. 23; Fregoso, 1993, p. xiv; Keller, 1994, pp. 201–202, 207–208; Massood, 1996; Chan, 1998). These films include:[3] *Lethal Weapon 1, 2, 3, 4* (1987, 1989, 1992, 1998), *Do the Right Thing* (1989), *Boyz N the Hood* (1991), *Grand Canyon* (1991), *New Jack City* (1991), *A Rage in Harlem* (1991), *Straight Out of Brooklyn* (1991), *Deep Cover* (1992), *Juice* (1992), *Passion Fish* (1992), *White Men Can't Jump* (1992), *Just Another Girl on the IRT* (1993), *Menace II Society* (1993), *Clockers* (1995), *Dangerous Minds* (1995), *Die Hard With a Vengeance* (1995);[4] *Zoot Suit* (1981), *Colors* (1988), *American Me* (1992), *Bound by Honor* (*Blood In, Blood Out*, 1993), *My Familiy/Mi Familia*, (1995), *My Crazy Live/Mi Vida Loca* (1994), *Set It Off* (1996).[5]

Interpretive Framework

Here I offer a critical race theory, cultural studies (Hall, 1996a, 1996b) analysis of a select number of these racially violent films.[6] My interpretations draw on my earlier treatments of ethnic minorities in recent American cinema (Denzin, 1991a, 1995a, 1997).[7] I will focus primarily on three ethnic and racial groups: African Americans, Hispanics, Latino/as, Chicanos, and Asian Americans.[8]

A several-part thesis organizes my argument. The twentieth century's history of cinematic race relations was shaped by what Myrdal (1944) called the American dilemma. This dilemma reflects a deep-seated conflict between a national creed that endorses the fundamental equality of all persons, and the segregationist and discriminatory realities surrounding the actual treatment of America's racial and ethnic minorities (Myrdal, 1944, p. 24; McKee, 1993, p. 227; also Friedman, 1991b, p. 12; Lyman, 1998; and Ellison, 1964, pp. 303–317; also Ellison, 1986, pp. 132–137; 1996a, p. 111; 1996b, pp. 553–554). Historically, this conflict has produced a two-sided race relations agenda, one played out both in real life and on screen. Myrdal's analysis pathologized the African-American community, finding dysfunction in a reactive, defeatist, overly emotional, and violent culture, including unstable family structures, inadequate schools, high crime rates, superstition, political provincialism, and unwholesome recreational activities (Myrdal, 1944, pp. 928–929).[9] The white man's burden obliges whites to lead non-whites into full assimilation. This will produce integration, 'Americanization' and a version of the melting pot that dissolves racial and ethnic differences (McKee, 1993, p. 131). Only individual prejudice and the absence of self-will and diligence will prevent this ideal racial order from coming into existence (see also Lyman, 1970, p. 6; 1972, pp. 119–120; 1977).[10]

The social science history of America's race relations has attempted to explain why full integration and assimilation have not occurred. This same history attempts to explain why multiculturalism, or the mutual respect of ethnic groups for one another, has been so infrequent (McKee, 1993, p. 264), while pluralism and segregative separatism have been normative.[11] And few predicted the race riots of the 1960s, 1970s, 1980s, and 1990s.[12] Current social science theory, along with Hollywood cinema, now struggles to define the meanings of such terms as separatism, diversity, pluralism, and multiculturalism (see Chapter 1; McKee, 1993, pp. 360–367; Friedman, 1991b, p. 20). Hollywood, like the rest of society, has not been immune to this social science utopian discourse (see below), and the politics of representation that shape it.

The hood movies of the 1990s are stitched into a contemporary version of the American dilemma. These films enact a post-civil rights racial politics. This politics shapes a cinema of racial violence. It contributes to the production of a new racial discourse that connects race to a culture of violence (see also Park, 1996, p. 497).

A majority of Americans know and understand the American racial order through the mass media.[13] Accordingly, those who control the media, including cinema and television, shape and define a society's discourses about race, and race relations. As Hall (above) argues (1996b, p. 473), there is 'no escape from the politics of [racial] representation.' Gray (1995) elaborates, contending that in the 1980s the New Right, under the leadership of Presidents Reagan and Bush, constructed notions 'of whiteness that … [made] appeals to … black male gang members, black male criminality, crumbling black families, black welfare cheats, black female crack users, and black teen pregnancy' (p. 14).

The New Right 'had to take away from blacks (and other persons of color) the moral authority and claims to political entitlements won in the civil rights movements of the 1960s' (Gray, 1995, pp. 17–18). Negative images of 'blackness' and 'brownness' (dark skin) were constructed, and cinematically arrayed 'along a continuum ranging from menace on the one end to immorality on the other, with irresponsibility located somewhere in the middle' (Gray, 1995, p. 17).

Persons of color co-mingled in this complex multidimensional space. But in white, popular, middle-class culture this was not a rainbow coalition; it represented, instead, a menacing blur of dark-skinned, non-English-speaking others, including African and Asian Americans, Mexican, Cuban, Puerto Rican, and other Spanish or non-English-speaking subaltern persons (e.g. Indian). Of course nothing is pure, solely white, black, or Hispanic, or Chicano, or Asian. Instead, hybrid cultural forms interact in the gendered racial and ethnic spaces of popular culture: Chicano and black rap,[14] the violent gang and gangsta rap, Chicano and black gangs, all-woman gangs (on this process see Hall, 1996b, p. 471). These cinematic and televisual representations of race, ethnicity and gender constitute, at the national popular level, America's system of race relations. Seemingly out of control classrooms are nonetheless managed by white women who are ex-marines (*Dangerous Minds*), and by the skin of his teeth, and the help of a good black man (*Grand Canyon*), a white man escapes from the violent racial ghetto streets of Los Angeles, a frightening place presented as if it were a bombed-out foreign city.

This cinematic version of the racial order situates race in the hood, the barrio, and in Chinatown. In these foreign sites the viewer confronts dark-skinned youth, baseball hats on backwards, driving low-riding cars. Threatening, cacophonous sounds reverberate from boomboxes, Chicano and black rap. Complex mixes of black and brown faces confront the white viewer – blacks, Asians, and Puerto Ricans; the subaltern threatening, youthful other is in my face.

The hood, barrio, and gang films of the 1980s and the 1990s answered to and attempted to salvage this political situation. Through the complex act of cinematic representation, these films defined this new (but old) racial order. African-American, Chicano, Asian-American, and white filmmakers produced a conservative cinema of racial violence, a cinema, and cinematic gaze, focused on the violent, destructive features of ghetto life, the very features stressed by the New Right: drugs, the cocaine wars, gangs, gangsta rap, drive-bys, and gang warfare (Sanders, 1994; Reeves and Campbell, 1994).[15] This gaze made the sexuality and violence of the black body the object of a system of spectacular display. This racial gaze was aligned with the laws of patriarchy and the state. It made a spectacle of law and order. It made transgressive black male bodies the subjects and objects of a white panoptic system of social control and surveillance. Thus did the cinematic gaze re-create a visual racial order of represssion and control.

How these films did this, and what its consequences are for race relations in American today, are my topics. Unfortunately, a majority of Americans know the United States racial order through these media representations of the violent ethnic, youthful other.

A New Racial, Cinematic Aesthetic?

Made by a group of young African-American, Asian-American, Chicana, Chicano, and Hispanic film directors (Diawara, 1993a, 1993b; Massood, 1996, p. 85; Keller, 1994; Fregoso, 1993), these films share several characteristics. According to Boyd (1997), the Black Arts Movement of the 1960s and 1970s resurfaces in the 1990s with a new generation of filmmakers.[16] Boyd (1997, p. 25) argued that these directors were using a version of a so-called 'new black aesthetic.' This movement was also called the 'new black realism' (Massood, 1996, p. 88; Diawara, 1993b, p. 23). These filmmakers use the visual and narrative styles of *film noir*; the use of *femme fatales*, a focus on lawbreaking, black rage, despair, violence, and decay (Diawara, 1993b, p. 534). Many examine the concept

3

of a black public sphere, focusing on the competing images associated with police and train stations, churches, barrooms, crack houses, basketball courts, and public housing developments (Diawara, 1993b, pp. 532, 534). These are coming-of-age stories located in the specific geographic boundaries of the hood, the inner-city ghetto, the barrios of South Central Los Angeles, Watts, Brooklyn, and Harlem. The hood or barrio is presented as an internal colonial ghetto, as a multiplicity of public spheres (Diawara, 1993b, pp. 532, 534), as a site of dystopia, of constant police surveillance, of economic impoverishment, racial segregation, and random gang violence (Massood, 1996, p. 88; Moore and Vigil, 1993; Diawara, 1993a, p. 9). These films (e.g. *Do the Right Thing*), like some of the blaxploitation films (*Sweet Sweetback's Baadasssss Song*), transform the bleak ghetto into a place where a moral community, in multiple black public spheres, is daily enacted through personal and group rituals (Diawara, 1993a, p. 9; 1993b, p. 534).

Linear narrative time dominates. The focus is on the present and the future, not the past, as is the case for many space-based narratives that celebrate black history, for example Dash's *Daughters of the Dust* (Diawara, 1993a, p. 13). The films tell coming-of-age, heterosexual stories about young African-American, Chicano, and Asian-American males. In their African-American version, these films are negative toward women (bitches and ho's; Massood, 1996, p. 97). Their soundtracks use and draw upon 'gangsta' and other versions of rap and hip hop musical culture (Rose, 1994; Dimitriadis, 1996; Boyd, 1997, p. 82).[17]

The aesthetic realism of the text is enhanced by the use of this music, the incorporation of hip hop culture into the text, and by the focus on ordinary people and their existential crises (Diawara, 1993a, pp. 13, 24).[18] Diawara (1993a) calls these movies the 'new realism films [because] they imitate the existent reality of urban life in America. Just as in real life the youth are pulled between the hip hop life style, gang life, and education, we see in the films neighborhoods that are pulled between gang members, rappers, and education-prone kids' (p. 25; also 1993b, p. 526b).[19]

In these respects the hood movies stand in contrast to the black action films (blaxploitation) of the 1970s (Diawara, 1993a, p. 11), which 'articulated a discourse of black empowerment ... directed toward a specific black urban audience' (Massood, 1996, p. 87). The black action films (*Shaft*, 1971, 2000, *Sweetback*) featured strong, sexualized black protagonists, and valorized black culture (Massood, 1996, p. 87; Diawara, 1993a, p. 11). These elements are largely absent in the hood and barrio movies of the 1990s.[20]

Between 1967 and 2000, from the post-civil rights period (1960s-mid-1970s) through the Reagan/Bush decade and the Clinton administration Hollywood aided in the containment of America's racial and ethnic minority population through the production of over 500 films featuring the violent ethnic other in a variety of stereotypical situations (for a sampling, see the filmography in the Appendix). In these films the dark-skinned male and female enacted a variety of stereotypical identities, many of which have long cinematic histories: Uncle Tom, Bigger Thomas, Jack Johnson, mammy, Jezebel, Aunt Jemima, prostitute, buck, mulatto, coon, gangsta, welfare queen, Sapphire, red hot lover, crack addict, gang member, low rider, greaser, dragon lady, asexual enuch, geisha girl, Asian rapist, laundryman, cook,

Jap, chink, Chinaman, Fu Manchu, gook, exotic flower (see Wong, 1978, p. 259), cantina girl, self-sacrificing mother or wife, vamp, bandit, gay caballero, faithful Mexican, lazy peasant, good badman, Hispanic avenger, Latin lover, wily señorita (Lopez, 1991, p. 406), colorful spitfire (Keller, 1994, pp. 40–69; Marchetti, 1993, pp. 1–3; Valdivia, 1996, p. 131; Collins, 1991, p. 7; West, 1994, pp. 119–120; Bogle, 1994, pp. 3–10).

These films simultaneously contributed to and helped define a sense of national crisis. A moral epidemic of violence was occurring in the nation's ethnic ghettos. This violence was spilling over into the nation's schools, and into its white suburbs (McCarthy et al., 1996). A culture of violent racial difference was produced. White America was placed on moral alert. Michael Douglas as D-FENS (*Falling Down*, 1993) spoke for many middle-class males when, on the day of his death, he refused to fall down any longer for this virulent, sick, violent ethnic other. (Of course, Douglas was the violent, sick other, killing innocent victims on his day of destruction.) These sterotypes reproduced and perpetuated oppressive images and understandings of the ethnic other. Keller (1994) is quite firm on this, noting that one of the side-effects of an international cinema is its ability to spread 'crushingly brutal ... stereotypical depictions of various outcast races and ethnicities ... to larger audiences than ever before possible around the nation and even around the globe' (p. 5).

The New Politics of Racial Difference

In perpetuating, even as they challenged, these images, these films set the stage for the 1990s attacks on federal affirmative action, social welfare, and education programs. The Republicans' 1996 Contract with America contained no space for the violent, dark-skinned ethnic other. 'Historians of American racial politics may rightly remember the final years of the twentieth century as the "Age of Repudiation" ... the 1990s mark the rejection of the always fragile civil rights [movement]' (Crenshaw et al., 1995, p. xxxii). Hollywood's culture of violent racial difference reinforced a larger conservative cultural agenda that had started in the 1980s.

This agenda was organized by a politics of cultural difference that manipulated the meanings brought to blackness and black- and brown-skinned people.[21] The Reagan/Bush presidencies and the Newt Gingrich agenda for Republican America demonized blackness by focusing on 'welfare queens, the aggressive black female, the menacing black male criminal' (Gray, 1995, p. 165), the cocaine-dealing violent youth gang. This discourse presented blackness and brownness as menaces to white society. In blurring the differences between black and brown skins, this project supported a simplistic racial politics that pitted whites against blacks and other persons of color.

But this approach partially undermined itself from within, perpetuating, while producing, the paradox of the acceptable dark-skinned other. By creating a category of the good dark-skinned other suited for the 1990s, it announced the end of the 'essential black subject' (Hall, 1996a, p. 444). It allowed the concept of race (defined by skin color) to be 'crossed and recrossed by the categories of class, gender and ethnicity' (Hall, 1996a, p. 444). Hall (1996a) addresses the implications of this move for the politics of racial representation: 'You can no longer conduct black politics through the strategy of a simple set of reversals, putting in the place of the bad old essential white subject, the new essentially good black subject' (p. 444). Now good and bad dark-skinned others could do battle with one another. Thus the question of the black or brown subject was both complicated and made more simple. The desire to place African Americans, Hispanics, Latino/as, Chicanos, and Asian Americans within the same simple dark-skinned racial category did not disappear.[22] But the new racial politics resisted such moves.

Still, as Gray observes (1995, p. 165), these strategies served to reinforce 'assimiliationist and pluralist discourses about blackness.' They either rendered blackness (and brownness) invisible (assimilation), or they celebrated exceptional blackness as it supported white values (e.g. Michael Jordan, Bill Cosby). Middleclass whiteness operated as the privileged position for viewing race and the world. This approach made racial and ethnic prejudice an individual problem, thereby repressing matters of economy, work, and racial inequality. It made a spectacle out of those racial moments where all elements of social control seemed absent, or black–white conflict was everywhere present (e.g. the Los Angeles riots; Gray, 1995, p. 170), or African Americans were on trial (O. J. Simpson, the Hill–Thomas hearings).

At the level of the national imaginary, this discourse essentialized racial (and gender) differences, creating a series of cultural oppositions, pitting the ethnic other against a mainstream white America. This discourse naturalized racial and ethnic differences. It contributed to a politics of representation that devalued racial and ethnic difference. It folded racial and ethnic differences into a larger cultural narrative that privileged full assimilation into the American racial order as the proper end-point for all minority group members.[23]

This utopian racial culture is repeatedly reified in the American media, and the hood movies could not escape it. In pitting dark skin against dark skin, they posited acculturation to white goals (education and hard work) as the preferred path out of the ghetto. The paradox of the acceptable dark-skinned other would not go away.

In these ways Robert E. Park's (1950a, p. 150) contested four-stage theory of race relations (which neglected gender) underwrote this representational model (competition, conflict, accommodation, assimilation). The idealized racial other knows his or her place in the racial order of things, and would be fully acculturated and assimilated into this system, including its separatist counterpart. These assimilated ethnic others neutralized previous negative images of the Asian-American, Latino/a, African-American other, and offered to minority group members (and Americans) a particular Americanized version of who they were and who they should be.

Park's highly influential theory (see Lyman, 1990b, 1990c; McKee, 1993, pp. 109–113, 350) was often contrasted with, while sutured into, the internal colonial and ethnic enclave models (see Portes and Manning, 1986; Blauner, 1972; *New Jack City, My Beautiful Laundrette*).[24] The ethnic enclave would be presented as a violent multicultural foreign land (*Do the Right Thing, American Me*) within the American city. Enclave and minority middleman minorities (e.g. Koreans) would mediate between immigrant and colonized minorities.[25] In turn a flawed family role-model theory of socialization (Moynihan, 1965; McKee, 1993, p. 182; Dash, 1996; see also Davis and Dollard, 1940; but see Sanchez-Jankowski, 1991, p. 39; and Fregoso, 1993, p. 127) would be applied to those wayward ethnic youth who fell into the trap of the urban gang, or into the worlds of drug and alcohol abuse (*Boyz N the Hood*, *New Jack City*).

A social and political constructionist view (Nagel, 1986, 1996, p. 243) of the assimilationist and conflictual ethnic identity (*Mississippi Masala*) would then be articulated. This helped to create the illusion of a fluid, pluralistic, utopian, multicultural community. Group violence would be presented as a matter involving territorial battles over the color line (Blumer, 1958, 1965; Lyman, 1990a, 1990b; Pinderhughes, 1997, pp. 14–15). Group prejudice would be defined in terms of a group's sense of social position, or ranking in the hierarchal racial order (*Do the Right Thing*, *Colors*, *American Me*). Individual prejudice would be presented as an issue operating at the personal, psychological level. Versions of the prejudiced authoritarian personality type would be invoked to explain such individuals (Adorno et al., 1950; Lyman, 1990b, p. 141; McKee, 1993, pp. 277–280).

These interpretive theories (which cover the full range of social science [but not cultural studies] race relations theories) can be read into the race and ethnic films of the 1980s and 1990s.[26] They complemented a larger conservative ideology that blamed the ethnic minorities for their problems (Giroux, 1994, p. 75). (This will be examined in greater detail in the next chapter.)

Gendered Group Violence

Gender and group gang violence were central to these films. In the ghetto gang the ethnic male developed a preferred masculine social identity. (Females were submerged into these gangs, often as hot-blooded lovers, while single mothers were presented as oppositional forces to the gang system, e.g. *Colors* and *Boyz N the Hood*). The Hispanic (*American Me*, *Zoot Suits*, *Colors*), Asian-American (*Year of the Dragon*, *True Believer*) and African-American (*Menace II Society*, *Boyz N the Hood*) youth gang was presented as an intermediate social structure standing between family, school, and society.[27] This structure worked against the assimilationist-utopian model (*Grand Canyon*) and was blamed for the failures of ethnic youth to find their proper place in white and non-white society.

A four-fold entangled oppositional system of discourse operated. Gangs were pitted against the family. Youth in gangs were contrasted to non-gang youth who were connected to the safe world of adults who had assimilated or acculturated to white values. Gang members were connected to mothers on welfare. Males were organized against females, and the assimilation model was contrasted to the self-destructive conflict model of internal colonial race relations.

The crack-cocaine wars of the 1980s and 1990s were stitched into this discourse, building on the larger moral panic that circulated in American society during the Reagan and Bush administrations (Reeves and Campbell, 1994). A simple model organized these texts: drugs = gangs; gangs = violence; gangs and drugs are destroying ethnic (and white) America. This destruction reaches out of the inner city into once safe white neighborhoods and schools. The new politics of race blamed America's racial problems on this hardcore inner-city racial order (McCarthy et al., 1996). Getting tough on crime meant getting tough on Asian-American, Chicano/a, and African-American youth.[28]

In these textual representations Hollywood operated and continues to operate as an internal 'orientalizing' agency for the larger American culture. Hollywood cinema worked, that is, as an institutional apparatus that created, described, taught, and authorized a particular view of Asian-American, Hispanic, and African-American culture, and the men, women, and families who live in these racial and ethnic enclaves. It created a system of discourse that represented the 'ethnic and racial other' (gang member) as an 'imaginary other' but 'real' threatening presence who killed not only his peers, but also middle-class white Americans. This view of the ethnic other as a threat to white society presented the ethnic male as a person who was simultaneously excluded and included within the mainstream conservative American cultural framework.

Multiple Systems of Discourse

At least two orientalizing cinematic systems of discourse operated during the late 1980s to 2000 time period. White male directors (Donner, Hopper, Kasdan, Kaufman, Sayles, Scott, Sheldon, etc.) offered their versions of an assimilationist-integrationist discourse (*Grand Canyon, Colors, Driving Miss Daisy, Lethal Weapon 2 and 3*).[29] This conservative discourse stood in almost direct opposition to the films made by a new generation of primarily black, Asian-American, and Chicano male film directors (Burnett, Dash, Duke, Harris, A. and A. Hughes, Lee, Naven, Olmos, Palcy, Parks, Jr, Rich, Singleton, Townsend, Valdez, Van Peebles, Wang, Whitaker; see Masilea, 1993, p. 107; Diawara, 1993a, p. 7; 1993b, pp. 526–528; Guerrero, 1993a, pp. 169–170; Reid, 1993, pp. 112, 128, 131–132).[30] These directors shifted the white man's burden for America's race problem onto their own shoulders. Their films mediated from within the new conservative racial politics, offering narratives that stressed not assimilation but local vernacular counter-racial narratives, and the metaphorical use of an embodied musical vocabulary. The destructive features of ghetto life were examined in realistic detail, as noted above.

Films produced by white male directors contained a kernel of utopian fantasy. As sites of ideological struggle, they projected a world where Americans and alien ethnic others could happily interact within a unified culture. In this culture (*Grand Canyon*) the facts of bigotry, racism, and discrimination were, if not absent, at least easily managed. These films operated as ethnic allegories. Assimilationist (*Grand Canyon*), pluralistic, and separatist (*Passion Fish, Rising Sun*) texts contained ethnic others who became positive stand-ins for the negative ethnic, violent other. At the same time, these characters critiqued and made a parody of the ethnocentric, Eurocentric, racist stereotypes (what Stuart Hall [1996a, p. 446] calls 'inferential racism') that were ascribed to them.

Films produced by ethnic directors were, in many cases counter-utopian (*Menace II Society, New Jack City, Boyz N the Hood*), stressing, in some cases, nihilism and violent self-destruction (*American Me*), while, in others, holding out for a dream of assimilation into or at least acceptance by a multicultural, conflictual racial order (*Mississippi Masala*).

However, as Hall (1996a, p. 443) observes in the opening epigraph to this Introduction, 'Films are not necessarily good because black people make them' (see also Bobo, 1992, pp. 66–67). An application of auteur theory (Guerrero, 1993a, p. 147; also Reid, 1993; Sarris, 1968) to minority filmmakers will not necessarily produce films that are more faithful to some set of so-called 'authentic' group experiences.[31] Films made by both white and non-white directors, with their shifting array of stereotypical heroes and heroines, are intricate constructions. That is, a complex play of voices, images, and sounds from the ethnic margins and the centers of white society interact in each film to produce characters who are not just unitary essences, but rather three-dimensional flesh-and-blood entities (Stam, 1991, pp. 253, 257–258). The ethnic others are not flat stick figures. They are always at the center of 'conflicting and competing voices' that constitute them as subjects within clashing racial and ethnic contradictions. At different moments within any of these films these characters are 'traversed by racist and antiracist discourse.' Each figure becomes a complex construction whose dialogical angle of vision on the American ethnic order is always at the very core of the 'American experience' (Stam, 1991, p. 259). In these ways these films mediate between white and non-white audience members, between insiders and outsiders. They perform 'two seemingly different functions: maintaining symbolic social distinctions and accentuating common American values' (Friedman, 1991b, p. 19). A kind of symbolic ethnicity, close to symbolic kinship, is created (Friedman, 1991b, pp. 19, 27; Gans, 1979).

On the surface Hollywood's internal Orientalist discourse distinguished the dark-skinned ethnic other from the white other, using terms of cultural and racial stereotyping. The white other was presented as the culturally known, familiar, comfortable other; dark-skinned persons were unknown, dangerous, and devious. White persons were rational, virtuous, mature, and normal; the ethnic other was irrational, depraved, fallen, childlike, immature, a danger to society. In these ways American cinema visually manipulated racial and ethnic color lines (see Wong, 1978, pp. 40–41). This perpetuated Hollywood's version of internal Orientalism. This version reinforced the notion of the impenetrable, violent ethnic enclave where youth gangs ran wild.

This Work

In this work I mediate these several discursive systems, seeking a site of cultural criticism that works against a simple oppositional reading of the late twentieth-century American racial order. As argued above, this book continues the project started in three earlier works (Denzin, 1991a, 1995a, 1997). In these works I called for feminist, performative, civic cultural studies that would address the key issues confronting a postmodern America. Race is the unraveled sign of the contemporary age, as Guerrero (1993a) argues, 'the great unspeakable, repressed topic of American cultural life [is] race and racism' (p. 146) Here I appropriate the gazing eye of a white cultural critic, critically reading selected cinematic instances of America's violent racial order. In the eight chapters that follow I hope to chart the way for a more humane, pluralistic, cinematic racial order.

Chapter 1 offers a critical, historical overview of Hollywood's cinematic treatment of African, Asian, Hispanic and Native Americans. I connect this history to the major social science theories of race and ethnicity, moving from images of the melting pot, to current conceptions of the disapora. This history is located in the recent Republican assualts on civil rights, and in the cocaine and gang wars of the 1980s and 1990s. Race is now connected to a culture of violence that is symbolized, at one level, by hip hop and rap music.

The three chapters in Part Two focus on those white moviemakers listed above: Donner, Hopper, Kasdan, Ruben, Sayles, Scott, Shelton, J. N. Smith, and their images of the hood; integrationist pictures of gangs, race, gender, violence, and friendship in the ethnic ghetto. Chapter 2 examines *Grand Canyon* (1991) and *White Men Can't Jump* (1992). These two films fold the problems of gangs and the hood into white, utopian, assimilationist stories about nature, sports, family, intimacy, and white men bearing the partial burden of the black man's situation. Chapter 3 connects race with gender and violence. In *Dangerous Minds* (1995), Michelle Pfieffer, the ex-marine, brings Bob Dylan, order, and intelligence to a classroom in the hood. *Passion Fish* (1992) is a story about a black and a white woman finding friendship and a home for themselves in the multiracial situations (black, cajun, Southern and Northern white) of the Louisana bayou. (Alfre Woodward brings the violence of the Chicago ghettos into this quiet bayou setting.) *A Rage in Harlem* (1991)[32] is based on a novel by Chester Himes (1909–1984), who created a Harlem-based crime and mystery series with two recurring black police detectives, Grave Digger Jones and Coffin Ed Johnson. A coming-of-age comedy, and urban gang film, *A Rage in Harlem*, with its virtually all-black cast, re-creates the vibrant cultural life of black Harlem, complete with 'period atmosphere' (Ebert, 1994c, p. 580), gangs, and violence. In so doing, it challenges the white version of the hood as a place from which to escape. Chapter 4 analyzes *Lethal Weapon* (1987, 1989, 1992, 1998), the quintessential cop-buddy film series of the 1990s, the unfolding story of Danny Glover's attempts to manage life with Mel Gibson. I examine how this series side-steps racial topics while dealing with forms of urban violence ordinarily located in the hood, that is, gangs and drugs. *Lethal Weapon* is a utopian, assimilationist story, only here the white man safely disappears into a black middle-class family.

Chapters 5, 6, and 7, in Part Three, examine black and brown versions of the hood. Chapter 5, 'Boyz N Girlz in the Hood,' focuses on the major African-American hood movies of the 1990s: *Boyz N the Hood* (1991), *New Jack City* (1991), and *Menace II Society* (1993). Chapter 6, 'Zoot Suits and *Homeboys* (and Girls),' studies the major Chicano/Latino barrio films of the 1980s and 1990s, including *Zoot Suit* (1981), *Colors* (1988), *American Me* (1992), and *Bound by Honor* (*Blood In, Blood Out*, 1993), and briefly *Mi Vida Loca* (1994), *Mi Familia* (1995), and *Set It Off* (1996). Chapter 7, 'Spike's Place,' interrogates Spike Lee's assertion that *Clockers* ends the cycle of hood movies. This chapter locates Lee's films within the new black aesthetic movement while criticizing his conservative racial politics.

Chapter 8, the only chapter in Part Four, returns to the cinema of violence and addresses again the problem of an ethnic cinema, a cinema that honors racial and ethnic difference. I revisit the Black Arts Movement of the 1960s and 1970s. I critically assess the hood movies in terms of the civil rights politics of that movement. In screening the race films of the 1990s, I hold them accountable for their images of racial violence, and their uncritical acceptance of a didactic film aesthetic based on social problems realism. I offer readings of two films that do articulate a radical film aesthetic, Zeinabu irene Davis's *Compensation* (1999) and Carl Franklin's *Devil in a Blue Dress* (1995), which is a film adaptation of Walter Mosley's novel of the same name.[33]

This project reflects two concerns. First, for over a decade I have been working with minority summer fellowship students at the University of Illinois studying the images and representations of ethnic minorities in contemporary American cinema.[34] Until recently, my students and I have been confronted by the absence of a coherent body of research in this area, including a basic filmography (but see Guerrero, 1993a; Diawara, 1993a; Reid, 1993; Bogle, 1994). This project attempts to fill part of this void, while building on this more recent work (see the Appendix).

Second, it is my belief that the current generation of college students has the opportunity to make a difference in the race relations arena. A multicultural society that truly values diversity is possible. If this generation is to make a difference, that difference will be defined, in part, in terms of its opposition, resistance to, and acceptance of the media's representations and interpretations of the American racial order. This study is intended to contribute to these understandings (and resistances).

Notes

1. Of course this is an international history. American cinema is a global industry, producing a commodity that circulates in the world community. In the arena of race relations this commodity often informs and defines the spaces of an oppositional Third World cinema (see Hall, 1996a, p. 447). In writing about these films and topics, I take my lead from Kellner (1997), who states 'I am aware that there can be problems with a white male professional in a privileged race, class, and gender position writing about African-American culture and politics, but I would argue that it is important for people of different identities to explore the terrain of difference and otherness' (p. 101).

2. Following contemporary linguistic convention, I will generally characterize blacks as African Americans, whites as whites, Hispanics as Latinos (or Chicanos), and Asian Americans as members of specific transnational groups, e.g. Korean American, etc. (see Ablemann and Lie, 1995, p. xii). After Ablemann and Lie (1995, p. xii), I argue that these racial and ethnic categories are constructed products of specific historical negotiations and struggles.

3. These are the films discussed in this study.

4. To this list of African-American hood films, I add the following films that focus on the barrio.

5. The barrio movies have not been systematically compared to the hood movies, although Keller (1994) observes of the gang movies that in the 1970s the 'Hispanic, or multiethnic versions of the genre really took off ... [and] other films of the general strip didn't single out Hispanics, but merely included them among other various and sundry riffraff: *Dirty Harry ... Fort Apache – the Bronx*' (p. 162). Ro (1996, pp. 5–6) historically connects current gangsta rap, hip hop fashion, and screen (video) images of the 'gangsta rapper' to Chicano gangs, with their concepts of the pachuco, 'cholo' or 'zoot suit' (Gonzales, 1993, p. 159) style of dress and speech, barrio (hood) pride, tattoos, low riders, partying, and cruising. Van Der Meer (1984, p. 6) notes how black and Hispanic youth came together

to create and forge hip hop culture in the early 1980s, and Rose (1994) argues that by the late 1980s Mexican, Cuban, Puerto Rican, and other Spanish-speaking rappers were making 'lyrical bridges between Chicano and black styles' (p. 59; see also Lipsitz, 1994, p. 23). Ro (1996) discusses the merger and overlap between Chicano and African-American gangs in Los Angeles from the 1970s through the 1980s when cocaine was introduced into the gang world (see also Sanders, 1994, pp. 129–130, 139–140). Moore and Vigil (1993, p. 42) trace the major Chicano gang systems in Los Angeles to the 1920s, noting, however, that by the 1990s black gangs like the Crips and the Bloods were receiving the bulk of the media attention. Sanders (1994) argues that the origin of contemporary African-American gangs in Los Angeles can be located in the 'late 1960s and early 1970s [in] the south-central and Compton areas' (p. 39), the site of the most recent Los Angeles hood movies (e.g. *Boyz N the Hood*). Lipsitz (1994, p. 23) discusses the recently formed pan-ethnic alliances connecting black, Chicano, and Asian antiracist, nationalistic youth groups in the Los Angeles area. McCarthy et al. (1996) observe that in Watts and South Central Los Angeles 'black people are outnumbered by Latinos and Asian Americans' (p. 131). But see Park (1996) on the racial conflicts and racial politics underlying recent Korean–Black relations in South Central Los Angeles.

6. This framework is informed by critical race theory in contemporary legal studies, that theory that is concerned with how race consciousness, 'race and racial power are [experienced] constructed and represented in American society' (Crenshaw et al., 1995, p. xiii). This theory takes the law as the site of analysis, attempting to construct engaged, adversarial, oppositional readings of the law and the ways in which the law has perpetuated regimes of racism in American. I apply these principles to Hollywood and the cinema of racial violence (see also Feagin, 2000, p. 204).

7. Terms, traditional definitions: *ethnicity*: 'the synthesis of biological, fictive ancestry, and cultural elements … a basis of diversity within and between racial categories' (Stanfield, 1994, p. 175); a cultural term (McKee, 1993, p. 132); 'the conscious and imaginative construction and mobilization of [cultural] differences' (Appadurai, 1996, p. 14); *ethnic group*: a minority group identified by language and religion (Healey, 1995, p. 542); 'a community of people who see themselves as descended from common ancestors and whom others consider part of a distinct community' (Nagel, 1996, p. 9); *race*: a biological term (skin color, hair texture) and social construct of dubuious scientific value (Healey, 1995, p. 24; McKee, 1993, p. 130); *racial minority group*: a group primarily identified by physical characteristics such as skin color; *racist cosmetology*: the use of cosmetics by whites to simulate other racial groups; the focus on external racial differences, e.g. the epicanthic fold, skin color, hair style; a racist method of representation that gives white actors the freedom to play non-white parts, while displacing minority actors from major (and minor) roles (Wong, 1978, p. 40); *racial slur*: name-calling based on racial stereotypes, e.g. gook, nip, slit-eye (Wong, 1976, p. 36); *racial disclaimer*: the use of racial slurs followed by a correction, or apology, or statement that 'racist terms are not intended to represent actual members of a racial group, living or dead (Wong, 1978, p. 39); *white racism*: the believe that 'white people are inherently superior to non-white people' (Wong, 1978, p. 3); *white racial prejudice*: the unquestioned acceptance of white racist beliefs (Wong, 1978, p. 5); *white racial discrimination*: the physical demonstration of white prejudice (Wong, 1978, p. 5); *individual racism*: the personal implementation of white racism (Wong, 1976, p. 6); *cultural racism*: the individual and collective coupling of white racism to notions of presumed cultural inferiority (Wong, 1978, p. 6); *institutional racism*: those institutional practices that exclude persons of color from full and equal participation in a society's institutions; those practices that reproduce, at the institutional level, racist ideologies and practices (Wong, 1978, p. 7); *racial (and ethnic) cultural politics*: the processes that challenge essential racial (and ethnic) identities (e.g. black), while connecting these identities to matters of class, gender, and sexuality (Hall, 1996a, p. 447). This process produces hybrid cultural identities. As Appadurai (1993) argues, America has become 'a federation of diasporas, American-Indians, American-Haitians, American-Irish, American-Africans … the hyphenated American might have to be twice hyphenated (Asian-American-Japanese, or … Hispanic-American-Bolivian)' (p. 424).

8. The following films represent, or make reference to, the violent, Asian youthful gang: *Chan is Missing* (1982), *Year of the Dragon* (1985), *Black Rain* (1989), *True Believer* (1989), and *Rising Sun* (1993). See Fung (1994) for a discussion of recent independent films produced by North American men and women of Asian- American descent.

9. Ralph Ellison (1964) rejected Myrdal's reactive analysis of African-American culture, asking 'But can a people (in its faith in the American Creed notwithstanding) live and develop for over

300 years simply by *reacting*? Are American Negroes simply the creation of white men ... why cannot Negroes have made a way of life upon the horns of the white man's dilemma?' (pp. 315–316).

10. This assimilation model has recently come under considerable attack: it essentializes racial identity; ignores the processes surrounding hybridity and diaspora; glosses gender; minimizes differences and heterogeneity within so-called 'mainstream' culture; reduces race (and ethnicity) to identity, thereby ignoring the politics of racism, and the ways in which race is transformed into power; and discriminates against separatist impulses, leading immigrants to suppress ethnicity in the name of opportunism (see Fine et al., 1997; Aguilar-San Juan, 1994, p. 9; Shah, 1994, p. 122; Radhakrishnan, 1994, p. 221; but also Du Bois, 1920; Garvey, 1969). Nagel (1996) contrasts right and left models of American race relations, noting that in the decades after World War II, 'social science thinking on both the right (assimilationist models) and the left (class models) predicted the end of ethnicity' (p. 19). But this did not occur. As Nagel notes, the melting pot did not assimilate most non-whites, and 'the resurgence of ethnic identification among American whties ... called into question both social science and popular assumptions about the inevitable decline of ethnicity' (p. 19).

11. This leads to the production of a complex vocabulary, a narrative that distinguishes types and stages of assimilation and pluralism. This language ignores the criticisms discussed in note 8. Thus, under this model, assimilation, defined as the process by which separate groups merge and intergroup differences decrease (Healey, 1995, p. 59), has two types; melting pot and Americanization (or Anglo-conformity). There are two stages to assimilation: acculturation and integration. Under acculturation, a minority group learns the culture of another group. In the process of integration a minority group enters and virtually disappears within the primary and secondary social structures of the dominant society. In contrast, under pluralism (Healey, 1995, p. 59), groups maintain their differences. According to this typology, there are three types of pluralism. Cultural pluralism exists when there is no integration or acculturation; different groups exist side-by-side in their cultural and ethnic differences. In structural pluralism, acculturation occurs, but without integration. Conversely, integrative pluralism occurs when groups are integrated into the primary and secondary sectors of a society, but acculturation does not occur. Enclave and middleman minority groups supposedly exhibit this type of pluralism (Healey, 1995, p. 59).

12. For example, two-thirds of America's black population live in segregated areas, and most black children attend schools with a black majority; one third attend schools that are 90–100 percent minority (Healey, 1995, p. 275).

13. And the obverse holds for the minority group member who knows the white other through media (and musical) representations (see also Allison, 1994, p. 451). Allison (1994) quotes Ice Cube, 'Most whites don't know what goes on in this world.... The record will be as close as most people get to us' (p. 451). This racial order was represented in the above films, and in such commercial television shows as: *The Jeffersons, The Cosby Show, Family Matters, True Colors, Frank's Place*, and *Living Color* (Gray, 1995, pp. 82–83). In these spaces white and non-white viewers reflexively encounter representations of whiteness and non-whiteness (Gray, 1995, p. 1640).

14. Precedents for contemporary Latin and black hybrid musical formations can be found in the Latin (Afro-Cuban) and Bossa-Nova jazz traditions. The first Bossa-Nova recordings appeared in 1954 (Laurindo Almeida). Afro-Cuban jazz can be traced to the early 1920s and extends into the present with the performances of Tito Puente, Dizzy Gillespie, Mario Bauza, and the current Afro-Latin world musical scene (e.g. Rubén González).

15. Salvation followed one of three paths: higher education, athletics, or the gang world, drugs and single parenthood (Massood, 1996, pp. 20–21). And each path combined competing images of race, ethnicity, and sexuality. As Marchetti (1991, p. 289) notes, race and sexuality are always intertwined in Hollywood cinema (as they are in real life). And race in the ghetto is never far from sexuality, and the threat of sexual contact between white and non-white racial, ethnic and economic groups (see Marchetti, 1991, p. 289).

16. I discuss the Black Arts Movement in detail in Chapter 8 (also see hooks, 1990, p. 104; William J. Harris, 1998, p. 1344; and Fuller, 1997).

17. This music appeals to a cross-over audience who 'idealize African Americans as primal, and exotic' (Staples, 1996). A key audience is white male teenagers, or 'wiggers' (Coleman, 1993), who seek to be hip by wearing the hip hop uniform, 'baseball cap turned backward, pants [that are] too big and [adopting] the swagger' (Staples, 1996; Wagner, 1996); images associated with the outlaw in this

culture (Dimitriadis, 1996, p. 188). This music is often violent, nihilistic, and misogynistic (see Gilroy, 1995, 2000). The films forge an immediate link between this music and the presence of violent gang members in any situation. Hence the presence of rap in a soundtrack lends authenticity to the representation (see Hall, 1996b, p. 469; also Perkins, 1996; Fernando, 1994; Toop, 1984). Recall the expression of fear on Kevin Kline's face in *Grand Canyon* when a car filled with black youth pulls up to his stalled vehicle. The viewer, with Kline, first hears gangsta rap, then sees the car. The connection between the music was further solidified by fact that rap performers (Ice-T, Tupac Shakur) also starred in hood films (*New Jack City, Poetic Justice, Gridlock'd*). In the late 1980s and early 1990s the music video medium (Dimitriadis, 1996, p. 188) carried this music into the homes of white youth (Yo, MTV, MTV Raps, BTV).

18. As Altman (1987, p. 62) notes, every film has two soundtracks: the diegetic, which carries realistic sound (traffic noises in a street scene), and the music track (instrumental and vocal accompaniment, the theme song played over the lovers' kiss). In the hood movies of the 1990s rap and hip hop music became a regular part of the diegetic soundtrack. In films like *White Men Can't Jump, Boyz N the Hood*, and *New Jack City* there is a constant cross-over between the two soundtracks: music appears in the diegetic track, and diegetic sounds are transformed into music. Thus these films broke down the 'barrier separating the two tracks' (Altman, 1987, p. 62). This had the effect of blurring the borders and boundaries between the real (the everyday) and the ideal (the musical).

19. A so-called 'new generation gap' in the black community centers on rap and hip hop culture (see Leland and Samuels, 1997).

20. In a parallel, but paradoxical, vein, the Chicano barrio gang films of the 1980s and 1990s (e.g. *Boulevard Nights*, 1979, *Zoot Suit*, 1981, *Stand Alone*, 1985, *The Principal*, 1987, *Colors*, 1988, *Hangin' with the Homeboys*, 1991, *American Me*, 1992, *Bound by Honor*, 1993) speak to a level of empowerment largely absent in the African-American hood movies. The 1980s was designated by the Coors Corporation as the 'Decade of the Hispanic' (Fregoso, 1993, p. 22), and several films in the gang genre were financed by Coors, including *Zoot Suit, Boulevard Nights, Defiance*, and *Walk Proud*. Four films released in 1987 and 1988 were dubbed by the industry and the mass media as 'The Hispanic Hollywood Phenomenon' (Keller, 1994, p. 163; Fregoso, 1993, p. 39). These films were *La Bamba* (1987), *Born in East LA* (1987), *The Milagro Beanfield War* (1987), and *Stand and Deliver* (1988). They were called a new cultural hybrid, and were seen as exploiting a 'wider "nostalgia" trend in popular (American) culture' (Fregoso, 1993, p. 39). Following Fregoso (1993, pp. xiv–xxi) and Keller (1994, p. 192), I will read the history and record of Hispanic, Mexican-American, Latin American, Latino, Puerto Rican, Cuban American, and other US Latino films back through the category of Chicano, connecting this re-reading to the emergence of a 'film culture *by, about*, and *for* Chicanas and Chicanos' (Fregoso, 1993, p. xiv, italics in original; but see also Noriega and López 1996, p. xiii; also Noriega, 1992a, 1992b).

21. After Gray (1995), I use blackness to refer 'to the constellation of productions, histories, images, representations and meanings associated with black (and non-white) presence in the United States' (p. 12).

22. This essentializing move was repeatedly challenged by the hood movies. Their politics of representation insisted on good and bad brown and black subjects.

23. Given the current state of affairs in America (see note 8 above), full assimilation is an utopian dream. In addition to the assimilation mode, Gray (1995, p. 84) argues that commercial television in the 1980s also represented pluralist (separate but different) and multiculturalist (upper middle-class diversity) racial narratives. These were clearly ideological texts, for throughout the twentieth century America ideologically endorsed an assimilationist model of race relations, but in reality employed residential, occupational, religious, and educational segregationist practices. Thus full assimilation meant dark-skinned persons disappeared into the racial order. Throughout the twentieth century miscegenation was forbidden. It was declared unconstitutional in 1967 (Cortes, 1992, p. 84), and prohibited by Hollywood's production codes until the mid-1960s. *Guess Who's Coming To Dinner* (1967) would break through this barrier to assimilation. See Cortés (1992, pp. 83–84), Marchetti (1991), and Wong (1976, pp. 23, 26) on the application of the code's miscegenation rule to Latinos and Asians (also Lyman, 1970, p. 143).

24. According to McKee (1993, pp. 135–36, 145–46, 350), Park's model also included the neglected notion that a race-conscious black population with a culture of its own would develop in America, and

this would involve 'an image of a racial future marked by militant action, conflict, and possible violence, instead of one of gradual, peaceful change leading to increased tolerance and social acceptance' (McKee, 1993, p. 146). But Park (1950b) also said that 'The Negro is, by natural disposition, neither an intellectual, nor an idealist.... His metier is expression rather than action. He is, so to speak, the lady among the races' (p. 280; see Ellison's [1964, p. 308] comments on this assertion).

25. This is dramatically represented in the treatment of the Korean grocer in Spike Lee's *Do The Right Thing*, who proclaims, after the race riot, 'Me no white. Me no white. Me Black. Me Black. Me Black' (see Fung, 1994, p. 167; also Park, 1996; and Reid, 1997a, p. 10).

26. *Do the Right Thing* presents the ethnic ghetto as an enclave, where Italian and Korean middle-men mediate community economic activity, groups and gangs battle over territorial boundaries, pre-judice is a result of flawed, psychological beliefs, and ethnic identities are carved out of constructed meanings brought to gender, age, dress, music, and public demeanor.

27 As Keller (1994, p. 161) observes, 'gang films, focusing on juveniles, date back ... to the silent period [in Hollywood], with the bad boy films'. Race-based gang films have been present since Griffith's *Birth of a Nation* (1915), and have gone through several cycles, stressing and then ignoring race: 1930s: our gang, depression-era representations (*Dead End*, *Tough Guys*, *Boys Town*); 1940s–1950s: post-war, social consciousness films (*Blackboard Jungle*); the non-gang, but 'Negro cycle' films of 1949 (*Home of the Brave*, *Pinky*, *Intruder in the Dust*, *Lost Boundaries*); 1960s: Hispanic youth gang (*West Side Story*, *The Pawnbroker*, *The Young Savages*, *Wild Angeles*); 1970s: Hispanic and blaxploitation gang films (*Shaft*, *Badge 373*); 1980s: black, Asian and Hispanic-focused gang films (*Year of the Dragon*, *Colors*, *American Me*, *Zoot Suit*, *The Principal*, *Do the Right Thing*).

28. In August 1996 Gary Webb, a journalist for the *San Jose Mercury*, published a series of stories alleging that the CIA 'had full knowledge of a ploy by South American drug lords to funnel cocaine to inner-city ghettos (and gangs – the Bloods and the Crips) as a means of funding the CIA-backed Contra rebels during the '80s civil war in Nicaragua' (Malinxe, 1997, p. 27; also Katz, 1996; but also Purdum, 1997, for amendments to this story).

29. Actually the films negotiated assimilationist, pluralist, and separatist multicultural racial spaces. At the same time they gave power and prestige to those who embodied white assimiliationist values and identities.

30. Reid (1993, pp. 135–136) argues for a distinction between studio-backed and black indepen-dent films, arguing that independent films are more responsive to the needs of the black community, while being subversive of the film styles and stereotypes that circulate in studio-distributed films.

31. Film auteur theory (and criticism) argues that a director's politics and cinematic style (use of *mise-en-scène*) shape the work in question. Each director has a personal/cinematic style (like a writer). At one level auteur theory would argue that only blacks or women can make accurate films about blacks or women, etc. (see Hall, 1996a, pp. 443–444; and on recent criticisms of auteur theory, Bordwell, 1996, pp. 4–6). But see Guerrero (1993a, p. 195) on attempts to turn Eddie Murphy into the next Cary Grant.

32. Directed by Bill Duke, an African American.

33. With his Easy Rawlins series, Walter Mosley, the author of *Devil in a Blue Dress*, has created for Los Angeles what Hines did for Harlem; namely the use of a white genre form (the mystery) to produce a celebration of black culture within a particular historical period and locale.

34. These students are called McNair Fellows and SROP Scholars.

Part One: reading race

1

The Cinematic Racial Order

Classic Hollywood cinema was never kind to ethnic or minority groups ... be they Indian, black, Hispanic, or Jewish, Hollywood represented ethnics and minorities as stereotypes.... Classic Hollywood film [is] ethnographic discourse. (López, 1991, pp. 404–405)

I want to read America's cinematic racial order through a scene from Spike Lee's highly controversial 1989 film *Do the Right Thing* (see Bogle, 1994, pp. 319–320; Guerrero, 1993a, pp. 148–154; Reid, 1997a). I will move backward and forward from this scene, offering a truncated genealogical history of America's cinema of race and ethnicity (see Friedman, 1991b). I will argue that the films constituting this cinema (see Table 1.1; also the Appendix) can be read as modernist realist ethnographic texts, stories and narrative histories that privilege whiteness, and an assimilation-acculturation approach to the race relations problem in America (see López, 1991, p. 405; Chow, 1995, p. 176; Denzin, 1997, pp. 75–78).[1]

These films are tangled up in social science theories of race, ethnicity, and the American racial order, including arguments about eugenics, nativism, race-relations cycles, melting pots, authoritarian personalities, internal colonial models, multiculturalism, and theories of disapora and pluralism. As realist ethnographies, as texts that perform situated versions of the racial order, these films have created and perpetuated historically specific, racist images of the dark-skinned ethnic other (see Wong, 1978). This racist imagery extends, like a continuous thread, from *Birth of a Nation* through *Boyz N the Hood*. How these films have done this and what its consequences are for race relations today is my topic. But first Lee's movie.

Doing the Right Thing

In a pivotal moment, near the film's climax, as the heat rises on the street, Lee has members of each racial group in the neighborhood hurl vicious racial slurs at one another:

Mookie to Sal: (and his Italian sons – Vito and Pino): Dago, Wop, guinea, garlic breath, pizza slingin' spaghetti bender, Vic Damone, Perry Como, Pavarotti.

Pino to Mookie (and the blacks): Gold chain wearin' fried chicken and biscuit eatin' monkey, ape, baboon, fast runnin', high jumpin', spear chuckin', basketball dunkin' ditso spade, take you fuckin' pizza and go back to Africa.

Table 1.1   *The Cinematic Racial Order and American Theories*
of Race Relations, 1900–2000 (representative films)

	African American	Asian American	Hispanic	Native American
Race theories (1900–1920): eugenics, nativism				
1900–1920	*The Birth of a Nation*	*Broken Blossoms*	*Martyrs of the Alamo*	*Squaw Man*
Race theories (1921–1930): race relations cycle, white man's burden, riots				
1921–1930	*Our Gang*	*The Mystery of Dr Fu Manchu*	*Davey Crockett at the Fall of the Alamo*	*The Scarlet West*
Race theories (1931–1940): melting pot, assimilation, cultural inferiors				
1931–1940	*Gone with the Wind; The Littlest Rebel*	*Charlie' Chan's Chance*	*Flying Down to Rio; Song of the Gringo*	*The Last of the Mohicans*
Race theories (1941–1950): black Metropolis, melting pot, riots, American Dilemma				
1941–1950	*Miracle in Harlem; Pinky*	*Bataan; Charlie Chan in Rio*	*Below the Border; Border Buckaroos*	*Red River; Duel in the Sun*
Race theories (1951–1960): authoritarian personality, desegregation, melting pot, personal prejudice				
1951–1960	*Porgy and Bess; The Defiant Ones*	*A Yank in Korea; Teahouse of the August Moon*	*Left-Handed Gun; Touch of Evil*	*The Big Sky; Apache; The Lone Ranger*
Race theories (1961–1970): civil rights, race riots, black power, miscegenation outlawed				
1961–1970	*Guess Who's Coming to Dinner*	*My Geisha; Green Berets; M*A*S*H*	*For a Few Dollars More; West Side Story*	*Comancheros; Geronimo*
Race theories (1971–1980): separatism, school integration, internal colonial models, Miami riots				
1971–1980	*Shaft; Cotton Comes to Harlem; Coffey*	*Tora! Tora! Tora!; McCabe and Mrs Miller*	*The French Connection; Dirty Harry; Badge 373*	*The Outlaw Josey Wales; Billy Jack*
Race theories (1981–1990): multiculturalism, gangs, cocaine wars, Miami riots				
1981–1990	*48 Hours; Clara's Heart; Lethal Weapon*	*Chan is Missing; Year of the Dragon*	*Zoot Suit; Colors; La Bamba*	*Dances With Wolves*
Race theories (1991–): pluralism, disapora, multiculturalism, affirmative action, riots				
1991–present	*A Rage in Harlem; Malcolm X*	*The Joy Luck Club*	*American Me; Mi Familia*	*Thunderheart; Geronimo*

Sources: Bataille and Silet, 1985; Bogle, 1994; Guerrero, 1993a; Keller, 1994; Richard, Jr, 1992; McKee, 1993; Boyd, 1997

A Puerto Rican man to the Korean grocer: Little slanty eyed, me-no speakie American, own every fruit and vegetable stand in New York, Bull Shit, Reverend Sun Young Moon, Summer 88 Olympic kick-ass boxer, sonofabitch.

White cop: You goya bean eatin' 15 in the car. 30 in the apartment, pointy red shoes wearin' Puerto Ricans, cocksuckers.

Korean grocer: I got good price for you, how am I doing? Chocolate, egg cream drinking, bagel lochs, Jew ass-hole.

Sweet Dick Willie to the Korean grocer: 'Korean motherfucker ... you didn't do a goddamn thing except sit on your monkey ass here on this corner and do nothin'. (see Denzin, 1991a, pp. 129–130)

Race and Ethnic Relations in Lee's World

Lee's speakers are trapped within the walls and streets of a multiracial ghetto (Bed-Stey). Their voices reproduce current (and traditional) cultural, racial, and sexual stereotypes about blacks (spade, monkey), Koreans (slanty eyed), Puerto Ricans (pointy red shoes, cocksuckers), Jews (bagel lochs), and Italians (Dago, wop). The effects of these 'in-your-face insults' are exaggerated through wide-angled close-up shots. The speaker's face literally fills the screen as the racial slurs are heard. These black and white, Korean, Puerto Rican, and Hispanic men, women and children exist in a racially divided urban world, a violent melting pot. Here there is little evidence of assimilation to the norms of white society. (There is no evidence of the black middle class in this film.) Complex racial and political ideologies (violence versus non-violence) are layered through subtle levels and layers of sexuality, intimacy, friendship, hate, love, and a lingering nostalgia for the way things were in days past.

Prejudice crosses color lines. But racial intolerance is connected to the psychology of the speaker (e.g. Vito). It is 'rendered as the *how* of personal bigotry' (Guerrero, 1993a, p. 154, italics in original). The economic and political features of institutional racism are not taken up. That is, in Lee's film, 'the *why* of racism is left unexplored' (Guerrero, 1993a, p. 154, italics in original).

Even as racial insults are exchanged, Lee's text undoes the notion of an essential black, white, Korean, Puerto Rican, or Hispanic subject. Each speaker's self is deeply marked by the traces of religion, nationality, race, gender, and class. Blacks and Koreans inhabit an uneasy, but shared, space where, in the moment of the riot, the Korean grocer can claim to be black, not Korean. Lee's world is a cosmos of the racial underclass in American today. This is a world where persons of color are all thrown together, a world were words like assimilation, acculturation, pluralism, and integration have little, if any, deep meaning. Lee's people have been excluded from the social, economic, and political structures of the outside white society.

In this little neighborhood's version of the hood, differences are ridiculed and mocked. Separatism is not valued, although intergroup differences are preserved, through speech, music, dress, and public demeanor. Indeed, like ethnic voyeurs, or middle-class tourists, the members of each ethnic group stare at one another and comment on how the racially and ethnically different other goes about doing business and daily life. These separate racial and ethnic groups are not merging into a single ethnic entity.

Only in a later film, *Clockers* (1995), will Lee take up the 'insidious, socially fragmented violence' (Guerrero, 1993a, p. 159) of the hood films of Singleton, Van Peebles, and the Hughes brothers. Cheap guns, crack-cocaine, gang and drug warfare are not present in *Do the Right Thing*. But a seething racial rage is, a rage that is deeper than skin color. This is a rage, even when muted, that attacks white racism, and urges new forms of black, Korean, Puerto Rican, Hispanic, and Latino nationalism.

Thus is evidenced a reverse form of ethnic nativism: disadvantaged racial group members stereotyping and asserting their superiority over the ethnically different other. Victims of racial hatred, they reproduce that hatred in their interactions with members of different racial and ethnic groups. The benefits of the backlash politics of the Reagan and Bush years are now evident (Guerrero, 1993a, p. 161). Fifteen years since Reagan came in of playing the race card, fifteen years of neo-conservative racial nativist national politics come home to roost. The nation's racist, crumbling, violent, inner-city ethnic enclaves have become 'violent *apartheid* environments' (Guerrero, 1993a, p. 159, italics in original).

And so *Do the Right Thing*, as realist ethnographic text, marks one ending for one history of the race relations story in America today: that ending that has race riots, and racial minorities attacking one another.[2] This ending demonstrates the paucity and tragedy of nativist and liberal assimilationist (and pluralist) desegregation models of race and ethnic relations (McKee, 1993, pp. 360–367). It is as if the clock had been turned back to 1915 and everyone was watching D. W. Griffith's *Birth of a Nation:* white men in Klan hoods attacking coons who are sexually threatening the sexuality and lives of white women. The birth of a new racist nation.[3] But how to start over?

In the Beginning: Creating a Cinema of Racial Difference

There is no fixed place to start the conjunctural history of America's cinematic racial order. Even before Griffith's *The Birth of a Nation* (1915), earlier silent films, including *Chinese Laundry Scene* (1894), *Uncle Tom's Cabin* (1903), and *A Gypsy Duel* (1904), were presenting racist views of American race relations (Guerrero, 1993a, p. 9; Keller, 1994, pp. 10–11), Nonetheless, by the mid-1920s Hollywood had firmly put in place a system of visual and narrative racism (Wong, 1978, pp. 2, 73–75) that privileged whiteness.[4] This system solidified what would be a near-century-long version of racial and ethnic stereotypes. These stereotypes would be fitted to the cinematic representation of African, Hispanic, Native and Asian Americans. 'Rarely protagonists, ethnics merely provided local color, comic relief, or easily recognizable villains and dramatic foils' (Lopez, 1991, p. 404). The effect of this marginalization produces the standard assessment. Hollywood's ethnic representations were (and are) 'damaging, insulting and negative' (Lopez, 1991, p. 404).

Here I offer one version of this cinematic history, a racial and ethnic genealogy that cross-cuts gender, class, geography, and social science writings on race and ethnicity (McKee, 1993). This is a structural history. It emphasizes key historical moments and structural processes that shaped the representations of minority group members in American cinema during the twentieth century. These processes operated differently for each racial and ethnic group.

Following López (1991), I argue that it is possible to 'pinpoint a golden or near-golden, moment when Hollywood, for complex conjunctural reasons, sees the light and becomes temporarily more sensitive to an ethnic or minority group' (p. 406). These moments vary for each minority group (see below): after World War II for Jews and Latin Americans; after the civil rights movement of the 1960s for Hispanic, Asian, African, and Native Americans (López, 1991, p. 406). In these moments history is rewritten. Previous stereotypical representations are rejected and new understandings and stereotypes are constructed (López, 1991, p. 406).

With Lopez (1991, p. 405). I want to read these films, and their historical moments, as situated, modernist, naturalistic ethnographies (see Denzin, 1997, pp. 75–76). These cultural texts factually, authentically, realistically, objectively, and dramatically present the lived realities of race and ethnicity. These films perform race and ethnicity (Lee's Pino talking to Mookie), and do so in ways that mask the filmmaker's presence. This supports the belief that objective reality has been captured. These texts bring racial and ethnic differences into play through a focus on the talk of ordinary people and their personal experiences.

These are ethnographies of cultural difference, performance texts that carry the aura and authority of cinematic mimesis. They 'realistically' reinscribe familiar (and new) cultural stereotypes, for example young gang members embodying hip hop, rap culture (on the dystopic features of rap, see Gilroy, 1995, p. 80). These representations simultaneously contain and visually define the ethnic other. This is a mimesis that rests on the conditions of its own creation: white stereotypes of dark-skinned people.

These texts are cultural translations; they exoticize strange and different racial worlds, often revealing the 'dirty secrets' (Chow, 1995, p. 202) that operate in these exotic worlds. Borrowing from Chow (1995, p. 202), who borrows from Taussig, contemporary race and ethnic films constitute a 'novel anthropology.' The object of these texts is not the exotic world itself, but 'the West itself mirrored in the eyes and handiwork of others' (Chow, 1995, p. 202). As translations, these films bring positive and negative attention to the ethnic culture in question (Chow, 1995, p. 202). In so doing, they risk betraying the very world they valorize, for its meanings have now been filtered through the lens of the filmmaker as ethnographer.

Structural Commonalities

Hollywood's treatment and representation of the ethnic other have been shaped by the following factors and processes: (1) nineteenth- and twentieth-century racist ideologies; (2) a pre-existing racist popular culture; (3) an early, racist silent cinema; (4) the advent of sound film (*The Jazz Singer*, 1927); (5) a widely understood racist performance vocabulary; (6) gender-specific cinematic racial stereotypes connected to (7) a series of film types and genres; (8) a segregated society that reproduced these cinematic stereotypes; (9) a pre-existing star system contained within a vertical integrated studio production system[5] (Keller, 1994, p. 112) that used a racist film production code; (10) the production of literary and dramatic works with racial themes that could be made into movies, including those in the post-World War II realistic social consciousness, social problems tradition (1947–1962; Cook, 1981, p. 401; Keller, 1994, p. 127); (11) minority directors, actors, and actresses seeking cinematic work, expanding minority theatre audiences, and the appearance of theatres in racial ghettos (Bogle, 1994, p. 105); (12) America's military history; (13) the civil rights and women's movements of the 1960s and 1970s.

A brief discussion of each of these dimensions is required. I will then argue that each minority group has a different history with these structural processes. These are disjointed histories. They are marked by ruptures and interruptions, by the absence of continuity.

Nineteenth- and twentieth-century racist ideologies affirmed the white man's burden in the arena of race relations; celebrated Anglo-Saxon nativism;[6] emphasized the uncivilized nature of dark-skinned persons, and their threat to white society (including women); favored a 'melting-pot' assimilationist philosophy of racial difference (Musser, 1991, p. 39; Keller, 1994, p. 5); set immigration quotas; endorsed laws against miscegenation and integration; and sustained a commitment to racial conflict and genocide, when necessary.

A preexisting oral (storytelling), print (comic books, dime novels), performative, and visual (vaudeville, minstrel shows) popular culture of racial differences shaped and supplemented the cinematic representation of America's racial order (Keller, 1994, p. 5). These cultural texts drew upon the above beliefs and provided early cinema with a repertoire of racist cultural images.[7]

Early, silent cinema (1900–1926; see Mast, 1976, p. 221), through the use of racial stereotypes, racial slurs, and racist cosmetology (blackface), told comedies and other stories about the racially inferior (and threatening) ethnic other. (On the ethnic and racial comedies, see Musser, 1991.) Silent cinema used white actors and actresses in blackface (Bogle, 1994, p. 26). This ended with the release of *The Jazz Singer* in 1927. This film signaled the need for 'real Negroes in Negro roles' (Bogle, 1994, p. 26)[8] and marked the popularity of film musicals, an idiom connected with black cultural life (Bogle, 1994, p. 26).[9] This opened the door for an indigenous American black cinema that flourished from the 1920s to the 1940s (Bogle, 1994, p. 105).[10]

These films helped shape an ethnically specific visual, racist performance vocabulary. This vocabulary has precise terms and looks for blacks (toms, mammies; see Bogle, 1994, p. 4); Asians (chinks, gooks; see Wong, 1978); Native Americans (redskins, good Indians; see Bataille and Silet, 1985); Hispanics (greasers, half-breeds; Keller, 1994, p. 13), and members of other ethnic groups (Jewish, Irish, Italian, etc.). As argued in the Introduction, this performance vocabulary was a central part of the cinematic racial gaze.

Visual (and vocal) excess were central to this performance vocabulary, which was historically specific (see below). Visual excess focused on costume, performance style, sexuality, and musicality.[11] Visual repertoires implemented racial and ethnic stereotypes; thus for blacks: stoop-shouldered, banjo playing, shuffling black males in blackface, wearing work clothes; for one version of the black women: jolly, smiling happy Aunt Jemimas; for Asians: opium dens, slant-eyed, self-deprecating, small-boned males with Fu Manchu moustaches; and for Asian women: reed-slender, kimono-garbed Madame Butterflies; for Native Americans: teepees, dogs, horses, mountains, brown-skinned men (and women) with painted faces, bows and arrows, and braided hair; for Hispanics: gay caballeros, zoot suits, greasy hair, guitars, sombreros, flowing, colorful skirts, guitar music.

Vocal excess emphasized the inability of the ethnic other to speak ordinary English. Garbled, slurred speech and racially coded phrases connected to each minority group were developed, including, for blacks: Yo, git, jest, Bro; for Hispanics: thick, impenetrable accents, the use of Spanish phrases, i.e. 'I keel ze man sis morning' (Keller, 1994, p. 65); for Asians: pidgin English. Wong (1978, p. 215) offers this example from *Chinatown* (1974). In responding to Jack Nicholson, a Japanese gardener observes, 'Salt water velly [very] bad for glass [grass].'

The speech of Carmen Miranda, the best-known Latin American actress of the 1940s, for example, was constantly characterized by the presence of 'cultural impurities … disturbing syncretisms … accents … shifting registers of tone and pitch … and linguistic malapropisms' (López, 1991, p. 416). As Valdivia (1996) observes for Latinos, 'the endurance of the accent in the stereotypes stems from the mistaken characterization of all Latinos as recent, and quite often illegal, immigrants' (p. 131). Broken speech places the ethnic other outside the American mainstream.

This visual and verbal vocabulary often defined otherness and difference in sexual, not racial or ethnic, terms (López, 1991, p. 410), thereby maintaining the theme of miscegenation while preserving barriers between whites and non-whites. Thus the bodies and sexual demeanor of classic Latin actresses (Delores Del Rio, Lupe Vélez) were defined as exuding smoldering, irresistible sensuality and sexuality (López, 1991, pp. 410, 412). Called 'hot-blooded Latin temptresses' (López, 1991, pp. 410, 412), these women were presented as being attractive to (and attracted to) Anglo men. On-screen miscegenation was not allowed (see note 16 below; and López, 1991, p. 412).[12]

This performance vocabulary was fused with stereotypical gender-specific identities fitted to each minority group. These identities were connected to the appearance of major and minor parts in American movies for blacks, Asians, Hispanics, Native Americans, and representatives from other racial and ethnic groups.

According to Keller (1994, pp. 37–69), eleven identities were developed for Hispanics, three for women (cantina girl, faithful, self-sacrificing señorita, vamp) and eight for men (greaser, bandit, bad Mexican, gay caballero, i.e. Zero, Cisco Kid, good Mexican, good badman, Hispanic avenger, Latin lover). As previously noted, Bogle (1994, pp. 3–4) lists five basic (and classic) black characters: tom, coon (pickaninny, Uncle Remus), tragic mulatto, mammy, brutal black buck.[13] Asian characters divide between Fu Manchu and Charlie Chan types, conniving businessmen, gang members, brutal military officers, laborers, cooks, dragon ladies, and Geisha girls (see Marchetti, 1991, 1993, Wong, 1978).[14]

These character types were stitched into film genres and film types. For Hispanics, this meant Latin musicals (and Latin lovers), Westerns, and films with themes such as the border, bullfighting, the Mexican Revolution, the barrio and gangs, prison, drugs, Acapulco, and family and immigration (Keller, 1994). Asian character types were primarily fitted to adventure, crime and mystery, war, and Westerns (Wong, 1978, p. 197), and the latter genre also reserved, of course, for Native Americans. Blacks, like Asians, have been cast in any film requiring a servant. While blacks have not been confined to a specific genre, black actors and actresses, until recently, have not been cast as major characters in mainstream Hollywood cinema. Unlike Hispanics, or Native Americans, blacks are not immediately associated with a specific genre (e.g. Latin musical, Western).[15]

A racially and ethnically segregated society (education, leisure, work, religion, residence) helped to define, embody, and reproduce the cinematic racial order and its pervasive stereotypes. These stereotypes were perpetuated by a segregated film industry. Central to the industry's racial self-consciousness was the development of a production code (1922–1934, 1968, 1972) that prohibited miscegenation and sexual relations between and across racial boundaries (see Cook, 1981, pp. 214–215, 266–267, 442–444).[16]

Hollywood needed stories to tell. There were ample literary works and dramatic plays telling stories about race and ethnic relations that could be adapted to the screen (*Gone with the Wind*, *Charlie Chan's Courage*, *West Side Story*, *The Last of the Mohicans*, *Dances with Wolves*) and to one or more film genres (comedy, family melodrama, Western, women's film).

Since the turn of the twentieth century there has been (especially for blacks) a growing pool of minority group talent to support these films: production companies (Reol, Gate City Film), theatres, directors (Micheaux), actors (Robinson, Gilpin, Moreland), and actresses (Horne, McKinney) who could direct or be cast in these films (Bogle, 1994, p. 105). This group would, after the 1960s, become more active in the cinematic representation of African Americans (see Guerrero, 1993a; Bogle, 1994; Reid, 1993; Keller, 1994; Wong, 1978; Marchetti, 1993).[17]

America's cinema of racial representation is intimately connected to wars and the military. Virtually every major American war (Independence, Civil, Native American, Alamo, Spanish–American, World Wars I and II, Korea, Vietnam, etc.) has occasioned attempts to align minority males with the American war effort, while often identifying the enemy as the self-same foreign, ethnic other. Thus there have been good and bad Asian (*M*A*S*H*),[18] Native American (*Thunderheart*), Hispanic (*The Alamo*), and black soldiers (*Glory*, *Soldier's Story*). The high death count of the ethnic other cannot be minimized. Wong (1978) notes that the film industry has emphasized the Asian death theme 'by way of kill ratios and filmic body counts. The assumed cheapness of Asian life is an integral part of America's cultural perception of Asia' (p. 239). (This theme has recently been extended to the hood movies, where the body count of dark-skinned youth is always very high.)

The civil rights and women's movements of the 1960s and 1970s challenged long-standing racist and sexist representations of America's major minority groups.[19] These movements helped create the conditions for ethnically indigenous political cinemas. Thus the 1970s and the 1980s were associated with politically self-conscious black, Asian-American, and Hispanic cinemas.[20]

Reading the Cinematic Racial Order

On the surface, Hollywood's version of the racial order appears to be seamless and continuous, a constant history of undifferentiated derogation and racist (and ethnic) stereotyping that applies across each racial and ethnic group (but see López, 1991, p. 404). This image is sustained, in part, because a series of common structural factors shaped Hollywood's representations of the ethnic other, including those discussed above: the sound, star, genre, and studio production system, the larger system of racism (and miscegenation) in American culture, the major foreign wars of the twentieth century, and so on. That is, each minority group was confronted with a racist system of cinematic representation.

However, a minority group's place in the cinematic racial order was (and is) shaped by how and when it entered this system of structural commonalties. In turn, each group's history is marked, as López (1991, p. 406) notes, by multiple moments of revisionist racial enlightenment, by new forms of representation and interpretation that are aligned with current perceptions.

This suggests that America's cinematic racial order is a fractured, discontinuous system of representation, a system that is constantly being revised in light of new understandings. These revisions move in two directions at the same time. In some instances they return to the beginning, to reinscriptions of those moments when the minority group is defined as entering American society.[21] In other forms, the revision attempts to correct, or alter, ongoing representations of the group, for example contemporary challenges to the violence in the hood movies (Weinraub, 1997), or claims that these films treat women in negative ways (hooks, 1990, p. 180). In both instances, the revision and its meanings are connected to other representations and anchored in specific historical contexts (see Hall, 1996c, p. 435).

Thus under the white Eurocentric model, African Americans entered the system as slaves, products of a plantation system and a civil war. Native Americans were treated as enemies of the state, to be placed on reservations, their native cultures destroyed. Asian Americans represented a threatening barbarian foreign presence in American culture (Wong, 1978, p. ii). They needed to be destroyed, assimilated, or otherwise put in the service of the state. Hispanics were a diverse group (Keller, 1994): Mexicans who wanted to control the Alamo, lawless, Mexican revolutionaries, greasers, half-breeds, part-Indians, Spanish and Latin aristocrats, Latin American politicians.

This historical relationship with the state shaped Hollywood's representations of each ethnic group. That is, this relationship defined how the group originally entered into the system of cinematic representation (slave, bandit, halfbreed, barbarian, etc.). Each group, in turn, fitted this relationship to its own structural history with the state and with Hollywood's cinematic apparatus.

African-American Cinema

The cinematic representation of blacks, decade by decade, from 1900 to the present alternates between four basic race relations models: pure segregation (plantation) stories (1930–1945 – e.g. *Gone with the Wind*); mid-century (1947–1962) social consciousness, assimilation films examining the negative consequences of segregation (e.g. the 'Negro Cycle' films of 1949); post-1970 movies that examine the positive benefits of assimiliation (the *Lethal Weapon series*); and post-1970 films that repudiate assimiliation, stressing, instead, black separatism and life in the hood (the blaxploitation films of the 1970s, and the hood films of the 1990s; see Table 1.1; also the Appendix, African-American films).

Bogel and Guerrero both note that by the early 1920s blacks had their own star and film production system, and were creating films that challenged racist images contained in Griffith's *Birth of a Nation*, and the earlier *Uncle Tom's Cabin*. The 1920s featured the comic Negro, the jester, the blackface tradition, and cute little black children.[22] The sound system in the 1930s created an important place for black (*Hearts in Dixie, Hallelujah, Porgy and Bess*) and Latin (*Flying Down to Rio, Mexicana, Carnival in Costa Rica*) musicals. The decade is represented by Mr Bojangles, Stepin Fetchit, Rochester, Hattie McDaniel, respectable servants and domestics in the kitchen, Paul Robeson, Butterfly McQueen, and ends with *Gone with the Wind.*

Two significant features defined the black 1940s. The first was the continued presence of black entertainers, including the sophisticated use of jazz performers (Duke Ellington, Count Basie, Louis Armstrong) and black singers (Lena Horne, Ethel Waters). These films used musical scenes unconnected to the narrative that could be cut if audiences objected to seeing a Negro on the screen (Bogle, 1994, p. 121).[23]

The second feature involved the emergence of the 'New Negro' film cycle, connected, in part, to the social consciousness film movement, which extended from 1947 to 1962. The Roosevelt administration forbade racial discrimination in war industries (Bogle, 1994, p. 137), and soon the film industry was offering more parts to blacks. A new group of black actors and acresses presented a 'New Negro' who challenged earlier stereotypes.[24] This figure emerged as a sympathetic human being, a strong woman, a feeling man, a doctor, soldier, minister, law student.[25] The 'New Negro' instances a significant revisionist moment in Hollywood's representation of African Americans. As noted in the Introduction (note 27), the 'Negro Cycle' films of 1949 (Cook, 1981, p. 401), examined previously taboo topics: passing as white, tragic mulattos, and racial intolerance. These films opened the spaces for the major (and minor) black stars of the 1950s.[26]

The 1950s: the Eisenhower decade, black and white television, the Korean War, the Supreme Court desegregation decision of 1954, bus boycotts, Jackie Robinson, Martin Luther King, federal troops march in Arkansas (Bogle, 1994, p. 160). This is the age of forced integration in America's schools, but not its residential neighborhoods, or the workplace. Dorothy Dandridge (*Carmen Jones*, 1954), Sidney Poitier (*Blackboard Jungle*, 1955), and Ethel Waters (*Member of the Wedding*, 1952) emerged as stars, blacks who could carry films to a mass white audience (Bogle, 1994, p. 161). Four themes dominated in these films: stories of the tragic mulatto (*Show Boat*, 1951, *Raintree County*, 1959); representations of the exotic, quaint, fake world of blackness (*Carmen Jones*, *St. Louis Blues*, *Porgy and Bess*); accounts of black–white male (and female) bonding (*Defiant Ones*, *Edge of the City*, *Member of the Wedding*); and tales of integration and its problems.

The national doctrine of integration created a space for an actor like Poitier, a model integrationist hero. Poitier was a paragon of black middle-class values. He was intelligent, educated, a conservative dresser. He did not carry the cultural baggage of the black ghetto, 'No dialect. No shuffling' (Bogle, 1994, p. 176). He did not threaten the white middle class. Poitier would move these non-threatening integrationist themes into the 1960s (*Raisin in the Sun*, 1961, *In the Heat of the Night*, 1967, *Guess Who's Coming to Dinner*, 1967).

The flaws in the simplistic doctrine of integration would be exposed in the 1960s, transition years, when racism 'would be revealed as a national sickness' (Bogle, 1994, p. 193). More deeply, the institutional roots of racism would be uncovered, and the limits of a personal, psychological approach to racism made apparent.

This is the decade of the civil rights movement, the great liberal experiment, televised violence on the evening news, Vietnam, the assassinations of Martin Luther King, Malcolm X, and the Kennedy brothers, the Black Panthers, Stokely Carmichael, H. Rap Brown, Angela Davis, riots in Watts, Detroit, Harlem, South Philadelphia, Cleveland, Chicago, Washington, DC, a racially divided society coming apart at the seams (Bogle, 1994, p. 219). It was liberally 'chic and hip to understand the black man's style, even to speak his jazzed-up dialect' (Bogle, 1994, p. 219), listen to his music, buy African art, and participate in civil rights and anti-war protests. At the same time, white audiences marveled at Poitier's elegance and Hepburn and Tracy's chic white gruffness in the last of the old-style integrationist films, *Guess Who's Coming to Dinner* (Bogle, 1994, p. 218).

But during the 1960s, mainstream Hollywood was primarily silent on civil rights (and Vietnam). Poitier's integrationist films (noted above) were major exceptions, as were Jim Brown's war and Western action films (*Rio Conchos, Dirty Dozen, Dark of the Sun*; Bogle, 1994, p. 221).

Four black art films at the beginning of the decade (*Shadows*, 1961, *The Cool World*, 1963, *One Potato, Two Potato*, 1964, *Nothing But a Man*, 1964), and four new-style black films released in 1969 (*Uptight Slaves, The Learning Tree, The Lost Man, Putney Swope*) marked the beginning of the black separatist movement that would define the 1970s (Bogle, 1994, p. 194). In these films the black film-making community, as it had done in the 1940s with the 'New Negro' films, quietly spoke out on the issues of mulattos and interracial marriage. Only now new elements were added to the mix: the emasculation of the black male by white society (*A Raisin in the Sun*), black matriarchs, drugs, violence, whores, hustlers, addicts, pimps, pushers, gangs, rage, and despair in the black ghetto (Bogle, 1994, p. 195).

The 1970s was a a revisionist decade for black cinema. It was called the decade of 'The New Black Hollywood' (Bogle, 1994, p. 257). For the 'first time in film history, the studios produced black-oriented films pitched directly at pleasing blacks' (Bogle, 1994, p. 232). The new black movie boom of the 1970s focused on the following types of films: blaxploitation (*Sweet Sweetback's Baadasssss Song, Shaft, Super fly* – action films with the pimp/outlaw/rebel as folk hero; Bogle, 1994, p. 236); black community comedies (*Cotton Comes to Harlem*); action and war films starring black athletes (O. J. Simpson, Rafer Johnson, Jim Brown, Fred Williamson); black family films (*Sounder*); women's films, including action (*Coffey*), and tragic romances (*Lady Sings the Blues*); Richard Pryor's black–white male bonding comedies (*Silver Streak*); black musicals (*The Wiz*).[27]

As argued in the Introduction, the blaxploitation and black comedies of the 1970s celebrated life in the black urban community (usually Harlem), including 'black roots ... and the trappings of the ghetto: the tenements, as well as the talk, the mannerisms, and the sophistication of the streets' (Bogle, 1994, p. 236; Boyd, 1997, p. 89). These films laughed at and with the old black characters (congenial coons, toms, painted ladies; Bogle, 1994, p. 234). They flaunted black power, crossed previously taboo class and sexual boundaries, and challenged racism at all levels of white society. In stressing a militant form of black separatism, some rejected the assimiliationist values of the black middle class. At the same time many of these films treated black women as prostitutes (Bogle, 1994, p. 236).

The 1980s, the 'tan decade' (Bogle, 1994, p. 268), can be read as a return to the 1960s, 'black performers in supporting roles in big-budgeted, general white releases' (Bogle, 1994, pp. 268–269): Louis Gossett, Jr (*An Officer and a Gentleman*), Carl Weathers (*Rocky*), Billy Dee Williams (*Nighthawks*), Gregory Hines (*White Nights*), Danny Glover (*The Color Purple*), Morgan Freeman (*Driving Miss Daisy*). With few exceptions (*Do the Right Thing*, 1989) the black activism of the 1970s, with its black rebels and folk heroes, was absent. Assimiliationist stories predominated, from male bonding and action films (*Lethal Weapon, Die Hard, 48 Hrs*), to black–white comedies starring Richard Pryor (*Stir Crazy*), Eddie Murphy (*Beverly Hills Cop, Trading Places*), and Whoopi Goldberg (*Jumpin' Jack Flash*). The concept of a corrupt racist system was not part of Hollywood's discourse under the Reagan/Bush administrations (Bogle, 1994, p. 267; also Page, 1997, p. 107). Films did all they could 'to make audiences forget the blackness of a black star' (Bogle, 1994, p. 268). Blackness was fitted to a white cultural context. Black stories (*The Color Purple*) were told within a white, Disney-like, Victorian melodramatic format (Bogle, 1994, p. 293).

Five films at the end of the decade took up blackness from a white revisionist perspective. *Cry Freedom* (1987), *Mississippi Burning* (1988), *Bird* (1988), *Glory* (1989) and *Driving Miss Daisy* (1989). A sixth end-of-the-decade film, Euzhan Paley's *A Dry White Season* (1989), examined racism in South Africa. Important new independent filmmakers emerged, who were examining blackness for a black audience: Charles Burnett (*To Sleep with Anger*), Julie Dash (*Daughters of the Dust*), Spike Lee (*She's Gotta Have It, School Daze, Do the Right Thing*), and Robert Townsend (*Hollywood Shuffle*). Denzel Washington was defined as the new Sidney Poitier. The decade ended with Lee's *Do the Right Thing*, a return, with new multicultural themes, to the militant black separatist films of the 1970s (Reid, 1997a).

Thus do Lee's texts segue into the hood moves of the 1990s: *New Jack City, Boyz N the Hood, Menace II Society*, rap, hip hop, and repetitions of old stereotypes towards women. New and previously established black filmmakers, actors, and actresses gain power and recognition.[28]

Hispanic Cinema

Now Hispanics. On the surface, Hollywood's treatment of Hispanics parallels its treatment of blacks; namely the reproduction of stereotypes (greasers, half-breeds, red-hot lovers) stitched into a discontinuous film history moving between segregation, assimiliation, and separatist narratives. However, the situations of the two groups cannot be easily fitted into a single historical model. Hispanics have a complicated relationship to Anglo cinema culture, a relationship that is confused by several factors.

The word 'Hispanic,' like the words 'Latino,' 'Chicano,' 'Mestizo,' 'Mexican,' and 'Spanish American,' contains multiple meanings, including those connected to such identity markers as race, ethnicity, gender, sexuality, and politics (Noriega and López, 1996 p. x).[29] These meanings blur with other factors involving language group (Castillian and Chicano Spanish, North Mexican dialect, Tex-Mex; see Anzaldua, 1987, p. viii), intermarriage (*Mestizo*), nationality (Mexico, Spain, Native American, the United States, Latin America, Cuba, Puerto Rico, Colombia, Dominican Republic, etc.), region, and city (Miami, New York, Los Angeles, Texas, Southwest, California, etc.).

Thus various accounts of 'Hispanic' cinema (Richard, 1992; Keller, 1994; Hadley-García, 1990; but see Noriega, 1992a, 1992b, 1996; Noriega and López, 1996; Fregoso, 1993) write this history through the word 'Hispanic,' and through the various 'Hispanic' themes that have been present in American cinema since the silent era (Keller, 1994, p. 1). This produces a series of discontinuous, decade-by-decade, regional, and genre-driven discrete histories that often cross-cut the above categories (see Keller, 1994, p. 3): the Zorro, Cisco Kid and Bronco Billy cycles; Hispanic, Spanish, and Mexican California; the Latin musical; Spanish classics (Don Juan, Carmen); Black Legend;[30] the Mexican Revolution of 1910; the Alamo, soldier of fortune, Mexican bandit, cowboy-Western,[31] half-breed, prison, barrio, immigration, drug, and Acapulco films.

The only constant throughout all of this are the stereotypes that spill over from one genre to another. These stereotypes cluster around a small set of negative meanings, including barbarian, greaser, lustful, treacherous, untrustworthy, lawless, and violent. In turn, these meanings circulate around those shifting points of reference marked by non-whiteness (dark and brown skin), impenetrable accents, and the words 'Hispanic,' 'spic,' 'Mexican,' and 'half-breed.'[32]

Noriega and López (1996) clarify this complex structure of meanings and factors, arguing that all Latino films 'be approached through the matrix of differential histories ... the ethnic or subnational (Chicano, Puerto Rican, Cuban American); the interethnic and interminority;[33] the panethnic or national ... (Latino, Hispanic); the mainstream, or national (American); and the hemispheric or international (Latin American)' (pp. xii–xiii).[34]

So there is no single 'Hispanic' cinema. There are only multiple 'Hispanic' cinemas that work back and forth against one another (and the white mainstream) in every decade and period since the silent era. Thus the (1898–1926) silent era (see Keller, 1994, pp. 5–12; Richard, 1992) is marked by films about Mexicans, cowboys, and Indians (*Eagle Dance*, *Pueblo Indians*, 1898, *The Life of a Cowboy*, 1906), noble savages (*The Redman and the Child*, 1908), the Spanish-held Philippines (*Filipinos Retreat from the Trenches*, 1899), the Spanish–American War of 1898 (*Battle of Manila Bay*, 1898), Hispanic gypsies (*A Gypsy Duel*, 1904), greasers (*The Greaser's Gauntlet*, 1908), miscegenation (whites, Mexicans, and Indians) and half-breeds (*The Half-Breed's Sacrifice*, 1912, *The Squaw Man*, 1914),[35] Aztecs (*The Fall of Montezuma*, 1912), the birth of Texas (Griffith's *The Martyrs of the Alamo, or The Birth of Texas*, 1915), and Latin lovers (*The Pleasure Buyers*, 1926).

As early as 1913 there were protests against the film industry and its negative representations of Hispanics. During the pre-World War I period the Mexican government, without success, called for more 'sensitive' portrayals of Spanish-speaking persons by Hollywood. In response to these and related complaints from other foreign markets, the film industry followed one of two strategies: the use of imaginary settings for their racist stories, or the removal of certain scenes that might be offensive to a particular foreign audience (Keller, 1994, p. 116). In 1922 the Mexican government formally banned all films produced by two American production companies (Famous Players-Lasky and Metro; Keller, 1994, p. 117).

These protests continued into the 1930s. The advent of sound created the space for Dolores Del Rio, Lupe Velez, Carmen Miranda, singing cowboys, B Western buddy films (Roy Rogers–Dale Evans, Gene Autry–'Smiley Burnett', Lone Ranger–Tonto, Red Rider–Little Beaver), the Latin musical and for the use of Latin actors and actresses who would speak with Spanish accents.

The Good Neighbor Policy (1933–1947) of the Roosevelt administration opened the door for friendly, less racist pictures of Hispanics (López, 1991, p. 407).[36] Over one hundred films made during this time period, including classic genre films (*Notorious*, *1946*), musicals (*Road to Rio*, 1947), and musical comedies, countered decades of representing 'Latin Americans ... as lazy peasants and wily señoritas who inhabited an undifferentiated backward land' (López, 1991, p. 406; but see Keller, 1994, pp. 117–119).

The social consciousness, social problems films of the 1947–1962 period produced sympathetic images of Hispanics, including youth gang films (e.g. *Blackboard Jungle*), courtroom (*The Lawless*, 1950) and boxing dramas (*Right Cross*; see Keller, 1994, p. 129). These films, like earlier texts in this tradition (*Bordertown*, 1935), were assimilitation narratives (Berg, 1992, p. 39), stories about Mexicans attempting to enter the American mainstream. They also positioned the marginal minority group member as a threat to mainstream culture, thereby perpetuating their version of the American dilemma (see Berg, 1992, p. 39).[37]

There was no 'Hispanic film' cycle in this period, as there had been for blacks. However, films like *Broken Arrow* (1950) and *The Searchers* (1956) addressed, even as they reproduced, previous negative images of the American Indian (Keller, 1994, p. 128).[38] A new wave (1949–1953) of Western (*The Ox-Bow Incident, High Noon, My Darling Clementine, Vera Cruz*), border (*Wetbacks*), and Good Samaritan films presented Anglos fighting bad Mexians on behalf of good, but defenseless and passive, Mexicans (e.g. *The Mysterious Desperado*, 1949) and wetbacks (*Headline Hunters*, 1955; see Keller, 1994, p. 131).[39]

Still, in films like *Lawless* (1950) and *Salt of the Earth* (1954), an important shift in the assimilation narrative occurs. The openly racist films of the silent and early sound era presented 'spics' as lazy and no good (Keller, 1994, p. 132). This justified the racist hatreds and scapegoating behavior of whites. Such a model ignored the institutional basis of racism. *The Lawless* and *Salt of the Earth* draw a connection between personal and institutional racism, showing 'the deplorable working and living conditions of the Chicano community ... [and showing] how Chicanos' rights were violated by Anglo industrial interests' (Keller, 1994, p. 132).

Four events in the 1960s significantly shape Hispanic film (Keller, 1993, pp. 150–151): the civil rights movement (see Noriega, 1992b, p. 141);[40] the repeal of miscegenation laws; the development (in Italy) of the Spaghetti Western directed by Sergio Leone and starring Clint Eastwood (e.g. *A Fistful of Dollars*, 1964, *For a Few Dollars More*, 1966, *The Good, the Bad, and the Ugly*, 1966); and the training of a group of Hispanic film professionals who would come of age in the 1980s (see Noriega, 1992b, p. 142; 1996, pp. 7–8).[41] For Hispanics, as for blacks, 1960s, would see Hollywood silent on civil rights. Indeed the Spaghetti Westerns reproduced old stereotypes about bad, lazy Mexicans (Keller, 1994, p. 153). A cycle of urban gang films (*West Side Story*, 1961, *Young Savages*, 1961, *The Pawnbroker*, 1965, *The Wild Angels*, 1966, *Change of Habit*, 1969) perpetuated these images. Hispanic actors (and actresses) seldom played the main character in these films (Keller, 1994, p. 161 (see also the Appendix, Hispanic, Chicana/o Films).

In the 1970s the Hispanic community did not generate its version of the blaxploitation films, although in *Mr Majestyk* (1974) Charles Bronson would play a half-Mexican, half-Slavic superhero (Keller, 1994, p. 160). The Hispanic and Chicano civil rights movement helped put the The Frito Bandito, Chiquita Banana, and José Jiménez to rest (Keller, 1994, p. 162). *The Ballad of Gregorio Cortez* (1982) and *El Norte* (1983), products of the Chicano Cinema Coalition, challenged classical treatments of the Hispanic outlaw and the 'illegal' immigrant.

Hispanic gang films, as if in anticipation of the black hood movies of the 1990s, gather force in the late 1970s (*Boulevard Nights*, 1979),[42] and continue through the 1980s (*Zoot Suit*, 1981, *Stand Alone*, 1985, *The Principal*, 1987, *Colors*, 1988). Such texts served to perpetuate the public myth that 'one of the major ways Chicanos become visible in public discourse is as "social problems" ... as greasers ... bandidos ... [as members of] gangs' (Fregoso, 1993, p. 29; see also Jankowski, 1991; Reeves and Campbell, 1994; Sanders, 1994). Fregoso (1993) is quite clear on this point. This discourse is part of the 'official race-relations narrative' (p. 29) in America. It has 'dominated media portrayals, and the social-science literature since the 1960s' (p. 29).

Four 1980s political films (*High Risk*, 1981, *Missing*, 1982, *Under Fire*, 1983, *Salvador*, 1986) and three comedies (*Romancing the Stone*, 1984, *Miracles*, 1986, and *Moon Over Parador*, 1988) emphasized American participation in Latin American affairs. These films examined human rights abuses, the media and

Third World journalism, drug-running, smugglers, and repeated traditional stereotypes about Latin Americans and their police and their dictators (Keller, 1994, p. 175).

Hispanic Hollywood   As noted in the Introduction (note 20), between the 'summer of 1987 and the spring of 1988' (Keller, 1994, p. 163) 'Hispanic Hollywood' arrived with the release of four films: *La Bamba, Born in East LA, The Milagro Beanfield War, Stand and Deliver* (Keller, 1994, p. 163).[43] Like the 'New Black Hollywood' films of the 1970s, the 'new' Hispanic Hollywood films of the late 1980s were produced by Hispanic filmmakers,[44] for a Hispanic audience, and starred Hispanics.[45]

These films, and those which would follow in the 1990s, challenged seven decades of negative representations of Hispanic culture. They actively engaged and criticized earlier genres that denied, repressed, or distorted Chicano/a history (e.g. greaser, Latin musical, Western; see Noriega, 1992b, p. 153; also Fregoso, 1993, p. 29). These texts also explored identities previously repressed, or negatively treated in Anglo culture and cinema, including 'the pachuco (urban street youth), the pinto (ex-convict), and the indigenous mostly Aztec warrior' (Fregoso, 1993, p. 30; see *Mi Familia*).

Each of these films was successful financially, and 'eminently Chicano' (Keller, 1994, p. 164). Each used intensive bilingualism, focused on Chicano characters, positively evoked the Chicano lifestyle, and made positive connections between Mexico and US Hispanic border culture.[46] Other Hispanic films, with some of these same characteristics, followed: *Old Gringo* (1989), *American Me* (1992), *Mambo Kings* (1992).

And the 1990s   Hispanic, Latin American, Chicano/a cinema, films made by Chicanos (and Chicanas) for the Chicano community, the Hispanic hood: *Hangin' with the Homeboys* (1991), *American Me* (1992), *Bound by Honor (Blood In, Blood Out)* (1993), *My Family/Mi Familia* (1995), *My Crazy Live/Mi Vida Loca* (1994).[47]

This new Latin American cinema uses the economic practices of Hollywood to produce a political cinema (Noriega, 1992b, p. 149), film as a tool to create critical race consciousness. In so doing it honors Chicano/a culture (in its multiple forms). A politics of opposition is presented, a politics that keeps the histories of this culture alive, attempts to reclaim a forgotten past. A realistic cinematic narrative is employed, the telling of stories based on true or historical events (Goldman, 1996, p. 84; Noriega, 1992b, pp. 152–153; e.g. *Zoot Suit*, 1981).

A specific set of film practices are associated with this project. Chicana/o filmmakers and screenwriters (i.e. Valdez, Villasenor, Young, Morales) improvise with narrative forms that are connected to long-standing Chicano traditions. *The Ballad of Gregorio Cortez* (1982) uses the *corrido*, or folk ballad (see Noriega, 1992b, pp. 152–153; Fregoso, 1993, pp. 70–76). Improvisation also occurs with specific cinematic forms, for example using *mise-en-scène* to fill the screen with Chicano images. Montage is often used in ways that manipulate bicultural visual and linguistic codes (English and Spanish).[48] Personal testimonials, life stories, voice-overs, and off-screen narration may then be employed to provide a film with overall narrative unity (Noriega, 1992b, pp. 156–159). These narrative and cinematic techniques allow filmmakers to celebrate and mark certain key elements in Chicano culture, especially the themes of resistance, maintenance, affirmation, and neo-indigenism, or *mestizaje* (Noriega, 1992b, p. 150).

Seeking an alternative to European and Anglo-American influences on cultural identity, recent Chicano artists have located their national origins in 'the racial mixture between the Spaniard and the Indian' (Noriega, 1992b, p. 150). They are the concept of *mestizaje* to describe the person who embodies border crossings, and challenges the dominant Anglo culture and its oppressive presence in Chicano/a life (Noriega, 1992b, p. 150). Many argue that the new dominant culture is a border culture (Noriega, 1992b, p. 151).

Assimilation and melting-pot narratives are contested by this new 'border cinema.'[49] But too often these texts stress the importance of machismo and the masculine identity (Fregoso, 1993, p. 29). This gives the impression that the 'Chicana subject is the object rather than the subject of the male gaze ... [she is] denied any active role in the discourse' (Fregoso, 1993, p. 94). Timeworn stereotypes persist: virgins, whores, supportive wives, home-girls (Fregoso, 1993, pp. 93–94).

The Los Angeles School of Chicano/a and Black Filmmakers

To summarize, by 1990 there are two new groups of filmmakers: the black and brown Los Angeles Schools (see Masilea, 1993; Noriega, 1992b, p. 142; 1996, pp. 7–8; Fregoso, 1993, pp. 31, 129). The barrio-hood (and Hispanic prison) films of the 1980s (*Zoot Suit*) and 1990s (*American Me, Mi Familia*) connect Hispanic gangs and community life to a unique regional and ethnic border culture. Border crossings and non-assimilation are key elements in these films. These features are largely absent in the social realism of the black hood films of the same period.

Nonetheless, the Los Angeles Schools of Chicano/a and black filmmakers share several characteristics (see Diawara, 1993a, pp. 9, 22–25): a concentration on the present; an opposition, at one level, to Hollywood studio practices; a telling of family stories (border crossings); the use of native cultural musical forms; challenges to simplistic assimilation narratives; a focus on the negative features of gang life; an examination of life in the hood and the barrio, including constant police surveillance; telling masculine, heterosexual coming-of-age stories.

The two schools implement a critical approach to cultural identity (see especially Fregoso, 1993, p. 31; Hall, 1989; also Masilea, 1993, p. 108; Noriega, 1992b, p. 151; 1996, p. 6).[50] The classic cinematic approach to ethnic identity assumed a core self with a fixed origin, an authentic ethnic essence located in a unified subject: a greaser, a coon, a mammy, a tragic mulatto (see Fregoso, 1993, p. 31; Hall, 1989, p. 69). The new filmmakers reject this essentializing approach, calling instead for a transformational model that sees identity in gendered, processual terms. This multi-sided identity is constituted 'within not outside [systems] of representation' (Hall, 1989, p. 68), including television and cinema (Fregoso, 1993, p. 32; Hall, 1989, p. 80).

This processual view creates the space for the reexamination of new and old forms of Chicano/a and black cultural identity (see below). Yet, as Fregoso (1993, p. 29) notes, even as this critical reappraisal occurs, a public myth is perpetuated. The 'offical race-relations narrative' (Fregoso, 1993, p. 29) in American today converges on a single point: the threats posed by black and Hispanic youth to white society. This myth privileges the ideology of assimiliation. Now to the Asian Americans.

Asian-American Cinema

The Asian-American cinematic story is at least as long as a century, the construction of the mysterious Orient as a site of desire, violence and intrigue, the Orient as a threat to the West (Marchetti, 1993, p. 27; Browne, 1989, p. 29). This is a history with variations on a single, but complex, motif: distorted, racist representations of Chinese, Koreans, Japanese, Filipinos, Vietnamese and Asian Indians (Wong, 1978, p. i). This theme is contained and repeated within three basic film genres: adventure films; crime, mystery, and spy stories; and war narratives (Wong, 1978, p. 195). Assimilation narratives are the norm for this so-called 'model minority group' (Healey, 1995, p. 404). Unlike Hispanic and black cinema, there is no extended positive revisionist period for the Asian-American community, no golden moment when Hollywood seems to see the light (see the Appendix, Asian-American Films).

Military representations gather force during each major war, extending through to the recent Vietnam revisionist film (*Heaven & Earth*, 1993). The recurring popularity of the war film is ideological. The major wars since the mid-twentieth century have been sites for the reproduction of negative Asian images. These wars are directly linked to America's ideological battles with fascism and communism. The Asian other is a political enemy, an internal (and external) threat to democracy and the principles of American capitalism (see Wong, 1978, p. 174).

Asian racism is located in more than three generations of wars (Russo-Japanese, World Wars I and II, Korean War, Vietnamese conflict),[51] religion (Christian, Buddhist, Confucian), immigration patterns and immigration laws (the 1982 Chinese Exclusion Act, the 1913 Alien Land Act), ethnic enclaves (Chinatowns), educational segregation, relocation camps, and laws against miscegenation (see Healey, 1995, pp. 436–441). It is a cinematic history of racial violence, a history that ignores cultural differences and presumes essential racial identities.

This history treats all Asians as if they belonged to the same ethnic, religious, and national group. It does not differentiate between Asian nationalities, for example between Korean, Chinese, and Japanese (see Wong, 1978, p. xvi). Nor does it address the complex and shifting foreign relationships between each Asian nation and the United States since the beginning of the twentieth century (Wong, 1978, p. 68).[52]

But like Hispanic (and black) history, many different narratives define the Asian situation, including an intermingling of hemispheres (East, South, and West Asia), nationalities (China, Korea, Japan, Vietnam, Cambodia, etc.), ethnicities (i.e. Vietnamese American, Cambodian American), national and local cultures, and religions and their missionaries. Negative, gendered stereotypes are folded into these histories: exotic China dolls and evil Dr Fu Manchu.[53]

Asians enter silent (and sound) cinema as Eurasian seductresses, Asian war brides, masquerading geishas (Marchetti, 1993, p. 9; also Browne, 1989, p. 29), spies, military officers, Oriental detectives (Chan, Moto, Wong), Asian warlords, opium dens, and drug kingpins, passive, cowardly coolies, 'pigtailed Chinese laundrymen' (Wong, 1978, p. 57), servants, lowly examples of the Yellow Peril, Oriental villains, and immigrating Asian hordes (Wong, 1978, pp. 30, 57, 59; also *Wild Bill*, 1995).

Two themes connected to the spy, mystery, and war genres intertwine in this early period, namely the criminal, military, and sexual threats of the Asian other to American (and British) Society. The sexual and rape themes, which sexualize racism (Wong, 1978, p. 23, 76), are powerfully presented in D. W. Griffith's *Broken Blossoms* (1919). This film is a virtual catalogue of sexual excesses (rape, incest, sadism, masochism, pedophilia, necrophilia, fetishism, voyeurism; Marchetti, 1993, p. 33). Indeed, Marchetti (1993, p. 34) argues that it should be read as a pornographic text.

It is also a catalogue of all that can go wrong in Asian–white interracial sexual relations (interracial couples smoke opium, drugged Caucasian women assume sexually provocative poses).[54] The film presents opium as a decadent, sensual intrusion into the West (Marchetti, 1993, p. 38). A pure white virgin (Lucy, played by Lillian Gish) is 'exposed and humiliated' (Marchetti, 1993, p. 38) by her contact and relationship with an Asian male (Cheng Huan, played by Richard Barthelmess, a white/Anglo actor). The character of Cheng Huan is feminized by Griffith through the use of dress, posture, gesture, 'soft focus and diffuse lighting' (Marchetti, 1993, p. 35). Montage and parallel editing are used to underscore the threats he poses for Lucy (shades of *Birth of a Nation*; Marchetti, 1993, p. 37).

The second predominant motif of the silent period, the criminal, detective (spy) and military theme, is given in the figure of Dr Fu Manchu, whose popularity increased with the advent of sound. Soon this figure would be complemented by the Oriental sleuth, who was virtually ignored in silent film. With the third Charlie Chan movie, *Behind That Curtain* (1929), the Asian detective became a staple of Asian-American cinema. This sleuth would work in the service of law and order, peace and justice and protect the world from sinister criminals.

Until the Chan figure, the concept of an Oriental hero was unthinkable.[55] Over the next twenty years there would be more than sixty films starring Charlie Chan, Mr Moto, and Mr Wong.[56] Chan, Moto, and Wong became positive stand-ins for the negative Asian other, and the 'Yellow Peril,' even as their characters critiqued and made a parody of the Eurocentric racist stereotypes that were ascribed to them (see also Shohat, 1991, p. 238). The mollifying influence of the Chan series is continuous, from the advent of sound to the present.

During the 1930s Hollywood ignored internal Asian struggles, and those wars when Asians fought one another, including the Japanese invasion of China in 1937. Indeed Hollywood ignored the Asian political situation until December 7, 1941 (Wong, 1978, p. 139). From that date forward 'Hollywood would completely put its cinematic machinery into high gear against the Japanese' (Wong, 1978, p. 131). Over forty war films featuring the Asian other were made between 1942 and 1949. (Indeed, more than 140 war films focusing on the Asian other were made between the years 1940 and 1970; Wong, 1978, p. 198).[57]

In the post-Pearl Harbor films, Japanese men are presented as 'fanatical, near-savages, sneaky, dirty fighters ... [as] repulsive, sadistic, libidinous little monkeys, grinningly bespectacled, and sporting king-size choppers' (Wong, 1978, pp. 156–157). In film after film (e.g. *Wake Island*, 1942, *Purple Heart*, 1944, *Dragon Seed*, 1944) an harmonious military force, a 'democratic ethnic mix' (Basinger, 1986, p. 61), consisting of white ethnics (usually Irish and Italians), one Jew, and one black, was presented (Wong, 1978, p. 163). This harmonious force was united in its struggles against the barbaric Asian.

The war genre films briefly ended in 1945, with the Japanese surrender, only to be taken up again with the Cold War (1947–1949), the Korean War (1950–1953), and the new war against communism (Wong, 1978, p. 169). In *The Sands of Iwo Jima* (1949) and the *Halls of Montezuma* (1951) the Japanese menace was resurrected and used as a vehicle for attacking the Chinese, 'a new Yellow Peril in Communistic garb' (Wong, 1978, p. 173). Charlie Chan notwithstanding, once again Fu Manchu emerged as a threat to the West (Wong, 1978, p. 175).

Americans seemed unable to distinguish the Japanese from the Chinese and the Koreans, although the Korean War would become the site for the construction of a new version of the Yellow Peril (Wong, 1978, p. 176). Prison camp (*Prisoner of War*, 1954; *Bridge on the River Kwai*, 1957) and brainwashing (*Time Limit*, 1957, *The Manchurian Candidate*, 1962) films were pivotal in this period. Films like these presented images of 'white men's minds being manipulated or destroyed by Asians' (Wong, 1978, p. 178). These texts suggested that the Chinese and Koreans were slaves of communist Russia. Thus were America's 'racial politics projected into the communist bloc' (Wong, 1978, p. 179).[58] (The fact that some POWs cooperated with their captors was explained by Korean treachery and the Asians' low regard for human life.)

Four films in the social problems film cycle of the 1950s partially corrected this negative treatment of the Japanese: *Go for Broke* (1951), *Japanese War Bride* (1952), *Bad Day at Black Rock* (1955) and *Three Stripes in the Sun* (1955) 'all dramatized the Japanese as victims of American bigotry' (Keller, 1994, p. 128).[59] This brief period of positive treatment did not carry over into the civil rights consciousness of the 1960s. Wong (1978) argues that 'the Asians were omitted from what was essentially a biracial consciousness (whites and blacks only) among film-makers' (p. 183). Indeed, the Vietnam conflict was an occasion for renewed negative treatments of the Asian other. This negativity was based in part on the fact that this war was causing so much trouble in America (Desser, 1991, p. 81).

The Asian conflict of the 1960s was located in one of three sites, which often overlapped: in Vietnam (*The Green Berets*, 1968, *A Yank in Viet-Nam*, 1964); in the American war protestor (*Alice's Restaurant*, 1969) or the damaged Vietnam veteran (*Who'll Stop the Rain*, 1978, *Coming Home*, 1978); or, as in the menacing figure of Dr No (in the James Bond film of 1962) or other Asian criminals. The Vietnamese enemy was a cliché, a construction based on previous cinematic treatments of the Japanese, Koreans, and the Chinese. He was a jungle-monkey. He hid in burrows. He lived underground. He lay in ambush of well-meaning American soldiers, and he emitted shrill cries when he attacked (Wong, 1978, p. 187).

Three decades of films have attempted to recover the meanings of the Vietnamese war for America (see Auster and Quart, 1988). The 1960s gave Americans John Wayne's super-patriotic *The Green Berets*. The 1970s offered the dark and deeply existential *The Deer Hunter* (1978) and *Apocalypse Now* (1979). Patriotic themes reappeared in the Reagan decade with the Rambo series: *First Blood* (1982), *Rambo: First Blood Part II* (1985), *Rambo III* (1988). Films like *The Killing Fields* (1984), *Platoon* (1986), *Full Metal Jacket* (1987), and *Born on the Fourth of July* (1989), however, challenged the 1980s Rambo narrative.

The memory of Vietnam lingers in the American imagination (Auster and Quart, 1988, p. 130). Comedies like *Good Morning, Vietnam* (1987) and sanitized television series like *China Beach* and *Magnum, P. I.* cannot erase the cinematic images of napalmed bodies, screaming children, and destroyed Vietnamese villages.

The 1970s and 1980s would work back and forth against the Vietnam narrative. Domesticated and exotic images of the Asian American would be given in the Western (*McCabe and Mrs Miller*, 1971) film noir (*Chinatown*, 1974), and disaster (*Airport*, 1975) genres. The Bruce Lee, Hong Kong, martial arts, 'chop socky' series (*Fists of Fury*, 1971, *Enter the Dragon*, 1973, *Return of the Dragon*, 1973) introduces a 1970s version of Mr Moto, a diminutive, violent Asian male, who uses martial (kung fu) arts for law and order.[60]

Lee's project would be countered by the Chuck Norris 1980s *Missing in Action* series (1984, 1985, 1988), a white man using martial arts against evil Asians. In turn, *The Karate Kid* (1984) and its sequels (1986, 1989) used karate for self-esteem and self-protection purposes, and the women's movement followed suit (*Tightrope*, 1984). The Asian 1980s ended with historical foreign spectacles (*Empire of the Sun*, 1987, *The Last Emperor*, 1987) and Asian gang (and drug) wars in New York City and Tokyo (*Year of the Dragon*, 1985, *True Believer*, 1989, *Black Rain*, 1989).

The late 1980s and 1990s revisit Vietnam (*Heaven & Earth*, 1993), the bombing of Nagasaki (*Rhapsody in August*, 1991), Indian Asians (*Mississippi Masala*, 1992), the life of a Chinese woman in China in the 1920s (*Ju Dou*, 1990), the Chinese cultural revolution (*Farewell My Concubine*, 1993), and another version of the Madame Butterfly story (*M. Butterfly*, 1993). American baseball travels to Japan (*Mr Baseball*, 1992), while Chinese and Taiwanese generational family conflicts are explored in two Wayne Wang (*Eat a Bowl of Tea*, 1989, *The Joy Luck Club*, 1993) and two Ang Lee films (*The Wedding Banquet*, 1993, *Eat Drink Man Woman*, 1994), respectively.

A fitting near ending to the Asian cinematic century is given in a penultimate moment in *Rising Sun* (1993). Wesley Snipes and Sean Connery are being chased by a gang of Asian youths through the alleys of South Central Los Angeles. Snipes detours through an alley and stops next to a group of African-American brothers who are just hanging out. He asks them for help. As if in anticipation of the Los Angeles riots of 1992, the black males attack the Asian males. This comic diversion allows Snipes and Connery to make a safe getaway. In this odd multicultural melting-pot fashion, the Asian and black communities do violent service for white society.

And beneath this narrative lurkes another, namely Vietnam's contributions to America's 1980s war on drugs, the crack-cocaine narratives (Reeves and Campbell, 1994, p. 26). The Vietnam experience introduced American soldiers to drugs (marijuana, cocaine, heroin). Drug networks extending from Vietnam (and Latin

America) to major American cities were established. Black, Hispanic, and Asian gangs took control of these distribution systems. Soon, so the story goes, the inner cities became 'contemporary versions of Southeast Asia – dangerous exotic places where even a child might kill you' (Reeves and Campbell, 1994, p. 26).[61]

Social Science and the Cinema of Racial Difference

Return to the beginning: America's cinematic racial order. The histories of black, Hispanic, and Asia-American cinema can now be inserted into the cultural and structural film practices outlined above, namely those practices connected to: America's violent, racist popular culture; its gender-based, racist performance vocabularies; the Hollywood sound system; race and ethnically linked film genres (black and Latin musicals); a segregated production system; miscegenation laws; the civil rights movements of the 1960s.

As realistic (and at times utopian) ethnographies of cutural difference, black, Hispanic, and Asian-American cinema transform and are transformed by these discursive practices. Each cinematic formation fits itself to a discrete set of moving racist historical circumstances, barriers that constantly filter, define, and redefine the cinematic racial self. Each ethnic cinema, as a set of performance texts, creates its version of the racial order; that is, it connects its historical, cultural, and social circumstances to these discursive practices.

To summarize These circumstances are familiar, and many of them cut across ethnic groups (religion, wars, drugs, gangs, miscegenation and immigration laws, multiple nationality groups, ghetto life). *For blacks*: slavery, strong black women, hustlers, specific film genres: musicals, social consciousness, comedies, blaxploitation, buddy, hood. *For Hispanics*: strong women, American and Italian Westerns, Latin musicals. *For Asian Americans*: geishas, Charlie Chan, the 'Yellow Peril,' adventure, mystery, and war films.

Thus, every historical moment, with its cinematic formations, articulates a version of the American racial system. And these moments and formations are of course tangled up in social science theories of race and ethnic relations.

Social Science Theories of the Racial Order

Each decade since 1900 (see Table 1.1; also McKee, 1993) has articulated its version of the white man's burden. To be specific, nativism and the eugenics movement dominate in the 1900–1920 period, the stuff of Griffith's race films. The notion of race as the white man's burden, coupled with theories of the race relations cycle, gains force in the 1921–1930 decade. This model presumed that those of dark skin would become like white persons, if given time and help. In contrast, from 1931 to 1940 the non-white other is regarded as a cultural inferior. Separate but equal social arrangements persist, even as melting-pot and assimilation theories are debated. In the 1941–1950 period, under democratic presidents, criticisms of the American system of segregation increase and contradictions in the American race system are exposed (Myrdal, 1944; see also Drake and Cayton, 1945; Frazier, 1957; Johnson, 1941).

Desegregation in 1954, coupled with the publicity surrounding the atrocities of the Holocaust, brings studies of personal prejudice and the authoritarian personality. The civil rights decade (1961–1970) turns race into a moral issue (Rogin, 1996, p. 266). Separatist movements begin, and civil rights leaders debate violent and non-violent approaches to the race problem. The laws prohibiting miscegenation are repealed, and the Immigration Act of 1965 'increased almost fourfold the allowable number of immigrants in any year ... and substantially increased [immigration] from Asia and Latin America' (McKee, 1993, p. 360). In the black power decade (1971–1980) internal colonial and separatist models are advanced, and connected to multiculturalism. The Reagan/Bush decade (1981–1990) produces the war on drugs, the Miami race riots, and conservative arguments against affirmative action and multiculturalism. The 1990s bears witness to criticisms of multiculturalism, the dismantling of affirmative action programs, and new race riots.

The failure of American social science to provide a solution to the race problem is finally recognized (McKee, 1993, p. 360). Assimilation models now appear dated (McKee, 1993, p. 361). A homogeneous American population is not developing, and ethnicity is not declining in importance (McKee, 1993, p. 362). The barriers to racial, economic, and educational equality have not been eliminated. It is no longer defensible to argue that 'any remaining inequalities are the problems of the minority groups and not the larger society' (Healey, 1995, p. 513).

Contemporary discourse emphasizes ethnic pluralism, many different diasporas (Appadurai, 1996), and 'some modes of separatism that once would have been called segregation are now encouraged' (McKee, 1993, p. 360). The new academic discourse argues against 'race' as a scientific concept, and 'in the new pluralism of ethnic groups' (McKee, 1993, p. 361) ethnic status is now conferred on black, Hispanic, Asian, and Native American. Thus is there an attempt to make a transition from a racial category to one grounded in 'ethnic' culture (McKee, 1993, p. 361). But a color-conscious, conservative America, 'still divided by a color line' (McKee, 1993, p. 361), will have none of this. Nor is everyone ready to accept the doctrines of ethnic and racial pluralism, of ethnic equality.

A Cinema of Resistance

A politically progressive, but discontinuous, narrative emerges from this truncated history. This narrative moves back and forth across the race relations models outlined above. These models repeatedly interesect with specific theories of race, culture, whiteness and non-whiteness, civilization, ethnicity, intelligence, cultural difference, violence, deviance, sexuality, gender, sexual appetitite, addiction, parenthood, and moral correctness. These terms, in turn, are folded, decade by decade, into specific cinematic texts.

Each ethnic cinema is characterized by brief moments of revision and resistance when past stereotypes are challenged, and more sensitive and complex stories are presented. These revisionist historical ruptures ebb and flow. They have greater influence in some decades than in others, for example black and Hispanic Hollywood.

However, these ruptures lengthened in the 1990s. From the civil rights movements came a multiplicity of resistance cinemas: black, Chicano/a, Native and Asian

American. These cinemas shape a politics of ethnic resistance. They frequently challenge mainstream Hollywood representations. Still, as argued above (also Fregoso, 1993, p. 29), an official race relations narrative runs like a long barbed wire through each of these histories. This narrative converges in those geographical spaces where America's black, Hispanic, and Asian ghettos criss-cross one another, where the rap, hip hop culture, the hood, the barrio, and Chinatown come together.

In the 1990s, a male, gang-based, multi-ethnic drug culture mediates this representational system. This culture is anchored in a political economy that extends deeply into the families and gangs in each ethnic ghetto. This political economy exploits the gang and gangster culture (Boyd, 1997, p. 85). In so doing it 'integrates the excesses' (Boyd, 1997, p. 85) of race and ethnicity directly into the larger economic, and cultural systems of the ghetto and of American society today.

In Conclusion

At the center of Wayne Wang's 1982 film *Chan Is Missing* are overlapping, conflicting, images of ethnic Asian-American identities: young women dressed like American teenagers, Chinese Richard Pryors, Chinese cooks singing 'Fry Me to the Moon,' *GQ*-dressed young Asian males, sad old Asian men and women. These images do not cohere into a single Asian identity that can be assimilated into the Western view of the mysterious Asian other. Indeed, in Wang's world assimilation is an impossibility. The self that dreams of fitting in loses itself, and in the end, while seemingly alive, is not only missing, but also dead.

Two scenarios. Spike Lee's multicultural ghetto is filled with prejudice, hatred, and viscous racial stereotypes. Wayne Wang's Chinatown is a lonely, quiet place where violence goes on behind closed doors, and in the public arena confused Asians stare past one another.

And as these two films confront one another, the plight of ethnic minorities in America's inner cities worsens – decaying neighborhoods, drugs, crime, poverty, violence (McKee, 1993, p. 364). The politics of a new ethnic diversity are now played out in the media, and in those sectors of the public sphere marked by the boundaries of the hood and the barrio. This is the stuff of the hood movies of the 1990s, the topic of this book. In the next chapter I examine two white versions of the hood: *Grand Canyon* and *White Men Can't Jump*.

Notes

1. However, like any realist text these films are not mimetic; they create the conditions of their own representation (see López, 1991, p. 405). Accuracy is not at issue; there are only competing and conflicting images of race and ethnicity (see Friedman, 1991a; also Cripps, 1979). Borrowing from Ryan and Kellner (1988, p. 12), race movies engage in a process of discursive, racial transcoding. These films draw upon existing racial understandings and stereotypes. They bring these understandings to the screen. This process transforms the original representations.

2. There are other endings, including the one about crack-cocaine, gang wars, and senseless self-destruction in the hood – Singleton's story.

3. Griffith is central to the cinematic construction of the American racial order. His films exploited nativist and miscegenation themes. He used white actors to play the parts of blacks (*The Birth of a Nation*, 1915), Hispanics (*The Martyrs of the Alamo, or The Birth of Texas*, 1915), and Asian

Americans (*Broken Blossoms*, 1919). The racist elements in *The Birth of a Nation* and films like *The Martyrs of the Alamo* (e.g. *Matero Murdered*, 1913) were immediately protested by blacks (Bogle, 1994, p. 15) and the Mexican government (Keller, 1994, pp. 115–117; and discussion below).

4. This system presented the dark-skinned minority male as a threat to white society, its women, and to racial purity. Parallel editing (Griffith's innovation), moving back and forth between alternate scenes, was a basic features of this cinematic system. It allowed Griffith to tell two stories at the same time: the story of the whites, and the story of the 'freed' black man who threatens the new society and its women (see Keller, 1994, p. 27; Rogin, 1986, p. 157; Clough, 1992, p. 52). These threats occur outside the main narrative, often located in those moments when the white woman is alone and stalked by the black man. In this way Griffith displaced race, locating it outside white society. Thus race (and women) entered American cinema under a system of visual and narrative displacement (see Clough, 1992, p. 53; Rogin, 1986, pp. 178–179).

5. In the 1930s this included MGM, Warner Brothers, Paramount, Twentieth-Century Fox, Universal, RKO, Columbia, and United Artists (Keller, 1994, p. 112).

6. Nativists believe that the 'United States should be reserved for native-born Protestant whites ... [and] some propose that all other groups be eliminated from society' (Healey, 1995, p. 550; also see discussion below of social science theories and race relations).

7. Bogle (1994) argues that early filmic representations of the Negro as coon, mulatto, mammy, and buck 'were merely reproductions of black stereotypes that had existed since the days of slavery and were popularized in American life and art' (p. 4; see Keller, 1994, p. 29 on dime novels and 'Wild West' films of the silent era).

8. In contrast, the advent of the sound system did not create a need for 'real' Native and Asian American actors, who, with few exceptions, were played by white actors speaking a version of pidgin English.

9. The new sound system functioned somewhat differently for Hispanics. By the 1930s (Keller, 1994, p. 119; Riós-Bustamante, 1992, pp. 22–23) the Hollywood film production system had a monopoly over film distribution in Latin America. The sound era required Spanish-language films for Latin America. However, it was impossible to create a single Spanish-language film that pleased the entire Hispanic public (Keller, 1994, p. 120). The solution was simple, use Latin actors and actresses who would use Spanish accents and speak broken or fractured English. Nevertheless, the Latin musical soon became a popular film category.

10. An indigenous Hispanic (Chicano) cinema would not appear until the 1980s, the 'so-called Decade of the Hispanic' (Noriega, 1992a, p. xvii), although a vibrant, active Hispanic film (and theatre) community existed in Los Angeles in the 1920s (see Rios-Bustamante, 1992, p. 24; and note 39 below). The Decade of the Asian-American film has yet to appear.

11. Early in Griffith's *The Birth of a Nation*, happy slaves pick cotton, and 'in their quarters dance and sing [Stephen Foster] songs for their master' (Bogle, 1994, p. 12). In these musical, carnival-like moments the presumably essential performative racial (and ethnic) self is enacted. This creates a moment of double racism. The essential self is being performed because the whites allow it to be performed and the performance is for the pleasure of the whites. This conclusion appears to hold for contemporary black and Latin musicals as well. In this site there is little of the Bakhtinian carnivalesque upturning of race relations that Hall discusses (1996b, p. 474).

12. Gender and nationality (e.g. Latin male lovers) complicates the miscegenation situation. On-screen Asian (*Black Rain*) and black males (*Jungle Fever*) could not have sexual relations with white women, but under certain circumstances black (*The Bodyguard*), Hispanic-Latin (*White Men Can't Jump*), and Asian (*Year of the Dragon*) women could have sexual relations with white men (see Bogle, 1994, pp. 13–14; Guerrero, 1993a, pp. 34–35; Keller, 1994, p. 32; Wong, 1978, p. 229). Wong (1978, p. 229) notes that when Asian males were seen as appealing to white women, white actors would typically play the Asian part. Of course white males could have sexual relationships with Asian and black females. When these rules are broken, 'there can be rape, but there cannot be romance' (Wong, 1978, p. 25).

13. He supplements this list with the following, more contemporary types: jesters, comics, servants, entertainers, militants, and action heroes.

14. Keller (1994) argues that Hollywood's formula system insured that the 'ethnic *other* almost invariably played the outcast and the evildoer' (p. 114, italics in original).

15. The black musical is an exception to this conclusion. From the 1920s to the present, blacks have been cast in Old South plantation stories, spirituals, musicals, family melodramas, ghetto adventures (blaxploitation), buddy and action films (see discussion below).

16. This code was explicit, 'Miscegenation (sex relationships between the white and black races) is forbidden' (Keller, 1994, p. 115). It was applied to Native, Asian, Hispanic, and African Americans (see Keller, 1994, p. 115).

17. A strong indigenous cinematic political economy associated with the Asian-American community apparently did not appear until the early 1980s (see Fung, 1994, p. 165; Marchetti, 1993, p. 216). Pioneering Asian actors (Wong, 1978, p. 247) include Keye Luke, Victor Sen Yung, Benson Fong, Miyoshi Umeki, and Nancy Kwan (Marchetti, 1993, p. 113).

18. Throughout the twentieth century Hollywood's identification of the Asian enemy shifted back and forth (depending on the war) from the Chinese to the Japanese, the Koreans, Vietnamese, and Filipinos (Wong, 1978, p. 221).

19. The gay and lesbian movements were part of this general civil rights history, and played key parts in the Hispanic, black, and Asian-American political (and cinematic) movements (see, e.g. Aguilar-San Juan, 1994, p. 11; also Negron-Muntaner, 1996, on the contemporary gay and lesbian Latino film community).

20. Native Americans have yet to fully enter this cinematic history (see Fiedler, 1988, p. 751), although each year since 1974 the American Indian Film Institution has held its Annual American Indian Film Festival (Nagel, 1996, pp. 203, 211). From 1945 to 1969 the federal Indian policy was based on the reservation model of assimilation, involving the 'termination of special treaty relationships between American Indian communities and the federal government' (Nagel, 1996, p. 214). Starting in 1970, a series of federal bills initiated the era of American Indian self-determination. This reversed the government's termination policy and ushered in the present red power period (Nagel, 1996, p. 217). The 1992 film *Thunderheart* explores some of these issues. The first all-Indian movie *Smoke Signals* began production in the spring of 1997 and was released in 1998 (see Dinitia Smith, 1997, p. B1).

21. Consider, in this context, Julie Dash's *Daughter's of the Dust* (1991); also the 1977 made-for-television film *Roots*, and, more recently, *Glory* (1989).

22. But as Bogle (1994) observes, there was a tendency for the black performer to 'not give a performance of his own, not one in which he interprets black life, but one in which he presents for mass consumption black life as seen through the eyes of white artists. The actor becomes a black man in blackface ... the blackface fixation' (p. 27). Spike Lee's 2000 film *Bamboozled* treats this issue in detail.

23. At the same time these black jazz performers continued to experience extreme prejudice and discrimination in their daily lives. White America was not prepared to accept black musicians and black vocalists in white bands, nor would it accept black musicians as stars in their own right (see Hampton, 1996, p. 126). Black jazz musicians also confronted grave racism in the American military during this period; the tragic case of Lester Young is an example (see Yanow, 1996, p. 795; Scott, 1996, p. 453; Porter, 1991, p. xiii; Hamond, 1991, p. 29; Giddens, 1998, pp. 179–181). (See also Davis, 1998, p. 192, for a discussion of Billie Holiday and her encounters with 'vitriolic expressions of racism' when she was a vocalist in Artie Shaw's all-white band; also Friedwald, 1990, p. 131.)

24. Juano Hernandez, James Edwards, Ethel Waters, and Clarence Brooks (Bogle, 1994, p. 137).

25. Still, the 'Huck Finn fixation' persisted (Bogle, 1994, pp. 140–141). According to Bogle, this complex aligns a good white man who is an outcast with a trusty black (also an outcast). The white man grows in stature through his association with the black man, who seems 'to possess the soul the white man searches for' (Bogle, 1994, p. 140). There are many examples, from *Casablanca* to *In the Heat of the Night*, and, most recently, the *Die Hard* and *Lethal Weapon* series.

26. Dorothy Dandridge, Sidney Poitier, Ethel Waters, Harry Belafonte, Pearl Bailey, Eartha Kitt, Ella Fitzgerald, William Marshall, and Ruby Dee.

27. Key directors, actors, and actresses in this decade included Melvin Van Peebles, Gordan Parks, Jr, Michael Schultz, Richard Pryor, Ossie Davis, Richard Roundtree, Ron O'Neill, Paul Winfield, Kevin Hooks, Pam Grier, Tamara Dobson, James E. Jones, Cicely Tyson, Diana Ross, and Billy Dee Williams.

28. The list is long and includes: Lee, Charles Burnett, Julie Dash, Bill Duke, the Hughes Brothers, John Singleton, Mario Van Peebles, Denzel Washington, John Amos, Damon Wayans,

Louis Gossett, Jr, Forest Whitaker, Cuba Gooding, Jr, Cicley Tyson, James Earl Jones, Whoopi Goldberg, Angela Bassett, Larry Fishburne, Kevin Hooks, Robin Givens, Samuel L. Jackson, Wesley Snipes, and Alfre Woodard (Bogle, 1994, pp. 359–367).

29. *Hispanic*: a census category; a term founded in socioeconomic politics (Noriega and Lopez, 1996, p. xii); of Spanish origin; to render in Spanish; Mexican. *Hispano*: Spanish-American. *Mestizo*: a person of Causasian and Native American ancestry. *Chicano*: Mexican Americans; the ideology of Chicanismo. *Mexican American*: of Mexican origin; one of the largest Spanish-speaking Hispanic groups in America. *Latino*: three communities: Chicano, Puerto Rican, Cuban American; a term founded in cultural politics (Noriega and Lopez, 1996, p. xii).

30. The Black Legend 'is a concept that refers to the negative image of Spain and Spaniards that arose during the reign of King Phillip II (1556–98) and his anti-Protestant policies.... [It] focuses on the alleged cruelty and intolerance of Spaniards' (Keller, 1994, p. 83).

31. Keller (1994, p. 31) identifies several variations within the Western genre: cattle empire, ranch, revenge, cowboys-versus-Indians, outlaw, law-and-order, and the conquest story. Wright (1975, p. 29) isolates four types: classical, vengeance, transition, and professional. The historical time-frame for the Western was short: 1860–1890 (Wright, 1975, p. 5). The Indian wars started in 1861 and by 1890 'all the American Indians had been exterminated or put on reservations' (Wright, 1975, p. 5). In 1862 the Homestead Act was passed. The great cattle drives lasted from 1866 to 1885 (Wright, 1975, p. 5).

32. Fear of miscegenation (white–Mexican/Indian) and Nativist beliefs stressing the inherent inferiority of Hispanics also operated (Keller, 1994, p. 32). This history is complicated by class. The negative features of 'Hispanic' were often erased in the figure of the non-corrupt Spanish aristocrat. The term 'Hispanic' is double-edged, containing within itself positive and negative meanings.

33. This would include gendered cinemas within each category (e.g. Chicana, Latina) as well as gay and lesbian cinema.

34. Region (e.g. Caribbean) and religion (e.g. Catholicism) must also be added to this matrix. This creates complex hybrid relationships between regional and religious (Latin, African, and Afro-Caribbean) cultures, including Rastafarian, Baptist, and Latin American Catholicism, and its mergers with Aztec and related belief systems.

35. A racist, gendered vocabulary fitted to the dark-skinned, dirty-skinned Hispanic quickly emerged. This language was also applied to Native Americans. Hispanic women were described as 'cantina girls, cantina cuties, hot tamales, hot peppers, ... señoritas, or in the case of Indianized Hispanics, squaws' (Keller, 1994, p. 14).

36. In his inaugural address Roosevelt referred to 'the policy of the good neighbor' in reference to Latin American initiatives pursued by his administration (Keller, 1994, p. 117).

37. That is, honoring democratic ideals while preserving white domination over minority group members.

38. In *The Searchers* (1956) Navajo Indians (and Jeffrey Hunter) play murderous Comanches who rape Natalie Wood. In an act of mercy, John Wayne allows Wood to reenter white society.

39. Keller (1994, pp. 134–141) discusses other genre films during this time, including Orson Welles's cult classic *A Touch of Evil* (1958), and such historical message and Mexican Revolution films as *Viva Zapata!* (1952) and *The Treasure of Pancho Villa* (1955). Pivotal Hispanic stars in this period, who were cast alongside the likes of Gary Cooper and John Wayne, included Natalie Wood, Anthony Quinn, Katy Jurado, Gilbert Roland, Rita Hayworth, and Ricardo Montalban (see Keller, 1993, pp. 142–149).

40. By 1965 the Chicano movement had coalesced, producing a series of protests in Los Angeles. The first Chicano film, *I Am Joaquin* (made for and by Chicanos) appears in 1969. In the early 1970s UCLA became a training ground for Chicano (and black) filmmakers. Noriega (1992b, p. 142; 1996, pp. 7–8) discusses the Chicano filmmakers connected to the UCLA program. Masilea (1993) discusses the Los Angeles School of Black Filmmakers (e.g. Burnett, Dash, Duke, Woodberry, Gerima). This program was based on a 1968 US Office of Economic Opportunity-funded program called New Communicators, designed to train minorities for employment in the film industry (Noriega, 1996, p. 7). In 1975 the National Chicano Film Festival was established in San Antonio and by 1978 the Los Angeles-based Chicano Cinemas Coalition (Noriega, 1992b, p. 43) was formed. Its participants would soon locate their work within the New Latin American Cinema (Noriega, 1992b, p. 145).

However, as Fregoso (1993) argues, 'Early Chicano films ... were made by Chicanos about Chicanos' (p. 129) [males], and not by and for Chicanas [females] but see Sylvia Morales' film *Chicana* (1981) (Fregoso, 1993, p. 16).

41. Rose Portillo, Daniel Valdez (Fregoso, 1993, p. 25); also James Edward Olmos, Rubén Blades, Emilio Estevez, Erik Estrada, Andy Garcia, Rosie Perez, Charlie Sheen, Jimmy Smitts, Madeleine Stowe, Lou Diamond Phillips, Esai Morales, Maria Conchita Alonso (Keller, 1994, p. 151).

42. Los Angeles Chicano student organizations protested *Boulevard Nights* and its negative depictions of gangs, Chicanos, and Chicanas (Fregoso, 1993, p. 23).

43. During the 1980s, the so-called 'Decade of the Hispanic' (as designated by the Coors Corporation), public funding sources for 'Chicano produced film and video ... were cut back under the Reagan administration' (Noriega, 1992b, p. 146; see also Fregoso, 1993, p. 22).

44. M. Esparza, M. Martinez, Sylvia Morales, Jesús Salvador Treviño, Gregory Naven, Edward James Olmos, Luis Valdez.

45. This presence was also felt (Keller, 1994, pp. 176–177) on American television (*Miami Vice, LA Law, Santa Barbara, Falcon Crest*).

46. The Cheech and Chong comedies (e.g. *Up in Smoke*, 1978, *Cheech and Chong's Next Movie*, 1980, *Cheech and Chong's the Corsican Brothers*, 1984) are an important antecedent to this series (but see List, 1992).

47. Although not a Hispanic film, John Sayles' *Lone Star* (1996) should also be added to this list, in part because it incessantly interrogates long-standing negative sterotypes of Hispanic (and black and Native-American) culture.

48. These two techniques merge mid-way through *Mambo Kings* (1992) when the two Cuban musicians appear on the *I Love Lucy* show. They pretend to not speak English. Their wives and friends back in New York City watch the two men lie to Lucy. The screen fills with the picture of the New York Cubans laughing at Lucy, laughing at the Mambo Kings, as they giggle and look out of the screen into the New York City living room.

49. But see John Sayles', *Lone Star* (1996), an assimilationist, melting-pot Texas border story with miscegenation and incest themes.

50. The films of Wayne Wang (Hong Kong), Ang Lee (Taiwan), and Mira Nair (India) add an Asian twist to this approach to cultural identity (the Asian self), see especially Wang's *Chan Is Missing* (1981), Lee's *The Wedding Banquet* (1993) and Nair's *Mississippi Masala* (1992) and *The Perez Family* (1995).

51. Indeed, Wong's (1978) history of Asian-American history is divided into two time periods: Asians in American films prior to World War II; and the mature years, from World War II, to Vietnam.

52. Higashi (1991, p. 124) and Lyman (1990d, pp. 154–159) present critical interpretations of the forms of institutional racism applied to Asians in the United States.

53. This figure would be reincarnated as the evil *Dr No* (1962), the first of the James Bond movies.

54. Marchetti (1993, pp. 8–9) argues that five rape (and miscegenation) narratives (captivity, seduction, salvation, sacrifice, assimilation) organize Hollywood's treatment of Asians and interracial sexuality.

55. This and the following paragraph draw from Denzin (1995a, pp. 89–90). Stanford Lyman (in correspondence) argues that Chan would develop as the reverse mirror image of Fu Manchu. Charlie is the tamed Oriental spirit working in the service of the Occident. Lyman observes that Chan's sons (who desire to become full-fledged Americans) are often aligned with Charlie's African-American chauffeur, usually played by Mantain Moreland, who embodies the 'coon' image of the black male.

56. The Asian sleuth, as wandering quasi-cowboy in kung fu garb, would return with a vengeance in the 1970s with the David Carradine TV show *Kung Fu*. Two other 1970s TV series, *Bonanza* and *Hawaii Five-O*, also Orientalized the Asian identity. Through the 1970s and the 1980s American television presented blacks (*Sanford and Sons, The Jeffersons, Goodtimes*), Asians (*M*A*S*H, Kung Fu*) and Hispanics (*The Freddie Prinze Show*) in assimilation and multicultural comedy contexts. This process extends from the 1980s into the 1990s with the Bruce (and Brandon) Lee *Dragon* films, and most recently with Jackie Chan (*Super Cop*, 1996).

57. The combat film, a basic form of the war movie, has undergone several transformations from World War I to the present, including the development of three basic variations within the genre: the comedy, musical, and women's combat film (see Basinger, 1986, p. 261). Ironically, some argue that *The Birth of the Nation* is the grandfather of all modern war film epics (see Auster and Quart, 1988, pp. 2–3).

58. This is painfully presented in *The Manchurian Candidate*.

59. By the end of the 1950s the communist Chinese had become America's major foreign enemy (Wong, 1978, p. 180).

60. Lee's son Brandon (1965–1993) would continue this project into the 1990s (*The Crow*, 1994).

61. Here resurfaces the CIA drug conspiracy theory discussed in the Introduction; the theory that in the 1980s the government furnished drugs to ghetto residents (see Boyd, 1997, p. 86; also the films *Deep Cover*, 1992, and *Panther*, 1995).

Part Two: racial allegories: the white hood

2

A *Grand Canyon*

Black gang member to Simon: Are you asking me for a favor cause you respect me, or cause I got the gun?
Simon to gang member: Man, the world ain't suposed to be this way.... You don't have the gun, we don't have this conversation.
Gang member to Simon: That's what I thought. No gun no respect, that's why I always got the gun. (*Grand Canyon*)

White men would rather win first and look good second, while black men want to look good first, and win second. (Billy to Sidney in *White Men Can't Jump*)

Lawrence Kasdan. Ron Shelton. Two white directors telling stories about the hood and race relations in the 1990s. *Scene One:* Lawrence Kasdan's 1991 film *Grand Canyon*[1] opens with the camera cutting back and forth between shots of Kevin Kline (Mack) at the Los Angeles Forum watching a Lakers NBA basketball game, and shots of his son (Roberto) at home watching the same game on a small portable TV. Each shot focuses on ten black men running up and down the basketball court, African Americans entertaining a white audience. Ninety seconds into the film, the game over, Kline takes a wrong turn out of the Forum parking lot. His car stalls on a dark street in South Central Los Angeles. He is soon hassled by five black youths who threaten violence. Within minutes Danny Glover (Simon), a tow-truck operator, comes to his rescue.

Two images of blackness: the controlled, aesthetically pleasing athletic body of the NBA star versus the violent, slouching, hip hop, trash-talking body of the young black male, rap culture on the loose in the LA streets. The first image of blackness is pleasing to the white eye: plantation negroes performing for their owners. The second image is jarring, disconcerting: black threats to whiteness.

Scene Two: The screen fills with the sights and sounds of NBA basketball: Magic Johnson, Larry Bird, Charles Barkley, Michael Jordan's 'Play Ground,' non-stop video action, NBA top guns, music video artists, the 'Dream Team,' Larry Bird's life story, Michael Jordan's 'Come Fly With Me,' Michael on the golf course, Michael on the courts, Aire Jordan, Dazzling Dunkers, Boyz II Men singing their music video 'Sympin' (Ain't Easy)'[2] as a trailer to *White Men Can't Jump* (1992),[3] LA street scenes flash on the screen (up against the wall), young black men on the basketball court, young black women cheering them on

('White Men Can't Jump' stamped on their buttocks). A Boyz II Men singer steps forth and speaks to the audience: 'This is another white man's story [song] Pretend you're at the movies.'

In this chapter I examine *Grand Canyon* and *White Men Can't Jump*, complementary images of whiteness and blackness, assimilation, white man's style, comfortable stories, fitting tales for a conservative decade. Their moral directives are simple. The race problems in American can be resolved if the races work together, although it may be up to the white man (and woman) to carry this burden on his (her) shoulders (Giroux, 1994, p. 81).

Moreover, sensible, sensitive adults can easily overcome matters involving race. Black urban teenagers in gangs are another question. As argued in Chapter 1, in the popular media black (and brown) youths are symbolically defined as threats to the social order (Rose, 1994, p. 126; Perkins, 1996, pp. 266–267). Their seemingly senseless rage and violence are directly connected to rap and hip hop culture (Rose, 1994, p. 125). This violent culture is self-destructive. The youth, left to their own devices, are unable to escape the effects of this culture. It is the black (and white) adult's burden to take young people out of this violent, hip hop culture. Strange bedfellows, the liberal white middle class converges with the cultural and religious Right. White and black youth must be saved from the rap attack (Perkins, 1996, p. 267).

I begin with Kasdan's *Grand Canyon*.[4] How these themes are central to the story he and Ron Shelton tell is my topic.

Lost in the Hood Again

Giroux's (1994, p. 75) reading of *Grand Canyon* is correct. The film is about whiteness and race, whiteness as privilege, as social construction, as domination (on whiteness see Fine et al., 1997, p. vii). *Grand Canyon* is about the new patriarchal, benign racism of the Reagan and Bush years. It is about a new politics of cultural difference. It is about the collapse of white middle-class civility and privilege in the public spaces of everyday life. This is a racism predicated on difference, on the strangeness of the other, on the death of the innocent black subject (Giroux, 1994, p. 76). This is a racism that is color-blind, even as it color-codes violence, locating white people on the margins of a violent, Third World, alien, dark-skinned culture, Los Angeles, no longer the city of angels.

This is a film that uses race for white purposes, to show that well-off whites can deal with life's contingencies, and with race at the same time. Hence its main characters (Mack, Simon, Davis, Claire, Dee, Jane, Otis, Roberto) wrestle with problems that constantly glance off of racial issues, including: marital, mid-life crises (Mack and Claire); young men coming of age (Roberto and Otis); the loneliness of single women (Dee, Jane); mistresses and one-night stands (Dee and Mack); interracial friendships (Dee and Jane, Mack and Simon); abandoned Third World babies (Claire); inner-city gangs, guns, and black mothers as single parents (Deborah); splatter movies, muggings, earthquakes, rampage in nice neighborhoods; police harassment (Otis); a mother in South Los Angeles 'matter-of-factly scrubbing a huge bloodstain off the sidewalk outside her home … police helicopers hovering "ceaselessly over nocturnal streets'" (Kemp, 1992, p. 50; also Ansen, 1991a, p. 57). Its all here: fear, danger, race coded as violent disorder, the Yuppie yearning for a safe life in the early 1990s.

The plot is simple, yet complex, involving several loosely connected storylines, each revolving around violence, race, gender, and white privilege. Two men, Mack and Simon, stand at the center of the narrative. Mack is a middle-aged successful immigration attorney. Mack is married to Claire, who fears the empty-nest syndrome because their son Roberto (named after Roberto Clemente) is about to leave home for college. Mack recently had a one-night affair with his secretary, Dee, who is in love with him. Dee's closest friend at work is an African-American woman named Jane. Simon is a middle-aged auto mechanic, a single parent, with a deaf daughter attending Gallaudet University in Washington, DC. Simon has a sister, Deborah, a single parent with a little girl and a teenage son, Otis, who has joined a gang. Mack's closest friend is Davis, 'a successful producer of gory, brutal films about big-city violence' (Balingit, 1992a, p. 159).

Kasdan's project is to forge a series of connections between the lives of these characters, Mack is the glue holding the story together. His point of view structures the narrative. The story begins, as noted above, with Mack taking a wrong turn into the ghetto and being saved by Simon. Over coffee and breakfast a few days later the two men form a bond from this chance encounter, a bond that is reaffirmed later in a one-on-one basketball game at Mack's house. In a drive-by, gang members spray Deborah's house with a barrage of bullets. Mack arranges for Deborah and her children to move from the ghetto into a safe, nearly all-white neighborhood. Mack introduces Jane to Simon, and they begin dating. Roberto goes off to summer camp and falls in love, comes home, and learns to drive his father's car. Claire discovers an abandoned baby in the woods one morning as she is jogging. Under some duress, Mack arranges for him and Claire to adopt the baby. Otis leaves his street gang. Davis, shot by a mugger, soon reneges on his vow never to make another violent film ('My movies reflect what's going on; they don't make what's going on'). Dee painfully accepts Mack's rejection and finds a nice policeman to hold her hand after she nearly has a nervous breakdown at a stoplight. At film's end, Mack – with new baby – Claire, Roberto, Jane, Simon, and Otis visit the Grand Canyon. Mack admits that life is not that bad after all. He has crossed the color line in his friendship with Simon, who has a new woman in his life. Claire is happy with their Third World baby, and Otis and Roberto may become friends. Everybody has purpose in his or her life and Mack can pat himself on the back.

Reading Kasdan's Moral Fable

The film's title functions at two levels. On the one hand it refers to the real place, the real Grand Canyon, a site that is visited by all of the principal characters at the end of the film. It represents an 'ancient landmark beside which humans dwindle in importance and size' (Billison, 1992, p. 35). As the Glover character says, 'When you sit on the edge of that thing, you realize what a joke we people are.'

At the same time the film turns this site, itself a product of great force, chaos, and violence, into a metaphor that stands for something else. The Grand Canyon represents life in Los Angeles today, a life defined by hysteria and fear and a toss of the dice, a violence that stands outside the natural order of things. On the surface it appears that only luck and fate protect us from chaos and destruction. So the film is about chance, risks, contingencies, well-intended white people who can turn good or bad luck to personal advantage; race and chance in the service of whiteness.

However, the conversations of Mack and Simon notwithstanding, risks are not randomly distributed in Kasdan's social structure. (Mack to Simon: 'There are just so many ways to buy it. It's amazing that at the end of the day anybody is alive in this city'; Simon to Mack: 'You never know when you will bump up against the big shark and he turns you into hamburger.') There are risky places, and if you go into them, you may be in trouble. This is the lesson Mack learned. Similarly, if you do not pay attention to what you are doing, trouble can reach out and hit you (Mack almost being hit by a bus). If you hang out with gangs, as Otis does, then you risk violence. If you are a young black man acting strange in a white neighborhood, the police will stop you. Single women who have affairs with their bosses get hurt and lose their jobs. There is a coded message: you risk danger when you take chances and stray from your own little world.

The fear and shock of violence, both black and white, unites Kasdan's characters. Indeed the film's moral turns on the symbolic manipulation of violence and its meanings. Kasdan valorizes Davis's violent movies, their blood and gore, brains smashed on the windshield of buses. This is safe white violence done in the service of white entertainment.

Kasdan abhors black violence, the violence and disrespect of the ghetto where black youth carry guns and threaten the lives of white (and black) men. (Recall the conversation between Simon and the gang member over the gun and respect quoted at the outset of this chapter.)

Violence in Kasdan's world exists on a continuum, from the emotional to the physical, and it crosses gender and race lines. It ranges from black on black (Otis and his gang, gang members to Simon) to black on white (gang member to Mack), and white on white (Davis being shot) violence. It moves from physical threats to actual violence, to the emotional violence involved in abandoning a newborn baby. It includes heart attacks and natural catastrophes: an LA earthquake. It involves almost being hit by buses (Mack), and barely avoiding auto accidents (Roberto turning left in front of ongoing traffic during a driving lesson with Mack).

In Kasdan's existential world every individual's fate is determined by the random play of trouble (Denby, 1992a, p. 46). Moral character is established in the face of life's contingencies. Thus Claire makes her claim to moral worth by bringing home the abandoned baby. Persons with strong character act with courage in the face of danger, for example when Simon faces down the gang member with the gun. And Mack takes a risk when he reaches out to Simon.

But there are different types of danger, and hence different types of moral character; indeed Kasdan codes danger in terms of gender and class. White women confront danger in the interpersonal and family realms: Claire and the baby, Dee and Mack. In Kasdan's world white people seem more frequently to confront the violence of nature, while black people confront the violence of their own culture

(Otis's mother being nearly killed in the drive-by shooting). On occasion this out-of-control black culture intrudes into the white world, as with Mack in the hood. When this happens, the white man must rely on the good black man to save him. Conversely, the good white man can help the black man get out of the nightmare of the hood. A strange interdependency thus connects black and white cultures; an interdependency born of the mutual need for survival.

Thus for Kasdan race in the 1990s has become something more than the white man's burden. In the white societies of cities like Los Angles race and violent disorder have become part of the natural order of things. This is unfortunate, and it increases the white man's burden. Sadly, there are too few Simons in this intrusive, explosive black culture; too many gun-toting, hip-hopping arrogant black youths. Kasdan fears that barbaric, disrespectful black youths are winning the war. This does not bode well for Mack and his yuppie crowd.

So in the end this moral fable resorts to the grandeur of the Grand Canyon to make its point. Things would be fine if we could all load up our families in a new recreational vehicle and visit this natural wonder. Things would be even better if we could take a black friend like Simon or Jane with us.

Race and Babyboomers

Balingit (1992a) suggests that Kasdan's *The Big Chill* (1983) was the 'original film anthem of the babyboomers' (p. 158) who were fresh out of the 1960s and moving into the 1980s. Angst, pain, confusion, disillusionment, drug use, sex, and wealth defined the obsessions and personal situations of the post-sixties radical yuppies in *The Big Chill*. *Grand Canyon* continues this narrative, taking up the same group, only ten years later, now 'more mature and economically stable, but hounded by the ghosts of spiritual longing they cannot satisfy' (Balingit, 1992a, p. 158). So this is a story about yuppies with New Age beliefs living in a troubled, edgy, violent Los Angeles, the city of fear (see Giroux, 1994, p. 84). Paranoia, traffic jams, smog, street crime, poverty, disorder, social inequity, earthquakes, and random violence define everyday life (Ansen, 1991a, p. 1). No one is immune from this state of affairs. Helicopters hover overhead; Los Angeles has become the site of the new Vietnam war (Balingit, 1992a, p. 160).

But this is not a story of life in the hood, the story Singeleton tells in *Boyz N the Hood*. This is a story about what the hood means for life in the white ghettos. It is, in this sense, perhaps a darker and deeper version of Steve Martin's satirical, whimsical *LA Story* (1991); that is, Kasdan's film affirms a 'final hopefulness – an affirmation of life in the city at fortysomething and of contemporary life in general' (Balingit, 1992a, p. 161). Like *The Bonfire of the Vanities* (1990), where a white man also takes a wrong turn into the ghetto, *Grand Canyon* is about the collapse of civic life in American today (Denby, 1992a, p. 46). But unlike John Sayles' *City of Hope* (1991), Kasdan's film refuses to connect race with politics, and politics with power and corruption. Kasdan's racial order, firmly rooted in the interpersonal realm, stands outside the political system.

Grand Canyon's story transcends time as it embodies today's conservative racial order. In so doing it repeats the adages and homilies of a 1950s melting-pot tale. The resolution of problems connected with race is reduced to the actions of well-intended individuals, even if blacks and whites live in residentially segregated communities. As with Mike Nichols' *Regarding Harry* (1991), *Grand Canyon* uses black men to rescue white men in need of help, including help in understanding that black men are men too (see Brown, 1991a, p. 52). Gentle black men lead anxiuous white males into new levels of racial- and hence self-sensitivity and self-awareness. Mack is a better father and husband because of Simon.[5]

In this sense Kasdan's film is even more whimisical and more utopian than Martin's *LA Story*. And more dangerous, for it reduces America's race problem to a nuisance factor in the lives of the fortysomething yuppie generation. At the same time, it repeats Hollywood's long-standing pattern of using the 'mellow and laid back' (Bogle, 1994, p. 275) black man as a symbol and model of stablity for the suffering, alienated white man; race in the service of whiteness (Bogle, 1994, p. 275).

Ron Shelton tells a slightly different story.

The Basketball Carnival

The time is now, the present. Cut to the boardwalk on Venice Beach. Another tequila sunrise.[6] Four black men ('The Venice Beach Boys'), with imaginary musical instruments, croon, 50s bebop style, 'Just a Closer Walk with Thee,' and pigeons gather on the street as the waves crash nearby, palm trees sway in the breeze, skateboarders roll by, weightlifters work out, and the sounds of 'Jesus Keep Us From All Wrong' lift to the clear blue sky. Billy Hoyle, a white man in baggy shorts, T-shirt, fancy sneakers, baseball cap, strolls by, basketball in hand, stops, listens, asks, 'This Venice Beach Court? Is this where Eddy the King Fardo and Duck Johnson used to play?' Turning away, he drops a dollar bill in one of the old men's hats, and says, ' My daddy was a preacher. I love this shit.'

Thus opens *White Men Can't Jump*, one of the most popular Hollywood films released in 1992, a 'comedy of great high spirits' (Ebert, 1992), a 'movie with appealing oddball characters and a grungy verisimilitude about small-time dreams' (Rozen, 1992), Siskel's (1992) pick of the week, a comedy about 'male braggadocio, sports bonding and good-natured race baiting' (Kehr, 1992; Clark, 1992).

From its opening pastel Venice Beach scenes, with Billy dropping a dollar in the hat, to its closing shots, when Sidney does the same, leaving $20 instead ('If I don't take care of my brothers, who will?'), *White Men Can't Jump*, like *Grand Canyon*, projects a utopian vision of American race relations. Basketball, the most successful of all US professional sports, is presented as the vehicle that can bond and bridge the racial gap between ordinary white and black American men. This bond overcomes prejudice, stereotype, and violence.

White Men Can't Jump foregrounds, as it neutralizes, race, class, and gender, making these terms central to the contemporary self and its emotional experiences (Denzin, 1991a, p. viii). In its tellings *White Men* co-opts contemporary black cultural practices, bringing its own white interpretations to bebop music, rap, hip hop, and playground basketball. The film asserts that white men have a rightful place in black street culture (see West, 1988, pp. 278–283). In Sidney's words, he and Billy are 'Ebony and Ivory.' Only a conservative racial ideology masquerading as white liberalism would contend that racial difference can be so easily transcended.[7] Thus does Billy parallel Mack of *Grand Canyon*, and Sidney becomes a more athletic version of *Canyon*'s Simon.

Two emotional versions of the postmodern self stand at the center of *White Men Can't Jump*. I call them the surface (impulsive) and the deep (expressive) versions or levels of the emotional self (Denzin, 1993). The person presenting a surface emotional self acts like a chameleon, staging performances that seem appropriate to the immediate situation. His or her self-expressions are often impulsive and action-oriented. Such individuals invest great meaning in action, thrills, and danger.

The deep emotional self, in contrast, creates emotional performances that produce authentically felt deep inner senses of moral worth (Denzin, 1993a, p. 74). This deep emotional self acts on the basis of an inner moral center. The surface self confuses style with success, favoring risks, chance-taking, and immediate mate-rialistic rewards. The expressive self blends style and performance with success, understanding that the two flow together.

These two versions of the postmodern emotional self are given racial form in Billy's argument to Sidney, as quoted at the beginning of this chapter. To repeat: 'White men would rather win first and look good second, while black men want to look good first, and win second.' Billy, the 'slow white geeky chump,' the 'scraggly white motherfuckin' Pilgrim,' has a superficially sloppy, awkward, nonchalant basketball style. It is Larry Bird-like. It vividly contrasts with the aes-thetic beauty of Sidney's Michael Jordon/Magic Johnson repertoire of moves. Sidney is the artist, Billy the clod with the surface, chameleon-like self. Sidney, the artist, performs a deeper, presumably more authentic self.

Cornel West (1988) clarifies this distinction. He contends that in black culture the athlete is an artist of great importance:

> The black player tries to *style* reality so that he becomes spectacle and performance, always projecting a sense of self ... smooth, clever, rhythmic, syncopated.... A lot of time and energy, and discipline goes into it but usually with a certain *investment of self* that does not express the work ethic alone ... whereas his white counterpart tends toward the productivistic and mechanistic. (p. 283, italics in original)

A great deal is at issue in the clash between these two versions of the emotional, racial self. If the white self 'can't jump' and 'can't hear Jimi [Hendrix],' as Sidney claims, then it does not have access to the inner and outer structures of experience that define the African-American emotional self. This self, embodied in Sidney, knows itself, knows its values, understands the worth of family, home, community, women, work, and ethnic pride. The white self, embodied in Billy, lacks all of these virtues, yet believes it can have them (and even hear 'Jimi') if it can just learn to dunk. But in the extended closing scene of the film, Billy does not understand why Sidney would drop $20 in the hat, while he only gave one.

At the end the film undermines its own premise. White men can't jump, and the racial barriers between whites and blacks in this culture are not so easily overcome.

There is more to the gendered racial self then being able to hear Jimi Hendrix. On race and the self, W. E. B. Du Bois (1903) argued, 'the Negro is ... born with a veil, and gifted with second-sight in this American world – a world which yields him no true self-consciousness, but only lets him see himself through the revelation of the other world' (p. 17). Du Bois argued that the color line in American creates a sense of double-consciousness for the African American. This is a racial self that is always looking at itself 'through the eyes of others' (p. 17). It is always measuring itself 'by the tape of a world that looks on in amused contempt and pity' (p. 17). Because of this double-consciousness, 'One feels his twoness – an American, a Negro; two souls ... two warring ideals in one dark body' (p. 17). The black self is mirrored back to itself through the imputed reflections of the white other.

White Men playfully and dangerously distorts this mirror. It does this when it suggests that Bily can look through the veil that separates Sidney from the white world. It contends that Billy has Sidney's double-consciousness. This is not what Du Bois had in mind.

African-American Spectacle

The Los Angeles ghetto basketball court is the center of *White Men Can't Jump*. Released just weeks before Los Angeles erupted in riots and fire after the Rodney King trial (see Ablemann and Lie, 1995, p. 6), the film presents the public basketball court as the site of moral community. A carnival-like atmosphere brings multi-ethnic, families together. Courtside, colorfully dressed dark- and brown-skinned mothers hold their children in their arms. Together they chide and cheer their muscular husbands and boyfriends, who twist, turn, and fly, à la Michael Jordan, up and around the basketball rim. The air is filled with the music of Jimi Hendrix, Aretha Franklin, James Brown, Ray Charles, Boyz II Men, College Boyz, Boo-Yaa Tribe, Bebe and Cece Winans, Cypress Hill, and The O'Jays.

This is pure separatist ethnic community. Family harmony. Pride, solidarity, no violence, no poverty. The basketball street carnival is presented here, not as the 'privileged arm [site] of the weak and the dispossessed' (Stam, 1989, p. 227). Nobody is dispossessed in *White Men*. Everybody is a winner. Basketball, the fantasized last court of resort for young, athletically gifted African-American males, is portrayed here as a place of joy, renewal, and triumph. This is utopian fantasy.

The humor of *White Men* lies, in part, in the verbal wit and ritual insults that are exchanged back and forth between the players on the court: 'Your mother so skinny she do the hula hoop in a Applejack.' 'Your mother so black, she sweat chocolate.' These men are doing the dozens (Labov, 1972, p. 133).[8] Labov (1972, p. 158) suggests that violence is probable when the ritual insult becomes personal. In dealing with strangers Labov (1972) observes that 'it is considerably harder to say what is safe ground, and there are any number of taboos that can be broken with serious results' (p. 158). Billy, as a racial outsider and hence stranger to Sidney's group, violates these rules without serious consequence, thereby pointing to another utopian theme in *White Men*.

White Men's Los Angeles is not the Los Angles of other late 1980s and early 1990s films located in this city, including *Colors* (1988), *Grand Canyon* (1991),

Boyz N the Hood (1992), *The Player* (1992), *Blood In Blood Out* (1993). The omnipresent helicopter (*Blue Thunder*, 1983), with its 'probing searchlight, and the propellers' [sinister] rhythmic concussions' (Balingit, 1992a, p. 159), are missing here. In *White Men*'s Los Angeles cultural differences do not produce fear, violence, or hatred,[9] and young children are not killed in front of their homes, their blood smeared on the sidewalks.

In attaching itself to the basketball court, and the struggles that occur there, *White Men Can't Jump* aligns itself, superficially at least, with other basketball films (*Hoosiers*, *Championship Season*) and male-bonding, sport-genre films (*Bang the Drum Slowly*, *Bull Durham*). At the same time, it is a black movie, keying with its stars (Wesley Snipes, Tyra Ferrell, Rosie Perez) on the recent popularity of such late 1980/early 1990s African-American-directed films as *Do the Right Thing*, *New Jack City*, *Jungle Fever*, and *Boyz N the Hood*. With Woody Harrelson as co-star, the film also connects itself to one of the most popular television shows of the 1980s, *Cheers*. This is a multi-ethnic, multi-media movie.[10]

In telling this white man's story, I cautiously take it back from its African American spokespersons, for in their telling, Boyz II Men suggest that 'sympin' ain't easy, and you may have to be black to do it.' But this statement is ironic and misleading. This is a white man's story told by a white man. Ron Shelton, director and writer, is closely identified with male-bonding, sport-genre films, having written or written and directed the screenplays for *Bull Durham* (1988) *The Best of Times* (1985), *Blue Chips* (1994), and *Cobb* (1994).

Four scenes are critical to the story *White Men* tells, but first a brief telling of the story.

Just Another White Man's Story

This is a white man's story. A small postmodern existential tale. From its opening to closing scenes, Billy Hoyle and his foibles structure the narrative. A gawky, goofy, down-at-the-heels hayseed basketball hustler, a one-time college talent who refused to throw a college game, he is on the run from the Stucci brothers – gamblers who seek their money ($8000) back. Billy kept the money for throwing the game and bought a car. Now he and Gloria (Rosie Perez) are seeking to win enough money to pay back the Stuccis, who want the car or the money. Billy's running companion is Gloria Clemente. Gloria is an energy-filled proud young Puerto Rican beauty from Brooklyn (a former disco queen), with a blaring nasal voice. She spends her days in run-down, cheap, sleazy motel rooms drinking vodka and studying the almanac (foods that begin with Q) in hopes of getting on *Jeopardy* ('my destiny') and winning a fortune that will launch her acting career ('I have more useless information in my head than any other human being on the planet! How many moons on Pluto? What is a solar eclipse? When was the hamburger invented?').

Billy meets and hustles Sidney in a one-on-one basketball game. Sidney holds down three jobs (cable TV, roofing, construction) plus basketball hustling. Billy and Sidney team up. Sidney taunts opposing players into making huge bets, while letting them pick his teammate. Naturally they pick white hayseed Billy (who is hanging around the court), and naturally Sidney and Billy clean up (Gabrenya, 1992, p. 16). In turn, Sidney hustles Billy out of the money he and Gloria are saving to pay off the Stuccis. Outraged, Gloria storms into Sidney's apartment and demands the money back from Sidney's wife, Rhonda. The two wives agree that their two men should be encouraged to enter and attempt to win the city-wide Two-on-Two Brotherhood Basketball Tournament. (The winners take home $5000.) Billy and Sidney win. In a one-on-one game with Sidney after the tournament it is determined that Billy cannot dunk a basketball. He loses his winnings to Sidney. An outraged Gloria leaves Billy. To help Billy get her back, one of Sidney's friends (a studio security guard) arranges for Gloria's appearance on *Jeopardy*. She wins $12,000, and she and Billy reconcile, Gloria vowing to help Billy get a regular job.

In an effort to help Sidney get money to move his family into a house, Billy and Sidney hustle Eddy the King and Duck Johnson. (Gloria threatens to leave if Billy gambles one more time.) Billy dunks the final, winning shot, thereby proving that a white man can both jump and dunk. Returning to the hotel, Billy finds that Gloria has left him once again. The Stucci brothers show up, demanding their money. Billy pays them off, and they stage his death, complete with Polaroid pictures of a faked murder. Billy asks Sidney for a job (which is given), and the two men are last seen (and heard) throwing a basketball back and forth as they do the dozens against a fading LA sunset. The O'Jays' song 'Can You Come Out To Play?' is heard over their verbal banter as the credits for the film begin to roll. A male-bonding tale from start to finish, the text finally answers in the affirmative its own question about white men and their ability to jump. Thus racial boundaries are erased on the basketball court.

Reading the Story

This is a woman's film with strong economic overtones. Underneath the male-bonding story there is the presence of a feminine moral position, a position that consistently moves across race and gender, and the political economy of work. In the end, Gloria leaves Billy because he will not grow up, stop gambling, and get a job. Rhonda, on the other hand, finally forces Sidney to allow her to work so that they can afford to move out of Vista View (which is neither a vista nor a view) to a home of their own. In the end Sidney is aligned with Rhonda's position. Billy never accepts Gloria's point of view. His impulsive self is always responsive to the lure and excitement of the next game, desires that arise from the immediate situation.[11] Four pivotal scenes bring race, gender, and economics together.

The first scene occurs shortly after Billy and Sidney have become partners. Billy and Gloria are dropping Sidney off at Vista View. Billy and Sidney have a conversation about Jimi Hendrix and his music ('Purple Haze').

> *Sidney:* You can't hear Jimi. You may may *listen* to Jimi, but you can't *hear* him!
> *Billy:* Hear this, Listen to George Jones man. [He plays Jones's *He Stopped Loving Her Today*] Hey man, Jimi's band was all white.
> *Sidney:* [*To Billy as he looks at Gloria*] Good woman.
> *Billy:* [*furious*] Keep your hands off her! I'll kick your ass!

Sidney: What's wrong? You're a cool customer on the court. Don't fall for that nigger shit! When it comes to your woman it's a different thing! You're just like all those other white boys I know.
Billy: [*screaming*] Shut the fuck up! You're just like all the brothers I know. You'd rather look good and lose, than look bad and win!
Sidney: It's a good thing I know this about you. It's your weakness.

Here the narrative comes up against race and gender (and sexuality) and then backs off, as it enunciates a stereotypical white attitude toward black males and white women. At the same time, it says that whites cannot hear (or understand) black music.

The second scene occurs in the Two-on-Two Brotherhood Basketball Tournament. Billy and Sidney are playing two black men. Billy engages the black opponents in a white man's version of a black man doing the dozens. Billy calls the black men racists, Oppie Taylors, Black Zorros, Rastafarians, corn-fed mules, pretty boys, black ball. He accuses them of throwing bricks up against the wall. He mocks black food ('Go back to Aunt Bea's, she fix you black-eyed peas and bean pie for your lunch'). Sidney angrily pulls Billy aside and yells, 'This is not a black and white thing. This is about money. I need five grand.' Billy retorts, 'You fuck'n' racist. I can hear Jimi.' Sidney replies, 'No you can't, dickhead!'

Their opponents physically and verbally threaten Billy, who claims he is in a zone. Billy and Sidney win the game. Once again Billy has crossed the racial barrier that divides whites and blacks. But in his performance he has broken three basic rules of doing the dozens: (1) do not make your teammate mad at you; (2) a white man does not do the dozens with a black man; and (3) in doing the dozens, one does not turn a ritual insult into a personal attack on the opponent (Labov, 1972, p. 148). In violating these understandings, Billy acts as if his skills as a basketball player give him the privilege to enter the black man's territory and act like a black man. Sidney refuses to accord him this right, but backs off when they win.

The third scene, and the film's penultimate moment, occurs when Gloria tells Billy she will leave him if he plays with Sidney in the match against Eddy the King and Duck Johnson. Billy is presented with contradictory demands. He wants to satisfy his friend and his lover. Sidney needs the money to buy the house Rhonda wants. Billy promises Gloria that he will win and that this will be the last time he gambles. She exclaims, 'I don't need the money. I don't want the money. I want you, you stupid sonofabitch. You gamble my money and we're through! I love you. Goodbye.' Gloria skates off, and this is the last time she is seen on the screen.

Billy, as an impulsive self, cannot answer to the deeper, loving self given in Gloria's demands. Ironically, when he and Sidney win, he confirms Gloria's earlier prophecy: 'Sometimes when you win you really lose. Sometimes when you lose you really win. And sometimes when you lose you actually tie. When you tie you actually win and lose. Winning and losing are part of one big organic globule from which one extracts what one needs.'

The fourth scene, the film's climax, occurs when Billy realizes that Gloria has left him. Billy has just recited Gloria's prophecy concerning winning and losing, saying he does not know what she means. Sidney keeps it brief:

Sidney: Listen to the woman.

Billy: What the hell does that mean?

Sidney: I didn't have to talk you into it [the last game]. I presented you with an option and you took it.

Billy: Who should I listen to?

Sidney: You're a grown man. Figure it out for yourself.

Billy: Gloria's not coming back.

Sidney: I know.

Billy: If I listen to the woman, do I have to agree with her?

Sidney: No. I don't want to stress you out.

Billy: I gotta get a job. Give me a job

Sidney: You got references?

Billy: Yah, you.

Sidney: You gonna be alright. Now you startin' to hear the music.

Billy: You mean I can hear Jimi now?

Sidney: No, you still can't hear Jimi.

Not hearing Sidney, Billy starts a game of dozens with Sidney ('Your mother is so stupid it takes her sixty, no it takes her two hours ...') and Sidney shuts him down, 'Don't hurt yourself man.' Billy offers, '$20 on this game?' So concludes the film.

In the end Billy thinks he has answered Gloria's demands, but as always he wants it two ways: to play ball, take chances, and have Gloria too. Now Gloria is gone and he is left to work for Sidney. In this gesture the film has Billy pass through its own thin racial barrier. Crossing the color line (Blumer, 1958), this white man has now become his version of being black. So race is once again erased, just as economics had previously displaced sexuality and gender. Billy's impulsive postmodern self finds a new home in a black world of his own making. Billy, the ambivalent renegade, has joined the colonized. He has colonialized himself.

This is the racial utopia *White Men Can't Jump* offers the white male viewer, but remember, 'Sympin' ain't easy.' If you learn how to do it, you learn that it is a gendered task, and the women you need may not do what you want them to do. Great risks are involved. Gloria, Billy's strong-willed lover, leaves him, and Rhonda demands that her traditional husband allow her to enter the workforce. Women's terms define the ground rules for 'sympin.'

The Postmodern Emotional Self

Back to the beginning. Social texts like *White Men* neutralize and displace the racial and gender crises that are everywhere present in America today. At the same time these texts enunciate two versions, surface and deep, of the post-modern emotional and racial self. The white late adolescent male seeks the deep emotionally rich self of the gifted black athletic male. White youth culture 'symbolically appropriates aspects of black culture through style and music [and sports]' (Tucker, Jr, 1993, p. 206; see also Gaines, 1991; Hebdige, 1984). But while the white man's self superficially crosses over into the terrain of black male culture, the self that is realized risks being superficial and emotionally barren.

Barthes (1972) suggests that the dominant culture operates by 'appropriation: it abstracts the specific signs of social groups into mere signifiers that are then recoded as general cultural myths' (Foster, 1988, p. 264). *White Men Can't Jump* appropriates the specific signs, symbols, and myths of black male (and African-American) culture and recodes these myths in terms of a white man's story. Black postmodernist practices end up 'highly packaged, regulated, distributed, circulated, and consumed' (West, 1988, pp. 279, 281) by white American male culture. In the process, the original African-American aesthetic and cultural practices are stripped of their radical meanings. They have been co-opted by the dominant culture. Thus the colorful carnivalesque athletic spectacles that define the center of *White Men* are always read through Billy's, not Sidney's, eyes, for this is a white man's story.

But this is a sad and 'soulful' story because the carnival Billy wishes to enter is about more than glitter, good sex with Gloria, bebop, rap, money, hustling, scams, quick bucks, and slam dunks. The street carnival played over and over again on LA basketball courts is a carnival about hope, family, and community. Basketball *is* community for the African-American community. It is public-life-as-spectacle. In it are enacted the deeply radical and practical elements of the hustling street culture (West, 1988, p. 282).

This street culture that Billy wants recognizes the performance art of the preacher, the musician, and the black athlete (West, 1988, pp. 281–283). Each of these artists aesthetically articulates the subversive energies, hopes, dreams, and promises of an oppressed culture that has been forced to fit itself to the racism and repressive political lethargy of American society (West, 1988, p. 281). Pageantry and spectacle are at the center of this culture. In its carnivals the dystopian realities of black life are re-created by performers who enact a collective deep, expressive ritual self that speaks for the community-at-large. This collective postmodern self flows through the three structures of religion (Billy's daddy was a preacher), black music (the Venice Beach Boys sing as preachers), and basketball. It synthesizes these three structures of meaning into a collective and individual self whose meanings are given in a commitment to family and community. This self is invested in performance art, basketball, dress, music, singing, dance, verbal wit, sounding, the dozens. These performances ritualize the collective racial self of the group. In them is produced the gendered, expressive postmodern African-American self.

This version of the self is denied Billy. His impulsive surface self inevitably seeks the challenge of another 'one-on-one' basketball game where a quick buck can be won or lost. Billy is addicted to the scene of action where the self puts itself on the line (Goffman, 1967). Rhonda immediately recognizes this, telling Gloria, 'Your man has a problem.' Billy can never go beneath the glitter of the dare, the thrill of the moment. He will never enact a deeper self that transcends the moment of action. He wants, but does not know how to get, what Sidney has.

So *White Men Can't Jump* is a story of two versions of the postmodern racial self. It is, in addition, a spiritual allegory, a moral fable, a sad story of yearning. The sadness is given, of course, in Billy. As the personification of all young white American males, Billy carries on his shoulders several burdens, including: the desire to be recognized, to be athletic, to be at one with himself, as the African-American male appears to be. For those drawn to the liberal's desire for racial integration, Billy shows one way that the black and white cultures can be merged. His way, which is to mock, while celebrating, black culture, is self-defeating. He wishes to deny the unique features of black culture (I can hear Jimi!), while honoring the superiority of his own (George Jones).[12]

At the same time Billy is drawn to the bravado, the macho, and the carnivalesque features of this black male street culture. His sloppy external bodily appearance mocks, while his physical movements emulate, the masculine beauty of the black male physique. Inwardly he seeks the certain superior gendered self of the macho black male. He too patronizes women, and uses them for his own pleasure. So in black maleness he finds all that he wants: being hip and cool. He is drawn to the externalities of this culture, while he keeps both feet in his own. Wanting both worlds at the same time, he is a victim of a popular culture that tells him this is how to be a man. In the final analysis eros and ego displace politics.

Herein lies the rub. Films like *White Men Can't Jump* are dangerous texts just to the degree that they carry and articulate the above set of messages and promises. They create false hopes for whites, and at the same time contribute to the commodification and destruction of black culture. But this is the way that ideology and capitalism always operate. They take up popular culture items and reduce them to the lowest common denominator. *White Men* sells black culture to white American males. Black culture resists this appropriation, knowing that the ugly, violent sides of racism are always just below the surface when black and white males interact.[13] The dream of integration is ideological whitewash.

So if *White Men* persuades, as it apparently does, it is because popular culture works its effects so effectively. Who does not swell with pride when Billy makes that last dunk shot that wins the money for Sidney? Billy has finally overcome his racial prejudice about looking good. This earns him the good will of a black man. Of course there is an internal contradiction here, a feeling of guilt, but on a deeper level, guilt is what *White Men* is all about (see also Giroux, 1992, p. 200). And behind the guilt lurks the larger question of the white postmodern racial self, and its attempts to seek an authentic mode of existence in this all too inauthentic world.

White Men Tell Racial Stories

It remains to compare the two films. The older racism relied on science and biology (hooks, 1996, p. 88) and the historical legacies of colonialism and modern slavery to justify white supremacy (Giroux, 1994, pp. 74–75). Whiteness was a universal marker representing goodness, being civilized; darkness signified pathology. The new racism shifts the argument from biology to culture, to the politics of cultural difference, the politics of representation (Giroux, 1994, p. 75). As argued in the Introduction, this situation has ushered in new regimes of cinematic racial representation. The race wars are now fought in the media, on TV, and in the cinema. The new cinematic racism argues for the end of racial differences, assimilation to the golden norm of whiteness. But it does so by creating moral panics, and reaffirming white power (hooks, 1996, p. 77). The white communities of America are under siege, 'young black men are spreading violence like some kind of social disease' (Giroux, 1996, p. 27).

This new cinematic racism is the space Kasdan and Shelton occupy. Indeed within this discourse they define the two ends of a liberal–conservative continuum. Kasdan is terrified by the black culture that Shelton valorizes. Kasdan's white babyboomers are under attack and in retreat. Shelton's lone outlaw, white man Billy, is on the loose in black public culture, but he poses no threat to the likes of Sidney. Shelton takes a romantic, liberal view of black culture, celebrating the spirited community life that surrounds street basketball. Kasdan dwells on white panic, racial difference coded as violence, finding little of value or beauty in Simon or Jane's black world. Indeed for Kasdan the only hope for blacks lies in escaping the ghetto, and they may need white help to get this done.

The need for white help is critical; black men can't make it on their own. Sidney needs Billy to get the money for his new home. On his own Simon cannot get his sister out of the ghetto. At this level subtle versions of supremacist patriarchal values organize both texts (on white patriarchy, see hooks, 1996, pp. 88–89). Black men envy what white men have. They understand that they must submit, at some level, to the authority of the white male if they are to have what he has. Interracial friendship arises out of this need, for black men also have something white men want but do not have, that is, 'soul.' In both films white patriarchy is stitched into stories about homosocial bonding, intimate connections between black and white buddies (hooks, 1996, p. 89). This bonding is not homoerotic; it is largely 'passionless passion' (Fiedler, 1966, p. 368), and for Sidney and Billy it is also economic.

In both texts this bonding is secured on the basketball court, one of the last ideological sites for interracial male bonding in America today. But basketball functions differently for each director. Shelton uses the game as a way of celebrating the beauty of black culture. The basketball court is a place where black males 'triumph over white patriarchy' (hooks, 1996, p. 89), even if Billy thinks he is better than Sidney. Kasdan is perhaps more mundane. Two men form a friendship over a few shared hoops, but white patriarchy does prevail.

Back to the beginning: white men telling stories about black culture. The politics of identity folded into a conservative cinema of racial representation. A cinema that masquerades as white liberalism. A great deal is at stake in these two films. Kasdan and Shelton navigate an essentialist discourse on identity and cultural difference. Both directors make appeals to common, yet essential, cultural differences: 'white men can't jump' and black youth carry guns. Each director constructs an essential gendered black and white racial self: black men have soul; white man have angst. Each director makes an appeal to a common civic culture where white selves freely circulate with one another. When invited, properly assimilated black men and women make brief appearances in this civic space. In these gestures, each director rejects any 'pluralized notion of culture with … multiple literacies, identities, and histories' (Giroux, 1996, p. 187). Under the guise of liberalism, both films reproduce coercive assimilationist politics.

A nation, Benedict Anderson (1992) reminds us, is an imagined political community, a community that is best understood as an intersection of history, power, political ideologies, gendered identities, racial, ethnic, material, and cultural practices (Giroux, 1996, p. 190). *White Men* and *Grand Canyon* imagine particular versions of community and the cinematic racial order in America today. Each film forges a complex relationship between civic community, shared national identities, a common white culture, and a culture of assimilation. This is an imaginary community based on essentialisms and rigidly exclusive membership terms. Such nationalisms, Giroux (1996) suggests, 'tend to be xenophobic [and] authoritarian' (pp. 187–188). And in the end, regrettably, these are the kinds of stories these two movies tell. But the story of xenophobia and coercive assimilation does not stop here, as the women's films to be analyzed in the next chapter reveal.

Notes

1. *Grand Canyon* (1991). Released by Twentieth-Century Fox, Director: Lawrence Kasdan; Screenplay: Lawrence Kasdan and Meg Kasdan; Director of Photography: Owen Roizman; Cast: Danny Glover (Simon); Kevin Kline (Mack); Steve Martin (Davis); Mary McDonnell (Claire); Mary-Louies Parker (Dee); Alfre Woodard (Jane); Jeremy Sisto (Roberto); Tina Liffard (Deborah); Patrick Malone (Otis); Sarah Trigger (Vanessa). This was a top video rental of 1992 and 1993. It was nominated for an Academy Award for Best Original Screenplay.

2. *Sympin*: a dance, a frame of mind, a yearning, a desire, something you have to get down on your hands and knees for. Michael Jordan has it. Boyz II Men have it.

3. *White Men Can't Jump* (1992). Released by Twentieth-Century Fox. Director: Ron Shelton; Screenplay: Ron Shelton; Cast: Wesley Snipes (Sidney Deane), Woody Harrelson (Billy Hoyle), Rosie Perez (Gloria Clemente), Tyra Ferrell (Rhonda Deane), Cylk Cozart (Robert), Kadeem Hardison (Junior), Ernest Harden, Jr (George), John Marshall Jones (Walter), Marques Johnson (Raymond). This was a top video rental of 1992 and 1993.

4. For reviews see Ansen, 1991a; Balingit, 1992a; Bernard, 1991a; Billison, 1992; Brown, 1991a; Denby, 1992a; Ebert, 1994b; Kemp, 1992; Mathews, 1991a; Sterritt, 1992; Turan, 1991a.

5. Gender follows race for males. In contrast, for females, gender follows the path of male patriarchy, regardless of race. Jane, Dee, Vanessa, Davis's girlfriend, and Claire all find fulfillment through their men, or through motherhood (see Giroux, 1994, p. 86).

6. My discussion of this film reworks and extends Denzin (1995b). Conversations with Nate Stevens, Katherine Ryan, and the critical comments of Carolyn Ellis and Michael Flaherty helped clarify the arguments in this section.

7. See also Warren Beatty's 1998 film *Bulworth*, where a white politician suddenly learns how to sing rap music and become one with the black community (see Hirschberg, 1998, p. 24; also Gates, 1998).

8. Labov (1972, p. 129) suggests that sounding, or doing the dozens, which consists of ritual insults involving a negative, often sexual, attribute directed to another's mother is 'primarily [within the male black community] an adolescent and pre-adolescent activity, and not practiced as much by young men twenty to thirty-years-old.' In *White Men* this practice has moved into the twenty-two-to thirty-year-old age group. The ability to do rapid-fire sounding is a direct measure of one's knowledge, competence, and status as a speaker in the group. Labov (1972, p. 158) suggests that this highly ritualized activity produces symbolic distance between participants while affirming in-group solidarity.

9. The two exceptions to this conclusion are given when Raymond attempts to hold up a local liquor store with his gun but ends up selling his gun to the owner for $250, and the brief sequence of scenes following the robbery at Sidney's apartment. The only real violence in the film (and this is broadly staged) occurs in the interactions between Billy and the Stucci brothers over the money Billy and Gloria owe them. Here race is irrelevant.

10. The film's text is thoroughly intertextual with contemporary television and popular music culture. Sidney calls Billy 'Brady Bunch,' Billy calls Sidney 'Gladys Knight and the Pimps,' Billy plays his version of the dozens during the Two-on-Two Brotherhood Basketball Tournament, calling black players 'Aunt Bea' (*Andy Griffith Show*) and 'Black Zorro.' Gloria appears with Alex Treback on *Jeopardy*.

11. For example, if Gloria wants to make love, they make love, but if there is a basketball game being played, Billy wants to be there. When he loses his winnings to Sidney he refuses to tell Gloria. In the tournament he tries to act more black-like than the black players on the court. Sidney, in contrast, fuses his outer self with the inner moral code of his black male community. He resists Rhonda's pressures to allow her to work, plays the dozens the right way, and views basketball as a means to something else. Billy lives for the moment of the game, and little else.

12. He may also be asking, Carolyn Ellis and Michael Flaherty suggest, that a space for his culture be created within the black community, thereby asserting even more superiority for his.

13. This assertation can be quickly confirmed by observations of black and white males on public basketball courts in any medium-sized American city. Within minutes, in any pick-up game there will be verbal outbursts and physical shoving as white men attempt to do their version of Billy Hoyle with a group of young black males.

3

Race, Women, and Violence in the Hood

> *Precious:* You don't see much colored help these days. It was the 60s, those riots up North.
> *May-Alice:* You can't keep 'em [Negroes] down on the farm after they've burned Chicago.
> *Precious:* Well, ours down here have certainly caught the attitude. (*Passion Fish*)

> Now you gonna try to psychologize me. I come from a broken home and we're poor. OK? I see the same fuckin' movies you do man. You gonna give me some good advice, Just say No. You gonna get me off the streets? How the fuck you gonna save me from my life? (Emilio to LouAnne in *Dangerous Minds*)

> You picked the wrong nigger to call nigger. (Slim to Lester in *A Rage in Harlem*)

Another version of race and the coming-of-age story, black and white women, gendered friendships, violence and intimacy in the hood, crack-cocaine, virgins, Jezebels, and *femmes fatales*, gay alcoholics, menacing black ex-Chicago drug dealers in the bayous of Louisiana, black patriarchy, Bob Dylan songs, Chester Himes novels, black women as single parents, con artists, blacks working for whites, colored help, Shakespeare plays, comedies, soap opera stars, Southern gothic dramas, violence in big city schools. This is the stuff of *Dangerous Minds* (1995),[1] *Passion Fish* (1992),[2] and *A Rage in Harlem* (1991),[3] the three films I examine in this chapter.

Following Fregoso (1993, p. 94), and the gendered performance model of race and ethnicity given in Chapter 1, I examine what happens when women in hood movies directed by white males are given an active place in discourses about race.[4] The cinematic screen, the reciprocal racial gaze, the narrative logic, and the visual fields of these three films complicate the usual image of woman. In each film she is allowed to take up multiple subject positions. She becomes something more than a traditional stereotypical black or white woman; something more then the simple object of the male gaze.[5]

Race stories told from a woman's point of view neutralize violence. The feminine standpoint reproduces and then disrupts the classic male narrative about race, gender, and disorder, even when white males tell the story. I contrast these feminist tellings about women and race to the masculine, utopian, assimilationist accounts of race, family duty, sports, and male bonding given in *Grand Canyon* and *White Men Can't Jump*.

LouAnne (*Dangerous Minds*), May-Alice, Chantelle (*Passion Fish*), and Imabelle (*A Rage in Harlem*) occupy shifting and complicated positions as the objects and subjects of the gendered racial gaze. LouAnne's male and female students are the focus of her gaze, just as she is the object of theirs. May-Alice gazes upon, and is the object of the intensive (and fleeting) gazes of Rennie, Chantelle, Ti-Marie, Precious, Kim, and Nina. Chantelle, in turn, gazes at and is the object of the looks of May-Alice, Sugar, her daughter Denita, and her father, Dr Blades. Imabelle is the sexual object of Jackson's gaze, even as she turns him into a sexual subject for her own visual pleasure.

Four propositions organize my analysis. The first is not new; it is supplemental to earlier arguments concerning women, race, and violence (see Pride, 1995, p. 6; Collins, 1991, pp. 140–143; Austin, 1995, p. 427; West, 1994, p. 66; hooks, 1994, p. 2). In neutralizing traditional conceptions of male racial violence, black and white women articulate the possibilities of a non-violent racial order. This is an order based on intuition, compassion, and deep feeling. A feminist moral ethic informs this gaze and its project. This is an ethic forged out of the conditions of pain, violence, racism, sexism, poverty, and addiction. It embodies the principles of love, empowerment, compassion, personal accountablity, trust, mutual caring, and dialogue (Collins, 1991, pp. 206–219). The female leads in these three films represent and enact these principles. In so doing they create the possibilities for a new racial order based on love, mutual respect, and trust.

My second proposition elaborates the first. By disrupting the traditional male narrative, women model non-aggressive behavior for men. They do this by engendering race with a critical, non-essentialist feminist ethical standpoint (see Haraway, 1997, pp. 198–199, 304–305). This standpoint defuses potentially explosive racial situations. It creates the possibilities for non-violent friendships that cross gender and racial boundaries.

The third proposition extends the second, and also combines race and gender. In challenging racial essentialisms, the feminist racial subjectivity continually transgresses gender stereotypes. In so doing it confronts the prejudices and fears surrounding the black male body, and black and white sexual intimacy (see West, 1994, pp. 117–118). This creates a space for the complex play of multiple feminine and masculine racial subjectivities; for the production of black and white women and men who are not just unitary racial or sexual subjects.

My fourth proposition extends the third. This new racial order questions the authority of the traditional masculine white racial gaze. It displaces this gaze, replacing it with a multi-perspectival, multi-sensual feminine subjectivity (see Denzin, 1995a, p. 141). This subjectivity, even when inscribed by the white male director, embraces a field of experience that looks beyond color and race. This subjectivity, when released into the cultural and cinematic racial order, threatens the status quo. But this is an unstable threat because it must always resist the power of the white masculine violent assimilationist narrative.

The women in *Dangerous Minds*, *Passion Fish*, and *A Rage in Harlem* stand at the center of competing and overlapping racial, racist, sexist, and sexual discourses. These texts locate black and white women in a reactionary post-feminist American racial and sexual order. This is a sexual order that constantly draws women back into traditional patriarchal family formations (hooks, 1994, p. 76). The women in these texts live these sexual and racial contradictions from within. Each woman struggles to find a form of subjectivity that transcends the pervasive presence of white supremacist patriarchy. Each fights to find a place within a non-sexist, non-racist social order.

Each film is organized around a double spectacular structure. This structure is focused on sexuality, and the female body as the site of multiple gazes. These sexual and racial looks are stitched into larger specular structures which make women the objects of the gaze of medicine (May-Alice), the law (Imabelle), and the state (LouAnne). In articulating gender and racial stereotypes, these looks serve to align the feminine figure with family, intimacy, and the laws of patriarchy.

Thus are women fitted into the visual structures of race and sexuality. However, in moments of narrative crisis their sexual and racial identities are submerged, folded into larger discourses about men and women, family, medicine, law, crime, intimacy, and friendship. This process of displacement produces new forms of racial and cultural integration; forms seldom realized in white male-bonding stories.

How these feminine and masculine racial narratives work back and forth across and against one another is the topic of the analysis that follows. I begin with *Passion Fish*, for here two women imagine and then create one version of this new racial order.

Passion Fish

It's a simple story, the stuff of soap operas, in fact *Passion Fish* is about a soap opera star, May-Alice Kohane, and what happens to her after she is hit by a New York City taxicab and left paralyzed from the waist down. Bitter and uncooperative, her life shattered, May-Alice discharges herself from rehabilitation and 'retreats to the now-deserted childhood home in the Louisiana bayous' (Kemp, 1993, p. 51). Drinking heavily, and watching television constantly (channel-surfing), self-absorbed and self-pitying, unable to care for herself, she hires and fires a series of women helpers. May-Alice meets her match in Chantelle, a black nurse, a recovering cocaine addict, and a single mother from Chicago.

> *May-Alice*: What did the others say about me, that I'm a bitch?
> *Chantelle*: On wheels.
> *May-Alice*: You been doing this long?
> *Chantelle*: No – you?
> *May-Alice*: I can't have sex I can feel. Unless I get into blowjobs.
> *Chantelle*: It's none of my business what you put in your mouth.

Passion Fish is the story of the evolving relationship between these two women, a kind of buddy movie for women (Corliss, 1993), a version of *Driving Miss Daisy* where the servant has a history, and talks back to the master (Brown, 1992a; Denby, 1993a; Ebert, 1994e, p. 540; see also Wilmington, 1992a). On a trip to town, Chantelle meets and forms a relationship with Sugar LeDoux, a blacksmith, a zydeco guitarist, and a ladies' man. On the same trip Chantelle meets an old high school boyfriend of May-Alice's, Rennie, a carpenter and swamp guide, a married man with five children and a wife who does not understand him. Rennie offers to help fix up May-Alice's house, and to build a ramp for her. May-Alice's gay alcoholic Uncle Reeves drops by and chats about selling real estate, 'Oh, what our dreams come to,' and tells May-Alice about the scheme his dear deceased friend had to manufacture 'homoerotic delftware with little Dutch boys in compromising positions.' Uncle Reeves shows Chantelle his old photography darkroom, and gives May-Alice an old camera. May-Alice is visited by two high school friends, Ti-Marie and Precious, and later by three actresses she worked with in daytime television, Dawn, Nina, and Kim. Luther, Chantelle's former black lover from Chicago, unexpectedly drops by.

Rennie takes the two women on a trip out into the bayou. A beautiful cinematic sequence, reminiscent of the photography in Julia Dash's *Daughters of the Dust* (1991), takes the women deep into the swamp. Light and darkness glance off the water. The sun shines through a clear blue sky. The wind slowly moves the women's hair. Soft Cajun music is heard on the soundtrack. Rennie and the women stop on a small island. He catches a fish, which he guts, producing two small fish. He tells the women to 'hold out your hands, squeeze the little fish, they're called passion fish, think about somebody you want love from.' They return home under the cover of darkness. Within days Chantelle is visited by her father (Dr Blades) and her daughter, Denita. May-Alice's former TV producer Vance suddenly appears and asks May-Alice to return to the soap opera, offering her a part as a blind paraplegic. She turns down the offer. In the film's final scene May-Alice and Chantelle take another boat ride.

May-Alice: We have to talk. Vance asked me to come back to daytime.
Chantelle: You could do it.
May-Alice: Yeah I could. So what did your father say?
Chantelle: He thinks you are a good influence on me.
May-Alice: Shows how much he knows.
Chantelle: I can't believe I still have to do whatever he says. I feel like I'm 13 years-old.
May-Alice: I played the faithful daughter in *Lear*, what's her name, Cordelia? Not much you can do but play it straight till its over. Think he'd let Denita stay with you this summer?
Chantelle: I have to have a job.
May-Alice: You have a job.
Chantelle: In New York City?
May-Alice: I turned them down ... If I'm gonna be here, I need you to work for me.
Chantelle: Bull shit.
May-Alice: If I'm lyin', I'm dyin'.
Chantelle: [*tears in her eyes*] Then we're stuck with each other.
May-Alice: Well, for the time being. Chantelle, you are gonna have to learn how to cook. [*smiles*]

The credits and cajun music play over a shot of the two women in the boat as a gentle white and orange sun sets on the shimmering waters of the bayou.

This is a racially gendered tale of self-discovery and self-destruction, a story of a friendship formed under the special circumstances of loss. It is a story about the refusal of one woman, Chantelle, to allow another woman, May-Alice, to become a bed-ridden, self-pitying alcoholic (Cormack, 1993, p. 290). This story is also about the refusal of a black woman to be treated as if she were the 'colored help' of a white woman. (Chantelle to May-Alice: 'I'm not your waitress … and I can't cook.')

Its title, passion fish, carries its other message. This is a film about love of self and love of others, a love that transcends stereotype and self-hatred. In the end each woman has learned to love herself, to love who she has become. This is a love whose origins lie in the maxim 'love is caring more about the other; then you care about yourself.' By getting outside herself, and entering the situation of the other woman, each woman has found self-respect. The wish on the passion fish comes true. Each woman finds somebody she wants love from, most importantly herself. And it matters a great deal that Rennie, Sugar, Denita, and Dr Blades hover in the background. (In a dream sequence May-Alice walks to Rennie on the dock, where they embrace and kiss.)

Four scenes, each involving a visit from the outside, bring race, gender, intimacy, love, and stereotype together. These scenes unfold against the initially hostile but progressively friendly and respectful relationship that develops between Chantelle and May-Alice. In each scene the women are turned into the object of another's gaze.

Scene One: 'I'm a Nurse, Not a Cook'

Shortly after Chantelle has arrived, two of May-Alice's old high school friends, Ti-Marie and Precious, arrive unannounced for tea. May-Alice introduces Chantelle as 'My assistant.' Precious asks, 'Did her people work for your parents? Wherever did you get her? She is such a jewel. You don't see much colored help these days. It was the sixties, those riots up North.' May-Alice sardonically replies, 'You can't keep 'em down on the farm after they've burned Chicago.' Precious agrees, 'Well, ours down here have certainly caught the attitude.'

After the two friends leave, Chantelle asks: 'Is there some rule all black folks gotta cook?… I'm a nurse, not your assistant.' May-Alice counters, in a mock cajun accent, 'Darlin' down here there is a rule dat everybody got to know how to cook! But I don't know what to call you. You are not my servant, my babysitter, or my housekeeper.' Chantelle keeps it brief. 'I'm not your friend … but you drink too much.'

Scene Two: Bad News Comes Calling and a Day Without a Drink

In response to May-Alice's physical helplessness, Chantelle insists that an exercise regime be taken up, including the use of weights. Days later, by herself in her wheel-chair (Chantelle is in town with Sugar), May-Alice is near the dock taking pictures with Uncle Reeves' old camera. A menacing black man, Luther, with goatee, sunglasses, and a black turtleneck appears out of nowhere, towering over her as she sits in her chair. 'Chantelle here?' He walks in front of May-Alice:

> *Luther*: You 'fraid of me? Don't be. She OK? She happy?
> *May-Alice*: Was she expecting you?
> *Luther*: No. You can't feel anything in your bottom half, that right? I felt that way once. Started in my knees, shot me right past into my head, couldn't feel nothin' down below. She finished with the detox? She made up her mind. That's good, she's

keepin' straight. Tell her I'm sorry I missed her. Tell her Bad News came calling. She'll know my name.

In this scene May-Alice is the object of Luther's gaze, a crippled white woman in a wheel-chair holding a camera as her only defense. Luther's threatening presence brings the racialized masculinity of the hood into May-Alice's world. Luther is unlike her other two gentle white male visitors, Uncle Reeves and Rennie. This black man intimidates through his language, his gaze, his dress, and by flaunting his physical presence. He sexualizes May-Alice's body ("you can't feel anything in your bottom half"). He lays claim to a relationship with Chantelle, revealing aspects of her history that had not previously been shared. That night, as Chantelle is making love with Sugar, May-Alice discovers a bottle of liquor in Uncle Reeves' dark room.

The next day, in response to May-Alice's constant drinking, Chantelle challenges her, 'Can you make it through the day without a drink?' May-Alice, 'Hey, I'm not the addict, you are!' Chantelle removes all the alcohol from the house. In search of the wine bottle, May-Alice screams, 'I'm not ready for this. ... I'm not strong enough.... Go get me the fucking wine. I hired you, I want you to do what I tell you to do.' Chantelle retorts,

> Dream on girl.... You can't even go one day without a drink. You miserable, TV watching dried up old witch. You're just fucking spoiled and you're not even a drunk yet. Most mornings when I wake up I want to get high so much, I can't even breathe!

May-Alice responds by breaking all the dishes in the countertop in the kitchen. Once again Chantelle refuses to be a servant. In challenging May-Alice to get sober, she uses her own recovery as leverage in the situation. Both are addicts, only Chantelle is recovering and May-Alice is not.

Scene Three: Uncle Tom's Condo

Race resurfaces when May-Alice is once again visited by friends from the past, in this case Dawn (Angela Bassett), Nina, and Kim, actresses from daytime TV. Nina treats Chantelle as if she were a maid, while May-Alice insists that 'She isn't my maid or anything.' Kim asks May-Alice if her place has a name, and Dawn jokingly remarks that her husband says their apartment in the Hamptons is named 'Uncle Tom's Condo.'

Dawn strikes up a conversation with Chantelle in the kitchen, discovering that they are both from Chicago:

Dawn: I went to Cooley High.[6]
Chantelle: DeSable, I lived on Euclid Street.
Dawn: Pill Hill, your father must have been a doctor? [*Chantelle nods*]. I'm from Cabrini Green [one of Chicago's infamous public housing sites]. That's a long way out.

Two twisted racial paths out of Chicago. The upper-class black woman becomes a drug addict and a single parent, mistakenly identified as the maid of a crippled white woman. The lower-class black woman from the Projects becomes a famous TV actress who vacations in Uncle Tom's Condo.

Scene Four: 'No Cooks in Our Family'

Chantelle is visited by her father and her daughter Denita. May-Alice fixes a special meal, remarking, 'Chantelle is such a wonder in the kitchen.' Dr Blades will have none of this, 'We've never had someone in the family work as a cook.' Chantelle is once again troubled by the label of cook, the traditional job of the black woman in the kitchen.

The visit from her father and daughter closes with Chantelle sorting through a montage of May-Alice's black and white photographs: pictures of the swamp, of the lane leading to the main road, a shot of the wheel on a wheel-chair, pictures of the water, the dock, shadows across the lawn, a photo of Denita that fades into her actually climbing on the bus back to Chicago, turning and waving goodbye.

May-Alice has discovered a new calling. She rejects the offer to reenter the world of acting ('The only thing I was ever any good at'). She moves to the other side of the camera. She has gone from actress to photographer, to filmmaker. She was previously a pawn in another person's make-believe reality. With Uncle Reeves' camera she takes control of her world. Now she creates the images, and the narratives. She becomes the artist who records the world and its meanings. The tiny corner of reality she claims as her own is the one given over by the wish on the passion fish. She tells Rennie, 'Why don't you come by and visit. You don't have to come over just to fix something you know.'

Engendering the Racial Gaze

Sayles' film refuses to enage in racial and gender essentialisms. Still, this male story about self-discovery and feminine interracial friendships constantly confronts the strength of racial and gender stereotypes. White women insist on calling Chantelle a maid and a cook. In resisting this identification, Chantelle articulates an Afrocentric feminist ethic of empowerment, dignity, and self-worth (Collins, 1991, p. 107). She communicates this ethic to May-Alice, insisting that her employer grow up and take responsibility for her own health and well-being. In so doing, she creates the conditions for an equalitarian interracial friendship modeled on self-respect and love. May-Alice's discovery of the camera and photography are a consequence of this empowering ethic.

In bringing Luther into May-Alice's world, Sayles superficially plays on the prejudices and fears surrounding the black male body and its threats to the white woman. But of course May-Alice is a cripple, and Luther's experiences with drugs have left him a damaged man. So there is no real threat, and we see this. Indeed, the viewer experiences a sense of mutual respect as Luther gazes down at May-Alice, and she up at him, and this is later seen in her photograph that captures him when he walks away.

The camera of Roger Deakins, Sayles' cinematographer, brings a sense of gentle grace and beauty to the bodies of Chantelle and Sugar as they make love. Like a spring flower, she blossoms under Sugar's gentle touch. His soft voice awakens within her a long repressed sensual beauty. This forthright display of black intimacy supports the film's contention that black men and women are complicated human subjects, not just unitary racial or sexual others. This awakening of Chantelle's sexual self is matched by May-Alice's sense that she is falling in love with Rennie, a married man, and that perhaps she can be sexual in ways she had previously not allowed herself to imagine.

The white men in May-Alice's world are not the usual models of masculine authority. Uncle Reeves is gay, and Rennie is a small slight man, with a downward gaze and a sweet smile. The interracial order that May-Alice and Chantelle create together is multiperspectival and multi-sensual. This order looks beyond gender and race, and constantly threatens the status quo. It dares to imagine a situation where a black and a white woman are friends. But this is an unstable threat because, as indicated above, every white visitor insists on turning Chantelle into some version of a servant.

When May-Alice gets serious with the camera, she begins to challenge the power of the traditional masculine racial and gendered gaze. Her camera records feelings, fleeting images, off-angled shots of country lanes, leaning trees, and docks extending out into the rippling water. Her camera engages the world, brings the world into play. It becomes a way of being in the world. With it she breaks down barriers between herself and others. This is a feminine gaze that imagines and captures and creates the world in new ways. And Sayles is firm on this point. From this gaze come the foundations of a new racial order, a new set of discourses, experiences, and conversations about race, gender, intimacy, and love. This interracial order is based on self love and self-respect, born out of pain, self-doubt, addiction, violence, and racism.[7]

I turn now to *Dangerous Minds*, which offers another white man's version of women, the hood, and the new interracial order.

Dangerous Minds

Of course, the films's title is a play on words, a moral fable. A mind is a precious thing. It can be dangerous in two ways, depending on what kind of ideas get inside it. Minds filled with violent ideas can kill. Minds filled with positive ideas can learn, grow, and also be dangerous, but in a positive sense. For LouAnne, our protagonist, a mind is like a muscle, to be exercised. If properly exercised, given the right ideas and rewarded for these ideas, the mind becomes a dangerous threat to those who would engage in violence and self-destruction. (LouAnne: 'The mind is your weapon in this unsafe world. I want to arm you.') *Dangerous Minds* is all about turning violent, dangerous minds into minds that can stand up to the self-destructive violence of the ghetto.

The opening sequence of this film is shot in a grainy monochrome. The camera moves through a series of familiar close-ups, taken-for-granted signifiers of ghetto life today: black teenage girls in atheletic jackets, hair in corn rows, gossip on the street corner; a black homeless men with a grocery cart breaks a glass bottle on the sidewalk; a faceless drug dealer takes money from a man in a car; graffitti is scrawled on the walls of run-down buildings with boarded-up windows (Francke, 1996). The city is unnamed, it could be any hood, but it looks like Los Angeles.

Rap music composed and performed by Wendy and Lisa blares in the background ('As I walk through the valley of the shadow of death ... I'll never live to see 24 ... The Ones we hurt are you and me').[8] This is another urban hood movie, not exactly a ghetto-action film, but surely 'gritty urban social realism' (Francke, 1996; see also Maslin, 1995; Buehrer, 1996; Mathews, 1995a; Medved, 1995; Taubin, 1995a; Turan, 1995b). This is an all too familiar utopian story, the one about the white teacher who uses unorthodox teaching approaches to reach disadvantaged and dispossessed students. (In fact it is based on a true story, the 1992 book by LouAnne Johnson, *My Posse Don't Do Homework*.) We've seen it before, only now the teacher is a woman:[9] *Blackboard Jungle* (1955), *Up the Down Staircase* (1967), *To Sir, With Love* (1967), *Conrack* (1974), *Stand and Deliver* (1987), *The Principal* (1987), *Lean on Me* (1989), *one eight seven* (1997).

The traditional student types are present, fitted to Hollywood's 1990 version of the racialized urban hood: Callie, the bright black young woman who is pregnant, and may have to drop out of school; Emilio, the charismatic Chicano boy who wants to break away from his gang, and tries to put a spell on his teacher; Raul, a shy, likable, articulate young Chicano, the first member of his family to graduate from high school.

Recently divorced, ex-US marine LouAnne Johnson gets a job as a substitute English teacher for a special education class in a ghetto school (Parkmont High) where her friend Hal teaches. Her first day in class is hell. The classroom is out of control. Hispanic, African-American, and white students are dancing, kissing, fighting with one another. A black woman calls her 'white bread.' Emilio sexually propositions her ('I'd like to eat you'). The next day LouAnne comes dressed in a leather jacket with cowboy boots. She takes control of the class by informing them that she is an ex-marine. She shows two of the male students how to do karate. She then tells them that 'as of today, everyone has an A. It is up to you to keep it.' She junks the approved reading curriculum in favor of Bob Dylan's poetry ('Mr Tambourine Man'). As the class analyzes the Dylan song, LouAnne tells them that Mr Tambourine Man was a code, 'You know this song is from the sixties when you couldn't sing about drugs.' The class reads Dylan's lyrics through the crack-cocaine culture, 'Hey, he's jingly and jangly, he needs a hit of crack, he needs Mr Tambourine Man to give him the drug.' She promises to take them on a trip to the amusement park if they continue to perform in class. She is disciplined by her principal (an African American) for her unorthodox methods. ('You can't teach karate in the class. We could be sued.') Undeterred, she promises a fancy dinner to the student who wins the Dylan–Dylan contest. (The winner must find a poem written by Dylan Thomas that is like a song written by Bob Dylan.)[10]

LouAnne stops a fight that breaks out in the hall between Raul, Emilio, and a rival gang member. The three men are expelled. The next day her class accuses her of ratting on the expelled students. She challenges them to leave, or talk about the Dylan poem she has brought to class. Emilio asks her to reread the Dylan poem.

'Mr Tambourine Man' plays in the background as the students work on the Dylan–Dylan contest, reading poems about death and dying to one another. The three winners, Raul, Callie, and Durrell. Each discover connections between Thomas's poem about dying and not going gently into the good night, and Dylan's song about death and pride 'Let me Die in My Footsteps' ('I will not go down under the ground cause somebody tells me that death's comin' round').

Durrell and Callie cannot join LouAnne and Raul for dinner. All dressed up, Raul is wearing a stolen leather jacket, costing $200. LouAnne loans him the money to pay for the jacket, on the promise that 'you pay me back on the day you graduate.' Callie later informs her that she is pregnant and moving to a school for mothers-to-be ('It's the rules'). LouAnne fights this school policy, and encourages Callie to stay at Parkmont ('Don't throw away all that you've become'). Meanwhile Durrell and his brother have stopped coming to class. LouAnne drives to their home, where she is confronted by their mother: 'You that white bread bitch been messin' with my babies' mind. You got them bringin' home poetry and that shit. They don't have time for that. They got bills to pay. Go find some other boys to save!'

Emilio is given a death threat by a gang leader on crack. LouAnne offers her home as a safe place for him to stay, and tells him to go the principal and ask for help. He is turned away by the principal. ('He didn't knock.') Emilio is shot to death three blocks from the school. Disillusioned, the next day, she speaks to her class:

LouAnne: I will not be here next year. I'm not coming back.
Raul: How come? Is it something we did?
LouAnne: No, No. I never intended to stay.
Raul: So if you never expected to stay, how come you made me promise what I promised?
LouAnne: At that time I thought I would stay.
Male Student: So how come you leavin'?
LouAnne: I have my reasons.
Female Student: Is it because of what happened to Emilio, Is it too sad for you?
LouAnne: [*cries, looks down, students avert their eyes*] Maybe, and Durell, and Lionel and Callie.
Raul: So if you love us so much, and you so interested in our graduating, how come you choose to leave? You're sad about Emilio and Durell, and Lionel and Callie. But we're here. How about us? None of us make you feel happy? We're working hard and we stayed in school. What about us?

The next day Raul helps LouAnne clear out her desk, 'What you did, when you gave me $200, that was the nicest thing anybody ever did. I don't know anyone else who would give $200 to a Mexican kid.'

On the last day of school, Callie returns to the classroom:

LouAnne: Did somebody talk you into coming, to talk me into staying?
Callie: Both, I wasn't really sure what I wanted to do until I heard you were leavin. Up until then I thought you'd always be here for me, whenever I came back. And I realized this is my last chance and we decided we're not just gonna let you leave.
Raul: We realized, just like the poem said, you can't give in. You can't go gentle, you got to rage into the night.
Male Student: Yeah, you got to go for yours, you know that!
LouAnne: No, no, I'm not giving in. I have no reason to rage against the dying of the light.
Callie: Cause you're not the one that's raging. We're raging. We see you as being our light.
Female Student: You are our Tambourine Man.
LouAnne: I'm your drug dealer?
Female Student: You are our teacher. You got what we need. It's the same thing.

Raul: All the poems you taught us say you can't give in. You can't give up. Well we ain't givin' you up.

Female Student: What we have to do. Tie you down to a chair, make you stay?

A male student gives her a candy bar, the class begins to chant, 'LouAnne LouAnne, LouAnne.' Everyone applauds and dances. LouAnne joins in the dance. She hugs Callie, and starts signing year books for the students who are graduating. Her eyes fill with tears.

In the last scene she and Hal walk down the hallway, arm-in-arm. He asks, 'How did they get you to come back?' LouAnne, 'They gave me candy and called me the light.'

Race, Gender, and Dangerous Minds

Dangerous Minds was uniformly panned by the critics: 'an old-fashioned white missionary movie' (Taubin, 1995a); 'stereotypical, predictable, and simplified to the point of meaninglessness' (Turan, 1995b; see also Mathews, 1995a); 'a fantasy' (Francke, 1996); 'appallingly sentimental' (Medved, 1995); 'false and condescending ... the schoolmarm is as attention-getting as Catwoman cracking the whip' (Maslin, 1995). Buehrer's comments (1996) are perhaps the harshest,

> It is an uplifting story ... but ... [i]t trades any raw force or true instructiveness for a plot that is much more acceptable to mainstream audiences (just as Bob Dylan will entice them more than Snoop Doggy Dogg). *Dangerous Minds* is heartfelt (and it has a great soundtrack), but it is too innocent for today's realities. (p. 124)

But at some level this simplistic, predictable, sanitized film works. It is a highly popular video rental. LouAnne Johnson's books sell well in the national chain bookstores (Barnes and Noble and Borders). At local libraries there are long waiting lists for *My Posse Don't Do Homework/Dangerous Minds*. This movie and Johnson's books tell a story many Americans want to hear.

The negative evaluations of the critics turn on two points: the film's failure to be realistic, and the decision to privilege mainstream audiences and their values (Bob Dylan) over black youth and rap music (Snoop Doggy Dogg). The critics presumed a single reality against which a filmic text is measured. But Stuart Hall (1989) reminds us that cinema is 'not a second-order mirror held up to reflect what already exists' (p. 81). Rather, the cinematic apparatus creates and constitutes its own version of reality, its own imagined sense of moral community, and the world out there. A film is to be judged not by its truthfulness, or its falsity, or its genuineness: rather, in terms of the moral meanings and cultural identities it allows us to see, and recognize, and take on as our own (Hall, 1989, p. 81).

Jameson (1990), Shohat (1991, p. 222), and Stam (1991, p. 253; 1989, p. 224) suggest that the works of mass culture are always 'implicitly or explicitly Utopian. They cannot manipulate unless they offer some genuine shred of content as a fantasy bribe to the public about to be manipulated' (Jameson, 1990, p. 29). This fantasy bribe simultaneously gratifies and represses wishes and desires that circulate in the political unconscious. Repression and wish-fulfillment work together (Jameson, 1990, p. 25). As cultural texts, films such as *Dangerous Minds* contain 'kernels of utopian fantasy whereby entertainment constitutes itself as a projected fulfillment of what is desired and absent within the status quo' (Shohat, 1991, p. 222).

Dangerous Minds succeeds as a gendered utopian text, another story about race and white missionaries. Its simplistic message allows its audience to believe that it is possible for hardworking students to escape the ghetto (Even if the hood comes into the school, students, not schools, must adjust). Further, well-intended female teachers like LouAnne are pied pipers who can lead ghetto youth into the promised land. School and educational issues still matter. Radical pedagogical practices can be successful, even using karate, Bob Dylan's poetry, and making house calls. Loving, committed teachers make a difference. Students who work hard can triumph over adversity. Race and gender are irrelevant to the project, just ask LouAnne, the ex-marine! She is firm on this point, 'There are no victims in this class' and 'I will allow no racial or ethnic or sexual slurs in this classroom' (Johnson, 1992, p. 28).

Of course race and gender do matter. With one or two exceptions, LouAnne's students are all African American or Latino, and she is that white bitch, 'white bread.' In telling its version of the 'White Missionary Racial Allegory' (hooks, 1990, p. 204), *Dangerous Minds* must first confront, and then erase, gender and skin color. In the end LouAnne becomes her posse's Mr Tambourine Man.

In turning her into a teacher who has what they need (the light), the film invokes the romantic poetry of the two Dylans, a poetry about choices, death, and dying. At the same time, the film ignores the Bob Dylan of the 1960s civil rights movement ('The Times They Are A-Changin', 'Blowin' In the Wind,' 'Masters of War'). In stressing the Dylan of the drug counterculture ('Mr Tambourine Man'), the film de-politicizes race and the politics of protest. It turns race into a matter of personal choice. In this existential move the film suggests that existence, how you choose to live, determines who you are, your essence. Hence, the two Dylans are read as arguing that existence transcends essence (Sartre, 1943, p. 626). In this way the film erases the so-called 'determinant effects' of race, class, and gender.

The message is clear. Dark-skinned people need to see through color to learn how to cooperate with hard working, well-intended white teachers and their unorthodox pedagogical practices. When this happens, race disappears, it becomes invisible (Ellison, 1952). When this does not happen, dark not white-skinned persons are to blame. This is how the gendered white missionary model of race relations works in America today.

The White Missionary Model of Race Relations

The classic missionary model presumes a morally superior white person who carries a message of salvation to the inferior, dark-skinned other. As one of God's chosen people, it is the white person's Christian duty to rescue and convert this other. Persons of color cannot do this for themselves. Left to their own devices, their lives become complete chaos, without order or meaning. The missionary brings the tools of culture to this situation, language, literacy, and the skills of reading and writing. Armed with these tools, the dark-skinned other accommodates and assimilates into the dominant white culture. Their mind and their soul has been saved by the white missionary.

This model is explicated in four critical scenes involving LouAnne confronting a dark-skinned audience and offering a message of hope and salvation. In each instance she speaks from a position of higher moral authority; an authority that transcends race and gender.

Scene One: Bring on Dylan and the Marines From the opening scenes of the film it is clear that these students cannot learn on their own. Their version of order is meant to be unacceptable to the viewer (and LouAnne as well). On days two and three of her class LouAnne uses karate (force) and Dylan (the drug song) as methods of getting their attention. In teaching them to read poetry and conjugate verbs, she gives them a language for making choices. These choices, as indicated, are existential: how to die with pride, how to fight to keep a teacher in the classroom. These are not political choices directed against the racial and sexual structures of oppression that operate in the complex cultures of the high school, the hood, and in the larger society. But in accommodating to LouAnne's existential system, the students direct their choices to the problems of literacy, language, and learning. Thus does Dylan's Tambourine Man lead LouAnne's posse out of the ghetto.

Scenes Two and Three: LouAnne Visits the Homeboys LouAnne's message is not uniformly accepted. On the one hand, Raul's parents respond favorably to her home visit, indicating that they are prepared to punish him for getting into trouble. But both parents are overwhelmed with emotion when LouAnne defends Raul, and states that not only is he one of her favorite students, but that she is very proud of him as well. Each parents smiles and becomes tearful. In this moment parent and teacher are aligned. Thanks to LouAnne, Raul will graduate. This brings great pride to his family. He and his family have been saved by this kind white woman.

The visit to the home of Durrell and his brother is met with less favor. The mother refuses to accept LouAnne's message. In calling her that 'white bread bitch' she states she does want her sons saved by this project that involves 'poetry and all that shit' ('They got bills to pay'). In this gesture the film reiterates its argument that the problems of the hood only disappear when dark-skinned persons learn to see past gender and skin color (Durrell and his brother get what they deserve).

Scene Four: Callie's Home The visit to Callie's house carries a somewhat different message. Here LouAnne's personal biography is made public, even as she attempts to persuade Callie to stay at Parkmount ('Don't throw away all that you can become!'). Callie challenges LouAnne, repeating the words of her boyfriend, 'Kimberley said you would probably try to talk me out of this. He said you probably don't even like men, that you are probably not even married, and that you don't want anyone else to be and that's why you are always messing in everyone else's business.' LouAnne will have none of this. 'I was married and I was pregnant. We got divorced and I had an abortion. He beat me.' Her parting words to Callie are bitter, 'Well, sometimes you start out wrong and just keep going.'

In giving LouAnne a marital and sexual history, this interaction engenders the films's race relations story. But irony is operating here. Callie is not drawn to LouAnne's position, even though they are both women. Indeed, she uses LouAnne's marital status (and gender) as an excuse for not listening to her message. Still, the film falters on this point. LouAnne's parting words leave the story at the existential level, suggesting once again that how race affects one's life is a matter of personal choice. These choices transcend gender.

Another White Woman in the Hood

I have suggested that race stories told from a women's perspective neutralize racial violence. So it is for LouAnne. As a white woman in the hood she constantly disrupts the classic male narrative about race, gender, and violence. In her use of poetry she tries to teach her students how to imagine a new racial order based on pride, personal choice, love, mutual respect, and trust. As a teacher she attempts to build non-violent friendships that cross age, gender, class, and racial boundaries. Nonetheless her non-essentialist, existential approach to identity leads to another version of the new cultural racism. This version, as argued in the previous chapter, emphasizes social, not biological, differences, suggesting that cultural 'difference should be overcome even as it reaffirms white power and domination' (hooks, 1996, p. 88).

The new cultural racism, as given in *Dangerous Minds*, builds on a reactionary post-feminist discourse. This discourse rejects feminism 'as a political movement that seeks to eradicate sexism, sexist exploitation, and oppression' (hooks, 1994, p. 98). Under the new cultural model feminism becomes 'simply "a theory of self-worth"' (hooks, 1994, p. 98). This is the theory LouAnne espouses, the one she conveys most forcefully to Callie, and indirectly to Raul and Emilio. This theory allows the film to not take up race as its subject matter. In LouAnne's world things will get better if you do things that lead to feelings of positive self-worth. In this version of the new racial order, race and gender disappear. And this is disquieting, for the problems of race and the hood will not go away just because students of color have read Bob Dylan's poetry.

Chester Himes, the author from whose book the next film was taken, understands this point very well. And he is also an existentialist. Unlike LouAnne, however, Himes' existentialism is connected to a critical theory of race consciousness.

A Rage in Harlem

Often compared to Zora Neale Hurston (and Raymond Chandler), African-American novelist Chester Himes (1909–1984), with Richard Wright, Ralph Ellison, and James Baldwin, articulates a black rage, a violent vision of the American racial order, a vision that is at once colorful, comic, and tragic.[11] In his essay 'The Dilemma of the Negro Novelist' Himes contended that the 'American Negro experiences two forms of hate. He hates first his oppressor and then because he lives in constant fear of this hatred being discovered, he hates himself – because of this fear' (Himes quoted in Williams, 1989, p. 3). In the second volume of his autobiography, citing Albert Camus, Himes (1977) asserted that racism introduces absurdity into the human condition. If one 'lives in a country where racism is held valid and practiced in all ways of life, eventually, no matter whether one is a racist or a victim, one comes to feel the absurdity of life' (p. 1). This absurdity produces violence, hatred, and self-alienation.

Like his recent counterparts Donald Goines (Guerrero, 1993a, p. 225), Walter Mosley, James Sallis, Gar Anthony Haywood, and John Edgar Wideman, Himes uses the autobiographical, pulp fiction, and hard-boiled crime genres to tell stories about life in America's post-World War II racial ghettos (Himes, 1945, 1957, 1959, 1960, 1965, 1972, 1977, 1998; Van Peebles, 1998, p. 16). Himes' nine novels set in Harlem in the 1950s and 1960s 'were attempts to portray the black ghetto subculture with its violence, hypocrisy, loose women, and crime … mob-sterism, gambling, and pimping' (Cormack, 1992, pp. 308–309).[12]

His novels are filled with black con artists, crooks, gangsters, flashy hookers, cross-dressing madames, law-abiding, church-going families, street-corner ministers holding Back-to-Africa ralleys, chattering old ladies, Amos and Andy look-alikes. Over these scenes often hover Himes' two African-American police detectives, Coffin Ed Johnson and Grave Digger Jones. And in the background the air fills with smoke and the smell of barbecued ribs, while elegantly dressed men and women dance and listen to 'Screamin' Jay Hawkins playing 1950s rhythm and blues at the annual Black Undertakers' Ball.

Released in 1991, the same year as three other ghetto action films (*Boyz N the Hood, Straight Out of Brooklyn*, and *New Jack City*, another Harlem-based picture), *A Rage in Harlem* is the fourth Himes novel to be adapted by Hollywood to the screen.[13] It's a crime caper, a coming-of-age story, a deal gone wrong, betrayals, double-crosses, a complex love story, a story about a reunion between two long-separated step-brothers, a tale about a beautiful black *femme fatale*, Imabelle, and her seduction of Jackson, a momma's boy, a virgin, an undertaker's accountant who falls head over heels for this 'cushioned-lipped, hot-bodied, banana-skin chick with the speckled-brown eyes of a teaser and the high-arched, ball-bearing hips of a natural-born amante. Jackson was as crazy about her as a moose for doe' (Himes, 1957, p. 6) (Each morning Jackson kneels at the foot of his bed and prays, 'Thank you Lord for letting me wake up in my right mind and for having gone another day without encountering the temptation of women').

With Jimmy Reed's 'Tell Me That You Love Me' playing in the background, the film opens in a cabin in the woods outside Natchez, Mississippi. The year is 1956. Slim, his scantily dressed girlfriend Imabelle, and his trusted sidekicks Jodie and Hank are inside the cabin with a trunk of stolen gold ore. They are meeting with a rival gang to exchange the gold for $200,000. A rival gang and the police disrupt the exchange. Shots are fired. Racial slurs are hurled back and forth, 'I don't do business with niggers!' Hoodlums are killed, throats are slit. Slipping through this fracas, Imabelle miraculously manages to escape with the trunk of gold in the back of a pick-up truck. She drives to Harlem, hoping to sell the ore to Easy Money, Slim's contact. 'But she is also running away from Slim … [and] from the kind of person that she has become … a double-dealing scam artist' (Cormack, 1992, p. 309) who uses her body to get what she wants from men.

Thus does the rage, in the form of Imabelle with the trunk of gold, arrive in Harlem. And as the title appears on the screen, Duke Ellington big band jazz in the background, the storyboards for the film unfold, a visual delight, each critical sequence given in lush, 'rich, velvety, smoky' colors (Brown, 1991b, p. 55), deep hues, oranges, reds, blues, pastels, larger-than-life characters, street scenes, pool rooms, men and women dancing, fighting, playing craps, firing guns, a 'sensual, surreal, cartoonishly violent and breathtakingly bawdy comic universe' (Turan, 1991b, p. 1). 'This is a highly styled comic thriller with exuberant cartoonish performances, beginning with Givens' sassy Imabelle and Forest Whitaker's quaking, god-fearing Jackson' (Brown, 1996, p. 55).

It's a criss-crossing plot. Penniless ('All I got is $4 to my name'; 'I needed a place to lay low, chump! So fuck you!'), and with no place to sleep, Imabelle is sent to the Annual Undertakers' Ball. Sidling up to the bar, she says, 'I'm looking for Easy Money.' Overhearing her voice, Jackson, a bow-tie-wearing, innocuous God-fearing virgin turns suddenly away from the bar and accidentially pours water down the front of her 'figure-hugging, scarlet dress' (Cormack, 1992, p. 307). Shocked, he apologizes as he attempts to wipe off her soaked dress, 'I'm sorry, I'm sorry.' She will have none of this, 'Get your goddamned hands off of me, chump!' and walks away. But seeing a place to sleep for the night, she returns and talks Jackson into dancing with her ('Just grab me and squeeze'). She then invites herself back to his apartment for the night, where photos of Jesus and Jackson's mother hang on the wall over the bed. As they start up the stairs, Jackson's landlady comments, 'If Christ knew what kind of Christians he got here in Harlem, he'd climb back on the cross and start over.' Imabelle stretches out on Jackson's bed. He gives her a foot rub. She strokes his chest with her foot. Imabelle seduces Jackson, but not before he takes the pictures of his mother and Jesus off the wall. She asks, 'Are you a virgin?' He nods his head yes. She replies, 'I can teach you.' And she does. In love, honorable man that he is, Jackson asks Imabelle to marry him. Slim bursts into Jackson's room ('You stretchin' that boy's jeans?'), and takes Imabelle and the trunk of gold. Slim persuades Imabelle to help him con Jackson out of his life savings. Posing as a policeman, Slim arrests Jackson after a fake money switch. Jackson buys his way out of the arrest by stealing money from Mr Clay, his undertaker boss.

Jackson enlists the help of Goldy, his older step-brother, promising the trunk of gold in return for his new love. Goldy and Jackson have not talked since their mother died, five years ago. Goldy, a con artist, passes himself off as a blind minister. His best friend is Big Kathy, a cross-dressing man and the owner of a bordello. At Big Kathy's club Jackson persuades Gus Parsons, Slim's contact man, to take him to Slims' place. Meanwhile Easy Money, with the love of his life, a cute little Pomeranian, arrives at Slim's and makes a deal for the gold. Jackson, Parsons, Goldy, and Big Kathy appear (with the police following them) just as Easy Money is leaving. Slim and his boys escape, and in a shoot-out Parsons is killed. Jackson and Goldy arrive and find Imabelle alone, trying to remove the gold in a hearse. Big Kathy, who is now helping Imabelle, is killed by Slim, who drives off with the gold. Imabelle next talks Goldy into helping her retrieve the gold, in return for half of the profit. Easy Money and Slim exchange the gold for the money. Goldy and Jackson arrive on the scene, and in a gunfight Goldy shoots Easy Money. Jackson challenges Slim for Imabelle ('I'll fight you for her, like a man. As God is my Judge I love her'). Slim has Jackson on the floor, and is about to slit his throat. Just as Imabelle shoots Slim in the back, saving Jackson's life, Coffin Ed and Grave Digger Jones burst into the room. They arrest Jackson and take him to jail for stealing Mr Clay's money. Mr Clay bails Jackson out, and thanks him for drumming up business (Slim, Easy Money, Big Kathy).

Imabelle escapes with the money, and runs to catch a train for Mississippi. In a locker in the train station she leaves Goldy half the money, and a letter for Jackson stating, 'You're too good for me' (Folded inside the letter is the cross from Jackson's mother, which he had given her when he proposed marriage). As Jackson runs for the train Goldy insists that he take some of the money Imabelle has left. 'You'll need this money. Take the money. Big Kathy wants you to have it.' Jackson turns down the offer, as he and Goldy hug and make up. 'I Love you Brother. God Bless. I forgive you.'

Jackson is reunited with Imabelle on the train. 'Excuse me, do you know who this cross belongs to?' he asks. Imabelle replies, 'Only you can answer that. You know Jackson, you really don't know me.' Jackson replies, 'Yes, I know, but it's a long ride to Mississippi. Tell me, do you know anybody in Mississippi who does a good foot rubbing?' Imabelle smiles. Chuckling, she slowly takes off her shoes, and begins to caress Jackson's thigh with her foot, 'You know, as a matter of fact I don't.' Jackson, with a sly grin, 'That's too bad, 'cause my feet are killing me.'

Reading Imabelle and Her Rage in Harlem

The appeal of this film, despite the shallowness of its characters and its convoluted plot, lies in its openness, in its willingness to be vulnerable in its celebration of black community life.[14] This vulnerability moves in two directions at the same time. It dares to use a Jezebel, a black *femme fatale*, named Imabelle as its leading lady. In its tale of Jackson's subtle seduction of Imabelle, the film creates a gendered space for an intimate, non-violent, loving relationship between a black man and a black woman. A truly loving, non-violent relationship emerges out of the violence surrounding this rage in Harlem. Indeed, the film constructs complex spaces for gender reversals – men who dress as women (Big Kathy) – and for men, like Goldy, who love men like Big Kathy.

At the same time, *A Rage in Harlem* refuses to be anything more than it is: a ribald, but tasteful, all-black comedy with loveable, larger than life characters, from sassy Imabelle and cuddly Jackson, to cross-dressing Big Kathy, Screamin' Jay Hawkins, Easy Money, and his lovable little Pomeranian. This all-black film is unwilling to cater to white audiences, for this is not a narrative about racial assimilation.[15] It reverently, and with great love and visual affection, respects all forms of life in Harlem, finding something good in everybody.

A ghetto-action comedy, it does not take its violence seriously. It does not take up the topics of the other early 1990s ghetto-action films, namely 'the rise of an insidious, socially fragmented violence driven by the availability of cheap guns and crack cocaine in the nation's partitioned inner cities' (Guerrero, 1993a, p. 159). Thus does *A Rage in Harlem* celebrate a prior moment in black cinema, namely black Hollywood of the 1970s (Bogle, 1994, pp. 224, 233–234, 342) and the comedies of Cambridge, St Jacques, Poitier, Cosby, and Pryor.

These high-spirited, boisterous films, as Bogle (1994) observes, 'were populated by a crew of congenial coons, toms and painted ladies ... [they] played up to black fantasies ... [and were] reminiscent of the best race movies – [they] managed to revive the old ethnic humor' (p. 234). And so *A Rage in Harlem* tells black audiences that it is 'all right to laugh at the old dum-dum characters' (p. 234). This move would have infuriated black consciousness audiences in the 1960s. But, as Bogle notes, for black audiences in the 1990s, an ironic double-consciousness seems to operate. 'Rather than cooning or tomming it up to please whites ... the black comic characters joked or laughed or acted the fool with one another. Or sometimes they used humor combatively to outwit the white characters' (p. 234).

This double-consciousness goes deeper than comic reflexivity. It cuts to the core of the gendered black identity, where passing, dissembling, and wearing masks (Guerrero, 1993a, p. 208) are basic to the black experience. Underneath the stereotypes connected to the identities of Tom, coon, mammie, and Jezebel (Bogle, 1994, p. 4; Collins, 1991, p. 77) are complex systems of self-understanding; no black man in this film is just a coon, no woman just a mammie, or a sexual aggressor, a Jezebel.

At one level Imabelle is presented as a sexually aggressive women, a *femme fatale*, a classic Jezebel, not perhaps an aggressor in the class of Pam Grier (*Coffy*, *Black Mamma*, *White Mamma*, *Jackie Brown*), but a Jezebel nonetheless. On the run from who she was in Mississippi, she creates a rage in Harlem because she thinks money will buy her happiness. Not one seduction, but two, two coming-of-age stories. For Imabelle stumbles and falls for a chump named Jackson, the person seduced seduces the seducer. It's a reversal of an old story, the story of the jaded man who finds love with an innocent woman.[16] In *A Rage in Harlem* the man becomes a woman, and the woman becomes the man. Through the love of an innocent, dumb man the jaded hooker finds humanity and a sense of self-dignity and self-pride. In a play on common cliché, here the hooker has a trunk, not a heart, of gold, but she finds a heart of gold through the love of a good man.

Imabelle tricks herself. With Jackson her mask falls off. Never intending to do him any harm, she becomes the kind of person she left Mississippi to find. When she tells Jackson that he does not know her, she is talking to herself, for she has allowed the Jezebel mask to determine who she is: a sexual self defined by its physical experiences with men like Slim.

When Jackson replies that it is a long train ride to Mississippi, he tells her to slow down, and that together they will discover one another. And this is what this slow-riding comic caper set in Harlem is all about. It is a story for a new generation of black filmgoers. It tells them to slow down (something Chester Himes was never able to do). It invites them to enjoy the fruits of the past, to take a slow journey of self-rediscovery into the past, a journey into a version of African-American cultural history that has been too long ignored. *A Rage in Harlem* is a detour through the past, so that the present and the future may be seen anew, so that old masks can be for ever let go of.

In this sweet little story, director Bill Duke (with Chester Himes) imagines an all-new black racial order, an order where the traditional white racial gaze no longer operates. Together Jackson and Imabelle teach one another how to experience multiple forms of feminine and masculine sexual selfhood. Each becomes the object of the other's sexual gaze. But each engenders this gaze with a loving sense of care and intimacy. And as Jackson transforms Imabelle, she transforms him. Together, they share a prideful selfhood. This selfhood, Duke seems to be saying, following Himes' lead, can only be given to blacks by other blacks. In this way *A Rage in Harlem* celebrates a cultural history that could have been, were it not for America's absurd, violent, racist, racial politics. And this is why this utopian film insists on representing all that is positive and good in black community life.

Gender and Racial Politics

White on black, three gendered utopian tales of race, women, and violence in the hood. Race stories told from a woman's point of view. Post-feminist reactionary tales of repression and wish-fulfillment. Feminism as positive self-worth. Of course utopian tales work because their fantasies make the unlikely seem likely. Thus do these three films play on cherished ideological beliefs. A white alcoholic paraplegic and a black drug addict become friends. A white female teacher brings order to a disorderly multicultural classroom. A chump seduces a *femme fatale*. The con artist is conned. Love prevails.

Three women's films, stories about women for women, three female protagonists, three women dealing with problems Hollywood has traditionally defined as female. The problems are familiar. They revolve around domestic life; sexuality; female spectatorship; women waiting for men to make their lives better; women making self-sacrifices for their family, marriage, children, or husband; women making difficult choices between duty and love; women dealing with crippling afflictions or illnesses (Doane, 1987, pp. 3, 35). But these are race stories told from a woman's point of view. And so each film remains within, while partially transcending, the genre of women's film, melodramas with imperfect happy endings (Gaines, 1997, p. 76).

Of course May-Alice has a crippling affliction, and she longs for a man in her life. Chantelle is an addict. She has made sacrifices for her daughter and father, and she is also looking for a good man to make her whole again. LouAnne is divorced, and her students have become her new family. She will go to great lengths to make this family better. Imabelle, in the end, must chose between running away with the money, or leaving a trail for Jackson to follow. She opts for Jackson and love.

So race tangles up these women's stories. Racial looks complicate each film. Each story gives power to a black woman. She uses her gaze and her agency as means of resisting (white) patriarchical control (hooks, 1996, p. 199). This oppositional black female gaze, these black looks, rupture the visual narrative of each film, and create a space for black spectatorship. Black men and women can enter *Passion Fish*, *Dangerous Minds*, and *A Rage in Harlem* precisely at those moments when Chantelle gazes on May-Alice, Callie fixes her eyes on LouAnne and Imabelle freezes Jackson with her seductive smile.

The black female presence in *Passion Fish* and *Dangerous Minds* confronts and resists the supremacy of the white gaze. Black womanhood is not erased in either film, although clearly the presence of Chantelle and Callie functions to serve and maintain the power of white womanhood. In the end the projects of May-Alice and LouAnne define the destinies of the black female other. Callie comes back to school, and Chantelle will learn how to cook.

Because of its all-black cast (except for Lester), *A Rage in Harlem* avoids these issues. Unlike Spike Lee (*Do the Right Thing, She's Gotta Have It*), Bill Duke does not turn the black female body into an object of erotic male sexual visual pleasure (on Lee's treatment of black women, see hooks, 1996, pp. 10–19, 227–235). The nude scenes with Jackson and Imabelle are neither pornographic, nor contained within a patriarchal tale (see hooks, 1996, p. 235). Rather these scenes show a tender, mutual sexually satisfying relationship between a black man and a black woman, and from them Imabelle emerges 'triumphant [and] ful-filled' (hooks, 1996, p. 235).[17] The same conclusions apply to Sayles' treatment of the sexual relationship between Chantelle and Sugar.

In both *A Rage in Harlem* and *Passion Fish* sexual relationships are presented as 'a source of mutual, nonexploitive erotic affirmation, and serve as catalysts for self-development' (hooks, 1996, p. 234). However, an irony operates. bell hooks (1996) suggests that during 'the early stage of [the] contemporary women's movement, feminist liberation was often equated with sexual liberation' (p. 229). Imabelle and Chantelle do not appear to endorse the political values of the femi-nist movement, yet they find fulfillment and empowerment in their sexuality. Thus is a reactionary feminist discourse on race and gender reproduced. To repeat, this is a feminism that turns the political into a personal agenda stressing actions which validate self-worth.

Back to the beginning. Return to our four opening propositions. A non-violent racial order is imagined and then created by each of our female protagonists. This racial order is based on a feminine ethics of personal care. Each women disrupts, but can never fully escape, the traditional male narrative that locates violence in the hood. In their explorations of black sexuality and intimacy, the films chal-lenge racial essentialisms. They turn their men and women into complex desiring subjects. Each protagonist resists and challenges the traditional masculine racial gaze. It seems impossible to ever fully escape the long arms of white patriarchy, unless you tell an all-black story, as Duke does in *A Rage in Harlem*. Under such circumstances a critical theory of race consciousness seems possible.

In the end, each film preserves a certain version of the status quo. Individuals not social structures and cultures change. It is a familiar tale, whether located in the deep South, in 1950s Harlem, or in the contemporary hood. Colored help must still learn how to cook. Success only comes to those youths willing to turn their backs on the ghetto and its gangs. Life in the ghetto can be a romp, especially if you have money and a good woman on your arm. This is one way the gendered cinematic racial order reproduces itself.

At a critical juncture in each narrative race and skin color become invisible, folded into stories about existential crises, seduction scenes, visits to bordellos, intimate relations, close friendships. In this way the films (and their filmmakers) show us that in the hood race disappears and the color line is crossed (Du Bois, 1903, p. 10) exactly at that point when the dark-skinned person willingly submits to white patriarchy. When gender takes over, race disappears. Intimacy, love, and friendship appear in the place previously occupied by race. Of course, simplistic, essentialist gender and racial stereotypes may persist.

When films by white directors tell stories about women, race, and violence in the hood, a conservative missionary discourse seems to dominate. This is what we found in the last chapter. I turn next to another version of the same story: white men dealing with racial violence in the hood, white cops and black, Asian and Latino gangs, cop-buddy stories (Bogle, 1994, pp. 275–276; Guerrero, 1993a, pp. 126, 134).

Notes

1. *Dangerous Minds* (1995). Released by Buena Vista. Director: John N. Smith; Screenplay: Ronald Bass, based on the book *My Posse Don't Do Homework*, retitled as *Dangerous Minds*, by LouAnne Johnson (1992); Cinematography: Pierre Letarte. Cast: Michelle Pfeiffer (LouAnne Johnson), George Dzundza (Hal Griffith), Courtney B. Vance (Mr George Grandey), Robin Bartlett (Ms Carla Nichols), Renoly Santiago (Raul Sanchero), Wade Dominguez (Emilio Ramirez), Bruklin Harris (Callie Roberts). Andy Garcia's role as as LouAnne's boyfriend was cut from the film (Buehrer, 1996).

2. *Passion Fish* (1992). Released by Miramax Films. Director: John Sayles; Screenplay: John Sayles; Cinematography: Roger Deakins. Cast: Mary McDonnell (May-Alice), Alfre Woodard (Chantelle), David Strathairn (Rennie), Vondie Curtis-Hall (Sugar), Leo Burmester (Reeves), Nora Dunn (Ti-Marie), Mary Portser (Precious), Sheila Kelley (Kim), Angela Bassett (Dawn), Nancy Mette (Nina), John Henry (Dr Blades).

3. *A Rage in Harlem* (1991). Released by Miramax. Director: Bill Duke; Screenplay: John Toles-Bey and Bobby Crawford, based on the novel by Chester Himes (1957); Cinematography: Toyomichi Kurita. Cast: Forest Whitaker (Jackson), Gregory Hines (Goldy), Robin Givens (Imabelle), Zakes Mokae (Big Kathy), Danny Glover (Easy Money), Badja Djola (Slim), John Toles-Bey (Jodie), Ron Taylor (Hank), Stack Pierce (Coffin Ed Johnson), George Wallace (Grave Digger Jones), Willard E. Pugh (Claude X), Himself (Screamin' Jay Hawkins).

4. Strictly speaking, *Passion Fish* is not a traditional hood movie. It is not located in an urban racial ghetto. However, it brings hood experiences into the complex racial (cajun, black, white) world of the Louisiana bayou, which is another version of a racial and ethnic ghetto. Of course *A Rage in Harlem* is directed by an African American (Bill Duke) who has directed other ghetto-action films (*Deep Cover*, 1992) and the comedy *Sister Act 2* (1993).

5. Compare here *Mi Vida Loca* (1994) and *Set It Off* (1996), two female hood movies. *Mi Vida Loca* (see Chapter 6), directed by Allison Anders, focuses on a group of single Latina mothers and gang members living in the Echo Park neighborhood of Los Angeles. *Set It Off*, directed by F. Gary Gray, is a blend of *Thelma and Louise* and *Boyz N the Hood*. Four African-American women attempt to escape the poverty of the ghetto by robbing banks, finding that crime does pay, up to a point.

6. Also the title of a 1975 film comedy about teenage life in an inner city Chicago high school, later made into a TV series, *What's Happening*!!

7. Sayles will continue to develop these themes in his 1997 film *Lone Star*.

8. The soundtrack, which reminds us again that 'Black music has always informed cinematic representations of African American culture' (Boyd, 1997, p. 63), is available as a CD. It features the work of Coolio, Aaron Hall, Big Mike, Mr Dalvin & Static, Immature, Rappin'4-Tray, Sista Featuring Craig Mack, De Vante, Tre Black, and 24-K.

9. With the exception of *Up the Down Staircase*, all of the teachers in these films are male.

10. It is significant that no African-American poet (Brown, Spencer, Hughes, Bennett, Brooks, Baraka, Giovanni, Angelou, Lourde) is mentioned in the film, even as poetry is extolled as the method for teaching English literature to students of color.

11. Himes spent the years 1928–1936 in the Ohio State Penitentiary for armed robbery. He began his writing career in prison, as would Malcolm X and Eldridge Cleaver decades later. In 1953, in part because of experiences with racism, Himes moved to France, where he was friends with other black expatriates (Wright, Baldwin, Demby, Smith, Yerby). Influenced by existentialism, he created black protagonists who were symbols of black rage, social, and moral protest against America's racism (Sallis, 2000, p. 101; Diawara, 1993b, p. 526).

12. In 1967 (Cormack 1992, p. 309) Samuel Goldwyn, Jr optioned seven of Himes' Harle novels, including *Love of Imabelle* (1957), *The Crazy Kill* (1959), *The Real Cool Killers* (1959), *All Shot Up* (1960), *The Big Gold Dream* (1960), *Cotton Comes to Harlem* (1965), and *The Heat's On* (1966). According to Cormack (1992) Goldwyn hoped to 'follow a trend started by Universal Picture's *In the Heat of the Night* (1967), which starred Sidney Poitier as a black Philadelphia police detective' (p. 309).

13. As Bernard (1991b) notes, *A Rage in Harlem*, unlike these other 'all-black-Harlem-based [films] ... isn't mean-spirited ... [it is] personal and fun [and] ... crowd-pleasing' (p. 38). (For other reviews see Ansen, 1991b; Brown, 1991b; Turan, 1991b; Mathews, 1991b; Romney, 1991; Guerrero, 1993a, p. 187; Bogle, 1994, p. 276; and most importantly, Diawara, 1993b.) Three other Himes novels were also made into films, *If He Hollers, Let Him Go* (1968), *Cotton Comes to Harlem* (1970), and *Come Back, Charleston Blue* (1972). The Himes films anticipated the black action (blaxploitation) films of the 1970s discussed in Chapter 1. The Himes comedies featuring Coffin Ed Johnson and Grave Digger Jones had much in common with three 1970s light-hearted films starring Sidney Poitier, Harry Belafonte, and Bill Cosby: *Uptown Saturday Night* (1974), *Let's Do It Again* (1975), and *A Piece of the Action* (1977).

14. Critics complained that the film displayed a 'laboured flipness' (Ansen, 1991b), 'was not driven by some burning social issue ... [and] plays as a loopy farce' (Bernard, 1991b). Cormack (1992) suggested that Givens' performance 'was overbearing and unnatural ... [and] not enough to make [the film] anything more than an imaginary story ... about the kind of criminal element that lived in Harlem during the 1950s' (pp. 309–310; but see Ebert, 1994c, p. 580).

15. Valerie Smith (1997) argues that films such as Duke's undertake many challenges, including 'revising the assumptions about black lives in earlier historical periods; addressing the complex nexus of issues of race, class and sexuality ... exploring how genre conventions are shaped when deployed within an explicitly racialized context' (p. 10). For example Diawara (1993b, pp. 534–535) reads Duke's film as film noir, and suggests that other 'recent Black films [also] participate in the discourse of film noir (*Joe's Bed-Stuy Barbershop: We Cut Heads, Deep Cover, One False Move, Juice, Illusion, Chameleon Street*' (p. 526). Diawara argues that the black rage that operates in Himes' novel (more than in Duke's film) 'is also present in the novels of Richard Wright as well as in *Straight Out of Brooklyn*, and *Boyz N the Hood*' (p. 528).

16. Johanna Bradley clarified this situation for me.

17. It is clear, however, that she enters the relationship with less than honorable intentions, even as she exerts her female sexuality as an act of liberation. Thus does this film challenge the usual negative Hollywood treatment of black women (and men) and their sexuality (see Tasker, 1998, p. 4; Guerrero, 1993b, p. 238; Jones, 1993, p. 254; Wallace, 1990, p. xxxvi; 1993, p. 260).

4

Lethal Weapons in the Hood

> *Uncle Zeus:* So who are the bad guys?
> *Cousins:* People with Guns. People with drugs.
> *Uncle Zeus:* So who's gonna help you?
> *Cousins:* We are.
> *Uncle Zeus:* So who's not gonna help us?
> *Cousins:* White people.
> *Uncle Zeus:* That's right. (Dialogue between Samuel L. Jackson and his two
> little cousins, *Die Hard With a Vengeance*, 1995)

> We're back! We're bad! You're black! I'm mad! (Mel Gibson to Danny Glover,
> *Lethal Weapon 2*)

A simple thesis organizes my reading of one version of the police and hood movies of the 1990s. Namely, when confronted in the eighties and the nineties with the matters of racial violence in America's inner cities, Hollywood responded in two predictable ways: through action-comedy serials and through social realism. On the one hand, the new black filmmakers (Lee, Singleton, the Hughes brothers, Rich, Dickerson, Harris, Van Peebles) used a traditional realistic social problems perspective to examine the destructive effects of violence, drugs, and gangs on black family life. Running alongside these films, in contrast, were two action-comedy serials: the Bruce Willis *Die Hard* series and the Mel Gibson–Danny Glover *Lethal Weapon* series. These two serials made race a laughing matter, while modeling an ideal form of the integrated black–white male friendship. Thus were the hood movies of the black filmmakers pushed to the side. In privileging an assimilationist norm, Hollywood once again attempted to whitewash America's race relations problems.[1]

In this chapter I examine how this happened, through a close reading of the eleven-year *Lethal Weapon* series (*LW1*, 1987, *LW2*, 1989, *LW3*, 1992, *LW4*, 1998)[2] film cycle, a series that has grossed over $1 billion for Warner Brothers, and has helped made Glover and Gibson millionaires.[3] This quintessential cop-buddy film series tells the unfolding story of Roger Murtaugh's (Danny Glover) attempts to manage life with Martin Rigg (Mel Gibson).[4] As indicated in the Introduction (pp. 10–11) *Lethal Weapon* is a reversal of the usual utopian assimilationist story. The white man disappears into the black middle-class family.

Cops in the Black Public Sphere

The opening sequence of the 1995 film *Die Hard With a Vengeance*[5] sets the context for my analysis: the black public sphere (Baker, Jr, 1995, p. 36), cops in the hood, male urban action films[6] (Brown, 1996; Chan, 1998; Tasker, 1993), hard bodies, stories of race, law, and order, tales of interracial male bonding; other versions of the black-buddy-as-mammy-nurturer narrative, the Huck Finn fixation (Bogle, 1994, p. 276); action as comedy, violence as farce, biracial assimilationist accounts fitted to the demands of the 1990s (Bogle, 1994, pp. 268–276; Guerrero, 1993a, pp. 127–135; 1993b; Tasker, 1993, pp. 44–48).

Hung-over and unshaven, dressed only in his undershorts, white socks, and black shoes, John McClane (Bruce Willis) is standing on the sidewalk of 157th street in Harlem. He is wearing a white billboard with the words 'I Hate Niggers' printed in large letters on both sides. Zeus (Samuel L. Jackson) is across the street in his electronic repair shop talking with his two little cousins. They have just agreed that they cannot depend on white people for any help. Leaving the store, the cousins see McClane standing across the street and call to Uncle Zeus to come look.

The following interaction occurs as Zeus walks across the street and confronts McClane:

> *Zeus:* Good morning sir, are you having a good day? Not to get personal, but anybody standing in the middle of Harlem with a sign that says I hate niggers has got to have serious personal issues, or all his dogs are not barking. You got about ten seconds before those guys [*points to eight black youths*] see you. When they do, they are going to kill you. Do you understand?
>
> *McClane:* I'm a policeman. I have to do this. Get away. You heard about that building that just blew up. I was told to come here with this sign, and if I didn't, another building will blow. Man get back, get away!

As promised, within ten seconds, McClane is confronted by the eight bare-chested black men, rap music playing in the background. The leader asks Zeus, 'Your friend?' Zeus replies, 'Man, he look like a friend of mine?' One of the black men hits McClane in the jaw. Another throws a basketball against the side of his head. A third says, 'This man here hates niggers, now what we gonna do?' A knife is thrown at McClane and he falls to the sidewalk. The straps holding up the billboard are slashed. It falls to the ground. Zeus is cut in the shoulder. A gun taped to McClane's back becomes visible. Zeus grabs the gun, waves it at the black men, and shouts, 'Get the fuck back, get back, back up, back the fuck up. I don't want to, but you know I will.' He pulls McClane up from the curb, and stops a cab. The two of them climb in the back of the cab. The rear window shatters as they pull away. The black men chase them down the street.

This is a complex scene. It is played out in one version of the black public sphere, ι sidewalk in Harlem. Its racist overtones are very strong. It aligns a black man (who has just said you cannot trust a white man) with a white policeman, with the state, and its laws.[7] In the name of law and order (McClane's plea for help), this scene turns the black community against itself. The black (male) point of view is negated. The black man 'makes a sacrifice to solve the White man's problems' (Guerrero, 1993b, p. 242). It is as if Zeus has suddenly become McClane's slave, or assistant, and McClane his master. Paraphrasing Guerrero (1993b), Zeus prefers to help solve 'the problems of a system which has confined and punished' African-Americans (p. 242).[8] The black youths who are Zeus' friends are transformed into his enemies. Only good fortune prevents him from shooting at them. And so begins another tale of interracial male bonding, a black man rescues a white man from danger in the hood. Just like *Grand Canyon*.

Now the series.

Race and the *Lethal Weapon* Narrative

The four films in the *LW* cycle can be read as a single text, successive chapters in an unfolding complex narrative about the lives, loves, and adventures of Roger Murtaugh and Martin Riggs, two detectives with the Los Angeles police force.[9] The unlikely friendship that forms between these two totally different men provides an unifying theme across the four films. In a combination of opposites (the odd couple), the suicidal, hysterical, manic-depressive, wildly unstable, irrational white hero is paired with the cautious, conservative, middle-class black man (Welsh, 1993, p. 213; Lewis, 1990, p. 219) (At the same time the black man is treated as an equal to the white man). As the series progresses, Murtaugh's children grow older, developing lives and loves of their own, and Murtaugh continues his attempts to take early retirement. In the first film Riggs grieves the loss of his first wife. In the second film he finds a new love who is killed. In the third film the series introduces a new woman, Lorna, whom Riggs marries in *LW4*. In *LW2* and *3*, Riggs moves beyond his suicidal state, the theme of *LW1*, but he remains as crazy as ever, a daredevil, constantly taking chances and risking harm, injury, and destruction to himself and to Murtaugh. As the series progresses, violence becomes farce. Indeed, by the third film, critics are reading the series as if it were a larger-than-life 'supersonic comic strip ... Murtaugh and Riggs have become the Abbott and Costello of buddy-cop flicks' (Kroll, 1992, p. 91).

The plot of *Lethal Weapon* is simple, a Christmas film containing the requisite elements of the contemporary action genre: old Vietnam drug connections, renegade Special Forces operatives, kidnappings, threatened rapes, extended torture sequences, multiple shoot-outs, displays of martial arts, a Christmas Day dinner. It, like *LW2*, has 'gimmicks out of "48 HRS," and "Magnum Force," a relationship out of the "Defiant Ones," and an incredibly silly kung fu showdown climax' (Wilmington, 1989, p. 1).

Martin Riggs, a narcotics detective, has become emotionally unstable since his 31-year-old wife Victoria Lynn (1953–1984) was killed in a car accident. He is perceived by the Department psychiatrist as being violent and unstable, even psychotic, although his Captain suspects he may be malingering. Riggs carries a hollow-point bullet in his pocket. In moments of depression, alone in his trailer staring at the TV, or holding his wedding picture, he loads his gun with the bullet and places it in his mouth. He dares hoodlums to shot him. He lives with his dog Sam in a small mobile home on the beach. He drinks beer for breakfast, and watches *Family Feud* and *Road Runner* cartoons on TV.

Because of his psychotic state, Riggs is transferred to the homicide division, and paired with Roger Murtaugh, a stable senior detective. Murtaugh owns a boat, and lives with his Cosby-like clan, wife Trish and three children, Rianne, Nick, and Carrie, in a large white house in the black middle-class suburbs. The family has a 'FREE SOUTH AFRICA, END APARTHEID' sticker on the kitchen refrigerator

(Dieckmann, 1987). Riggs resents being taken out of narcotics ('Hey, I'm fucked!!'), and Murtaugh, who has just turned 50, sees Riggs as a threat to his stable middle-class life ('God hates me. I'm too old for this shit!').[10] Because of Riggs's violent history, including his participation in the Phoenix Project in Vietnam, the 9 millimeter Barretta he carries, and his love of martial arts, Murtaugh suggests that we 'should register you as a lethal weapon.' Hence the film (and series) title (and four scenes later, after Riggs has jumped off a ten-story building, Murtaugh observes, 'You're not trying to draw a psycho pension, you really are crazy').

The two men investigate the apparent suicide of Amanda Hunsaker, a 22-year-old prostitute who jumped from her apartment window (In fact she ingested poisoned cocaine). Her father saved Murtaugh's life in Vietnam when they were in the Special Forces together. He demands that her killers be found. Riggs kills her drug dealer in a shoot-out. Murtaugh invites Riggs to his house for dinner. Rianne develops an instant crush on her father's new partner. She cannot take her eyes off of him, leading her sister Carrie to make up a song with the line, 'My sister's in love with this man named Martin.' After dinner, sitting in Murtaugh's boat in the driveway, both men share Vietnam experiences. Riggs still has nightmares. Murtaugh has put the war experience in his past. The next day an explosion devastates the house of the woman who saw Amanda jump. It is witnessed by four little black boys, and one of them, Alfred, noticed a meter man with a Special Forces tattoo at the scene prior to the blast. Murtaugh attempts to interview Alfred, who tells him, 'Momma says police shoot black people. Is that true?' Murtaugh confronts Amanda's father. He confesses that he uses his bank as a front for a heroin operation run by former CIA agents and mercenaries. Amanda was killed to keep Hunsaker from leaving the operation. Hunsaker is killed by Mr Joshua (Gary Busey) just as he is about to give the two men the location of the next heroin shipment. Murtaugh's oldest daugher Rianne is kidnapped by Mr Joshua and the General, who controls the heroin operation. Murtaugh and Riggs almost save Rianne, but are captured. The General threatens to rape Rianne ('That's a real good lookin' young woman you got there'). Riggs is tortured by Joshua and his Vietnamese assistant ('He knows more about inflicting pain then you will ever know'). Riggs gets free and kills the assistant. He, Murtaugh, and Rianne escape, but not before Riggs does a word pun with Murtaugh, 'What did the one shepherd say to the other shepherd? "Let's get the flock out of here."' Murtaugh kills the general.

The detectives chase Mr Joshua and capture him at Murtaugh's house. Riggs challenges Mr Joshua to a final 'shot at the title.' An extended martial arts scene is an acrobatic display of fast-moving bodies colliding and hurling through Murtaugh's front yard. A search light from the police helicopter shines down on the yard, but a spewing fire hydrant makes it almost impossible to see the two men fighting (Noriega, 1988, p. 212). In the end, Mr Joshua attempts to shoot Riggs. In a slow-motion sequence Murtaugh and Riggs draw their guns, each 'trying to save the other' (Noriega, 1988, p. 212). Riggs collapses into Murtaugh's arms. The film ends the next day, which is Christmas. Riggs visits his wife's gravesite. 'Merry Christmas Victoria Lynn. I love you.' He stops by

Murtaugh's house to give him a present. Rianne answers the door, and he hands her the hollow-point bullet. 'Give this to your father. Tell him I won't be needing it anymore. You have a nice Christmas.' Murtaugh stops him.

> *Murtaugh:* After all we've been through if you think I'm gonna eat the world's lousiest Christmas turkey by myself, you're crazy.
> *Riggs:* I'll let you in on a little secret. I'm not crazy.
> *Murtaugh:* [smiling] I know.
> *Riggs:* Oh good. Lets' eat. You know somethin'. I think your daughter kind of likes me.
> *Murtaugh:* You touch her and I'll kill you.
> *Riggs:* OK if I bring a friend?
> *Murtaugh:* Yeah.

Riggs whistles for Sam, who comes running across the lawn. Elvis Presley sings 'I'll be Home for Christmas' on the soundtrack. The film closes with the following lyrics, 'Killing you, that's the last thing love was ever meant to do, to become a lethal weapon.'

And so the film reflexively turns in upon itself, giving a double meaning to 'Lethal Weapon,' a term that describes love, and life, as well as death. This is more than an action, cops and robbers, interracial buddy movie. It is a meditation on the meaning and purpose of life. A story about despair, the consequences of losing a loved one. It is about the meanings of friendship, and love, the recovery of purpose through action in the world and the love of a family.

The friendship bond that forms between Murtaugh and Riggs starts first when Riggs saves Murtaugh's life. This bond is thickened when Murtaugh takes Riggs home for dinner. There Riggs finds love, even if it is the teenage infatuation of Rianne for an older man. But this black man's family makes a place for Riggs, and the next day Martin awakens Murtaugh with a fresh cup of coffee. Rigg's crazy acts become less and less frequent as he becomes more and more a member of the Murtaugh family. It is clear that his insanity was produced, in part, by his loneliness, by his self-absorption in the pain of losing Victoria. The loss of her love had killed his desire to live. Her love had become a lethal weapon. He, in turn, had become a lethal weapon, a man trained to kill by the forces of the Vietnam war.

But underneath his craziness lurks a friendly, likeable man who loves his work and his fellow human beings. He likes to joke and pull tricks on people. He loves language. He likes to pun. He is a punster ('Beverly Hills, where the rich and the shameless live'). He, like Murtaugh, is a person you come to care about, and the two of them together, like Jim and Huck Finn, are a lovable couple.

So *LW1* is about friendship, sanity, insanity, the recovery of self through family. It is the beginning of a story that may be about the beginning of a beautiful friendship, to steal a line from Claude Rains in *Casablanca*. Race functions as a subtext throughout. The Oriental other, Mr Joshua's Vietnamese assistant, is presented as a stereotypical Asian who inflicts pain on good white people. Thus Riggs reenacts a Vietnam torture scene at the hands of the Asian assistant. Race is openly confronted when Alfred tells a black policeman (Murtaugh) that his mother says the police shoot black people. Race is indirectly taken up when Murtaugh tells Riggs to keep his hands off his daughter. Of course she is a teenager, but then he is also white.

And so *LW1* is not just another action movie. In a sense, as Ebert (1988a) notes, 'It is not about violence at all. It is about movement and timing, the choreography of bodies and weapons in time and space' (p. 457). It is about two men learning how to come together in a way that celebrates difference and 'eccentric personal rhythms' (Ebert, 1998a). It is about a black man and a white man, and a black man's family. In this, it is about how race stands aside when honest personal relationships are allowed to form.

At this ideological level *LW1* aligns itself with all of those other race films that say race stops mattering when common values can be shared. Regrettably, the values of *LW1* seem to be those of the white middle class. The problems of race, the violent Asian other, cops killing black people, are really not problems of white (or black) society. Those are problems confined to the hood, or the ghetto, or to the violence that naturally occurs in the worlds of international drug trafficking.

So the action of *Lethal Weapon* functions at two levels. On the one hand Riggs and Murtaugh are repeatedly put in situations where they risk life and limb for one another. In saving one another from death or great injury they further cement the bond that ties them together. But of course their work places them in risky situations. These situations require that they take chances. Herein lies the other source of action for the series: these two men are lethal weapons who will go to any length to stamp out evil in the world. They will never be too old to do this shit.

Lethal Weapon 2 begins with no introduction of the characters. Riggs and Murtaugh are in the middle of a car chase on the crowded LA freeway. Riggs is calling for more speed, and Murtaugh yells, 'Man, we gotta be careful, this is Trish's new station wagon.' During the chase a German voice comes over the police radio. This leads to an exchange between Murtaugh and Riggs.

Murtaugh: What the hell language is that? German, Japanese?
Riggs: It's a Japanese radio, maybe they bought the LA police force as well.
Murtaugh: Yeah, they own everything else.

The chase ends, of course, with a crash scene.[11] As they attempt to open the trunk of the vehicle they have been pursuing, gold kruggerrands spill to the ground. The film introduces Joe Pesci as a chipmunk-grinning, fast-talking pip-squeak, a self-deprecating (Ebert, 1998b, p. 457) but lovable character named Leo Getz ('Whatever you need, Leo Gets. Get it?'. 'OK, OK, OK, OK, I like you guys'). Leo is a hysterical accountant for a South African mob.[12] The gold kruggerrands are linked to Leo, who is under protective police custody. He has laundered half a billion dollars of drug money for a group of white supremacist drug-dealing South African diplomats (headed by Arjun Rudd and Peter Vorstedt) who have diplomatic immunity and cannot be arrested. Riggs and Murtaugh begin harrassing the South Africans. Riggs calls Arjun 'Aryan,' Aldolf, and a leader of the master race. Riggs joins a group of poster-carrying marchers ('End Apartheid Now') protesting in front of the South African Embassy. Rudd informs his secretary, 'The policies of our government are not popular in this country. The police department of this city is overrun with Blacks. They hate us.'

The South Africans set a bomb under Murtaugh's toilet, leading Murtaugh to say to Riggs: 'First time in twenty years I got the bathroom all to myself' (The explosion of the bomb allows the two men to end up in each other's arms, providing

91

another occasion to prove that they are not gay, but that they are the closest of friends. Riggs: 'Get off me man. I don't want anybody to see us like this').

Leo and Murtaugh visit the offices of the South Africans. Leo tells a consular official that he has a friend who wants to emigrate to South Africa. The official replies, 'This will not be a problem.' Leo then introduces Murtaugh to the official:

Official: Oh, you don't really want to go to South Africa.
Murtaugh: Why?
Official: Because you are black.
Murtaugh: Of course, that's why I want to go, to be with my oppressed brothers, to take up the struggle against the racist, facist, white minority regime. One man, One vote. Free South Africa! You dumb sonofabitch!'[13]

At this point white South Africans drag Murtaugh out of the building. Later the South Africans attack Murtaugh in his garage and he kills two of them. Riggs's trailer is blown up. Leo is kidnapped. Riggs falls in love with Rika, Rudd's assistant. Vorstedt captures Riggs and makes a devastating revelation:

I changed the course of your life. Four years ago when you were a narc down at Long Beach you were getting too close to us. I put a contract out on your life.... I forced your car straight off the road. Imagine my surprise when I pulled back the bloody body out of the car. It was your wife. Right?

Riggs vows vengeance against Vicki's killers. Rika is killed. Riggs and Murtaugh rescue Leo from Rudd's house, and then race to the docks, where Rudd is loading a South African freighter with the profits from his drug deals. Riggs and Murtaugh destroy the money. Riggs kills Vorstedt. Rudd shoots Riggs. Murtaugh kills Rudd, and then comforts a wounded Riggs in his arms. Lyrics from Bob Dylan's 'Knockin' on Heaven's Door' play on the soundtrack. Rigg and Murtaugh have this final exchange:

Murtaugh: Riggs, You're not dead until I tell you.
Riggs: I'm not gonna die in your arms. The bad guys did you get 'em?
Murtaugh: They been de-caffeinated. [*laughs*]
Riggs: Hey Rog [*looking into his eyes*], did anyone tell you, you really are a beautiful man? Give us a kiss before they come.

Lines from George Harrison's song 'Cheer Down' play as the credits roll: 'I can see by the smile on your face, by the grin on your face, no tears to be shed.'

LW2 is about the deepening friendship between the two men (Lewis, 1990, p. 218); it is about Riggs being less of a lethal weapon, being less crazy and less self-destructive. Straight out of Hollywood gender mythology, the film is about the core of male bonding, two men facing death (the toilet bomb scene and the final shoot-out in the ship) and the 'intense affection' (Lewis, 1990, p. 220) they obviously feel for one another. Men who experience and express this bond can do so emotionally, and with good humor. They need not be fearful of showing their inner self-feelings. They can even cry. In this way the film argues that race need not stand in the way of male friendship. And thus does the loving Murtaugh family find a space for Riggs, this man who is an outsider to white society.

Together, Riggs and Murtaugh fight racism. The vile white South Africans, as modern-day Nazis, represent 'the ultimate facist/racist incarnation of evil' (Lewis, 1990, p. 218). The police may shoot black people in America, as Alfred tells Murtaugh in *LW1*, but Rudd and Vorstedt, as representatives of apartheid South Africa, are pure evil. In a subtle and complex process of racial transcoding (Ryan and Kellner, 1988, p. 12), *LW2* constructs a violent racial other, the South Africans who kill whites and blacks for profit and pleasure. But in the deployment of this racist stereotype, which is coupled with Nazism, the target of violence ceases to be defined solely in racial terms. The evil South African kills anybody who stands in his way. Indeed, Rudd and Vorstedt do not confine their attacks just to blacks, Riggs is also the target of their violence, and they have killed both his wife and his new love interest. And so the film fails to sustain its initial criticisms of apartheid as a form of institutional white racism.

Nonetheless, *LW2* attacks racism and racial violence on two fronts. Murtaugh, as a black policeman, continues to correct the impression initiated in *LW1* that all police shoot black people. At the same time Murtaugh aligns himself with his black brothers in South Africa, even suggesting that he wants to move there to help the cause. But before he can do that he must put an end to the racist (and non-racist) violence the white South Africans spread in America. In this struggle he calls upon his old friend, the lethal weapon named Riggs.

Still, an irony operates in the series. *LW1*, as noted above, confined the problems of racial violence to one of two settings, either the hood or the world of white and Asian men engaged in drug trafficking (On occasion, *LW1* suggested that drug-based violence merged with the violence in the ghetto). *LW2* sustains this theme, for once again white men are trafficking in illegal drugs. Only now the venality of these men is shaped by racial ideology. The new Nazis are from racist South Africa, and the illegal international drug trade now seems to by-pass both Asia and South or Latin America (Newman, 1989). Hence the irony: racist white men kill other white men (and women). Indeed, no blacks are killed in *LW2*.

The third film in the series starts with a bang – a building blows up (Riggs: 'A cat-astrophe!') – and then moves to a car chase, actually armored trucks chasing one another, Riggs hanging on to one, Murtaugh a passenger in the other. Demoted after the bomb incident, the detectives are back on the job investigating the armored car robbery and the theft of illegal firearms from a police warehouse. Leo returns as a realtor. He is trying to sell Murtaugh's house ('Hey, I have to disclose everything, OK. Hey, that picture window is new. A drug dealer drove right through it, OK. And hey, the bathroom upstairs has been completely remodeled due to bomb damage. OK?'). A fourth character is added, Lorna Cole (Rene Russo), a tough cop from Internal Affairs, which Riggs calls 'Infernal Repairs.' A running gag involves Riggs's attempt to stop smoking. He uses dog biscuits as a substitute for cigarettes ('Hey, they taste pretty good, want one? … but I'm ready for some human food'). In one scene he tames a ferocious guard dog with his biscuits. A new but unreciprocated love interest appears for Murtaugh. Delores Hall plays a large black lady cop who has a crush on him ('Don't you worry about nothin' baby, I got somethin' for you'), and embarrasses him at work with her show of affection ('You tell that good-lookin' lovely Sergeant Murtaugh that he is the jam in my jellyroll').

The plot turns on four interconnected themes. First, the retirement story. Murtaugh is seven days away from retirement, and Leo as a realtor is trying to sell his house. Second, the robberies are being organized by Jack Travis, a drugs-, arms-, and gun-dealing renegade cop who runs a construction company as a front. Third, the drugs are connected to youth gangs and gang violence. Travis, through Tyrone, a black drug dealer, is selling the drugs that are falling into the hands of young gang members who are killing each other with these automatic weapons. If the police can stop Travis, they can save the lives of some of these young African-American men. Fourth, Riggs finds a new love interest in Lorna Cole. Travis is being investigated both by Internal Affairs (headed up by Lorna), and by Riggs and Murtaugh. This produces conflicts (Riggs to Lorna: 'Hey, we are both cops, let us in on what you know!'). Travis is building a subdivision for whites in the desert east of LA (Travis to Tyrone, in a play on the title of a nineties hood movie: 'We are sinking all our money into this subdivision because nobody wants to live next to people like you. You are a menace to society').

Reminiscent of *Boyz N the Hood*, Murtaugh's son Nick becomes friendly with a drug-dealing street gang, which includes Darryl, a young black friend who has dropped out of high school (Darryl, who wears a heavy gold necklace, to Nick: 'We take care of ourselves man, me and my crew, that's the rule'). Riggs, Murtaugh, and Leo chase Travis to a hockey game, where he escapes. In a shoot-out with gang members in the middle of a drug deal Murtaugh kills Darryl.

> *Murtaugh:* Call an ambulance, and pray. Oh God don't do this to me. I know this kid, he's Nick's friend.
> *Riggs:* It was a clean shoot, he was going to do you, he was gonna do me.
> *Riggs to Lorna:* There are kids out there with automatic weapons. They are killing each other).

Riggs, Murtaugh, and Lorna discover that the weapons are being stolen by Travis from the basement of police headquarters.

Lorna and Riggs team up. She is as good at karate as he is. In a tender scene they compare body scars, leading each to undress. Thus she to him, as she traces the scars on his shoulder, 'That's impressive.' And he to her, as he touches her thigh 'Wow, that must have hurt.' This is all a prelude to the sex that follows (*Riggs:* 'A serious ethical breach here, I never made it with another sergeant before.' *Lorna:* 'Shut up Riggs!').

Murtaugh is racked with guilt over the killing of Darryl:

> *Murtaugh:* I killed that kid. You don't kill boys like Nick. Three days before I retire and this happens.
> *Riggs:* We are partners, what happens to you happens to me. When you retire, you retire us. You're the only family I have. You got beautiful kids. I love 'em. Trish does my laundry. I live in your refrigerator. What am I supposed to do when you retire?
> *Murtaugh:* I didn't realize my retirement was going to screw you up.
> [*The two men hug.*] You know I love you.

The next day, just before Darryl's funeral, Nick tells his father, 'I love you dad. I don't blame you. I blame Darryl.' At the graveside, surrounded by Darryl's large family and members of the police force, a choir singing in the background, the black minister speaks, 'My God remove the scourge of violence that is taking the lives of our children.' Murtaugh is slapped in the face by Darryl's mother. Darryl's father tells him, 'You wanta do somethin' Sergeant Murtaugh, you find the man that put the gun in my son's hands.' That night Murtaugh goes to Tyrone's house, with Darryl's gun. 'Where did this gun come from motherfucker? You know the word genocide? You folks are killing each other and I'm tired of it.'

Riggs and Murtaugh chase Travis to Mesa Verde, his housing development. Lorna is shot by Travis. Riggs destroys the center of the building, and starts a fire that sends the entire site up in flames. Riggs kills Travis. Riggs announces his love for Lorna:

> Honey, open your eyes, what ya tryin' to prove out there, uh? You're supposed to grow old with someone, not because of them. I'm gonna be with ya. I wanna be with ya. What ya got to lose? Hey Lorna, let's live to regret this. I love you. [*She smiles, and then passes out*].

In the next scene Murtaugh is in the bathtub. The family breaks in, 'Happy Retirement Daddy.' Nick gives him a cake, with a candle for every year he has been on the force. 'I can't retire. I thought I wanted to, but I can't.' Rianne: 'Well, the streets will be safer for the next couple of years.' Leo appears, announcing he has sold the Murtaugh house. Murtaugh tells him the house is off the market, 'We are staying here another ten years.' Leo leaves, and Murtaugh pulls Trish into the bathtub.

Riggs and Murtaugh have a familiar closing scene.

Murtaugh: Why weren't you at my retirement party?
Riggs: I knew you wouldn't retire.
Murtaugh: Stay away from my daughter.
Riggs: Hey, she finds me irresistible. Hey, I'm spoken for. I'm going to pick Lorna up from the hospital this afternoon.

The film ends with Elton John singing 'Runaway Train.' In a final scene the two men pull up in front of an apartment house, which suddenly explodes. Together they exclaim, 'Oh, I'm too old for this shit!!'

With *LW3*, the series comes of age as an action comedy (or a comedy with action). It has moved from 'hard-boiled thriller to explosive comedy' (Kermode, 1992). In *LW2* and *LW3*, the Pesci character, like a knock-around clown, functions as comedy detective who tells the hapless Murtaugh and Riggs where to go next (Kermode, 1992). The plot of *LW3* appears to swerve from one action set-piece to another. There is no apparent coherence linking one scene to the next, other than a sense of urgency connected to Murtaugh's impending retirement, Riggs' fear of losing his best friend, and the desire to end Travis's crime wave.

Yet underneath this apparent mayhem, for the first time *LW3* squarely locates itself within the 'hood' movies of the 1990s. Not only does it invoke a film from that series (*Menace II Society*), but it brings hood life directly into the Murtaugh family with the death of Darryl. In so doing it offers personal, racial, and systemic (political economy) criticisms of gangs and drugs. On the personal level, Nick blames Darryl for his own death, and Nick's mother blames Murtaugh for killing her son. At the level of race, Murtaugh tells Tyrone that blacks are engaging in group genocide, and there must be an end to this tragedy. At the level of political economy, the black minister asks God to remove this scourge of violence from his community. The scourge, at the systemic level, connects Travis to Tyrone to Darryl.

Thus does *LW3* weave the personal through the political and the racial. In so doing it suggests that the police must do what the family cannot do; that is, stop this scourge of violence in the black public (and private) spheres, this violence that unites black youth with gangs and drugs. Thus does the state mediate race in the hood.

Of course the film's other story involves Riggs falling in love again, not only with Lorna, but more deeply with Murtaugh as well. Riggs cannot imagine life without the Murtaugh family. They have civilized him ('I live in your refrigerator'). But more deeply Riggs has discovered a renewed purpose in living. He is no longer a depressed suicidal manic. He has the love of Murtaugh and his family to thank for that, even if Murtaugh tells him to 'Stay away from my daughter!' This love allows Riggs to open up to Lorna. Indeed the fear of losing Murtaugh increases his attachment to her ('You're supposed to grow old with someone.... I love you'). So in imagining its ideal racial and gender order, *LW3* validates the importance of the black–white male bond, but keeps the male–female interracial bond off limits.

LW4 is also about families, black, white, Asian, and extended. It is also about friendship, sons-in-law, fathers, mothers, and their children. Chris Rock is added to the series, playing a police officer (Lee Butters) with a psychology degree. Leo is back, only now as a private investigator who does contract work for Riggs and Murtaugh. Three interconnected plot lines organize the narrative. The first plot brings Asia and the newest international martial arts star, Jet Li, into the series. The dialogue makes the Asian other the object of Western scorn (Riggs to Chinese businessman: 'You speakie English? You eat fried lice?'). Although the film stigmatizes the Asian other, it suggests that African-American gang-bangers and their violence in the ghetto are worse than Asians killing one another on the LA waterfront (Butters to Riggs and Murtaugh: 'Fuck man, we got people killed left, and right and center in this town, now we are importing them. Hey, those gang-bangers want to kill each other, no problem. Occupational hazard').

Riggs and Murtaugh stumble upon a scheme to smuggle illegal aliens from China to work as virtual slaves in the United States. In the LA harbor Murtaugh's boat (*Code 7*) crashes into a freighter from China. A fight occurs, and Murtaugh's boat sinks. The freighter is filled with 400 illegal aliens, each of whom has paid a fee of $35,000 to be brought to America. Murtaugh discovers the Hong family (father, wife, grandfather, son, daughter) hiding in a rowboat near the pier. He adopts the family and takes them home ('It is my chance to do something about slavery. I'm freeing slaves like no one did for my ancestors'). It seems that Uncle Benny, Chinatown's mob boss, has imported Chinese slaves to pay for an artist to create counterfeit Chinese currency that the Triads (led by Jet Li) will use to buy the Four Fathers (heads of the Triad) back from the Chinese military. Mr Hong is an artist who has been brought to the US to help make the counterfeit money to buy back the Four Fathers.

The second plot involves parallel pregnancies. Lorna and Riggs are living together. She is pregnant, and wants to get married, but does not want to pressure Riggs, who is not ready to marry again. He still grieves for his first wife (Vicki) and blames himself for her death ('She's dead cause I'm a cop'). Rianne,

Murtaugh's oldest daughter, is pregnant and secretly married to Butters. Butters is very friendly with Murtaugh, constantly trying to impress him. Riggs convinces Murtaugh that Butters may be gay, and is making gay overtures to him (Riggs: 'Hey, he likes you.' Murtaugh: 'Likes me like that?!'). She is afraid to tell her father about her marriage because he does not want her married to a policeman, he doesn't want her to get hurt.

In plot number three Murtaugh is suspected of being on the take by Internal Affairs. Murtaugh's wife has become a successful writer of women's fiction (with soft pornography). She has made a great deal of money from her first two books, and it is some of this money that Murtaugh is spending. Throughout the film Riggs quizzes Murtaugh about his extra funds. Not until the final shoot-out with Jet Li is it revealed that Trish is writing the novels that Lorna is reading, the novels with sex scenes that have stirred Riggs' imagination.

The narrative moves through a series of spectacular stunt sequences and fireworks, including: a chase scene where Gibson is dragged behind a trailer truck on the freeway on an upside-down round coffee table attached to a long sheet of plastic; a scene where everybody is tied up on the floor of Murtaugh's house, which has been torched by Jet Li and his associates; an underwater fight and rescue (twice Murtaugh saves Riggs); a scene where Murtaugh and Riggs crash straight through one building into another; dazzling martial arts sequences involving Jet Li; an outrageous extended scene involving laughing gas in a dentist's office where Murtaugh finally learns that Butters is his son-in-law (Butters: 'Your baby is having my baby!!').

In the end all the bad guys are dead. The two aging detectives have once again proven that 'We are not too old for this shit!!' Riggs visits Vicki's grave with Murtaugh, and tells her he is in love with Lorna. Leo shows up and tells Murtaugh about 'Froggie' his pet frog, and best friend, in childhood,

> I really loved Froggie. I took him everywhere with me. One day he jumped out of the basket on my bike and I ran over him with the back tire and I killed him. I was heart broken. He was by best friend. And then I met you and Roger and you guys looked out for me. Now you and Roger are my family, my friends. Not better friends than Froggie, just different.

Riggs looks up and speaks to Vicki, 'I got the message. I'll always have you.' At this moment he seemingly decides to marry Lorna. He and Leo race to the hospital. Lorna demands to be married before she has her baby, 'I want to be a wife before I am a mother.' Leo finds a rabbi to perform the service. Seeking a glass to consecrate the ceremony, Leo then takes a paper cup containing urine out of the hand of an elderly black man in a bathrobe who is walking down the hall ('Hey, you sonofabitch, that took me all day! Bring that back right now!'). Leo drops the cup on the floor and he and Murtaugh stomp on it as Lorna is taken into the delivery room. Riggs soon emerges with his son in his arms. Murtaugh and Butters rush in looking for Rianne's baby, just as Captain Murphy appears bearing gifts for both babies (and families) from the police department downtown. Murphy reports that the Hong family has been granted residency by the Immigration Service. A black doctor steps forward and takes a camera out of Leo's hands. He turns to the entire group and asks, 'Are you friends?' and they shout, 'No!!! We are family'.

Thus the film, at its end, has a predictable trajectory, with Riggs and Lorna married and Murtaugh happily accepting his new son-in-law.

The film credits play over a series of photographic stills and snapshots of the cast as the musical soundtrack booms out 'Why can't we be friends? The color of your skin, no matter to me, as long as we can live in harmony. Why can't we be friends?' A final photograph of the entire cast and production crew fills the screen, and thus does the film, with its multicultural themes, end.

Two speeches by Butters help frame the film's stance toward race and the hood. In the car with Riggs and Murtaugh, he says of his childhood,

> There were about 150,000 bullets zinging around my neighborhood when was I growin' up. You couldn't go near a window. I lived on the floor man. Ate on the floor. TV on the floor. I didn't learn how to walk until I was 10 years old. Not the crime! It was the Goddamned floor that pissed me off!!!

Leo pulls up alongside the police car. Butters is sitting in the back seat.

Leo: Who's the perp?

Butters: Oh, you see a young brother in the back of the police car. Automatically I'm a perp. Look at my suit. Look at my tie. What do I look like, a fuckin' Crips accountant? Bitch!

Leo: Hey, German Jews didn't have it any easier when we were kids. Don't think you're the only one. Besides I knew you were a cop. I was just kidding. Hey, I can smell a cop a mile away.

Butters: Oh, so now I smell bad?

Leo: Stop turning everything around. Don't be so damned touchy. These guys will tell you we got a history together.

Butters, with his psychology degree and his secret marriage to Murtaugh's daughter, has left the projects. In invoking the German Jews, Leo raises the racial ante, telling Butters that he too his experienced racial violence and prejudice. Thus does the film attempt to forge an alliance between African Americans and members of the American Jewish community (West, 1994, p. 104). For the first time Leo is identified as being Jewish.[14] His retort to Butters accomplishes two ends. It announces a Jewish sympathy for blacks and their suffering, while suggesting that historically Jews may have been treated worse then blacks.

The film returns to the black–Jewish theme in the extended hospital wedding scene cited above. Suddenly, in three short scenes, the film, and by implication the series, has gotten itself tangled up in issues of race, religion, and black–Jewish relations.

This is not exactly a call for a 'principled alliance between Jews and Blacks' (West, 1994, p. 106), but within the terrain of popular culture it makes black–Jewish relations a matter of public discourse. This gesture, when combined with Murtaugh's efforts to adopt the Hong family, indicates that *LW4* indeed attempts to define family in a multicultural way. Nonetheless, the film's playful treatment of gay African-American males suggests a passive homophobia and an alignment with the norms of heterosexuality. Still thinking Butters is gay, Murtaugh observes (to Butters), 'People have to do what ever makes 'em happy. Just don't expect me to like it too.'

The *Lethal Weapon* narrative comes full circle with *LW4*. From the beginning this self-reflexive series has been about the same small set of topics, about friendship, family, and race, about race and human relations in a historical moment defined by violence, greed, drugs, and guns. It has been a series focused on how the black family (and now the white family) reproduces itself through love, action, care, and comedy. It has been about fitting two genres, action and comedy, into a third, a hybrid, the cop-buddy-action race film.

Race as Action-Comedy

If the *Lethal Weapon* series is action-comedy, then its treatment of race must, in the main, be read through the comedy framework. It is white, not black, racial comedy that structures the series. White racial humor (Ellison, 1986, pp. 184–185) reproduces long-standing stereotypes, making the person of color an object of white verbal slander and abuse. This is an old tradition: comic Negroes playing racially derogatory characters, jesters, buffoons, pure coons, toms, Aunt Jemimas, little pickaninnies (Bogle, 1994, p. 24). Ellison (1986) suggests that 'In the Lear-like drama of white supremacy Negroes were designated both clowns and fools' (p. 185). This led to the creation of a comedy of the grotesque. But blacks 'fooled' whites, Ellison argued. Even as they played fools and clowns, blacks maintained their own sense of reason and pride within this absurd racist system. Thus did they produce their version of the American Joke (Ellison, 1986, p. 186); they turned the tables on white society.

The black-produced comedies of the late 1980s and 1990s (*Mo' Money, Livin' Large, Rage in Harlem, Hollywood Shuffle, Boomerang, Strictly Business, House Party*) elaborated this version of the American Joke (Guerrero, 1993a, pp. 190–191). Through a complex process of transcoding,[15] these films told their stories from the perspective of the white middle class. They allowed 'complex, pent-up racial fears and energies to be transcoded into simplistic entertaining formulas and solutions' (Guerrero, 1993a, p. 190). These solutions maintained the racial status quo while mocking and reproducing white 'perceptions and expectations' (Guerrero, 1993a, p. 190).

Ellison (1986, p. 185), employing a functional safety-valve theory of comedy, argues that the greater the racial tension in a society, the greater the need for racial comedy. Comedy allows the members of the society to become observers of their conduct, helping them see real and imaginary racial conflicts, tensions and obstacles. Racial action-comedy texts, such as the *Lethal Weapon* series, provide such a forum. But their comedy framework does not challenge the dominant racial order.

Indeed *Lethal Weapon* gives the white man the traditional black comedy part. Riggs is the clown and the fool, and Murtaugh is the straight-faced conservative moralist. In this reversal of racial parts, the series has Murtaugh model the preferred racial order; the black man as a solid member of the middle class (Of course Murtaugh lives in a racially segregated neighborhood). But more deeply, his blackness is not given a racial identity. His blackness is not part of who he is. Race is the unnamed signifier, the label that is never attached to Murtaugh or his family. Only the South Africans and Jack Travis dare speak its presence. Like Michael Jordan, Danny Glover does not have a racial identity. But race is present, even when it goes unnamed.

Glover as Murtaugh is a black man who is not black. He is a black man who is white. Like Michael Jordan, he enacts a racially neutered identity (Andrews, 1996), a black version of a white cultural model. This is an understated racial identity that privileges Glover's superior skills as a physical comedy actor. Glover plays a character who seeks to be regarded as a good person, rather than as a good black man. In this gesture, blackness dissolves into goodness, thereby allowing action and comedy to take over the race story.

Thus the race relations narrative of *Lethal Weapon* must be read through its comic moments; moments that refuse to give a face to race. These moments emerge (with few exceptions) in times of action and crisis, or just after a crisis has been managed. In these scenes the meanings of race, gender, and sexuality are negotiated within a comedy framework. Black and white, male and female bodies get tangled up in incongruous, laughable situations that disrupt the taken-for-granted meanings of masculinity, femininity, homosexuality, and miscegenation. These scenes and their conversations are folded into action sequences. This sexual and racial discourse and banter is presented as an afterthought, as the aftermath, the dessert, the reward for successfully negotiating a moment of danger. And the banter further seals the bond between Murtaugh and Riggs and the audience.

At the same time each film is marked by its comic representations of race as farce. And like Mark Twain's Jim (of Huck Finn), Roger Murtaugh is a man to be envied, a human being to be admired, an everyman who 'expresses his essential humanness in his desire for freedom [from the LA police force], his will to possess his own labor, in his loyalty and capacity for friendship and in his love for his wife and [children]' (Ellison, 1964, p. 31). Riggs has the Huck Finn fixation, but Murtaugh refuses to play Jim to his Huck.[16] At the same time, Murtaugh refuses the traditional 'white dictum that Negro males must be treated either as boys or "uncles" – never as men' (Ellison, 1964, p. 51). Indeed, Riggs plays the part of the boy, counterpart to Murtaugh's manliness.

Two key scenes in *LW1* establish this framework for the entire series.

After the shoot-out with Amanda's drug dealers, Murtaugh invites Riggs home for dinner. In that first family scene Rianne develops an immediate crush on Riggs. Her brother and sister sing a song with the lines, 'My sister's in love with this man named Martin.' In this song Nick and Carrie mock Rianne's doe-eyed infatuation with Riggs. Looking back from *LW4* to *LW1*, it can be seen that in making this a laughing matter the series is announcing its desire to be relentless in the treatment of white–black relationships, including miscegenation.

The closing sequence of the film, the comedy by-play between Riggs and Murtaugh over Christmas dinner, returns to this theme. Riggs states, 'I think your daughter kind of likes me,' and Murtaugh replies, 'You touch her and I'll kill you.' Murtaugh repeats these lines in *LW3*. This reflexively links the two films, while underscoring the notion that this race business, including male–female miscegenation, is clearly more than something to be just joked about.

In *LW2* key comedy scenes revolve around Rianne's TV condom commercial, and the extended bathroom bomb sequence. The condom commercial, with all black actors, suggests that Rianne, Murtaugh's baby, is no longer a virgin. Murtaugh's outrage over this fact leads the entire family to laugh at him behind his back, as Riggs joins in, 'In one ear, out the rubber.' The rubber tree at his office continues this comedy routine, forcing Murtaugh to accept his daughter's sexual maturity.

The bathroom bomb scene occasions homosexual banter. Riggs tells Murtaugh, 'Get off me man. I don't want anybody to see us like this.' In this scene the film embraces a theme that will extend throughout the entire series; namely homosexuality, manliness, male bonding, homosocial (Fuss, 1989, p. 45), not homoerotic relations (Fiedler, 1966, p. 366). Race is unnamed in these scenes. The heterosexual taboo against same-sex relations overrides the racial theme. A white and black man can be friends, but not lovers.[17]

In *LW3* Delores Hall develops a crush on Murtaugh, giving him a big red lipstick kiss after the chase with the armored trucks. She later brings him flowers at work ('You tell that good-lookin' lovely Sergeant Murtaugh that he is the jam in my jellyroll'). This sexual statement, with its implicit racial coding (jellyroll), of course embarrasses Murtaugh, confirming, at the same time, his heterosexual identity, as well as his attractiveness to another black woman.

The humor of *LW4*, as indicated above, turns again on sexual and racial discourse, and includes Murtaugh's mis-identification of Butters as a homosexual, racial slurs directed to Asians ('Speakie English?'), the laughing gas episode in the dentist's office, the hospital wedding, and the final family photography scene, when Leo is made part of the Murtaugh–Riggs clan, 'We are family!'

In its call for interracial harmony ('Why can't we be friends?'), *LW4* functions as an ideological text that imagines a racial utopia. In this multicultural world, skin color, religion, sexual orientation, and cultural differences no longer matter. We can all become friends if we become color blind. In this perfect world of racial integration ugly racial slurs are reserved only for the bad guys, those evil Asians, those violent, drug-dealing gang members in the hood. Thus does *LW4* imagine a world divided into two parts, good and evil, with good winning out in the end. These two old guys, Murtaugh and Riggs, these two lethal weapons, will never get too old to do this shit! And in these ways this series inscribes an ideal racial order for the new century.

Reading Interracial Cop Stories

It remains to offer a framework for reading the *Lethal Weapon* cycle, for interpreting interracial buddy-action-cop-comedy films. The following propositions, extending the arguments of previous chapters, are suggested.[18] First, as stated in Bogle (1994), utopian, interracial buddy texts like *LW1–4* function as 'wish-fulfillment fantasies for a nation that has repeatedly hoped to simplify its racial tensions' (pp. 271–272). Historically, such film friendships 'have held to one dictum: namely that interracial buddies can be such only when the white buddy is in charge' (Bogle, 1994, p. 272) (Of course this is the model operating in the *Die Hard* sequence described above). The *Lethal Weapon* cycle exploits this dictum by moving power back and forth between Murtaugh and Riggs, as when in *LW1* Murtaugh moves over and lets Riggs drive the police car.

Thus integration (and assimilation) function under the sign of the white man, as the two male friends enact the new racial order. The dark-skinned male has become white. At the same time, the black male has what the white man wants, a respectable middle-class home and a stable family life. This means the two men must resolve racial conflicts in order to get on to the more important matters involving law, order, and justice in the capitalist system (Guerrero, 1993a, p. 126; Bogle, 1994, p. 276). Still, the resolution of these problems will be within terms set by the white (and black) middle class, and its family and law and order agenda.

In the *Lethal Weapon* cycle, Murtaugh and Riggs never engage in a direct dialogue about race. Murtaugh carries the banner of civil rights for blacks and other minorities. He laments the genocide of the ghetto, seeks freedom for South African brothers, and sees Asian refugees as being like black slaves on board a slave ship. Open racial discourse is left for the other black–white cop pair, Leo and Butters. Only Leo, the Jew, and the college-educated black Butters directly confront race, and in their caustic back-and-forth dialogue they resolve their racial conflicts ('Hey, the Jews had it bad too'). Once this is put to rest, they get down to the business of finding the bad guys.

Second, consistent with the racial politics of the 1990s (Bogle, 1994, p. 268), these bi-racial comedy buddy films simultaneously side-step racial topics while taking up forms of urban violence ordinarily located in the hood; that is, gangs, guns, violence, and drugs. This focus on gang violence, as noted in Chapter 1, reproduces America's official race relations narrative; the narrative that locates America's racial problems in a dysfunctional political economy of violence. This system of violence extends from the hood to white (and black) suburbia. This focus on the political economy of violence means that in the bi-racial buddy film there is little analysis of a corrupt racial order.[19]

Furthermore, in these films, black (and brown) characters are treated as if they where white. They are isolated from the larger African-American (Latino and Asian) community, contained within the white work and community environment (Guerrero, 1993b, p. 244). Yet in those moments that focus on the spectacular display of violence, the film may take masochistic pleasure in seeing a black man almost blown up; for example, the bathroom bomb scene in *LW1* (Guerrero, 1993b, p. 242). In such moves, these films neutralize race and racial matters, much as the women's films analyzed in the previous chapter.

Third, these movies are shaped by the narrative legacies of Vietnam, Southeast Asia, and international drug cartels. As argued in Chapter 1, three decades of Hollywood films have yet to secure firmly the meanings of the Vietnam war for American society. The Rambo/Chuck Norris model of manhood defines one version of masculinity that circulates in these action films. This version of manliness is established in the face of the torture and pain inflicted by the barbaric Asian male, for example Riggs' torture scene in *LW1*. But Vietnam gave America more than troubled men with hard bodies. It also gave us drugs, drug wars, and new versions of gang (Asian, black, Hispanic) warfare. The CIA, the Special Forces, and a Laos-based heroin operation established during the Vietnam war are central to the story told in *LW1*. It is as if, as Noriega (1988) notes, 'Vietnam has come home to Los Angeles' (p. 211). Thus do these interracial buddy cop comedy films keep the Asian presence alive in American culture.

Fourth, these movies combine unlikely social types. Lewis (1990) observes that the concept of the 'unlikely friendship is one of the staples of the adventure film. Two people of very different personalities are plunged into a situation of tension and pressure in which their survival depends on mutual cooperation' (p. 218).[20] The action hero, or central protagonist, is often presented as a tragic figure. He may, like Riggs, have lost his loved one to the violence and terror that permeate this contemporary late modern world. He is marked by this violence; it has turned him against himself and society. This figure will be paired with and contrasted to a more stable, less troubled opposite. The resolution of the conflict between the two characters provides an underlying subtext for dramatic action, comedy, slapstick, and physical humor, romance (and romantic comedy), and on occasion melodrama and tragedy.

Fifth, as action films, the *Lethal Weapon* cycle celebrates violence in its multiple forms: personal, political, social, cultural, and material. Muscular, masculine bodies are cut up, kicked, smashed, thrown from speeding automobiles/trucks; characters like Riggs jump 'Indiana Jones-style back and forth between moving vehicles' (Flamm, 1992); people are hung by meat hooks in freezing lockers. Buildings explode, cars crash into one another, windows are blown out, homes burn down, dumpsters are dropped on people. There are machine-gun killings, surfboard decapitations, death by carpenters' nail guns, bombs wired to toilet seats.

Loud rap music plays in the background as menacing young black males drive through middle-class black and white neighborhoods. Racial politics are thereby engendered, played out in an almost exclusively heterosexual masculine public space (Brown, 1996, p. 52; also Tasker, 1993, p. 17; 1998, p. 73). Violence between racial groups is subordinated to these larger narratives that locate violence at the level of the relationship between corporate capitalism, the racial order, the state and its agents, the drug trade, the police, gangs, individuals and their personal property (see Chan, 1998, p. 38).

Sixth, this masculine space makes an erotic – and on occasion comedic and parodic – spectacle of the hard male body (Tasker, 1998, p. 73). These bodies are anchored in a racially engendered heterosexual narrative. But a homoerotic subtext lurks beneath the surface, as in *LW3* when Gibson asks Glover, just as the closing credits roll, 'Give me us kiss before they come' (Levy, 1992).

Tasker (1998) elaborates on the homoerotic theme, noting that many of the buddy films of the 1990s often opt for 'a comic buddy partnership defined by a tongue-in-cheek, eroticized banter' (p. 73). Thus Riggs and Murtaugh joke about exchanging kisses, but never really cross this interracial barrier, although they pat each other on the shoulder and share tender glances (Tasker, 1998, p. 75; also hooks, 1996, p. 89).

This kind of 'hip riff on the homoerotic undercurrents of male bonding cop movies' (Wilmington, 1989) supports Fiedler's (1966, p. 503) contentions that the American male directs his emotional intimacies to another male, not his wife. He does this because he has been defeated in his attempts to deal with the love (and loss) of a woman (but see Ellison, 1964, p. 51). At the same time, the buddy-action film avoids anxieties over the male's masculinity (and sexuality) by deploying 'parodic enactments of war movie death scenes' (Tasker, 1993, p. 47), where men hold dying (or wounded) men in their arms (*LW2* and *4* have these wounded scenes, with Murtaugh telling Riggs he can't die. In *LW3* it is the wounded woman [Lorna] who ends up in the man's [Riggs'] arms).

Of course the playful homoerotic patter in this mock-death scenes between Gibson and Glover by-passes the taboos against male–female miscegenation. Further, it is handled with a grin, like the person who tells a dirty or racist joke, and 'then winks and says he knows they're bad; he's heard them before too' (Wilmington, 1989, p. 7).

Black, brown, or white, the heterosexual hero (here Riggs and Murtaugh) and heroine (Lorna) have well-displayed muscles, unbelievable acrobatic skills, and strength. He or she is able to endure inhuman torture. He or she is an unstoppable two-fisted force of destruction, fearlessly wielding his/her muscles and guns as lethal weapons. This spectacular display of masculinity codes black, brown, and white male and female bodies in the same way; they are turned into objects of the cinematic (racial) gaze (Brown, 1996, p. 56). Yet the 'contemporary action cinema has tended to erase or to play down the figure of the suffering hero, though he has not disappeared. The hero (or heroine) is treated as something of a joke' (Tasker, 1998, p. 73).

Paradoxically, this lighter 'tone in American action films has ... allowed a space for female characters to take on more central action roles' (Tasker, 1998, p. 73). Thus, as noted above, in *LW3* Lorna and Riggs compare battle wounds and scars before they make love.[21] At this level there is no gender difference between the black, brown, and white body. The female body is as masculine as the male body. The masquerade that fosters gender and racial difference is thereby exposed. In masculinizing, eroticizing, and engendering the racial body, the bi-racial buddy film neutralizes race and racial politics. And, regretfully, only in all-black films does the black action hero get the beautiful leading lady. Riggs gets Lorna, and Murtaugh gets to go home and take a bath (although somehow his Trish gets into the tub with him).

However, seventh, unlike the white buddy movies of the late 1960s and 1970s, women, and feminine sensibilities, are central to the bi-racial cop-comedy movies of the 1990s. Guerrero (1993b, p. 239), citing Woods (1986, pp. 227–230), argues that the white buddy films of earlier decades marginalized women, and could be read as negative reactions to the women's movement (*Easy Rider, Butch Cassidy and the Sundance Kid, Midnight Cowboy*). Guerrero (1993b, p. 239) suggests that the white buddy movie of the 1970s mutated into the feminized biracial film of the 1980s (and 1990s).

The feminization of the biracial film in the 1990s is complex. Consistent with earlier eras, a black man (Murtaugh) still takes on the duties of a nurturing black woman. He takes care of his reckless white pal (Riggs). Often the black buddy is located in a stable family system.[22] In turn, the white action hero, due to personal tragedy, is presented as being outside any intimate family system. His work has become his life. Nonetheless, this figure learns how to share his emotions. It may be painful to do so. Murtaugh and Riggs can get drunk together and slobber all over one another, sharing their innermost fears and self-doubts. Thus does the nineties action film open a space for the new sensitive male of the twenty-first century.

Eighth, to summarize, building on Altman's (1986, pp. 32–34; 1987, p. 95) and Tasker's (1993, pp. 1–13) structural and critical feminist approaches to genre study, it can be argued that these hybrid, interracial, male-bonding comedy texts are defined by the following semantic (common traits, characters, shots, locations) and syntactic (structural-relational) elements. Many of these features derive from the classic Western, detective, and conspiratorial film traditions (Tasker, 1993; Jameson, 1992; Denzin, 1995a, pp. 7–8). The cop-comedy-action films exhibit these characteristics:

- a preoccupation with spectacle, physicality, the military array of weaponry and hardware; less concern with dialogue, but a focus on witty lines and wise-cracks (Tasker, 1993, p. 6);
- a preoccupation with the male body as the site of pleasure, sexuality, pain, and torture (Tasker, 1993, p. 77);
- corrupt characters (violent arch-villains, foreigners, corrupt insiders) who threaten the established moral order and the state, and inflict great pain upon and create staggering obstacles to be overcome by the action hero and heroine, and his/her buddy;
- a larger than life action hero (usually an outsider to the moral community) who is characterized by good looks, quick wit and wise-cracks, a strong, muscular body, is marginally successful with women, but has a strained relationship with the police and the official institutions of society; knowledgeable, nonetheless, about violent weapons of destruction, committed to justice and the values of the moral community;
- a referential narrative that reflexively pays tribute, through comedy, jokes, parody, and pastiche, to current and classic popular culture and action heroes;[23]
- violent scenes of discovery that undo earlier scenes of misrecognition (where bad guys were taken to be good guys; see Tasker, 1993, p. 63); these scenes disclose the underlying conspiracy that caused trouble in the first place, and they are often preceded (and accompanied) by multiple deaths;
- a treatment of violence and spectacle as farce; a merger of violence-as-spectacle with scenes of dramatic resolution; the action hero causes a violent spectacle, and in that spectacle justice is wrought, and the conspiracy is destroyed;
- a visual style and code that highlights explosions, bomb and fire scenes; visual pyrotechnics; the use of long telephoto lenses, wide high-angle subjective shots, reverse and close-up camera shots, bright scenes lit for night, broken glass, blood, guns, moving vehicles, mutilated, dead bodies, tension emphasizing ticking clocks (on bombs), parallel editing, crowd scenes, physical torture, clashes between humans and machines, and advanced information technologies (computers), framing devices using doors, windows, mirror reflections, a constant concern with visual and physical danger.

This visual code highlights physicality, action, the emotions of death, danger, pain, the senseless destruction of lives and property.

The interracial, buddy-action-comedy film deploys an investigative narrative structure that presupposes a damaged male hero and a moral outsider. This figure is in search of the truth of an event; an event that has caused moral and physical danger for the local moral community. That event, in turn, will be connected to a sequence of increasingly larger spectacular violent events, culminating in a final grand explosion (as in the climaxes for each *LW* film). This visual (and narrative) code stresses the importance of:

- action defined in male terms with violence connecting the male to the public sphere; the male must prevent something from happening (a man-made disaster) in order to save the moral community; in so doing he places himself in grave physical danger;
- women as objects of the male's investigative-action work, as well as objects of desire, and sometimes companionship; a romantic involvement of the male character with women defined as *femme fatales*, or wives, or recent- or long-suffering girlfriends
- a corresponding emotional attachment between the two male figures, an attachment that connotes love without homoeroticism, and that erases race as an object of attention.

Sex, Desire, and Race

Within the above framework, the interracial buddy-action comedy film proposes to entertain in masculine ways. In so doing it takes up and reproduces standard answers to the problems of law and order and justice under a patriarchal, capitalist, racist system.

So the *LW1-4* cycle is all about ideology and utopia, and idealized racial orders. 'We are family!' the crew of *LW4* exclaim. In the end it all comes back to black and white bodies that matter, to race and sex and gender, to love, intimacy, and family, to male and female bonding, to taboos surrounding miscegenation, to male desire.

And here it gets complicated. In every scene in the *Lethal Weapon* cycle where homoerotic banter occurs it is the white man, Riggs, who utters the words of desire to the black man, Murtaugh. But then this is not surprising. Paraphrasing Fiedler (1966), 'In dreams of white men ... the forbidden erotic object tends to be represented by a black man' (p. 365). Further, in our popular national American cinema, literature, and culture there is a repressed symbolic demand that configures the sacred male bond in 'inter-racial as well as homerotic' (Fiedler, 1966, p. 366) terms (but also see Ellison, 1964, p. 51).

Profound sociological consequences follow. As Fiedler observes (1966, p. 366), the interracial male bond models one solution to the race problem in America. The black male is accorded full freedom in his homosocial relations with the white man; no longer slave, he is the white man's equal. Thus do the agendas of the civil rights and gay liberation movements overlap (Fiedler, 1966, p. 366).

And so Riggs and Murtaugh are joined, 'soul to soul rather than body to body' (Fiedler, 1966, p. 368) ('Get off me man. I don't want anybody to see us like this,' Riggs mutters to Murtaugh). In this joining, a non-erotic but noble passion is presented. This is a manly passion that joins the white and black men in a pure intermingling of the races, a pure miscegenation, a friendship blind to race, Huck and Jim all over again. No wonder Riggs fears Murtaugh's retirement, for if

Murtaugh goes, Riggs loses his pure soul-mate. And clearly Lorna is an intended substitute for Murtaugh, but in the end she is a woman, and somewhat fragile. And their sexual lust for one another is ignoble when compared to the love between Murtaugh and Riggs.

The new racial order? A new public sphere, black on white? Black and white men *Get on the Bus* (1996), a new Million Man March to racial equality? Is this what the new racial order will look like? Black men leading white men out of racism. What would James Baldwin say?[24] Fun and games, 'Give us a kiss before they come.' In the next chapter I turn to what the black filmmakers and the boyz in the hood say about all of this.

Notes

1. King (1999) argues that, taken as a group, the *Lethal Weapon* series 'hardly erases racism or celebrates white supremacy. They are, instead, white male responses to their own guilt, rage and need' (p. 117). He offers a valuable reading of previous analyses of this series (pp. 115–116, 260), noting that '*Lethal Weapon* is the most often analyzed movie in cop action, having received more attention than even the 'Dirty Harry' movies' (p. 115).

2. *Lethal Weapon* (1987). Released by Warner Brothers. Director: Richard Donner; Screenplay: Shane Black; Cinematography: Stephen Goldblatt. Cast: Mel Gibson (Martin Riggs), Danny Glover (Roger Murtaugh), Gary Busey (Mr Joshua), Tom Atkins (Michael Hunsaker), Darlene Love (Trish Murtaugh), Traci Wolfe (Rianne Murtaugh), Jackie Swanson (Amanda Hunsaker), Damon Hines (Nick Murtaugh), Ebonie Smith (Carrie Murtaugh). (For reviews and commentary, see Fiorillo, 1987; Noriega, 1988; Wilmington, 1987; Wootton, 1987; Ebert, 1987; Gelmis, 1987; Schickel, 1987; Dieckmann, 1987; Tasker, 1998, pp. 75, 82–83; Guerrero, 1993a, pp. 126, 134; Bogel, 1994, pp. 274–276, 326; hooks, 1996, p. 88.)

Lethal Weapon II (1989). Released by Warner Brothers. Director: Richard Donner; Screenplay: Jeffrey Boam, based on a story by Shane Black and Warren Murphy and on characters created by Black; Cinematography: Stephen Goldblatt. Cast: Mel Gibson (Martin Riggs), Danny Glover (Roger Murtaugh), Joe Pesci (Leo Getz), Joss Ackland (Arjen Rudd), Derrick O'Connor (Peter Vorstedt), Patsy Kensit (Rika Van Den Haas), Darlene Love (Trish Murtaugh), Traci Wolfe (Rianne Murtaugh), Steve Kahan (Captain Murphy). (For reviews and critical commentary, see Lewis, 1990; Fiorillo, 1989; Wilmington, 1989; Newman, 1989; Edelstein, 1989; McGrady, 1989b.)

Lethal Weapon III. (1992). Released by Warner Brothers. Director: Richard Donner; Screenplay: Jeffrey Boam and Robert Mark Kamen; based on a story by Boam and on characters created by Shane Black; Cinematography: Jan De Bont. Cast: Mel Gibson (Martin Riggs), Danny Glover (Roger Murtaugh), Joe Pesci (Leo Getz), Rene Russo (Lorna Cole), Stuart Wilson (Jack Travis), Steve Kahan (Captain Murphy), Darlene Love (Trish Murtaugh), Traci Wolfe (Rianne Murtaugh), Damon Hines (Nick Murtaugh), Ebonie Smith (Carrie Murtaugh), Gregory Millar (Tyrone), Mary Ellen Trainor (Dr Stephanie Woods). (For reviews and critical commentary, see Welsh, 1993; Canby, 1992; Edwards, 1992; Rainer, 1992; Denby, 1992b; Flamm, 1992; Anderson, 1992a; Kroll, 1992; Kermode, 1992; Levy, 1992; Tasker, 1998, p. 83.)

Lethal Weapon IV (1998). Released by Warner Brothers. Director: Richard Donner; Screenplay: Channing Gibson, based on a story by Jonathan Lemkin, Alfred Gough, and Miles Millar, and on characters created by Shane Black; Cinematography: Andrzej Baartkowiak. Cast: Mel Gibson (Martin Riggs), Danny Glover (Roger Murtaugh), Joe Pesci (Leo Getz), Rene Russo (Lorna Cole), Chris Rock (Lee Butters), Jet Li (Wah Sing Ku), Kim Chan (Uncle Benny), Steve Kahan (Captain Murphy), Darlene Love (Trish Murtaugh), Traci Wolfe (Rianne Murtaugh), Damon Hines (Nick Murtaugh), Ebonie Smith (Carrie Murtaugh), Mary Ellen Trainor (Dr Stephanie Woods).

3. The figures are tentative, dated, and do not always include rentals, or all of the non-US revenue. *LW1* grossed $95 million, *LW2*, $327 million, *LW3*, $319 million, and *LW4* (as of 1 November 1998), $267 million. In the first week of February 1999, *LW4* was the fifth highest grossing US film in terms of rentals and sales.

4. Danny Glover brings a cinematic racial history to the character of Roger Murtaugh. Through his performances in such films as *Places in the Heart* (1984), *The Color Purple* (1985), *Witness* (1985), *To Sleep With Anger* (1990), *A Rage in Harlem* (1991), and *Grand Canyon* (1991), he has mediated and helped define America's complex cinematic racial formations of the 1980s and the 1990s. He has been a sharecropper, a violent husband, a corrupt policeman, a con artist, an action hero, and a single parent. He represents one version of the black male hero. In the Murtaugh part he becomes the black patriarch who is the butt of family jokes and the target of Riggs's sadistic humor.

5. This is the film third in this Bruce Willis series.

6. Following Tasker (1993, pp. 54–72), it is possible to distinguish several narrative and representational variations within the contemporary hybrid action film genre, including: (1) muscular, post-Vietnam narratives (*Rambo*); (2) *Indiana Jones* adventure serials; (3) black action texts (*Superfly*); (4) black male buddy-bonding stories (*Die Hard*, *Lethal Weapon*); (5) kung fu tales (*Enter the Dragon*, the Jackie Chan films); (6) comic strip heroes, heroines, action figures, supermen and super-women (*Superman*, *Batman*, *Conan the Destroyer*, *Cleopatra Jones*, *Terminator 2*, *Robocop 2*; *Red Sonja*); (7) women, heroine action films (*Thelma and Louise*, *The Long Kiss Goodnight*); (8) action, male-bonding, detective narratives (*Black Rain*, *Rising Sun*); (9) comedy–parody (and pastiche) action tales (*Lethal Weapon*); (10) urban gang, ghetto movies (*New Jack City*, *Boyz N the Hood*, *Colors*). As a hybrid genre, any given action film can construct itself in reference to any of these representational, 'iconographic and narrative traditions' (Tasker, 1993, p. 57). Conspiratorial themes are basic to the genre, things are never as they appear to be, good guys are bad guys, bad guys are good people, and so on. Conspiratorial evil forces (personal, political, medical, national, economic) are often at work.

7. Previous films in this series connected the McClane character to Al Powell (Reginald Veljohnson), a good-natured, chubby Los Angeles police officer (Tasker, 1993, p. 44). The use of black males as supporting players to white male actors is a long-standing Hollywood tradition, and includes such famous pairs as: Bing Crosby and Louis Armstrong, Will Rogers and Stepin Fetchit, Jack Benny and Rochester, Frank Sinatra and Sammy Davis, Jr, Sidney Poitier and Tony Curtis (*The Defiant Ones*), Sylvester Stallone and Carl Weathers, Clint Eastwood and Mario Van Peebles (*Heartbreak Ridge*), Bruce Willis and Damon Wayans (*The Last Boy Scout*), Eddie Murphy and Nick Nolte, and, more recently, Will Smith and Gene Hackman (see Bogle, 1994, pp. 271–272; Tasker, 1993, pp. 44–45). This tradition in American literature can be traced back (at least) to Mark Twain and Huck Finn and Huck's relationship with Jim (see Ellison, 1964, p. 31).

8. Guerrero is interpreting the actions of the Eddie Murphy character in *48 Hours* who chooses to not escape from Nick Nolte when he has the chance (1993b, p. 242).

9. Once again we encounter Danny Glover.

10. 'I'm too old for this shit!' will become the mantra for the series, and for the Murtaugh character. It becomes a major theme of *LW4*; that is, have the men become too old for this line of work?

11. Subsequent scenes show Riggs watching TV with the Murtaugh family, having breakfast with Trish, coming home from work with Roger. He has become part of the Murtaugh family, and no viewer needs any introduction to the storyline. An early gag-line involves Murtaugh's daughter Rianne, who is pursuing an acting career. The family gathers in the television room in anticipation of her first TV performance, which turns out to be an ad for condoms ('When the time has come, remember: use Ramses extra condoms'). A few days later Murtaugh's friends at work cover a plant on his desk with condoms, 'Hey Sarg, how do you like your new rubber tree?' Riggs: 'Oh, sorry, Sarg, you're too old for that stuff.'

12. An early scene shows Riggs alone with his dog Sam in his tiny housetrailer by the ocean watching *The Three Stooges* on TV. Their slapstick humor becomes point–counterpoint for Riggs' over-the-top physical acrobatics, which involve taking insane chances (see Newman, 1989). At the same time, Rigg's maniacal, masculine hysterical conduct is contrasted to Leo's feminized hysteria, including his high-pitched squeaky voice. Of course Murtaugh whines, like Leo, and at this level, these three characters complement one another.

13. This statement recalls *LW1* with its shot of the 'FREE SOUTH AFRICA, END APARTHEID' sticker on the Murtaugh kitchen refrigerator.

14. It is now possible to reread Leo and Roger Murtaugh's embassy scene with the South Africans in *LW2*. In confronting their racist attitudes toward blacks, in invoking the image of the Nazis, Leo is also challenging the South Africans' alleged anti-semitism.

15. To repeat, in racial transcoding a film draws upon existing racial understandings and stereotypes. These understandings are brought to the screen. This process transforms (transcodes) the original representation (Ryan and Kellner, 1988, p. 12).

16. For an explanation of the Huck Finn fixation see Chapter 1 n. 25.

17. On the homophobia and racism of black and white, gay and straight films, and the invisibility of gay black men in cinema, see Van Leer (1997, pp. 158–159).

18. This framework applies to the several categories of the hybrid action film discussed in note 5 above.

19. A classic exception is the famous Eddie Murphy scene in the redneck country and western bar in *48 Hours* (Guerrero, 1993b, p. 242). This scene, as Guerrero notes, recalls the Gene Hackman 'rousting of a "ghetto" bar [scene] in the *French Connection* (1971)' (p. 242).

20. Still, as Lewis (1990) observes, 'the pairing of opposites ... goes beyond action ... teams such as Stan Laurel and Oliver Hardy developed the comic potential inherent in the clash of disparate outlooks ... in the comic-book realm, there have been a host of partnerships, usually of unequal status or social class' (p. 218). The list is long: Batman and Robin, Lone Ranger and Tonto, Green Hornet and Cato, Red Rider and Little Beaver (Lewis, 1990, p. 218).

21. *The Long Kiss Goodnight* (1996) pairs Geena Davis and Samuel L. Jackson, and foregrounds the sexual aggression of the Davis character, who attempts to seduce Jackson.

22. However, as Bogle (1994) notes, in the interracial male-bonding movies 'black women rarely had a chance for important roles' (p. 291). In contrast, by the third film in the *Lethal Weapon* cycle, Rene Russo has become Gibson and Glover's partner and Gibson's lover, an action heroine (tomboy) in her own right (see Tasker, 1998, pp. 82–83; but in contrast consider the Pam Grier and Tamara Dobson black superwoman, macho female action films of the 1970s, including *Cleopatra Jones* and *Foxy Brown*, and, most recently, Grier's low-keyed 1997 film, *Jackie Brown*; see Bogle, 1994, pp. 251–252).

23. *Parody:* burlesque and imitation with a satiric thrust; *pastiche:* parody without criticism, blind imitation. Thus the final exchange between McClane and the sneering villain in *Die Hard* has McClane correcting the villain, who does not know his Western heroes. Villain: 'This time John Wayne does not walk off into the sunset with Grace Kelly.' McClain: 'Gary Cooper, asshole' (Tasker, 1993, p. 60).

24. In *Another Country* (1962) Baldwin merged the gay and civil rights movements.

Part Three: racial allegories: the black and brown hood

5

Boyz N Girlz in the Hood

> One out of every twenty-one black American males will be murdered in their lifetime. (On-screen opening statement, *Boyz N the Hood*)

> If we in America don't confront the problem – realistically – without empty slogans and promises, but by examining what motors the human soul on the course of spiritual self-destruction – then ... we shall be forever doomed to despair in the shadows. (On-screen epilogue, *New Jack City*)

> Death doesn't give a shit about color. (Nick to Scotty in *New Jack City*)

> My dad sold dope. My mother was a heroin addict. Instead of keeping me out of trouble, they turned me on to it. (Caine in voice-over, *Menace II Society*)

> *Cop:* Hey, homeboy, why don't you leave the gang life and try something more productive?
> *Grand Bush:* Yeah, I could quit the gangs.... Maybe go to Hollywood and be Eddie Murphy. (*Colors*, quoted by Guerrero, 1993a, p. 157)

> I go to see this so-called black film, OK? Twenty minutes of comin' attractions, all black films, all violent! And I'm talkin'about black brothers shootin' brothers. (Marcie Tidwell to Rod Tidwell, *Jerry Maguire*)

Now the black filmmakers, and their reading of the hood: John Singleton, Mario Van Peebles, Allen and Albert Hughes. My topic, the new urban ghetto gangster film cycle:[1] *Boyz N the Hood* (1991),[2] *New Jack City* (1991),[3] *Menace II Society* (1993).[4] A celebrated group of ghettocentric narratives, excessively violent, nihilistic, misogynist male coming-of-age stories, hip hop culture, a critical social realism, the hyperreal ghetto, hyperghettoization (Boyd, 1997, pp. 92–93; Diawara, 1993a; Massood, 1996; Watkins, 1998, pp. 11, 196, 212, 230, 276; Bogle, 1994, pp. 341–347; Guerrero, 1993a, pp. 166–167; Valerie Smith, 1997, p. 3; Reid, 1993, pp. 133–135; George, 1998, pp. 74, 108–110, 166–167; McCarthy, 1998, pp. 94–95). Depressing existential tales, living and dying in the wastelands of the postindustrial American city, the ghettos of Los Angeles, New York, Chicago. A warning, a call to arms; paraphrasing Roger Murtaugh, this generation of African Americans is committing genocide. These filmmakers are here to tell this story, and the story is not pretty. No comedy here, no cop-buddy stories like the *Lethal Weapon* series.

These films enact both a new and an old black cinematic aesthetic. These are black gangster films for the nineties, a re-doing, an imitation of the blaxploitation movies of the seventies. But these texts are blank parody, there is little criticism of the genre itself. They exhibit what Jameson (1991, pp. 16–18) calls pastiche, or imitation without satire, a cinema of excess racial violence turned into spectacle. The spectacle is parody, montage, death scenes up-close, dead bodies moving through space, blood on sidewalks, drive-bys in slow-motion. These movies are fitted to the era of post-civil rights. They respond to the black backlash of the eighties, day jobs at McDonald's and Jack 'N the Box, the Nation of Islam, gangs and cocaine, Crips and Bloods, black filmmakers issuing a wake-up call to black (and white) America: 'Do something now! Stop the violence.'

A single thesis, based on six arguments, structures my interpretation of this film cycle. These realistic social-problems texts fueled conservative racist discourse. They helped fearful white Americans blame blacks for the problems of the inner city. They suggested that blacks caused their own problems. The problems of the ghetto were not problems shared by the larger society. How these films contributed to these understandings is the topic of this chapter. Now my six arguments.

First, as Valerie Smith (1997, p. 3) suggests, there is a direct lineage between the hood movies of the 1990s and the gangster and 'blaxploitation movies of the 1970s (*Shaft, Superfly*).[5] The 1970s films 'established inner cities as context, drug and gang violence as themes, and rhythm and blues as the sound track of black cinema' (p. 3). The 'new jack pictures of the 1990s – such as *New Jack City* ... replaced heroin with crack, and rhythm and blues with hip hop' (p. 3).

Second, these 1990s films are complicated social problems texts. Simultaneously utopian and dystopian, they contest and reproduce dominant conservative and liberal racial discourses about the hood and the black public sphere (Watkins, 1998, p. 230). They criticize the economic, social, education, housing, and family conditions of the new ghetto. They present the hood as an overly militarized, coercive police state, a site that represses, entraps, and illegitimately disciplines young black men (Watkins, 1998, pp. 222, 230). These movies challenge those who blame the hood for its own problems. They locate responsibility for the hood's problems with the media, the police, and other apparatuses of the state. These films make these structures at least partially responsible for the pathologies that are located in the violent drug-dealing street gang and the fatherless black family.

Nonetheless, in the public imagination, these films became part of a national moral panic surrounding crack-cocaine, gang drug wars, and racial genocide in the ghetto (Reeves and Campbell, 1994, pp. 18–19; Reinarman and Levine, 1997, p. 42). America's crisis with cocaine started in the mid-1980s with news stories connecting an epidemic of crack-cocaine spreading from the inner cities to the suburbs. This epidemic gave rise to a national war on drugs. This soon shifted to the argument that the use of crack-cocaine was confined to the inner city, the racial ghetto. According to this narrative, ghetto gangs of young black, Latino, and Asian men were dealing in drugs and killing one another with automatic weapons (Reeves and Campbell, 1994, pp. 235–247). By the mid-1990s, it was commonly believed that Singleton was correct when he asserted that 'one in every twenty-one young men will die of gunshot wounds, and most of them will be shot by other young men' (Ebert, 1994a, p. 93). By the late 1980s this dramatic increase in gang-related homicides was attributed to the 'crack-cocaine wars' (Sanders, 1994, p. 59; also Jankowski, 1991, pp. 147–149; Bourgois, 1997, pp. 65–66).[6] These media narratives are central to the hood movies.

Still, by presenting negative images of welfare mothers and violent gang members, the films in this cycle also reproduce long-standing conservative criticisms of the black family; namely the inability of black mothers to raise black sons who do not become infected with the pathologies of the hood (Watkins, 1998, pp. 222–223). In telling coming-of-age stories about young black males who make it out of the ghetto (*Boyz N the Hood*), the cycle keeps alive the conservative myth that individuals with strong father figures can lift themselves up by their bootstraps and escape the hood's violence (Watkins, 1998, p. 224; see also Anderson, 1997, p. 35).

These texts implicitly criticize an economic system that makes dealing in drugs more attractive then working for minimal wages in the fast-food industry (Watkins, 1998, p. 208; also Anderson, 1978, 1990, 1999; Dash and Sheehan, 1998). This criticism is complex. Drug-dealing gangs are connected both to power and to prestige, and to violence and death at an early age. However, it is not clear if the gangs will get you out of the ghetto, although the time-worn conservative paths of sports and higher education (and musical entertainment) may, if you are lucky.

Third, these ghettocentric narratives glorify violence. In elaborating the urban gangster film genre, they celebrate a violent, misogynist masculinity; a gender politics that turns women into crack addicts, ho's, bitches, and lazy welfare mothers (Watkins, 1998, pp. 201, 230; hooks, 1994, p. 116; also Margolis, 1999, p. 51). However, as hooks (1994) observes, the sexist, misogynist, patriarchal values of these films are the same values that have been created and sustained by a 'white supremacist capitalist patriarchy' (p. 116). It is inappropriate to read these sexist practices as endemic to black youth culture. Still, black (and white) males 'must be held politically accountable for their sexism' (hooks, 1994, p. 116; also Giroux, 1997, p. 384).

This is a cinematography of violence: *Pulp Fiction* meets De Palma's *Scarface*, Cagney and Raft, *The Untouchables* (Pelecanos, 1991), *Bonnie and Clyde*, *GoodFellas*, *Reservoir Dogs*, *U-Turn*. *A Rage in Harlem* with real guns, real violence, real tough guys. A ghetto so violent that nobody gets out alive. Black gangsters, black Godfathers, Al Capone for the hood, *Hoodlums* (1997) style. This is not the celebratory experimental violent cinema of Quentin Tarantino. These black filmmakers are not in awe of the violent gangster and his genre. These violent tales are not for the squeamish, nor are they playful, or intended to be ironic.

But by invoking the genre, stylistic conventions, and narrative devices of the classic and new gangster films (*The Public Enemy*, *White Heat*, *Reservoir Dogs*, *Pulp Fiction*), these black filmmakers 'fall prey to the same … stylistics of violence' that they appear to be working against (Massood, 1993). This erodes the power of their moral and cinematic position; namely that this violence on the screen is meant to be a deterrent to real violence in the real hood. As Massood observes, the effects of this cinema might have been better achieved if filmmakers like the Hughes brothers had 'consistently resisted the masterful, pleasurable and *familiar* cinematography of violence' (Massood, 1993).

Fourth, these films use ethnographic and cinematic realism to achieve their ideological effects; dirty violent ghetto culture seen up close. These effects are produced through the use of close-ups, voice-over narration, vernacular speech, realistic dialogue, slow-motion photography, telephoto lenses, and overhead steadi-cam shots. The signifers from black youth culture, from baggy pants, sun-glasses, long-billed baseball caps on backwards, and rap music are everywhere present, including the use of rap stars in the cast (Ice Cube, Ice-T). Shots of hovering helicopters, searchlights beamed down on houses, and speeding police cars with shrill sirens present the hood as a site of inner-city violence (see Pelecanos, 1991; Massood, 1993, 1996, p. 90; McRobbie, 1994).

These cinematic techniques support the belief that filmmakers have cap-tured objective reality, that they are giving viewers an 'authentic portrayal of ghetto life ... official transcriptions of the lived experiences of poor black youth' (Watkins, 1998, p. 226). Of course, as argued in Chapter 1, this is not possible.

Fifth, the hood movies geographically locate contemporary urban ethnic rela-tions within a historical framework. *Menace II Society* is set in 1990s' Watts, but opens with footage from the 1965 Watts riots. *Panther* (1995) begins one version of its narrative in Oakland in 1966. *Boyz N the Hood* starts its story in 1984[7] in South Central Los Angeles; *Straight Out of Brooklyn* (1991), in Red Hook, a housing project in Brooklyn. The early scenes of *New Jack City* are located mid-way in Reagan's second presidential term. This suggests, although the theme is not explored, that the 1990s violence and drug cultures of the hood were fueled by Reagan's welfare policies (Pelecanos, 1991).

Rodney King was arrested on 3 March 1991, just after the release of *New Jack City*. The King jury returned its verdict on 29 April 1992. The Los Angles riots continued for three days after the jury brought in its verdict of not guilty (Ablemann and Lie, 1995, p. 2). The hood movies are situated squarely within this moment in recent race history. They take up and re-present the 'post-Watts history of the hood – the LAPD's militaristic methods of fighting inner city ... the Reagan and Bush Administration's war on drugs, and the right's negation of self-rehabilitation as a possibility for those convicted of selling and/or using drugs' (Massood, 1993). These scripts update and accommodate earlier blax-ploitation drug narratives, those focusing on heroin and Harlem. The new hood movies continue this narrative by examining the place of gangs, the police, and the state in the current crack epidemic (i.e. *Panther*).

The music is key. These filmmakers use rap, the 'current revolutionary poetry of the young black masses' (William J. Harris, 1998, p. 1362), to authorize their films, creating texts that speak to the black hip hop generation. Thus John Singleton is quoted as saying, 'I'm just saying the same thing that the hard core rappers are saying. They say it on wax, and I'm saying it on film' (quoted by William J. Harris, 1998, p. 1364). Since the 1980s, rap artists have 'criticized America for the perpetuation of racial and economic discrimination against African Americans, especially in the form of police brutality' (William J.

Harris, 1998, p. 1363). During the late 1980s, performers such as Ice-T, Ice Cube, Snoop Doggy Dogg, Tupac Shakur, and other

> Los Angeles rap groups from Compton and Watts ... developetd 'gangsta rap,' a West Coast style that narrates the 'Inner City Blues' realities of the typical young, poor, black male of the ghetto ... these rappers frequently and irresponsibly celebrate gang violence and violence against women and use offensive and misogynist language. ... They have come under attack by the media and various national organizations. (William J. Harris, 1998, p. 1363; also Gilroy, 1995; hooks, 1994, p. 116; Rose, 1994, pp. 183–184)

At one level, the hood movies re-enacted the music of the streets, going so far as to turn male rappers into on-screen performers (e.g. Ice Cube in *Boyz N the Hood*, Ice-T in *New Jack City*).

As historical texts, these movies privilege the hood as a geographical space within Los Angeles and New York City. These texts make the hood and its male coming-of-age stories center-stage. In so doing, they undermine the usual Hollywood and Los Angeles narrative, which locates the racial ghetto on the margins of Beverly Hills, Malibu, and Venice Beach (Massood, 1996, p. 89). In this move, filmmakers like Singleton, Van Peebles, and the Hughes brothers 'link representation to power by questioning the images which have been reified by mainstream Hollywood cultural production' (Massood, 1996, p. 90).

At the same time these movies present the hood as a heavily-policed geographical site that limits the movements of African-American males. For example, street signs reading 'One Way' and 'Do Not Enter' convey 'the message that free passage is not allowed' (Massood, 1996, p. 90). Ubiquitous police presence marks the outer boundaries of the hood. Those contained within the borders of the hood are armed and dangerous gang members. They are fair game for the police, including the African-American policeman in *Boyz N the Hood*, who mutters, 'one less nigger out on the street we won't have to worry about' (Diawara, 1993a, p. 22). Further, any black man found outside the hood is instantly a criminal, as when Caine and O-Dog are stopped by the LAPD 'for driving the wrong car in the wrong place ... are beaten and taken out of the hood to be dropped in a neighboring Mexican American barrio' (Massood, 1996, p. 92). There is no sacred, safe black public sphere, no safe place on the corner (Anderson, 1978).

Sixth, in telling stories about police injustices and police violence, these films criticize the current American system of racial justice. This separates them from the *Lethal Weapon* series, which, in many senses, blames the ghetto for its problems. Nonetheless, these films have helped create a version of reality viewers have come to associate with the new ghetto.[8] The filmmakers presumed a black (and white) audience familiar with the hood and its problems. Their films sent a message to black youth, and to white America: we want an end to racial genocide in our black communities (hooks, 1992, p. 6).

But in so doing they have done a great disservice. They have suggested that the hood, with its violent sights and sounds, has become the best metaphor of the African-American experience. They have given this cinematic image to a conservative racist culture that has been all too willing to believe that this is really the way things are in the ghetto (Massood, 1993; 1996, p. 94).

In this these films backfired, but this is always the risk of the social problems text. In drawing attention to the hood and its problems, these movies reinforced white racist criticisms of blacks in America today. In so doing they reassured white and black middle-class audiences that their identities were stable, and their stances towards race and the hood were correct (Margolis, 1999, p. 59). Thus, in the final epigraph to this chapter, Rod Tidwell's wife can openly complain (paraphrasing) about all those 'black films where brothers are killin' brothers.' A commitment to assimilation and hard work has allowed her and her husband successfully to escape the hood and its problems.

To summarize, taken together these six arguments suggest that the hood movies failed to meet the critical challenge for black filmmakers; namely to 'expand the discussion of race and representation beyond debates about good and bad imagery' (hooks, 1992, p. 4; also quoted in Margolis, 1999, p. 50). Now the films.

Boyz N the Hood

It's an old story, a familiar myth fitted to the African-American ghetto in the 1990s. An attractive young man comes of age under the most difficult of circumstances. The story, divided into two parts, spans seven years in the life and friendship of three boys. Tre, Ricky, and Doughboy, are 10 years old when the film begins. In Part One Tre Styles has just been handed over by Riva, his mother (who is getting here Master's degree), to his father, Furious (Furious runs his own finance and small home mortgage company). Tre has gotten into another fight in the classroom. His teacher tells Riva that 'your son is very intelligent, but he has a very bad temper. Perhaps he needs therapy.' Riva confronts Tre, 'You've broken our agreement. You have gotten into trouble in school. Now you will go live with your father.... I just don't want to see you end up dead, or in jail, or a drunk standin' in front of one of those liquor stores.' Riva believes Tre needs to learn how to be a man, and Furious must do this ('I can't teach him how to be a man. That's your job').

Ricky and Doughboy, who are half-brothers, live across the street from Tre and Furious with their mother, Mrs Baker, who is a single parent, and does not seem to work outside the home (Wallace, 1992, p. 123). Furious teaches Tre self-respect, and to take responsibility for his own actions: 'Any fool with a dick can make a baby, but only a real man can raise his children.' Tre learns three rules: always look a person in the eyes; never be afraid to ask for anything, stealin' isn't necessary; and never respect anybody who doesn't respect you back.

Part One insists 'on the necessity of a male authority figure, a father figure, to teach and reinforce responsible behavior for young men' (Balingit, 1992b, p. 56). At the same time it establishes the differences between the black middle and underclasses, even when the members live across the street from one another. The neatly maintained Tre and Furious household, with its buppie artwork on the walls and VW in the driveway, is contrasted with the disorganized Baker home. In the Baker house the TV blares, plastic sheets cover the furniture, paint is peeling off the front porch steps, and Mrs Baker is constantly berating her sons, especially Doughboy: 'You don't do shit. You just like your daddy. Think I'm your maid? Boy, don't get smart with me. I'll knock your ass into the middle of next week. You little fat fuck. You ain't got a job.' Fathers, not mothers, command respect from their children.

Furious would never talk this way to Tre:

I'm tryin' to teach you to be responsible. Friends across the street, they don't have any-body to do this. Tre, you're the prince, I'm the king ... I wanted to be somebody you could look up to. That's why I went to Vietnam. But don't ever go into the Army. Black man got no place in the Army.

Part One ends with Doughboy being taken off in a police car for a petty crime. A strong father figure protects Tre from the violence and crime that circulate in the neighborhood. Tre's language is properly middle class, in contrast to Doughboy, who swears and speaks street slang ('I'm gonna smoke that mother-fucker'), and sees no value in working ('I can make more money doin' nothin'').

In Part Two the story moves forward seven years. Ricky and Tre are about to graduate from high school. Ricky is his mother's favorite son. She hopes he will go to college on a football scholarship. Ricky has fathered a 1-year-old son. He and his wife and son live with Mrs Baker. Doughboy is hanging with the home-boys, drinking and doing drugs. Tre is the star of the neighborhood. He has a job, he is a good student, and he has a nice Catholic girlfriend named Brandi. In the fall the two of them will go to college.

In an extended scene Furious lectures Tre and Ricky on the facts of economic life in the hood. They are standing on a street corner under a large billboard that reads, 'Cash for your Home/Seoul to Seoul Realty'. Furious speaks,

This is the 90s ... look at that sign. Cash for your home. The message – gentrification – property values of a certain area are brought down, buy land at a lower price, move all the people out, raise the property values and sell at a profit. We need to keep everything in our neighborhood black. Black owned, black everything. Just like the Jews, the Italians, and the Mexicans.[9]

An older black man joins the conversation. A group of young black men loiter in the background. The older man speaks, 'Ain't nobody from the outside bringin' the property down. Its these fellas shootin' each other and sellin' that crack rock and shit.' A gang member responds, 'What we supposed to do? They gonna kill us, less we smoke 'em back.'

Furious will have none of this:

How do you think that shit gets in here? We don't own any airplanes or boats. I know, every time you turn on the TV that's what you see. Black folks selling the rock. It wasn't a problem until it showed up in Iowa, and on Wall Street. You wanta talk about guns? Why's there a gun shop on every corner and a liquor on every corner? Why do they want us to kill ourselves? You go out to Beverly Hills, you don't see this shit. They want us to kill ourselves.

And thus does Singleton invoke a conspiracy theory involving the CIA, guns, drugs, gangs, and the hood (see Purdum, 1997; also Denby, 1991).

By accident at a strip mall Ricky insults a gang member. The gang respond with machine-gun fire from their car. Ricky and Tre run for cover. On their way home they are stopped by a cruel African-American policeman who jams his gun into Tre's throat: 'I hate little fuckers like you. I can blow your head off. That's why I took this job.' The next day Ricky is gunned down in an alley by the gang. Doughboy and his gang vow revenge. Tre attempts to steal his father's gun, but Furious talks him out of it:

Oh, you bad now, gotta shoot somebody now. Shoot me, shoot your dad. Shoot me. I'm sorry about your friend, but that's their problem. You're my son. You're my problem. Give me the fuckin' gun Tre.

Tre hands the gun to his father, but minutes later he climbs through his bedroom window and jumps into Doughboy's car. Just before the rival gang is spotted, Tre gets out of the car. Doughboy murders the three gang members.

The next morning in Tre's front yard Doughboy reflects on what has happened,

I know why you got out of the car. You don't want that shit to haunt you. I turned on the TV. They had this show on livin' in a violent war. They showed all those foreign places. They don't know, they don't show, they don't care about what's goin' on in the hood.... I don't know how I feel about it. Shit just goes on and on. Next thing, somebody smoke me. Don't matter. All gotta go sometime.

The screen informs the viewer that 'The next day Doughboy saw his brother buried. Two weeks later he was murdered. In the fall Tre went to Morehouse College in Atlanta, Georgia, with Brandi across the way at Spelman College. Boyz N the Hood. "Increase the Peace."' At the end of the film's credits, the USC Film Writing Program is thanked, followed by, 'Dealing a new hand. The new deal has arrived.'[10]

A New Deal in the Hood

And a new deal it is, for Singleton proposes to take on the hood and its problems, to inform viewers that the passive acceptance of destructive racial violence will no longer be tolerated. His stance, typical of a social problems film, becomes didactic (Balingit, 1992b, p. 58), at times heavy-handed. Furious is the 'obvious mouthpiece for Singleton's concerns' (Grant, 1992). His solutions move in several directions at the same time: some connect them to Farrakhan (Denby, 1991b), others to Malcom X (Sterritt, 1991b), and others to Spike Lee (Balingit, 1992b, p. 58). There is a conspiracy against blacks, and at one level only blacks can help themselves. Racist capitalist practices are inflicted on blacks by whites, and these practices have worked their way into the black community itself (Sterritt, 1991b).

Singleton begins with the black public sphere. The hood must be transformed into a safe civic space where members of the black community, the elderly, the young, teenagers, husbands and wives, mothers and daughters, fathers and sons can interact without fear. This public sphere will not be controlled by roaming gangs of violent young men. This reign of terror connected to the sights and sounds of gun shots, dead bodies, blood on the sidewalk, screeching automobiles, and blaring hip hop music must stop. Guns, drugs, and gangs must go. Gang life is not an acceptable substitute for a stable family home, with a firm father figure. Indeed, left to their own devices, young black men in gangs are killing one another.

Black men must become responsible fathers and role models for their sons and daughters (Balingit, 1992b, p. 58). Birth control and safe sexual practices must be followed. Furious lectures Tre: 'You been usin' the rubber I gave you, ain't ya? I ain't ready to be a granddaddy. You had some pussy? Girl tells you she on the pill, you use somethin' anyway.'

Singleton connects safe sex practices to AIDS. Doughboy and his friends Little Chris and Dooky are at a neighborhood barbecue, drinking and eating and playing cards:

Dooky: I want some of them hootches over there. I get more pussy than you.
Doughboy: Dooky you full of shit, you been gettin' that dope-head pussy.
Dookie: I let 'em suck my dick. They got AIDS and shit.
Doughboy: You can catch that shit from lettin' 'em suck your dick too.
Dookie: I ain't sick. I ain't skinny and that shit.
Doughboy: You can die five years from now.
Dookie: Can you really get that shit by lettin' 'em suck your dick?

Men are expected to treat women with respect. As food is about to be served at the picnic, Tre tells Doughboy and his friends: 'Act like gentlemen and let the ladies eat first.' Doughboy replies: 'Let the ladies eat. Ho's gotta eat too.' A young woman responds: 'Why you callin' me a ho? I ain't no ho.' Doughboy: 'Sorry bitch.'

Education, solid family values, and hard work are the only paths out of poverty and violence. Blacks must take pride in their homes and their neighborhoods. They must not allow members of other racial and ethnic groups to buy up their houses and their neighborhoods, no black Korea in South Central (Gilroy, 1992, p. 308).

Blacks cannot trust the government, including the institutions of the military, the police, and the schools. Schools and their tests are culturally biased against blacks. The police encourage racial genocide in the ghetto. The Army sends black men off to fight other men of color. The CIA is behind the flow of cocaine into the hood.

Underneath this didactic coming-of-age story lies an existential theme. As Ricky's absurd death reveals, Singleton flirts with notions of existential complexity, chance encounters, and the meaning of life (Balingit, 1992b, p. 57). Ricky just happened to be in the wrong place at the wrong time. But despite the play of chance in daily life, Singleton contends that blacks can control their own fate if they follow certain instructions. Ricky did not have a father at home when he was growing up. In the time of crisis, Furious was there for Tre, persuading him not to take the gun out of the house.

Singleton acknowledges his debt to Spike Lee, 'who paved the way for other African-American directors to tell stories about their own experiences and about African-American communities' (Balingit, 1992b, p. 58). Ironically, some of the criticisms that have been brought to Lee's project are now directed at Singleton.[11] But like Lee, Singleton also understands that race is given its most powerful meanings in media representations.

Negative images of welfare mothers, fatherless homes, and gang murders must be replaced with stories about good black families, about good young black men. But there is a risk here, the risk of reproducing conservative myths about individuals who get out by luck and hard work. While some responsibility for the hood and its problems must be located in the apparatuses of a racist society, black men and black women still make their own problems. The media are not inventing these problems.

But the situation is complex, and it goes beyond the issue of whether or not these films (and the media) are correctly imitating life. As Giroux (1996) observes, films like *Boyz* 'reinforce the popular perception that everyday black urban life and violent crime mutually define each other ... black men and their community are the central locus of the American scene of violence' (pp. 42, 56). The inner city, the hood, and its rap music[12] have become the central metaphors for social disorder and social violence in our culture today. Young black men have 'become agents of crime, pathology and moral decay' (Giroux, 1996, p. 56).

While Singleton distances himself from the misogynist talk of Doughboy and his buddies, he reproduces their discourse of ho's, bitches, and hootches nonetheless.[13] And he, like Lee, must be held accountable for this sexist practice. And herein lies another risk of reproducing vernacular speech. By having characters engage in code-switching, using words and slang from the so-called 'everyday, real world,' the filmmaker makes a text that is taken to be literal and authentic. In Singleton's case, this creates the impression that educated middle-class blacks like Furious and Reva use such words and phrases as 'ain't,' 'pussy,' and 'sit your sorry ass down.' Thus does his film fuel white fears and stereotypes about blacks.

John Singleton's advice for young African-American filmmakers trying to break into the industry is 'know your history, know where you're from' (Balingit, 1992b, p. 55). But the history he is referencing is not film history, nor is this the history of black politics in America (see Baraka, 1993). Singleton's history is personal history, autobiography, for, like Tre, Singleton grew up in South Central (Mathews, 1991c; Balingit, 1992b, p. 55). *Boyz N the Hood* is a storied version of his childhood. The issue is clear. Framed as a question, it asks, 'Where does Singleton's gendered didactic text and its promise of a New Deal gets us?'

Lisa Kennedy (1992) rephrases the question as a challenge:

[w]here are the women?!? From *House Party* to ... *Mo Better Blues* to *Boyz N the Hood*, the sons are working overtime to secure the place of the father, and in doing so, themselves. If ever there was a symbolic effort to counteract a sociological assertion – that of paternal abandonment – it has been these films, which depict a world of fathers and sons.... Word to the brother: I will not have some twenty-three-year old man-child in LALA land telling me I must forgo a career to be a good mother, that it's my responsibility to the embattled black family, just because he made a moving film. (p. 110)

Singleton's project brings black men back to their fathering tasks. In so doing, it gives black women a narrow range of identites: bitches, ho's, crackheads, or buppies. In stating that women are not up to the challenge of raising their sons, Singleton ignores decades of gendered black history. In this history, single black mothers function 'as complex individuals' (Collins, 1991, p. 74), negotiating many different tasks and identities, including being breadwinners, models for their children, leaders in their churches and communities, artists, performers, writers, singers, musicians, actresses, lovers, and so on. So Singleton's 'New Deal,' his story, like Lee's story, is familiar. It is the story of the black male middle class, the 'upwardly mobile Black, petit bourgeois professional' (Baraka, 1993, p. 146). And this is a story and a history that is confined, like Lee's, to the present, to the contemporary moment.

This is a black art that mocks (or lacks) a revolutionary black politics; not even a Malcolm X on the horizon. Quite the opposite (Baraka, 1993, p. 146). This is a conservative film that manipulates the meanings of family, masculinity, and gender. The discourse on race and community (Furious's lecture to Tre and Ricky about black property in the hood) and race, manhood, and family (Furious's birth control lectures to Tre) interpret the crisis of the black community and 'black politics and social life as a crisis solely of black masculinity' (Gilroy, 1992, p. 312; also Boyd, 1997, p. 98).

The fatherless home is the site for reproducing 'the cultural dysfunction that disables the race as a whole' (Gilroy, 1992, p. 312). This cultural dysfunction can be easily repaired by 'Instituting appropriate forms of masculinity and male authority' (Gilroy, 1992, p. 312). By intervening in the heterosexual family structure, the black race can be rebuilt, and only black men can do this. As Gilroy observes (1992), this position is 'complacently comfortable working within ... deeply conservative codes' (p. 313).

Furious's (and Singleton's) politics, in the end, turn out to be speeches about safe sex practices, and keeping other ethnic groups out of the hood. No one can doubt the virtue of his cause, stop the genocide in the hood. But in making that plea, his version of 'real' life, his 'reel' hood, somehow distorts the everyday in unsettling ways (see Baraka, 1993, p. 147; Kennedy, 1992, p. 110; hooks, 1996, p. 9). From beginning to end this coming-of-age story is one long conservative male fantasy. But gender cannot be so easily sequestered in the hood, or in cinema, and sadly Singleton's New Deal does not seem to understand this.[14]

Now Mario Van Peebles and *New Jack City*, a film that actually preceded *Boyz N the Hood* by a few months in the theatres.

New Jack City

New Jack City is a cop-buddy story with black (Scotty: Ice-T) and white (Nick: Judd Nelson) partners, a 'gangster thriller about the cocaine trade in contemporary Manhattan' (Wilmington, 1992b). Wesley Snipes – no longer a playground basketball hustler as in *White Men Can't Jump* – is now a black gangster, a larger-than life comic book figure who wears a satanic wardrobe of brilliant primary colors (Pelecanos, 1991).[15] Set between 1986 and 1989, this is another story of greed and violence under the Republican presidencies of the 1980s (Nino: 'You gotta rob to get rich in the Reagan era'). This is also the decade of the cocaine epidemic in the hood, and, as an anti-drug, didactic text, the story repeatedly draws on the cocaine addiction narrative. But ironically the 'script, updated to accommodate the crack epidemic, apparently began as an examination of 1970s Harlem drug king Nicky Barnes' (Wilmington, 1992b).

Van Peebles' reverence for the hood-drug-gang narrative includes a nod to the stars in and the remakes of the gangster movies of the thirties: George Raft, and James Cagney; De Palma's *Untouchables* and *Scarface*; Coppola's *Godfather* trilogy.[16] Thus do we watch Nino watching Pacino in *Scarface* ('The world is mine, all mine'). Later in a scene modeled after De Niro in *The Untouchables*, in a violent tirade Nino drives a sword through the hand of an innocent gang member, whom he then nearly strangles. As Guerrero (1993a) observes, Van Peebles' film, with Bill Duke's *A Rage in Harlem* (see Chapter 3), is one of the first 'black gangster movies since the wane of Blaxploitation in the mid-1970s' (p. 187), although some termed it 'unblaxploitation ... because it does not glorify the outlaw mystique' (Pelecanos, 1991). It does, though, seem to capture 'the milieu, manners and morals of the young, black inner-city drug-dealing gangster culture as *GoodFellas* does for the white gangster class' (Benjamin, 1991).

Unlike his father Melvin's legendary *Sweet Sweetback's Baadasssss Song* (1971), Van Peebles' *New Jack City* has no 'sexualized rebel outlaw fighting the injustices of police occupation in the black community' (Guerrero, 1993a, p. 187). Indeed, in *New Jack City* the violent undercover biracial buddy cop team is presented as the solution to the black community's drug and crime problems (Guerrero, 1993a, p. 187).[17]

The story starts in 1986. To the sound of rap music,[18] an off-screen news broadcaster reports that 'unemployment is at an all-time high, the rich are getting richer, hopelessness is at an all-time low, and last night two 7-year-old boys were killed in Harlem when a drug-deal went wrong.' The camera cuts to two men. What follows is a sequence that almost succeeds in translating comic book action to film (Pelecanos, 1991). Scotty, an undercover policeman, and Pookie,[19] a petty thief, are making a drug deal, which turns into a chase that ends in a school yard. (Three years later, Scotty makes friends with Pookie.) Nino Brown, a cocky, gold-chain-wearing, hip black drug dealer, is told by his friend Gee Money that the future for the drug business is in crack-cocaine ('Man, the bitches go crazy for it, they suck my dick all day long.... Times like this people want to get high real fast, this is gonna do it'). With the help of Kareem, a computer expert, Nino and Gee Money take over the Carter Apartments. They turn this brick fortress into a drug lab and a crack-house that is monitored by a high-tech system and protected by its own armed security force. Over the next three years crack catches on in Harlem. Nino emerges as the wealthy and powerful head of the Cash Money Brothers Syndicate (CMB), a million-dollar-a-week operation (he lives in a baronial mansion). Nino kills his Jamaican competition ('Dumb dread-locks'), and breaks with Frankie Needles, Dom Armeteo, and the Italian mob ('Silly spaghetti-eatin' asses').

In 1989 Scotty and Nick are recruited to become part of a crack task force (Commissioner: 'The system was not ready for this kind of epidemic ... get Nino Brown.... It's a war out there. We need New Jack Cops to take down a New Jack gangster'). Scotty locates Pookie, who has become a crack addict ('Crack-shit got me man, it got me'). Scotty takes Pookie to a treatment center and to NA meetings (Pookie: 'When I get out I'm gonna take everything one day at a time').[20] Pookie volunteers to go undercover and get evidence against Nino and CMB ('Man you saved my life. I need to be a part of something. Let me help you bring Nino down'). Through lavish excess Nino alienates his CMB associates, rejects his former girl ('Hey, you got no claim on me'), and insults the Italian mob by stealing Frankie's girlfriend, Uniqua. Pookie wears a wire into the Carter, and is warned by Scotty that he better not relapse:

> I don't know what you got left in your little rehabilitated body, but you owe me man, you owe a lot of people. You owe the community. A little junkie just like you killed my mother. Took her life.

Back in the Carter, surrounded by vials of crack, Pookie relapses, and gets high, as Nick and Scotty watch him on tape. In a play on the title of Gordon Parks' 1972 film, Nick asks Scotty, 'Hey Superfly, what's wrong with your boy Pookie?' Gee Money kills Pookie and destroys the Carter, eliminating all evidence against CMB. With seconds ticking down to one, Scotty and Nick, in a scene reminiscent of the Riggs and Murtaugh *Lethal Weapon* bomb episodes, defuse a ticking bomb wired to Pookie's dead body.

In a male-bonding scene, drunk together after Pookie's funeral, Scotty and Nick vow to get Nino:

Nick: I used to be Pookie, I was poor a white trash Pookie. This whole drug thing. It's not a black thing. It's not a white thing. It's a death thing.... You don't have to like me. I don't even know if I like you, but we're in this together now partner.

Scotty: You know a drug dealer is the worst kind of brother man. He won't sell it to his sister. He won't sell it to his mother, but he'll sell it to one of his boys on the street. I'm ready to kill Nino Brown. Are you with me?

Scotty goes undercover as a Peruvian drug dealer. He and Nick convince Frankie Needles to introduce them to Gee Money. Scotty gets close to Nino, who tells him about the first time he killed someone,

When I was young I was a member of a gang called the LA Boys. I had to snuff somebody to prove my membership ... an ordinary mob. ... I walked up on this lady, I was so crazy and Pow [*points gun at Nick*], I shot her, didn't even stay to see her body drop.

In a scene that foreshadows his death, Nino hands out money to little schoolkids. An elderly black man comes for his grandson. 'Get your butt out of here right now.' He turns to Nino, 'You're an ignorant bastard. You're committin' genocide on your own people with your silk suits and fancy cars.... You're an idol worshipper. You're killin' your own people.'

Nino challenges him. 'In the next two years they be markin' your gravesite.... And what can you offer them, another "I have a dream" speech? You the fool old man.'

Gee Money becomes addicted to crack. Nino offers Scotty Gee Money's job. Lounging in a large in-door swimming pool, fed grapes by Uniqua, Nino says of his lifestyle: 'This is some fine shit man. George Raft, James Cagney type shit.' In the shadows of a *Godfather*-style wedding, the Italian Mafia kill Gee Money's new bride, Keisha. Nino, now called Mr Untouchable by the DA's office, retaliates with a St Valentine Day's massacre, murdering Don Armeteo and ten of his henchman. Kareem recognizes Scotty, and tells Nino. Nino shoots Gee Money point blank in the head ('You been suckin' that plastic dick. You betrayed me'), but not before Gee Money tells him, 'I loved you man, let's be family again, You're all I got.'

Another shoot-out follows, at Nino's new headquarters. Nino and Scotty fight, a crowd gathers on the sidewalk. Scotty throws Nino off the fire escape into a pile of garbage. The crowd cheers. Scotty holds a gun on Nino: 'That teacher you killed, that was my mother. This is for all the people you have killed. This is personal. I want to shoot you so bad my dick is hard.' Nick pulls Scotty away from a bloodied Nino, who promises: 'I'll be out in week. You're a dead man.'

In court Nino plea bargains his case by offering testimony against Kareem and the other members of CMB. But justice prevails. As he is leaving the courthouse he is confronted by the old man whom he had previously insulted ('You the fool old man'). The old man shouts, 'Your soul is required in Hell,' and fires his gun, killing Nino, who falls to the floor. As spectators gaze down at Nino's body, the following words appear on the screen: 'Although this is a fictional story, there are Nino Browns in every major city in America. If we don't confront the problem realistically ... without empty slogans and promises, then drugs will continue to destroy our country.'[21]

New Jack Culture

New Jack City is an anti-drug didactic film that is 'deplorably violent' (Sterritt, 1991a) and 'unbelievably ruthless ... toward women of any color' (Bernard, 1991c).

In its own way it is also racist, both toward the 'spaghetti-eatin'' Italians, and 'in its casting of the most dark-skinned cast members as the primary villains' (Pelecanos, 1991). It wants to be two things at once: to be a positive-message action film that glorifies New Jack street culture while not glorifying drug dealers (Pelecanos, 1991). It does this, in part, by casting former gang member/rapper Ice-T as the number one cop, and by dressing Ice-T and Judd Nelson as *Miami Vice* look-alikes (Pelecanos, 1991). Ice-T is street-wise and authentic, and Nelson, hiding behind sunglasses, plays a perpetually stoned Nick who periodically asks Scotty, 'Is this a black thing?' But the cop-buddy story never really comes off as it does for Murtaugh and Riggs.

And Nick is wrong. The whole drug thing is a black thing, not a death thing, and a black thing that is an economic thing. It is about the 'historical disenfranchisement – socially, educationally, and economically – of the nonwhite American population, a disenfranchisement that has nearly destroyed an entire generation' (Pelecanos, 1991). Sadly New Jack street culture answers this economic violence with vigilante retribution, the answer to violence is more violence, more death (Pelecanos, 1991).

This is a hood movie that fails on its own terms. It is as if Van Peebles asked, 'What happens to the members of street gangs, when the gang members become gangsters, when petty street drug culture turns into organized crime, and petty thiefs become crime lords?' Side-stepping the blaxploitation films of the seventies, he found his answer in the old gangster movies of the thirties, Cagney and George Raft. Crime doesn't pay; law and order does. The answer for inner-city drug crime lies in black and white cop-buddy teams who stamp out evil black drug dealers. A conservative reactionary story, oddly compatible with the Reagan Law and Order Decade. Say No to drugs, and let the police do the dirty work. Ironically, Van Peebles ends up endorsing the very politics his film initially attacks. In the process he suggests that, left to its own devices, black culture is unable to deal with this genocidal epidemic. Only the state and its police can rid the ghetto of this scourge.

Van Peebles, like the rest of us, wants an end to the drug thing, down with the Nino Browns of the world. But unlike Singleton's *Boyz N the Hood*, *New Jack City* never reveals its version of the Martin Luther King 'I Have a Dream' speech. The standard answers are missing. Nobody here goes off to an all-black college in Atlanta, or is offered an athletic scholarship to play football for the local university.

So this is a two-message film fitted to the narrative structure of the gangster movies of the thirties. People who use drugs get addicted, and addicted people do demeaning things, and then they die, or are killed. People who sell drugs have power and prestige. They also dress, eat, and play well, have beautiful girlfriends, and live the good life. But drugs are evil, and evil people must be punished; drugs are sinful, so drug dealers must die. Sadly this tale from the hood, this little Harlem story, offers little hope for those who were disenfranchised by the Reagan/Bush administrations.

Now *Menace II Society*.

Menace II Society[22]

Set in 1990s Watts (with footage from the 1965 Watts riots and location shots from Jordan Downs Housing Project),[23] this is the story of the short and violent life of

Caine (*co*-caine) Lawson. Caine, a recent high school graduate, has been raised by his grandparents, and a surrogate father Pernell, who is in prison. Caine's father, a drug dealer, was killed in a drug deal when Caine was 10. When he was 5 years old, Caine watched his father kill a man in the family living room ('That was the first time I saw my father kill anybody, wasn't the last'). Caine's mother, a heroin addict, died from an overdose. Like his father, Caine is a drug dealer.

The film opens with the murder of a Korean grocer and his wife. Caine and his friend O-Dog ('America's nightmare: young, black and didn't give a fuck') have gone to buy beer, and in a fit of anger O-Dog kills the two Koreans (Wife to O-Dog: 'I feel sorry for your mother.' O-Dog: 'What did you say about my momma?'; Caine to viewer: 'I went into the store to get a beer, came out an accessory to murder and armed robbery. After that I knew it was gonna be a long summer'). O-Dog takes the video tape of the killing, and replays it for friends. On high school graduation night Caine kills a gang member who murdered his cousin during a carjacking. Caine and O-Dog are later arrested for stealing a car, but the charges are reduced to joyriding. Caine's fingerprints are found on a beer bottle in the Korean grocery store.

Sharif, a Muslim, and his father, Mr Butler, befriend Caine and ask him to come to Kansas with them. On a whim, Caine sleeps with Ilena, who becomes pregnant. Caine denies responsibility ('It ain't mine'). Ilena's cousin comes looking for Caine ('I'm Ilena's cousin. She don't like the way you been doggin' her. I don't either'). Caine falls in love with Ronnie, Pernell's girlfriend. He also becomes a mentor for Anthony, Ronnie's little boy. Caine shows Anthony how to hold a gun. Ronnie accepts a job in Atlanta, and asks Caine to move there with her and Anthony. Caine's grandfather insists that Caine move out of their home ('You got to go. I want you out of here by tonight'). Caine is murdered by Ilena's cousin and his gang in a drive-by on the day he is preparing to leave for Atlanta with Ronnie and Anthony.

Another didactic film. The video copy I purchased opens with Charles S. Dutton (who plays Mr Butler in the film) speaking directly to the viewer. His speech is framed with these lines, 'Institute for Black Parenting: A Special Message from Charles S. Dutton.'

> Hi, I'm Charles S. Dutton. I want to talk to you about our future. The murder rate among young men is sky-rocketing. Why? Because guys who think they're tough lose their cool and settle every argument with a gun.
>
> Listen to me. I know, 'cause I've been there. I spent time in prison because of it. Turning away from violence and rebuilding the community is your responsibility, not somebody else's. That's why I'm working with the Institute for Black Parenting. To help turn things around.
>
> (The following on-screen message appears: 'For more information on how you can support the Institute for Black Parenting, Please call 1-800-367-8858.')

This message is followed by a trailer for *Menace II Society*, 'The hardcore movie of the year.'

This is Caine's life history, his autoethnography. He narrates the film, which, as noted above, begins with flashback scenes of the 1965 riots in Watts, then presents scenes from his parents' home in Watts, late 1970s, before turning to the present, Watts, 1993. Caine is about to graduate. Sitting in a classroom, his beeper goes off. 'I'm a drug dealer,' he states. Later he elaborates, 'Workin' for minimum wage was never my style. I learned how to mix drugs when I was little: heroin, cocaine, all of it. My dad taught me.'

Before this summer of his high school graduation is over, Caine will be dead. Another coming-of-age story, *Menace* moves through a sequence of moments, each marked by graphic violence, murder, and death. In episode one Caine's father kills a gambling associate. This murder segues into the murder of the Korean grocers, which glides into episode three, the murder of Harold, a close friend. In episode four, Caine and O-Dog kill the men who killed Harold. In the final episode, Caine, Sharif, and Stacey (also a friend) are murdered in the drive-by. Each violent episode is interpreted by Caine, who functions as an off-screen narrator.

In episode two (as noted above), he reports, 'I went into the store to get a beer and came out an accessory to murder.' After the murder of Harold's killers he says, 'I seen lots of people killed, but I never done it myself. ... I thought killin' those fools would make me feel good.... I just knew I could kill somebody.' And of his own murder, he comments:

> I knew. I was gonna have to deal with that fool someday. I never thought he'd come back like this, blastin'. I said it was funny like that in the hood. You never knew what was gonna happen. I'd done too much. It was too late to turn back and I'd done too much to go on. I guess in the end it all catches up with you. My grandpa asked me one time if I care whether I live or die. Yeah, I do, and now it's too late.

The screen goes black, and the viewer reads (and hears) the language and lyrics of gangsta rap:

> Wake your punk ass up ... ain't nothin' but a Compton thing, y' all, and we ain't nothin' but niggaz on the run ... a fucked-up childhood is what got me the way I am. I'm just another victim of the ghetto. Homie from the hood ... he shot my nigga in the fuckin' head.

Virtually plotless (will Caine move with Ronnie to Atlanta?), *Menace II Society* is a photo-montage of scenes and slices from the hood, scenes that are marked by gun shots, drive-by killings, drug dealing, teen parties, picnics in the park, and occasional lectures by well-meaning adults who are attempting to help Caine find purpose in his life. And although, in the end, he appears to accept advice, it comes too late.

Caine is like an anti-hero in a Camus existential novel, a man without purpose or goal, who moves from one moment to the next, carried only by the flow of current events. He moves inexorably to his certain death. In the Hughes brothers' version of the hood, all the men die young. And they are so young, still babies, hardly young men at all. They are victims of a senseless, violent culture. Headstrong, they are unable, and unwilling, to listen to the wisdom and advice of their elders, and other significant persons in their lives.

This wisdom is passed along to Caine in three key moments. Early in the film Caine's grandfather speaks to him and to O-Dog: 'I want to talk to you about the trouble you're been getting into. The Lord didn't put you here to be shooting and killing each other.' Caine replies: 'I ain't never killed anybody.' O-Dog is critical of God: 'God doesn't care too much about us, or he wouldn't put us here.' Caine comments (as an off-screen narrator): 'My grandpa was always comin' at us with that religion, and everythin' in one ear and out the other.' His grandfather replies: 'Caine, do you care whether you live or die?' Caine: 'I don't know.' Outside his grandparent's house, Caine apologizes to O-Dog, 'Sorry about that man.... I mean sitting there prayin' to a white Jesus.' O-Dog agrees: 'Black people got too much damned religion as it is.'

Ronnie criticizes Caine's language. When he says to Anthony, 'Boy, I gonna whip your ass,' she says, 'He's 5 years old! He has no business talking like that.'[24] Caine disagrees: 'You gotta be hard growin' up out there.' Ronnie: 'That has nothin' to do with bein' hard. He gets that crap from you, O-Dog, and that fool Stacey.'

In an extension of this scene, Ronnie confronts Caine, who is showing Anthony how to hold a gun: 'What the hell you doing? I don't want my son learning to pull drive-bys.' She turns to Anthony: 'If I ever catch you with a gun in your hand, I'm gonna break your tail.' To Caine: 'You need to be glad you've graduated from high school, that you're alive at 18 and you need to do something with yourself.'

Mr Butler tells Caine the same thing:

> What you gonna do with your life? Sharif used to get all kinds of shit before he found the Nation. I agree with some of the things they say about black people and if Allah can help make him a better man than Jesus, then I'm all for it. Whatever changes you have to make, just do it. You have to think about your life. Being a black man in America isn't easy. The hunt is on and you're the prey.

Caine gives an off-screen response. 'Mr Butler had me thinking. Only one came at me like he gave a damn. Grandpa always pitches that religious stuff. My Dad never said anything. Parnell showed me how to survive on the streets. Mr Butler was talkin' about survival for good!'

Ronnie finally convinces Caine to come with her to Atlanta, but not without difficulty. Ronnie: 'I was hopin' you'd come with us. You ain't doin' jack shit here. The way I see it, you'll be dead or in jail.' In an off-screen response, Caine states, 'Bein' in the streets was cool, but I cared about Ronnie and Anthony reminded me of me when I was little. I didn't want him to go through what I've been through.' To Ronnie (and John Singleton) he states, 'Ain't nothing gonna change in Atlanta, just another nigger from the ghetto. You act like Atlanta ain't in America.... Yeah, I'm gonna go.'

Reading Menace

The film received considerable praise: 'With this film, the Hughes brothers have achieved one of the most impressive directorial debuts in the late twentieth century' (Delalis, 1994, p. 228); 'perhaps the most striking directorial debut in the history of black cinema' (Denby, 1993b). But it was not without its critics: 'thoughtless filmmaking ... none of the film's characters extend beyond ghetto stereotypes' (McRobbie, 1994); 'irritating and maddening ... I dislike *Menace*'s racism ... riddled with psychological implausibilities (Brown, 1993); 'generic homegirls' (Massood, 1993); 'semi-documentary veneer' (Rainer, 1993); 'the story is relatively simple, to the point of being nonexistent' (Anderson, 1993).

The film indulges a cinema of graphic violence. It draws on and exploits the 'violent imagery of rap' (McRobbie, 1994). It is homophobic. O-Dog guns down a male addict who offers to 'suck his dick' for a hit (McRobbie, 1993). The story's treatment of women is also aggressively sexist. With the exception of Ronnie and Caine's grandmother (who is silent), women are sex objects, bitches, or ho's. Ronnie, like Reva, Tre's mother in *Boyz*, is also a single parent. But unlke Reva, Ronnie has few skills, although she has found a job in Atlanta, the Mecca of the

South. But Caine cannot think his way into this so-called 'Southern paradise.' On this level the story is hopelessly nihilistic and bleak. The most violent character in the hood, O-Dog, survives. The hood is Hell. There is no way out.

The use of flashbacks and off-screen narration (voice-overs) gives depth to Caine's character. This privileges his point of view (Watkins, 1998, p. 203), thereby allowing the Hughes brothers to speak directly to the viewer. Thus does Caine give us his views on poverty, the absence of father figures in his life, the underground drug economy, fast-food jobs and menial labor, education, women, sex, children, religion, the Nation of Islam, black expressive culture, gangsta rap, capitalism, and race (Watkins, 1998, pp. 203–212). Caine becomes the spokes-person for poor black youth, giving meaning to the crisis situations that occur in their lives. We read their lives through his eyes and voice, as he 'presides over this fictional representation of the hood' (Watkins, 1998, p. 203).

John Singleton, S. Craig Watkins (1998, p. 205), and Elijah Anderson (1999, p. 324) are correct. The conflicts and crisis situations that Caine confronts revolve around the disappearance of 'decent daddies' (Anderson, 1999, p. 180) and older father figures who function as moral authorities 'in black urban communities (Watkins, 1998, p. 205). Caine refuses to grant his grandfather any power or authority in his life. Caine's father taught him how to mix drugs. Parnell showed him how to hold a gun. Mr Butler finally got through to him, but it was too late.

Historically, decent daddies and older male heads of the family, as Anderson notes (1999, pp. 180, 324), teach young men the values of religion, family life, hard work, and personal responsibility. Traditionally, these men are listened to, but in today's hood these are the values Caine and O-Dog reject. As Watkins (1998, p. 205) and Anderson (1999, p. 323) note, this rejection can occur when young black men find that good housing, respectable work, and gainful employment are not present in the ghetto. Young black men conclude that the 'moral lessons of the old head con-cerning the work ethic, punctuality and honesty do not fit their circumstances … [these] moral urgings are generally viewed as antiquated and irrelevant means of improving the material conditions of their lives' (Watkins, 1998, p. 205). Hence does Caine apologize to O-Dog when his grandfather talks of religion.

Like Nino Brown, Caine embraces the concepts of wealth, commodity con-sumption, and membership in the leisure class. He wants a flashy car, expensive clothes, gold chains, a pretty girlfriend. He does not want to work, beyond deal-ing drugs now and then. His code of the street (Anderson, 1999), is simple: 'you dis me, you die' (Anderson, 1993).

At this level, the film simultaneously celebrates and criticizes black youth expressive culture. The gangsta elements of the culture reject the assumption that hard work produces freedom and upward mobility out of the ghetto. The black expressive body should be a site for and an instrument of pleasure. Wage labor is a form of servitude (Watkins, 1998, p. 210). These are Caine's beliefs. At the same time, people who work and save have hope. They are not dying violent deaths. But if capitalism cannot 'incorporate poor youth, it will continue to pro-duce young "Menaces II Society"' (Watkins, 1998, pp. 211–212; also Boyd, 1997, pp. 100–102). And black expressive culture, including gangsta rap, will provide the music at their funerals.

Ironically, Caine's 'cynical rejection of old-head authority, religion, and black political ideology is strongly reactionary' (Watkins, 1998, p. 207). This individualistic stance rejects the avenues and methods blacks have traditionally used to achieve escape from poverty, namely family, church, education, sports, and community. But the value system that replaces the one that is rejected is self-destructive. It is not one that builds community, or family, and it is not life affirming. Only in the moment of death can Caine answer his grandfather's question, 'Yes I want to live.'

I disagree with those who read *Menace* as an amoral film, devoid of hope, or moral outrage (Anderson, 1993). This is a moral story. Caine is killed precisely at the moment when he turns his back on God, Ilena, his grandparents, and only reluctantly joins Ronnie. His refusal to honor his obligation as a father is punished. Is some grand cosmic scheme at work here, or is the world totally random? Is God laughing, this God who saves O-Dog and Anthony, and has Caine die? The messsage is clear. Life in the hood is not fair. The hood is cruel. Violent things happen in this grotesque out-of-control ghetto world, with its guns and gangsta rap music, and its violent street code.

O-Dog, America's nightmare, may be a menace to society, but this hood society is also a menace to its members. This is the film's moral message. Reagan and Bush's race relations polices have produced a society that is devouring its young. So it is necessary to return to the Charles Dutton speech that opens the film. This is an anti-violence movie. 'The murder rate ... is skyrocketing ... [b]ecause guys who think they're tough lose their cool and settle every argument with a gun.... Turning away from violence and rebuilding community is your responsibilty.'

In Conclusion

Quoting hooks (1992, p. 4), I have suggested that the hood movies have failed to expand the discussions of race and representation beyond debates about good and bad imagery. This failure has led conservative Americans to blame African Americans for the problems they have experienced since the civil rights movement. So at one level these films have backfired. But that is a simplistic reading.

These movies and their filmmakers are located at the intersection of multiple discourses on race, including: ethnographic realism; the blaxploitation films in the seventies and the gangster movies of the thirties; hip hop culture, rap, and gangsta rap; the cocaine and drug addiction narratives; welfare mothers; race riots; life in the projects; drive-bys; the Crips and the Bloods; homophobia; misogyny; Asian Americans; Korean realtors; Vietnam; police brutality; Rodney King; the American system of racial justice; black patriarchy; the African-American family; Martin Luther King; the Nation of Islam; Christianity; multiculturalism; assimilation; black power; separatism; nationalism; Afro-centrism.

Race in America today is no longer a simple matter. It is a topic that refuses to be contained within a single narrative framework. The old race relations models no longer operate. Indeed, unlike the white filmmakers (Donner, Kasdan, Shelton, Smith, Sayles), the black hood directors are saying there is something deeply troubling with these models, including the ideology of assimilation. As a model of the American racial dream, assimilation to the white norm has once again become problematic. For Americans of color the promises of democracy and capitalism stopped working sometime (and somewhere) between the civil rights movement of the 1960s and the election of Ronald Reagan as President in 1980. America's race relations agenda collapsed. These hood movies record, represent, and offer stories about the effects of that collapse.

Singleton believes that a commitment to the old values will help you get out of the hood. Van Peebles disagrees. At one level he says take the drug money and run, we are all going to die anyway. The Hughes brothers just want people to put down the guns and get honest day jobs. The filmmakers agree on this: white society cannot help; blacks must do this for themselves, and they should not seek, as they did under the old assimilation model, to disappear into white culture.

These films are clear on a single point: big capital has moved out of the inner city. Fast capital has moved in. Menial labor in the service sectors of the economy has become the norm. A pervasive underground drug economy stretches from East Los Angeles and Harlem, to Latin and South America, to Asia and Vietnam. Gangs have excessive power in daily ghetto life. And new narratives need to be written. Race in these three movies stands inside all of these narratives.

So these tales from the hood can be read as retellings of *The Way of All Flesh* (Butler, 1903); sons relive the sins of their fathers. Each generation is doomed to reproduce the tragedies of the previous generation ('a fucked-up childhood is what got me the way I am. I'm just another victim of the ghetto'). This is another version of the social disorganization theory of black underclass life (Anderson, 1999, p. 323). Dysfunctional black family life reproduces itself. Black men are doomed to die. The code of the street generates an oppositional culture that leads young black men to reject the standard teachings of school, church, and family (Anderson, 1999, p. 323).

This is not news; this is an old story, tragic, sad, and violent. These hood movies retell this story, and in their tellings they bring a certain sadness to every heart. Why must Americans continue to re-enact this tragic racial drama? Why can't it be otherwise?

In the next chapter I examine how Latino filmmakers have taken up these issues, as they tell stories of the barrio, gangs, drugs, the police, family, and community.

Notes

1. Watkins (1998, pp. 172–173) locates four key films in the ghetto film cycle of the 1990s: *Boyz N the Hood* (1991), *Menace II Society* (1993), *New Jack City* (1991), and *Straight Out of Brooklyn* (1991). Other films in this cycle include those listed in the Introduction: *Clockers, American Me, Zoot Suit, Bound by Honor, My Family/Mi Familia, My Crazy Live/Mi Vida Loca*, as well as *Colors, Black Rain, Juice, King of New York, Sugar Hill*, and *Deep Cover*. In 1991 'twelve feature films by African American directors were released' (Green, 1993, p. 192; also Georgakas, 1992, p. 375; see also the Appendix).

2. *Boyz N the Hood* (1991). Released by Columbia. Director: John Singleton; Screenplay: John Singleton; Cinematography: Charles Mills; Cast: Cuba Gooding, Jr (Tre Styles), Ice Cube (Doughboy), Morris Chestnut (Ricky Baker), Larry Fishburne (Furious Styles), Angela Bassett (Reva Styles), Tyra Ferrell (Mrs Baker). With *Boyz N the Hood* John Singleton became the first African-American nominated for as Oscar as Best Director, 'as well as the youngest directorial nominee ever' (Bogle, 1994, p. 347). He was 23 years old when the film was released. It was produced at a cost of $6 million, and within its first five weeks of exhibition earned $42 million (Watkins, 1998, p. 190). Theatre violence

'in roughly 20 of 829 theatres where the film was playing' (Denby, 1991), involving gang-related fights and shootings, accompanied the release of *Boyz* and *New Jack City* (Guerrero, 1993a, p. 183; see also Balingit, 1992b; Sterritt, 1991a, b; Hoberman, 1991). *New Jack City* was controversial during its opening week. At one theatre in Brooklyn, shots were fired and a man was killed. In Los Angeles at the Westwood Theatre, a riot broke out when 1500 persons were turned away on opening night. Van Peebles appeared on local television 'assuring viewers that such random violence and shootings had nothing to do with the film's content, pointing out that similar outbreaks had accompanied other films as well, such as *Godfather, Part III* ... and *Superman II*' (Welsh, 1992, p. 260).

3. *New Jack City* (1991). Released by Warner Brothers; Director: Mario Van Peebles; Screenplay: Thomas Lee Wright and Barry Michael Cooper, based on a story by Wright; Cinematography: Francis Kenny; Cast: Wesley Snipes (Nino Brown), Ice-T (Scotty Appleton), Chris Rock (Pookie), Judd Nelson (Nick Peretti), Mario Van Peeples (Detective Stone), Allen Payne (Gee Money), Christopher Williams (Kareem), Vanessa Williams (Keisha), Tracy Camilla Johns (Uniqua). Produced at a cost of $6 million, it earned $33 million in its first five weeks of distribution (Watkins, 1998, p. 190; see also Welsh, 1992; Benjamin, 1991; Sterritt, 1991a; Pelecanos, 1991). According to George (1998, pp. 165–166) and Benjamin (1991), Barry Michael Cooper introduced the concept of '*New Jack City*' in a series of 1988 stories in the *Village Voice* on Detroit's violent drug scene and New York City's black street scene. The script for the 1991 film by this title fitted Cooper's story about the Detroit drug scene to a '"new jack" Harlem drug dealer for the go-go '80s' (George, 1998, p. 166). Cooper 'dubbed the music of record producer Teddy Riley New Jack Swing' (Benjamin, 1991). In another version of slang 'jack' refers of course to money.

4. *Menace II Society* (1993). Released by New Line Cinema. Directors: Allen and Albert Hughes. Screenplay: Tyger Williams, based on a story by Allen Hughes, Albert Hughes, and Williams; Cinematography: Lisa Rinzler; Cast: Tyrin Turner (Caine), Larenz Tate (O-Dog), Jada Pinkett (Ronnie), MC Eiht (A-Wax), Marilyn Coleman (Grandmama), Arnold Johnson (Grandpapa), Samuel L. Jackson (Tat Lawson), Glenn Plummer (Pernell), Bill Duke (Detective), Charles S. Dutton (Mr Butler). Produced at a cost of $3 million, it earned $20 million in its first six weeks of distribution (Watkins, 1998, p. 192). The Hughes brothers were 21 years old when the film was released (Delalis, 1994, p. 228; see also Rainer, 1993; Denby, 1993b; Anderson, 1993; George, 1998, pp. 34, 74, 108; McRobbie, 1994; Massood, 1993; Brown, 1993). Since 1993, Albert and Allen Hughes have directed *Dead Presidents* (1995), *From Hell* (1999), and *American Pimp* (1999).

5. Thus, in *Menace II Society*, a man just released from prison says to Caine's father, 'Who the fuck do you think you are nigga, Ron O'Neal or somethin'?' As Boyd (1997) observes, Ron O'Neal is the actor 'who became famous for his starring role in *Superfly*' (p. 101).

6. Juvenile homicide rates would continue to rise throughout the 1990s. In Washington, DC, for example, 'the homicide rate involving victims ages 15 to 19 increased 700 percent from 1985 to 1995' (Dash and Sheehan, 1998, p. A1). In this war of violence young black men paid a high price: 'Ninety percent of the victims of young black killers are other young black men' (Dash and Sheehan, 1998, p. A1). At the same time, the escalation of the war on drugs contributed to the militarization of the American police system. This included the use of heavily armed SWAT patrols deployed in the ghetto (Egan, 1999, p. A16). As noted in the Introduction and Chapter 1, a counter-cocaine narrative continues to circulate. This is the story connecting the CIA to efforts to funnel cocaine into inner-city ghettos.

7. In an opening scene, Tre and his friends walk up to the scene of a shooting. On the wall above the blood on the sidewalk are posters of Reagan and Bush '84.

8. Here the words of Pete Wilson, former Governor of California, are relevant. Immediately after the 1992 LA riots, he told George Will that 'everyone in America should see *Boyz N the Hood*. In that movie a strong father figure makes the difference for his teenaged son ... that movie says ... we need a strong father figure and welfare is no suitable replacement for that' (Wilson, quoted in Reeves and Campbell, 1994, pp. 246–247; see also Watkins, 1998, p. 224).

9. *Furious* indirectly addresses the issue of discrimination against minorities in the housing market. In 1998 'African-Americans were twice as likely as whites and Hispanic-Americans one-and-a-half times as likely, to be denied a conventional, 30-year home loan' by mortgage lenders (Kilborn, 1999).

10. The soundtrack includes 'Jam On It,' 'Sunshower,' 'More Bounce to the Ounce,' 'Sucker M.C.'s,' 'Ooh Child,' 'Work It Out,' 'Too Young,' 'Mama Don't Take No Mess,' 'Hangin' 'Out,' 'Growin Up in the Hood,' 'How to Survive in South Central,' with performances by Ice Cube, 2 Live Crew, and Compton's Most Wanted.

11. These criticisms (see Kellner, 1997, for a review) of Lee include his sexist stereotypical treatment of women, his use of flat, cardboard masculine characters who define themselves through extreme violence, a privileging of heterosexual relationships and practices, a quasi-separatist stance towards interracial romantic relationships, the relegation of women to the private sphere, an emphasis on a politics of identity that does not engage a radical program of empowerment and social change, a neglect of macro-class-based issues (for comparisons between Lee and Singleton, see Wallace, 1992; also hooks, 1990, p. 179; 1996, p. 158; 1992, p. 105; Baraka, 1993; Guerrero, 1993a, pp. 185–186; Bogle, 1994, pp. 346–347; Watkins, 1998, pp. 218–226; Massood, 1996, p. 93). Wallace and hooks have focused on Singleton's narrow treatment of women.

12. Ice Cube's acclaimed performance as Doughboy helps give the film its sense of authentic realism (see Dyson, 1996, pp. 172–173).

13. Wallace (1992) observes that

before *Boyz N the Hood* there were two kinds of black female characters in film – whores and good girls ... [now] a third kind of black female character appears ... single black mothers who are white identified and drink expresso (the Buppie version), or who call their sons 'fat fucks' and allow their children to run in the street while they offer blow jobs in exchange for drugs (the underclass version). (p. 124)

14. Singleton's films since *Boyz* (*Poetic Justice*, 1993, *Higher Learning*, 1995, *Rosewood*, 1997, *Shaft*, 2000) have continued this nationalistic examination of race, gender, and the hood.

15. See Bogle (1994, pp. 364–365) for a review of Snipes' film career, which includes *Mo Better Blues* (1990), *Jungle Fever* (1991), *King of New York* (1990), *Passenger 57* (1992), *Rising Sun* (1993), *Drop Zone* (1994), *Sugar Hill 9* (1994), *Murder At 1600* (1997).

16. Boyd (1997, pp. 88–89, 92) contends that the blaxploitation films of the 1970s made the black gangster a media staple, and this presence would be fitted to the so-called 'black gangsta culture' in the 1990s, as given in rap and gangsta rap music, and in new gangsta hood films like *New Jack City*.

17. In subsequent films, Van Peebles offers politically correct versions of the standard Western (*Posse*, 1993), and a nostalgic examination of oppression against Black Americans during the Vietnam era (*Panther*, 1995). His other recent films include *Standing Knockdown* (1999), *Love Kills* (1998), and *Gang in Blue* (1996, TV).

18. Here, as in the other hood movies, rap (and gangsta rap) music functions as part of the film's diegetic soundtrack. Songs performed by NWA and its former members (Ice Cube) also authorize the soundtrack.

19. As Pelecanos (1991) notes, Pookie rhymes with Mookie, Spike Lee's character in *Do the Right Thing*. Of course we earlier (Chapter 4) confronted Chris Rock (Pookie) in *Lethal Weapon 4*.

20. The film becomes especially didactic during the treatment-center group therapy sequences. One mother reports, 'I have a crack baby,' and another says 'I ho'd [whored], I did everything for that crack. I sold my babies' pampers for crack.'

21. The music soundtrack includes 'New Jack Hustler (Nino's Theme),' 'New Jack City,' 'I'm Still Waitin,' 'I'm Dreamin,' 'The Love of Money,' 'I Wanna Sex You Up,' 'In the Dust,' 'Get It Together (Black is a Force),' 'Lyrics and the Rhythm,' 'Facts of Life,' 'The Show,' 'The Redhead One,' and 'Straight Outta Compton,' with performances by NWA, Ice-T, Queen Latifah, Color One Bold, 2 Live Crew, F.S. Effect, Esssence, Doug E. Fresh, and the Get Fresh Crew.

22. The soundtrack includes 'Trigga Gott No Heart,' 'Straight Up Menace,' 'Packin' a 'Gun,' 'Death Becomes You,' 'Luck Dem Muthaphuckers,' 'Homey Love,' 'Can't Fuck Wit' a Nigga,' 'All Over a Ho,' 'Fly Away,' 'Only the Strong Survive,' 'Love and Happiness,' 'Dopeman' (Remix), 'Atomic Dog,' 'Stay Strapped in South Compton,' 'Hot Wired Oldie,' and 'Got to Give It Up,' and performers include NWA, Al Green, Isley Brothers, Jerry Butler, Marvin Gaye, Smooth, R. Kelly and Public Announcement, Hi Five, MC Eiht, Ant Banks.

23. In the footage, guns are blazing, storefronts burn, the sky is filled with smoke, police are firing at black men, armed tanks come down the streets. It looks like a battlefield. Caine, the off-screen narrator reports, 'when the riots stopped, the drugs started.' The camera cuts to Caine's father lighting a cigarette, and his mother shooting up heroin. The narration continues, 'My father sold dope. I caught onto the criminal life real quick' The time is the late 1970s, the place is Watts.

24. Sharif also criticizes the language that Caine and his friends use: 'You need to stop callin' yourselves niggas.' Stacey objects, 'That's Black Power shit!'

6

Zoot Suits and Homeboys
(and Girls)

> Control the inside – and you own outside. (J. D. to Santana in *American Me*)
>
> There's a cancer in this subculture of gangs. Either you treat the cancer or it'll eat you alive. (Edward James Olmos quoted in Fregoso, 1993, p. 123)

Luiz Valdez, Edward James Olmos, Gregory Nava, Joseph Vásquez, Dennis Hopper, Taylor Hackford, Allison Anders, the brown hood, Hispanic and Anglo filmmakers, and their readings of the barrio and its gangs. My topic is the Hispanic barrio-gang-prison-gangster film cycle: *Zoot Suit* (1981),[1] *Colors* (1988),[2] *American Me* (1992),[3] *Bound by Honor* (1993).[4] East LA, California prisons, hangin' with the homeboys, zoot suits,[5] pachucos, Zapata outlaws, Aztec warriors, low riders, the Mexican Mafia, macho-gang violence, Crips and Bloods, Latinas, Chicano Godfathers, gang rapes, greasers. Another celebrated group of misogynist, violent coming-of-age stories set in the hyperreal barrio, fatherless, dysfunctional families, homoerotic intimacy, social realism in the service of didactic messages: the cancer in the Hispanic gangs is killing all the brave young men. The gendered barrio, one more version of the racial order; rape and violent sexuality. A series of wake-up calls to the Latino community: do something before it is too late (Turan, 1993).[6]

A single thesis with several supporting arguments structures my interpretation of these films. Like the hood movies, these didactic texts give support to conservative criticisms of Hispanics and their presence in American culture. Brown and black skins blur together in the national imagination. Greasers and gang-bangers and boyz n the hood are a menace to white society. The barrio movies make this fear real. How they do this is the topic of this chapter.[7]

Reading the Barrio Films

These films make the threat to white society concrete by embracing even as they deconstruct and criticize the gang-gangster-prison genre (see Goldman, 1996, p. 83). They turn the genre back against itself, taking up and then rejecting a cinema of violence, much as the Hughes brothers did in *Menace II Society*.

In so doing, they embody an oppositional cinematic aesthetic. This aesthetic marks key elements of Chicano culture, including the themes of family, gangs, community, church, resistance, cultural affirmation, and border crossing (see Horowitz, 1983, pp. 75–76; also Fregoso, 1993, p. 25). This aesthetic challenges traditional assimilation narratives. It makes the Hispanic presence in the culture simultaneously real, foreign, and threatening.

Still, these texts can be read politically, as calls for racial equality, self-determination, human rights, and social justice for (and in) the Hispanic community (Fregoso, 1993, p. xix). But these are male-centered narratives. They represent versions of a Chicano cinema; a cinema made by, for, and about Chicanos (Fregoso, 1993, p. xix). These are not stories about the experiences of Chicanas, in any systematic sense (Fregoso, 1993, p. xix). These are narratives that deal with relationships between men. Like the hood movies, they blame men for the problems of the barrio.

This is a cinema that 'documents social reality through oppositional forms of knowledge about Chicanos' (Fregoso, 1993, p. xv; Goldman, 1996, p. 83). These prison-gang films are based on actual historical events, for example the zoot suit riots of 1943 in Los Angeles. They tell stories about real historical persons (Noriega, 1992b, p. 153; also Goldman, 1996, p. 84).[8] At the same time these films invoke and 'rework Latin American and Latino cultural forms, such as the melodrama/*telenovela*, autobiography/*testimonio* ... [Latin] music [and] camp' (Noreiga and Lopez, 1996, p. xv).

The use of voice-overs, translations of Spanish texts into English, off-screen narration, and montage establish connections to Chicano culture. Paraphrasing Noreiga and Lopez, (1996, p. xvi), these traditional cinematic devices affirm and define diverse forms of Chicano identity while marking Chicano participation in a larger, racist and dominant culture. This discourse speaks out against 'prevailing stereotypes in the U. S. news and entertainment media' (Noriega and Lopez, 1996, p. xvii).

The barrio films, like the black hood movies, speak to the era of post-civil rights in America. Ironically, these movies anticipated the enormous brown backlash of the California nativist movements of the 1990s, even as they were used as ammunition for conservative racist policies.

With the hood films, these stories establish links to the gangster genre, for example Santana in *American Me* functions as a Chicano Godfather (see Boyd, 1997, pp. 92–93). This link to the gangster genre produces a violent gender politics. This is a politics that turns men against men, races against races, whites against blacks and Chicanos, blacks against Chicanos, and Chicanos against Chicanas. Of equal importance, as noted earlier (see Introduction, Chapter 5), these films served to mark further the cinematic and popular culture shift away from the ethnic Italian gangster of Coppola's *Godfather* trilogy, to the racialized gangsta of the black and brown hood. The barrio movies, like the hood films, increased racial paranoia by solidifying the ideological link between crime and race (Boyd, 1997, p. 88).

These films problematicize the male–female bond. Violent Chicanos do not know how to have intimate relationships with women. They are unable to accept the kindness and love of a woman. A gender-segregated racial order operates. In this bleak society men rape and kill one another. Thus these films disrupt the traditional male–female narrative. They directly and indirectly draw upon the traditions of homophobia, homosociality, homoeroticism, gayness, and homosexuality in

Latino culture (see Negron-Muntaner, 1996, p. 61). In confronting and presenting the Chicano body as a site of violent desire and sexuality, these films create a space for the appearance of complex and multiple masculine and feminine subjectivities. The concept of a unitary sexual subject disappears in these works. But like the women's films analyzed in Chapter 3, the barrio movies locate brown women in a reactionary, post-feminist racial and gender order. That is, Hispanic women are placed in traditional patriarchal family and sexual formations.

Each film, also like the women's films in Chapter 3, is structured around a double spectacular structure. This structure is focused on sexuality, and the Chicana/o body as a site of rape. In the moment of rape, violence, and gender are linked. They are coded within patriarchy, and the racism of Anglo society (Newman, 1996, p. 97). In *American Me* and *Bound by Honor* there are multiple rape scenes (see below). At one level these scenes can be read as representing 'Chicano internalization of Anglo oppression' (see Newman, 1996, p. 99).

It is an error to read the barrio cycle as being supplemental to, or compatible with, the hood movies of this period. They are more than a 1990s version of the 'typical gangxploitation film' (Fregoso, 1993, p. 125). The barrio cycle differs from the black hood films in several significant ways. First, and most obviously, these movies honor Hispanic religion, history, culture, and family life. They invoke cultural and family connections to Mexico, Cuba, Puerto Rico, Spain, Latin and South America.

Second, except for *Colors*, these are prison stories that connect gang violence and crime to life inside and outside the walls of San Quentin and Folsom Prison. *American Me*, in particular, contrasts the prison and community worlds, emphasizing the place of homosociality and homosexuality in a society of imprisoned males (see Fregoso, 1993, pp. 132–133).

Third, these films draw on and interrogate long-standing Hispanic cultural stereotypes, especially those associated with macho Chicano maleness (e.g. Pachucos, Zapata outlaws, Aztec warriors). In each film there is an 'unflinching treatment of Chicano masculinities' (Fregoso, 1993, p. 123). There is a corresponding refusal to 'romanticize the defiance of the masculine heroic figure' (Fregoso, 1993, p. 123). The male homosexual bond is celebrated. This problematizes the male–female sexual bond. In turn, this challenges the taken-for-granted heterosexual intimate relationships that stand at the center of the black hood movies.

Fourth, in taking up the dark, violent sexual underside of Chicano prison culture, these films present a version of violence that is coded in gruesome and brutally realistic detail (Fregoso, 1993, p. 125). Further, both *American Me* and *Bound By Honor* (also *American History X*, 1998) focus on violent and complex connections between Hispanic, black, and white Aryan gang members. (The white Aryan presence has been largely absent in the black hood movies.) In so doing, these films present prison as a multicultural arena. In its complexities, this site magnifies ethnic and racial tensions that exist in the outside urban world.

Fifth, like the hood films, these barrio stories are didactic texts that use realistic cinema to create a critical race consciousness. But finally, to repeat, like the hood films, these movies are sexist and paternalistic in their representations of women.

Now the movies.

135

Zoot Suit

Zoot Suit 'is a story of the racism and intolerance that is deeply rooted in the culture of Los Angeles' (Broeske, 1982, p. 389). Its themes and genesis make it a milestone in Chicano cinema history (Broeske, 1982, p. 389). The Chicano barrio film cycle is indelibly shaped by this film. *Zoot Suit* was written as a stage play by Luis Valdez. Opening in August 1978 at the Mark Taper Forum of the Center Theatre Group of Los Angeles, it was 'an unqualified hit that ran for nine months' (Broeske, 1982, p. 389). It then moved to Broadway, where it flopped. The movie is a filmed version of the play. It was filmed in a fourteen-day period at the Aquarius Theater on a budget of $2.5 million (Broeske, 1982, p. 389).

The play is based on an embarrassing slice of Los Angeles history (Broeske, 1982, pp. 389–390; Moore and Vigil, 1993, p. 42). On August 2, 1942, 'a Chicano teenager named Jose Diaz was found dead after a fight between rival Chicano gangs at a ranch house near an abandoned gravel pit at the end of Los Angeles Street in Baldwin Park' (Thomas, 1981). The gravel pit was used as a swimming hole by teenagers, and the area was a lovers' lane. It was called Sleepy Lagoon in a popular Harry James song of the day. The police arrested 600 Chicanos, and twenty-two were put on trial for murder, 'despite the absence of any substantial evidence' (Broeske, 1982, p. 389). The trial became a mockery of justice, and the judge was nicknamed the hanging judge. Twelve Chicanos were sentenced to life terms in San Quentin. 'A defense committee was formed and an appeal was won; the boys were released eighteen months later' (Broeske, 1982, p. 390).

A year later, beginning on June 3, 1943, the 'zoot suit riots' occurred when members of the oldest Los Angeles Chicano gang, El Hoyo Maravilla, and invading sailors confronted one another outside the barrio (Moore and Vigil, 1993, p. 42; also Turner and Surace, 1956).[9] The riot was precipitated by a series of allegations, each group alleging that they and their girlfriends had been molested and insulted by members of the other group (Turner and Surace, 1956, p. 15). In particular, a group of sailors asserted that they had been beaten by pachucos, Chicano youth in zoot suits. In retaliation, some two hundred sailors from the Naval Armory in Chavez ravine hired twenty taxis and headed for East Los Angeles. Accompanied by 'civilian mobs, who "egged" them on ... they roamed through downtown streets in search of victims' (Turner and Surace, 1956, p. 15). They were looking for Chicanos wearing zoot suits. The streets became a battlefield. Zooters were attacked and forced to disrobe. Streetcars and buses were stopped and searched (Turner and Surace, 1956, p. 16). Civilian gangs of 'east-side adolescents organized similar attacks against unwary naval personnel' (Turner and Surace, 1956, p. 16).

'This was the moment when California attorney general Earl Warren interned all of the state's residents of Japanese heritage, when Angelenos of Mexican extraction who had lived in the city decades longer than the arriviste Okies were subject to discrimination for not being real "Americans"' (Rickey, 1982). It was a time when, as El Pachuco (a.k.a. El Bato) in *Zoot Suit* says, 'The Japs have sewn up the Pacific, Rommel has Africa, and the mayor is waging war on Chicanos.'

Using the zoot suit riots and the Sleepy Lagoon murder case as defining events, Luis Valdez, founder of El Teatro Campesino, 'fashioned what he calls his "construct of fact and fantasy," the play "Zoot Suit"' (Thomas, 1981). *Zoot Suit* tells the story of Henry Reyna (Daniel Valdez), a man between two cultures. The film (and the play) criticizes official versions of the Sleepy Lagoon case and the zoot suit riots, presenting Chicanos as victims of a rampant cultural and biological racism (Fregoso, 1993, p. 22). Henry is a zoot suiter, leader of the 38th Street Gang, and about to join the Navy to fight for America. The night before he is to report, he gets involved in a fight between his and a rival gang during a dance at the Downey Club.[10] Later that night a boy is murdered at Sleepy Lagoon. Henry and his gang are arrested and forced to stand trial. They are convicted of committing first- and second-degree murder, and sentenced to life imprisonment in San Quentin.

Zoot Suit merges music and dance, using the format of the Hollywood musical to present 'affinities to a Mexican vernacular tradition' (Fregoso, 1993, p. 26). The big band dance hall music of Harry James and Benny Goodman plays in the background, invoking a patriotic nostalgia for 1940s wartime America. As Henry's trial unfolds, past, present, and future blend into one another. In the trial white and Hispanic versions of youth culture are placed in opposition to one another. Mexican youth are presented as loving to use knives to kill, and 'this in-born characteristic,' the state's attorney argues, 'comes down from the bloodthirsty Aztecs.'

Throughout the trial Henry is advised by a strutting zoot-suited figure named El Pachuco (Edward James Olmos). El Pachuco wears a black suit, red shirt, a broad-brimmed hat, and a gold-chained cross. He acts as stage manager, advisor, and a one-man Greek chorus. He is a magician: with a snap of his fingers, action stops; twirling, he turns and confronts the audience, 'Hey, carnal! Relax! It's just a show!' He struts and sings the 'Zoot Suit Boogie' and gives 'calculated meaning to the lyrics of 'Marijuana Boogie' (Broeske, 1982, p. 390). He tempts and taunts Henry, tells him to carry a switch-blade, makes fun of his entering the military, gives him crude advice about his girlfriend. Interrupting the narrative and flow of action, El Pachuco directly addresses the audience. In his speeches and actions he privileges a positive masculine cultural identity, thereby reversing the dominant cultural discourse, which focuses on Chicano gang members as pathological greasers (Fregoso, 1993, p. 37).

Henry is defended by George, a civil libertarian attorney, and Alice, a representative for the Congress of Industrial Organizations. Alice forms the Sleepy Lagoon Defense Committee, and repeatedly visits Henry in prison. She attempts to break through his negative feelings toward Anglos. He writes her a love letter. On this point the film transgresses racial boundaries, normalizing the love between an Anglo woman and a Chicano male.

The film closes with Henry's release from prison, as El Pachuco speculates about his future, suggesting that drug addiction, murder, and another prison term are what he can expect. The story closes on a positive note, with Alice imagining a glowing future for Henry, his bride Della, and their five children, three of whom, she says, 'will go to college and come to call themselves Chicanos.' El Pachuco has the last word, telling the audience that Henry the zoot-suiter, the man, the myth, still lives.

Zoot Suit is about memory, official and unofficial ethnic histories, assimilation, American justice, and race prejudice; it is about the 'insurmountable obstacles to assimilation. Is Henry a Pachuco or an American? He's both' (Rickey, 1982). But can he be both? Can he retain his ethnic identity as a zoot-suiter, speaking Pachuco slang, and also be a sailor defending his country. To be a sailor he must leave the zoot suit behind, and become *persona non grata* among his peers. Fashion becomes metaphor for assimilation (Rickey, 1982). As El Pachuco/El Bato says, 'Don't hate your ass more than you love the gringo's.'

In the end, *Zoot Suit* imagines a future that draws on the ideologies of a Chicano nationalism. Digging deep within himself, after ninety days in solitary confinement, Henry asks, 'Where am I? What am I doing here?' And El Pachuco answers, 'You're here to learn to live with yourself, Hank.' Henry learns that he is his own worst enemy. To himself he says, 'You're the one who got me here.' At this moment, a group of sailors gang up on El Pachuco, violently beating him and stripping him of his clothing. He writhes on the floor in a fetal position. Turning to face the audience, El Pachuco is transformed into Henry's brother, and then back again into an erect Pachuco, dressed only in the loincloth of an Aztec warrior. This figure moves toward the Aztec sun.

The reflections of Henry's brother and El Pachuco as Aztec warrior are super-imposed on one another. Fregoso (1993) suggests that this image 'signifies the symbolic convergence of two historical moments: the sailors' attack on pachucos (1943) and the Spanish conquest of the Aztec nation (1519)' (p. 36). The film inscribes the identity of the Aztec warrior on the body of the Pachucco. This new warrior is the revolutionary subject of Chicano cultural nationalism. This identity is buried deep within the unconscious soul of the Chicano subject. It can only be recovered through an inward journey (Fregoso, 1993, p. 36).

Fregoso (1993) rejects the outcome of this journey, suggesting that *Zoot Suit* 'ultimately offers a masculine discourse that masks itself as politics' (p. 37). This discovery of self in ancient Aztec and Mayan rituals reconstructs identity as essence. The dangers are obvious, including subsuming the female subject within a 'universal Chicano male cultural identity' (Fregoso, 1993, p. 38).[11]

Colors

Before *Boyz N the Hood* and *Menace II Society* there was *Colors*, Dennis Hopper's black and Chicano hood movie. In Hopper's telling we have homeboys, the Crips, the Bloods, and the 21st Street Chicano gang killing another in night-time drive-bys with Uzis and AK-47 rifles (Benson, 1988).[12] This is a familiar cinematic world. The narrative is defined, in part, by a pounding rap soundtrack in the background (Ice-T performs the title track). Black and Chicano crack dealers wear 'plaid shirts with tails hanging out and a variety of messy headbands ... talking in a profane jargon not always comprehensible to the outsider' (Denby, 1988). It's all here, the usual 'matrix of race, drugs, guns, territorial disputes and peer-group pressure' (Jenkins, 1988); the required ingredients of the urban hood film. (These are the very ingredients that would soon be taken to new levels by the black filmmakers.) Gang members are identifiable by their blue and red 'colors,' leading the police to say, 'they fly their colors, we'll fly ours,' hence the film's title.

Colors is *Lethal Weapon 3* and *4* without the comedy, a cop-buddy-race-in-the-hood film. The plot is formulaic (Ebert, 1988). Hodges (Robert Duvall), nearing retirement, is a seasoned, level-headed, nineteen-year veteran of the Los Angeles Police Department reassigned to CRASH (Community Resources Against Street Hoodlums), a special unit intended to handle street gangs. He is partnered with hotheaded Danny 'Pacman' McGavin (Sean Penn). McGavin has a Chicana girlfriend, Louisa Gomez. The two men patrol the streets in uniform, but in unmarked cars. Craig, a member of the 'Bloods,' is killed by the 'Crips.' Hodges and McGavin round up gang members, including Rocket, one of the killers. They later find a Blood (High Top) dealing drugs to a Crip, but Hodges lets him go. They also meet Frog, a veteran gang member of the Chicano 21st Street Gang. Frog, who befriends Hodges, is fearful that his younger brother Felipe is becoming a gang member. The Crips stage a drive-by after Craig's funeral. Crips are killed in a car chase involving McGavin and Hodges. McGavin and Louisa visit Hodges at his home. Hodges tells him that they can only act as professionals on the street, 'Otherwise, you're just like them, nothin' but a gangster.' McGavin views this as giving in to the gangs. In a drug bust an informant gives High Top's name to McGavin and Hodges. McGavin abuses a young drug dealer, and angers Louisa when he spray-paints her cousin's face. Frog persuades Hodges to remove Felipe's name from a police computer list of gang members. Frog is arrested for non-payment of traffic tickets and High Top is sent to prison, where he names Rocket as Craig's killer. Rocket's girlfriend is killed in a police raid. Frog learns that the Crips think McGavin did the killing. He passes this information along to Hodges. Rocket and the Crips machine-gun Frog's house. McGavin argues with Lousia about her involvement with the 21st Street Gang, which Felipe has joined. The 21st Street Gang attempt to kill Rocket. The police surround the Chicano gang. Frog suspects that Hodges has betrayed his confidence. Hodges is killed by Bird, a young gang member. (Hodges to McGavin, as he is dying: 'catch my breath, call my wife, ready to roll.') McGavin kills Bird. In a closing scene McGavin is teamed with a new aggressive black partner (Jenkins, 1988).

The Critics

The film met with controversy even before it was released. Some, incorrectly, viewed it as the 'first movie to reflect the vicious escalation of gang violence in America' (Ansen, 1988). Law officials in Los Angeles were apparently prepared to go to court to ban the film from opening (Gelmis, 1988). It had to be first screened by the Los Angeles Police Department, where the District Attorney stated that 'Los Angeles is the gang capital of the United States and there are over 600 street gangs with 70,000 members' (Gelmis, 1988). In 1987 in Los Angeles, 'in gang-war shootouts … there were there 387 murders. Sixty percent of the victims were innocent bystanders caught in the crossfire' (Gelmis, 1988). Hopper's film entered this space, and authorities were fearful that the film would cause the kind of violence that had earlier been associated with the release of Walter Hill's 1979 film *The Warriors* (Jenkins, 1988; Benson, 1988; Gelmis, 1988).[13]

Critics praised Hopper's stylish, realistic, and dark direction, arguing that he 'doesn't pay homage to the gangs, nor does he make heroes of the cops ... *Colors* offers no explanations, no solutions, just graphic imagery and language' (Fiorillo, 1988; see also Benson, 1988; Jenkins, 1988). If the film is 'melodrama in realistic clothing,' it also does very little to 'sketch in the social and economic pressures that lead kids to see gangs as the only brotherhood in a bleak and hopeless world' (Benson, 1988).

Hoberman (1988) was even more critical, claiming the film

delivers the delirious kill ratio of a Depression gangster film with the grim pseudo-doc purposefulness of a Phil Karlson 'B.'... [A] liberal cop film may be a contradiction in terms ... even so ... *Colors* has something to offend everyone ... two beleaguered honkies ... an inescapably racist view of the ghetto ... the slums of LA are a kind of zoo ... unreconstructed '60s chauvinist.

A nihilistic thread opens and closes the film. Everyday life in this East LA Third World country is defined by random, senseless murder, a repetitive cycle of death and replacement, endless encounters between police and gangs, drive-bys, murders, stand-offs, betrayals, stints in prison, and the beat just keeps going on (Jenkins, 1988; Hoberman, 1988). Occasionally the pattern is broken, but only momentarily. An older cop mentors, in father-like fashion, a young hothead cop. Then the father is murdered, and the young cop steps up to mentor his replacement.

Hopper's film succeeds in showing how the system of honor, pride, and violence in the gang produces a profound alienation 'from anything like a normal existence' (Denby, 1988). There is nothing to hold these young gang members to life. They are bound only by a loyalty to the gang. They are doomed by the very values that define them: honor, courage, and loyalty. But, as with O-Dog and Caine, 'once an act is committed against them, they must retaliate' (Denby, 1988).

Boyd (1997) locates Hopper's film within America's cinematic racial history. He suggests that 'in many ways *Colors* served the same function for gangsta culture that *Birth of a Nation* served for the early stages of African American cinema' (pp. 87–88). Both films used armed militia as an answer to the perceived black threat. *The Birth of a Nation* used the Ku Klux Klan, and *Colors* used the racist LA Police Department. He further observes that the film turned a local Los Angeles problem involving gangs, drugs, and drive-bys into a national epidemic.

American Me

The film you are about to see is inspired by a true story. The events depicted are strong and brutal, but they occur every day. (Opening on-screen lines in *American Me*)

Hard, disciplined male bodies, tattoos, zoot-suiters, brown, black, and white gangs, prison (pinto) poetry, drugs, Godfathers, ethnic gangsters for the nineties – it's all here. Also nihilistic, *American Me* is a didactic, anti-gang, anti-drug film. Narrated through the use of voice-overs and flashbacks, it is about 'the depraved and ruined Chicano *familia*; a savage vision of Chicano gang life' (Fregoso, 1993, p. 123). This is a film with multiple beginnings. It starts days before Santana is murdered, as he listens to the voice of his girlfriend in his prison cell.

It then jumps to 1943, skipping next to 1959, when Santana is a teenager. The story starts again in the present and then backtracks over the previous thirty years. Sifting through a box of old photographs and letters, Santana leads us through his life (Turan, 1992).

Directed by Edward James Olmos, who also stars as Santana, *American Me* can be read as a terrifying continuation of *Zoot Suit*.[14] Olmos' film is rooted in the same historical events: Santana's mother was repeatedly raped by sailors during the 1943 zoot suit riots.

The film opens with an off-screen male voice telling prison inmates to:

Hold your hands out in front of you. Reach down and lift up your nut sack. Drop your nut sack, skin-back your dick. Bend over, spread your cheeks.

This voice is replaced by a woman's:

You're like two people; one's like a kid who doesn't know how to make love. That's the one I cared about. But the other one I hate, the one who knows, one who has this rap down, who runs drugs, who kills people....

As these words are spoken, Santana is shown holding a book written by Tolstoy. Santana's story begins before he was born. His off-screen voice narrates:

Until now I would have thought it a sign of weakness to even listen to what you said to me that night. But I see that you were right. I am two people. One was born when I met you. The other one began in a downtown LA tattoo parlor. My father Pedro was showing his love for my mother, Esperanza. My mother was a beautiful woman. They were pachucos, zoot suiters, and proud of it. In June of 1943 America was at war, not only overseas, but with itself. Racial tension was running high against anyone who was different.

The screen cuts to Santana's father getting a tatoo, and then moves to the brutal beating of his father, and the violent rape of his mother by US sailors. The film traces Santana's 'downfall to this primal rape scene' (Fregoso, 1993, p. 132). The narrative then jumps forward to 1959, when Santana, age 15, forms a gang with two barrio pals, J. D. (a white male) and Mundo. (The sign of the gang is a cross that is tattooed on the web of the left hand, between the thumb and forefinger.)

Zoot suits, new suits. I had no clue
what they had been through.
But to be 16 in '59
Stayin' away from home
Even if I didn't have a dime
The old man was just waitin'
To give me a piece of time
Drove me to the streets
Just to save my mind

The three young men swear allegiance to one another, affirming that 'Our gang is the only thing we've got. It gives us respect'. Santana, J. D., and Mundo wander into the territory of a rival gang. A fight ensues. The boys break into a café. J. D. is shot. Santana and Mundo are sent to juvenile detention. Santana's off-screen voice narrates, in the lyrics of prison, or pinto, poetry, 'Thought I knew it all, sent to juvie hall, and the shit got even deeper' (Fregoso, 1993, p. 130). Santana is raped by a white teenager. He kills his rapist, and is sentenced to eighteen years in prison. A year later Santana and J. D. are reunited. With the lyrics of 'Rockin' Robin' in the background, the screen fills with shots of wholesome young Latinos exercising and playing games in a sunny prison courtyard. As Santana hits a handball back against a high wall, the scene suddenly shifts to Folsom State Prison. The same handball game is going on, only now the young boys have tattooed bodies, life weights, and are dressed in prison garb. Armed guards patrol behind barbed-wire fences high above the prison yard. Santana narrates, 'The choices we made to survive, got Mundo, J. D., and me, 10 to 25.'

Santana, J. D., and Mundo create their own prison gang, known as 'la eMe' or the Mexican Mafia. Santana, the Mexican Godfather, says of the gang,

> The Aryan Brotherhood and Black Guerilla Family shared the yard, but Folsom Prison belonged to us, the oldest gang, the Mexican Mafia. Power became our game, power to provide anything you find outside – extortion, gambling, prostitution – power to make every inmate pay rent, and the biggest money-maker of all, drugs.

Members of 'la eMe' must swear absolute allegiance to the Godfather. His power is enormous. A prisoner who steals drugs from 'la eMe' is burned to death. In order to restore respect to the Mexican Mafia, Santana orders the murder of several members of a rival Chicano gang. The brutal murders are carried out as the prisoners watch a Walt Disney 'Woody Woodpecker' cartoon in the darkened cafeteria.

J. D. is released from prison. Shortly thereafter Santana is visited by his little brother, who reports that their mother has died. Santana laments,

> You never stop to think
> of what life has meant
> til reality hits hard
> you ride behind pride
> thinking you can hide.
>
> I had years on the tier to think how my life had effected my mother.

Upon release from prison Santana is met by J. D., who is driving a Cadillac, and reports that the Italian Mafia, led by Scagnelli, is controlling drugs and gambling in the barrio. While Santana's father will not talk to him, his little brother, with a show of great deference, brings him a shoebox full of letters that he received while Santana was in prison. 'I read them to my homeboys. They are like poetry, the way you write.'

Santana enters the outside world like a 'fish out of water' (Theodore, 1993, p. 37). He does not know how to act in the straight world. (He does not know how to drive a car. He can't dance. He has never been to the beach.) His macho ethics begin to crumble when he meets Julie at a community dance. She asks him to dance. He awkwardly follows her onto the dance floor. 'When was the last time you danced?' she asks, and he replies, 'I never really tried it you know.' Although he is treated with a great deal of respect in the barrio, his prison codes of loyalty and vengeance seem out of place. When he tries to buy a pair of shoes, the salesman treats him curtly, and he takes offense ('Hey, look at me when I'm talking').

He attempts to explain himelf to Julie:

> *Santana:* You know when I got to Folsom, I smiled and looked around, and said, 'I've finally made it to the big time.'
> *Julie:* How did you survive there?
> *Santana:* I got the gang going. I had anything I wanted there. Before, if somebody wanted something from you, cigarettes, or your manhood, and they were stronger than you, they just took it. We changed all that. We made it better for our people in the joint.

Julie: You never finished school.

Santana: But I fed myself – history, politics, biography – anything I could get a hold of to help me forget about myself – to think about something else – La Raza, our people, the revolution, the movement. I loved it in there. I had whatever I wanted.

Julie: Yeah, how about walking outside, or going out with a girl?

Santana: I didn't know about that. Didn't care either.

Julie's brother overdoses on heroin and dies. In retaliation, Santana's gang rapes and murders Scagnelli's son in prison. Reminiscent of Francis Ford Coppola's use of parallel montage in the *Godfather* trilogy (Fregoso, 1993, p. 132; Kroll and Wright, 1992), Olmos cuts back and forth between Santana's love-making with Julie, which turns violent, 'with Santana attempting to sodomize Julie' (Fregoso, 1993, p. 132), and the rape and murder of Scagnelli's son. (She is the first woman he has ever been with.) As Santana climaxes, an inmate rams a Christmas tree-shaped knife into the rectum of Scagnelli's son, and Julie screams, 'Stop it!' while pushing herself away from him.

Santana and his father meet accidentially in the cemetery. Standing at his mother's grave, Santana seeks his father's forgiveness, 'Whatever I did to you or momma that made you hate me. I'm sorry.' His father replies,

Your mother was a beautiful woman. She made me feel proud. She was 19 years old when she was raped by sailors. After it happened, we never talked about it. We got married and we tried to forget it. When you were born I tried to love you, but every time I looked at you, I wondered who your real father was. I wondered which sailor's blood you carried within you.

Responding to his son's murder, Scagnelli releases uncut heroin into the barrio. A violent chain reaction follows. The Black Guerilla Family are working with the Italian Mafia. At J. D.'s request, the Aryan Brotherhood attack the Black Guerilla Family. Santana objects, saying that they are sending the wrong message. 'We are spending all our time dealing with the situation, instead of with our people and getting them out and keeping them out.' J. D. does not agree, 'If we don't fight now, we'll lose it all later. ... You are starting to show weakness.'

In a voice-over Santana speaks to Julie, 'For weeks I wanted to tell you how I felt, but I couldn't find the courage.' Julie speaks to him at Santana's little brother, Little Puppet's wedding. This is the last time they see one another. Like Ronnie in *Menace II Society*, Julie criticizes Santana's way of life (Boyd, 1997, p. 93).

Julie: I don't know what to say to you. You're like two people.

Santana: [interrupting] I don't have to listen to this shit. If you were a man...

Julie: Oh no, you'd kill me. Oh no! You'd fuck me in the ass, and then kill me.

Santana: I guess we got nothing to say to each other.

Julie: You know when I met you, I was impressed, You talked about La Raza, education, and the revolution. You don't care about any revolution, do you? You're nothing but a fucking dope dealer. Your business kills kids.

Santana: What the fuck you want from me? Do you want me to start over? Get a job. Become a citizen?

Julie: There's no fucking hope for our barrio with people like you around!

As Julie finishes her speech, a police car stops. Santana is frisked, picked up, booked, and sent back to Folsom.

In prison J. D. and Santana quarrel. J. D. again asserts that Santana has lost control over the gang ('They're saying you're not showing them anything').

Santana asks J. D. to remember when they first formed the gang as teenagers: 'Whatever we lost, we gave it away. Nobody took it from us.'

He reads a letter he has sent to Julie. On a split screen she reads the letter while he narrates:

> Dear Julie, Maybe the reason I learned to read and write was so I could write you this letter here in this cage, behind these bars. I can read. I can learn. I can even make love, but it's distorted. I thought that what I learned on the inside was everything I needed to know, even on the outside.... You scared me by showing me a glimpse of what my life might have been.

As Julie reads the letter, in another sequence of parallel montage, Little Puppet is strangled to death behind trees in a grassy and tree-lined expanse along the road. (This space is not unlike the New Jersey saltmarsh area where Sonny is killed in the first *Godfather*). And as Little Puppet dies, Santana is called from his prison cell and stabbed to death by his friends, a death that was ordered by J. D.

The narrative cuts back to the barrio. Like *Menace II Society*, *American Me* ends in a senseless drive-by shooting. Carlito, Santana's little brother, and Julie's young son are in a car with friends using drugs and drinking. They drive randomly through the neighborhood. Julie's son leans out of the car and fires a gun at a family in its front yard. The screen fills with these words: 'In 1991 it is estimated there were more than 3000 gang-related deaths in the United States. Although this film was inspired by a true story, specific characters and certain events are fictional.'

The Critics

The film has been praised for its 'almost documentary sense of ... verisimilitude' (Turan, 1992); its moments of Shakespearean power (Anderson, 1992b); its 'impassioned study of the deadly Latino East L. A. gang structure' (Kroll and Wright, 1992); its refusal to romanticize the pachuco, or celebrate the Chicano Nation; its brutally realistic violence; its tragic, horrific portrait of Chicano male culture; its ability to capture the sounds and rhythms of prison speech (pinto poetry); its skill in representing 'the stylized walk and prose of the pinto' (prisoner) (Fregoso, 1993, p. 130). The authenticity of the film apparently touches viewers, especially mothers and fathers who have sons in prison (Fregoso, 1993, p. 131).

In turn, it has been criticized for its clichéd situations (Turan, 1992); its macho bullheaded violence (Denby, 1992; Theorore, 1993, p. 38); its ponderously trite dialogue and one-dimensional characters (Farolino, 1992); its neglect of economics; its argument that the dysfunctional family is the cause of the barrio's social problems (Fregaso, 1993, p. 126). Indeed, Fregoso (1993, p. 127) suggests that Santana's emotional cemetery scene with his father perpetuates the myth of the absent father being the cause of juvenile delinquency.

The scene can be read differently. Olmos is criticizing those values that celebrate macho masculine sexual prowess, prize feminine virginity, and regard male offspring as the most important measure of one's manliness.

At the same time he is placing the blame for the barrio's problems squarely on the shoulders of white racist capitalist patriarchy.

144

Boyd (1997, pp. 92–95) elaborates the implications of this reading of racism and capitalism. J. D. is the only white member of the Mexican Mafia. Early in the film Santana endorses J. D.'s membership in the gang, saying he is family, he is one of us. At the end of the film, J. D. refuses to hear Santana's messsage, the messsage he has learned from Julie, namely the gang's 'business kills kids.' Ironically, it is J. D.'s whiteness that authorizes Santana's murder. Thus whiteness is sutured into the opening and closing sequences of the film. The American military oppression of Mexican Americans starts the story, the original rape scene. The story comes full circle. Santana is killed by a representative of this self-same violent white society.

In its history and politics, *American Me* convincingly argues that systemic, institutionalized racism and white supremacy are the 'real root evil in American society' (Boyd, 1997, p. 94). It is this understanding that separates the politics of *American Me* from the 'bourgeois politics of *Boyz N the Hood*, and the nihilistically apolitical *Menace II Society*' (Boyd, 1997, p. 94).

Finally, and regrettably, *American Me*'s model of spectatorship invokes images of women as passive subjects (Fregoso, 1993, pp. 128, 132). Julie emerges as the only hero in the film, but in a traditional way. The Chicanas in *American Me* carry double duty: first as origins of Santana's downfall (his mother's rape), and second as 'vehicles for his salvation' (Fregoso, 1993, p. 133). But Julie's help comes too late. Santana can neither understand nor accept her love. If his story ends before hers, the final close-up of the film signals her untold story. She has a cross, the sign of the gang, tattooed on her hand. She has survived the hard life. But the story of her oppression and her resistance is not on the screen (Fregoso, 1993, pp. 133–134).

Bound by Honor

Bound by Honor is another wake-up call to the Chicano community. Taylor Hackford's three-hour epic on East Los Angeles Chicanos is part '*Godfather*, and part *Riot in Cell Block Eleven*' (Blackburn, 1993). It does not work.[15] The film is filled with violent, cartoonish characters, contrived melodrama, and cinematic clichés connected to the East LA prison and gang genres: blood-oath alliances, tattoos, gang rumbles, murders to pay off debts, drug running, misogynist homosocial bonding, homophobia and rough prison sex, racial tensions, hackneyed phrases, dialogue reduced to mumbled phrases like 'homeboy' or 'loco' (Bernard, 1993; Turan, 1993). Still, the 'electrically charged camera work of Mexican-British cinematographer Gabriel Beristain vividly captures the warmth, spice and diversity of East LA life' (Medved, 1993).

The film opens with a soundtrack of street noises and soft Latin guitar music, cutting quickly to Aztec dancers wearing Day of the Dead masks and great plummed headdresses performing in a street festival. Hackford moves back and forth between the dancers, families shopping, food markets, and a montage of colorful murals on the sides of neighborhood buildings, including images of mothers holding babies, Christ and Madonna figures, serpents, great eagles in flight, jungle scenes, angels, and industrial workers united under the signs of labor.

A cab pulls over a bridge and stops; out steps a young blue-eyed young man (Miklo) with light hair, 'This is East LA, a whole different country.' The year is 1972. Miklo has returned to the barrio and his Chicano mother, after a fight with his Anglo father in Las Vegas. He is on parole from prison.

The plot parallels *American Me*. This is another barrio movie about a Godfather behind bars, a brown San Quentin don (Turan, 1993; Mathews, 1993; also Blackurn, 1993; Morales, 1993). Three young Chicano men tell their now familiar story against the backdrop of the East LA barrios and San Quentin prison. This is a film that wants to be two things at once: a 'depiction of late twentieth century Chicano life' (Tepper, 1994, p. 49), and a story about 'the tragic consequences of crime in the urban Latino community' (Tepper, 1994, p. 49). It fails at both levels.

The story unfolds over a span of twelve years in the lives of Cruz, Paco, and Miklo. The three men are linked by blood relationships, by their deep devotion to one another, and their commitment to their gang, 'Los Vatos Locos.' Cruz and Paco are half-brothers and Miklo is their cousin. Paco is a street fighter, a boxer who is called the Black Rooster. Cruz is a brilliant artist-painter. Miklo, a product of Anglo and Latino cultures, is a trouble-maker. He is called 'Milkweed.'

The story begins as Miklo rejoins his old gang, and they have a fight with their rival gang, 'Tres Puntos,' which is led by Spider. A shoot-out leaves Cruz badly injured and in chronic pain. Miklo kills Spider, and is sent to San Quentin. The scene is familiar: black and brown men with hard bodies lifting weights and working out in the prison yard. And in contrast, gay black men dressed as women, hair in curlers, swish down the aisles in the cafeteria. Two violent sub-cultures. Paco escapes prison by joining the Marines. In prison Miklo is adopted by Popeye, who tries to rape him. The prison is governed by three gangs: the white Aryan Vanguard (AV), the Black Guerilla Army (BGA), and La Onda, the ruling Latino gang led by Montana.

Back in the barrio, Cruz achieves success as an artist. However, he has turned to the use of painkillers for the pain in his back. He slips deeper and deeper into heroin addiction, in part because of the guilt he feels over the death of his younger brother, Juanito, who overdosed and died on heroin left in his studio. Cruz is banished from his family by his father, who says, 'You are dead to me.' Paco, who has returned from the Marines, becomes an undercover narcotics policeman.

In prison, Miklo becomes the lover of Big N, the prison cook, who is also the prison bookmaking kingpin. To win favor with La Onda, Miklo kills Big N. He then becomes a lieutenant in La Onda's ruling council, heading up the prison gambling operation, while studying and obtaining his GED. In La Onda Miklo finds acceptance and recognition, becoming a prison Godfather of sorts, controlling gangs and drugs and relations between rival gangs. Not unlike Santana in *American Me*, he mediates between the AV, the BGA, and La Onda.

Prior to his initiation into La Onda, Miklo is brought into Montana's inner circle. Montana explains the significance of La Onda, and addresses the film's title:

> For 500 years we've suffered the oppression of our people. But here, by organizing ourselves, we're gonna stop this disaster. Because this land is ours. Blood for Blood. Blood in Blood out.

In 1982 Miklo is paroled and returns to the barrio. His attempts to go straight fail. A crooked foreman at the tire plant where he works skims off his paychecks. He lives in a 'squalid flat inhabited by Popeye and a coterie of Chicano hoodlums' (Blackburn, 1993). He takes part in an armed robbery, which is busted by Paco, who shoots him in the foot (which later has to be amputated) as he attempts to escape.

Miklo is sent back to San Quentin, where he learns that Montana, the leader of La Onda, refuses to become involved in the cocaine trade. A war with the BGA breaks out and spreads back to the barrio in East LA. Montana forms a truce with the BGA, hoping to weaken the hand of the AV. Montana is killed by a BGA member. To avoid a war, the governor of San Quentin and Paco convince Miklo to make a truce with Bonafide, the leader of BGA. In alliance with BGA, on the Day of the Dead, La Onda wipes out the AV, and then, in a double-cross, destroys the BGA at the same time (Blackburn, 1993). In this extended sequence, obviously influenced by Francis Ford Coppola, Hackford (like Olmos) cuts back and forth between the assassinations in the prison, engineered by Miklo, and the Day of the Dead festival in East LA (Mathews, 1993).

On the same day, Cruz's stepmother forgives him for his brother's death. In San Quentin the members of La Onda are about to be dispersed to other prisons across the country. Miklo destroys evidence that he ordered Montana's murder. Back in the barrio, Cruz and Paco are reunited. The film ends in 1984, with the two men standing beneath a mural of them and Miklo painted twelve years earlier by Cruz. They have the following conversation.

Cruz: Ten years star trekking in twilight zone. I thought this [*points to mural*] would help me find my way back. Damn! We were all so innocent.

Paco: It's all gone. It's a dream, a fantasy. It's not like that any more.

Cruz: You think you use brotherhood up, drink it like a shot of tequilla and its all gone?

Paco: Look, you showed me your mural. You're a great artist. The best. Come on, let's go. I see a dream, a fantasy. Three *vatos* lookin' for somethin'.

Cruz: We stood by each other. We trusted each other. *Familia* homes.

Paco: Never again. Miklo and I are finished. Now I hate that fucker.

Cruz: No matter how much hate. You are still connected. The same blood pumps through your hearts. That's a bond you can never break. Neither can Miklo. Miklo is just trying to be like you, the baddest Chicano.

Paco: Are you sayin' its all my fault the way things turned out?

Cruz: You think you got that much power, you can control everybody?

Paco: I set him up. I made him go after Spider.

Cruz: Relax.

Paco: Your back wouldn't be all fucked up. Miklo wouldn't be in prison.

Cruz: I forgive you.

Paco: I don't want your forgiveness.

Cruz: That's your problem. You can't forgive yourself. You need that guilt. It's what keeps you going. I know. I fed mine through a needle for ten years. ... Miklo is hating his own white skin. He's got it worse than both of us. Cut it out. It's worse than poison. That's what we are [*points to mural*]. Three *vatos locos* full of *carnelismo*, tryin' to survive in a fuckin' war zone. I need my *familia* to do it. We all do. Even you (they hug). Life's a risk. You said it. We are from East Los Angeles. We come out chased by hounds, round and round we go wearin' a rabbit's foot for luck [*dances, jabs the air*], just ahead of the hounds. Hey, we got somethin' better than a rabbit's foot. We got *familia*! [*They hug each other.*] Man, you still can't dance. [*They shadow box.*] Hey, I'm a lover. Not a fighter.

The camera pulls back from the two men at the base of the canal, moving to the mural on the hill, dissolving into a long shot of the LA highway landscape.

Reading the Film

The criticisms have been noted above. This epic text seems politically shallow. It does not articulate the politics of rage that organizes the other major films in the barrio cycle (*Zoot Suit, Colors, American Me*). It does not treat the gangs as a cancer, even though it does connect the drug narrative to gangs in prison. But the violence that the gangs do to one another does not spread deeply into the barrio, as it does for *Colors* and *American Me*. The outrage at senseless violence that organizes the films of Hopper, Olmos, Singleton and the Hughes brothers is missing in Hackford's film.

Hackford reduces the problems of the barrio to problems of the individual and his self-image, to self-forgiveness, self-guilt, and blood relationships. The larger political economy of gangs, gang warfare, drugs, guns, and violence is ignored. In Hackford's world the problems of the barrio can be resolved through family, by being loyal, and by letting go of self-hate. But the ability of the person of color to let go of hate is not easy. Fanon (1986) reminds us that those with black skin wear white masks, and the white mask invokes self-hatred. Thus does Cruz's monologue calling for self-forgiveness ring hollow.

The images of black, white, and Latino masculinity and sexuality that Hackford's film constructs are homophobic and racist. In the public spheres of the prison, homoerotic interracial male bonds are modeled. But these are cruel, loveless parodies, filled with self-loathing. They are coded within the homophobic racism of conservative white society. This prison world, filled with black and brown bodies, is a profane site. The gay masculinities that circulate on parade here are presented as gross, even comic, caricatures of normal white male masculinity (see Nero, 1998; Jones, 1998, pp. 216–217; Van Leer, 1997, p. 158; Jones, 1993, p. 247). These images must be read through the lens of a reactionary, conservative, post-feminist racial and gender order.

Following Foucault (1978, p. 155), it is clear that in the prison, sexuality is a linchpin for the administration and control of an all-male population. Power flows through sexuality and its representations, it is endowed with 'the greatest instrumentality' (Foucault, 1978, p. 155; also quoted in Jones, 1993, p. 247). And the hysteria that is associated with its deployment, especially in its gay forms, is a white hysteria, born of a fear of the black and brown body. Thus do the prison narratives in the barrio film cycle reproduce repressed sexual fears that circulate in America's conservative white male culture.

At this level, as Newman observes (1996, p. 99), these narratives seem to represent the black and Chicano internalization of Anglo oppression. But remember this is a white filmmaker telling the story. Hackford is projecting some set of white stereotypes onto these black and brown forms of masculine sexuality.

So in the end, the hounds chase the *vatos locos* back into the barrio. There, now safely home, and free of guilt, behind the walls and masks of white America, these brown men create their own free society. In this utopia there are wandering street musicians playing soft Latin music. Couples stroll past one another, smiling and holding hands. Children play on the sidewalk. And in the distance are wildly colorful murals painted on the sides of little grocery stories depicting an idealized Latino culture.

In Conclusion: Godfathers in the Hood

I want to read the barrio movies through Jameson's (1990, pp. 32–34) analysis of gangster films, and the Mafia narratives in American culture, especially Coppola's *Godfather* trilogy (1972, 1974, 1990).[16] Jameson's thesis is well known: works of popular culture are always ideological and utopian. Shaped by a dialectic of anxiety and hope, such works revive and manipulate fears and anxieties about the social order. At the same time they offer kernels of utopian hope. They show how these anxieties and fears can be satisfactorily addressed by the existing social order (Jameson, 1990, p. 30). Hence the audience is lulled into believing that the problems of the social have in fact been successfully resolved.

The *Godfather* trilogy functions ideologically by first reworking earlier versions of the gangster paradigm. The gangster films of the thirties and forties located sick loners in a struggle with a society of essentially wholesome people. In contrast, the post-war gangster films invest the loner with a sense of the tragic, a pathos experienced as a result of reentering a rigid, petty, and vindictive social order (Jameson, 1990, p. 31; see also Boyd, 1997, pp. 84–85).

The Mafia/*Godfather* films of Coppola replace this figure of the sick, pathological loner with the concept of an ethnic family patriarch and the story of his family's struggles. This is a saga with recurring episodes 'involving legendary figures returning again and again in different perspectives and contexts' (Jameson, 1990, p. 31). Coppola further extends the gangster genre by folding ethnicity into his story, for his trilogy is an assimilation narrative. The history of the Godfather's family, and the intricate complex leadership structure of the Mafia itself, can be traced back to nineteenth-century feudal Sicily.

Coppola's trilogy is about the utopian and gendered fantasies and fears of this family as a collectivity, about its attempts to overcome the prejudice, scorn, and contempt of white middle-class America. It is the story of how the members of one Italian-American family disappear into the deep fabrics of American culture. Driven by this desire, by this version of the American Dream, Michael Corleone and his father Vito use the wealth and power attained through the operations of the family to achieve symbols of wealth and acceptance. Within this framework, the crimes of capitalism somehow seem less evil, because they are serving this greater good (Jameson, 1990, p. 32).

Thus the family's ethnic solidarity speaks to a previous moment in American culture, the pre-war period before anomie and social fragmentation took their toll on the white middle class. Coppola's films offer hope, utopian fantasies that say that the fears surrounding the loss of community in America are unfounded.

Community still exists in the tightly knit ethnic family, a model for the rest of us. Indeed, the Mafia's version of the ethnic family projects images of morality, stability, and social integration. Furthermore, the Godfather always acts ethically. He is always searching for a way to serve and protect his family.[17] Of course this is done at a price. He is constantly seeking to advance the project of the Mafia, while maintaining his leadership position in that structure and also being a moral leader of his family.

Boyd (1997, p. 84) extends Jameson, anchoring the gangster and *Godfather* films in American racial and ethnic cinema. Hollywood's classic American gangsters (*Little Caesar, Public Enemy, Scarface*) have been defined as deviant because of their ethnicity, as opposed to their race. Thus in *Godfather II* Michael is verbally abused by 'Senator Geery of Nevada because of his Italian heritage' (Boyd, 1997, p. 84). In Coppola's narrative, this prejudice and discrimination led the Italian immigrants to use their own cultural traditions and the underground economy as 'vital means of sustenance in the face of ethnic, religious, and cultural oppression' (Boyd, 1997, p. 85). By the end of the second film Michael is indistinguishable from the 'America that surrounds him' (Boyd, 1997, p. 85). By authorizing the murder of his own brother, he places the interests of capitalism and business above family.

Boyd (1997) suggests that ultimately the *Godfather* trilogy is about how American society forced these 'turn-of-the-century immigrants to reject their own culturally distinct voices' (p. 85). Hypocritically, Americans willingly incorporated the excesses of 'ethnically defined gangster culture, especially from an economic standpoint, into the structure of larger American society' (Boyd, 1997, p. 85).[18] More deeply, the films 'foreground the continued rejection of race as a component of the metaphoric "melting pot" – because it is the challenge of race that accelerates the assimilation process of ethnicity' (Boyd, 1997, p. 85).

Hence at the end of the first *Godfather*, Vito Corleone rejects drug trafficking in the African-American community. The Mafia leader from Kansas City disagrees, arguing that the 'dark people' are 'animals anyway, let them lose their souls.' Boyd (1997) argues that many African Americans found these lines prophetic, because in the early 1970s there was an upsurge 'in underworld drug activities throughout African American ghetto communities' (p. 86).

Boyd pushes this argument to the next level: that is, the assimilation of ethnicity was achieved at the expense of race. Furthermore, the racialized drug culture would now become an important part of the national discourse on race, violence, and gangs in America.

Brown and Black Godfathers

The blaxploitation films of the 1970–1973 period (which Jameson ignores) would develop this connection, presenting a black protagonist who opposed a corrupt white police or Mafia figure (Boyd, 1997, p. 89).[19] This protagonist was a black gangster and Godfather, an outlaw and a rebel. He was also presented as a pimp, dope dealer, and hustler. But he was an outlaw hero, nonetheless, a rebel attempting to wrest control of the alternative drug economy from his white counterpart. The blaxploitation films (*Sweet Sweetback's Baadasssss Song, The Mack, Coffy,*

Cleopatra Jones, Superfly, Shaft, Cotton Comes to Harlem) established the black gangster as a key cultural icon. The flowering of the cinematic and everyday gangsta culture (and music) in the late 1980s and early 1990s can now be traced to these films, and to their historical antecedents in the Hollywood gangster film and the *Godfather* series.

The focus on race and not ethnicity creates the space for the hood and barrio movies to critique the Mafia and Coppola *Godfather* narrative.[20] In these contemporary moral tales crime ultimately does not pay. The Godfather is always murdered, usually by one a member of his own community. In this move these films harken back to the Bogart, Cagney, and Robinson gangster movies of the pre- (and post-)World War II era. That is, no brown or black Godfather rises to a position of public power and respect. These black or brown Godfathers are not anchored in a complex ethnic and family culture as was the case for the Corleone family. In no instance does the black or brown Godfather become the moral leader of a local ethnic or racial community.

For the barrio Godfathers family becomes gang, not family *per se*. (This is the underlying counter-narrative in the *Godfather* trilogy as well.) Santana holds to the utopian belief that he and his gang bring respect to the barrio. But gang in *American Me* is not family. Gang is a group of men being violent to and with one another. Gangs do not have homes (except for prison yards and prison cells), children, neighborhoods, or family traditions. Gangs are violent homoerotic structures; systems that allow men to experience emotion without intimacy.

Only at the end of his life, because of Julie, does Santana come to realize that his business as the Godfather is corrupt, that his gang and its code are killing family, killing the members of his moral community in the barrio. Michael Corleone never comes to this understanding.

Herein lies the power of the brown and black hood movies. They lay to rest the myth of the Mafia, the myth that says we do this for family and for community. In the ghettos and the barrios the Mafia and its values are doing just the opposite. As Santana says, 'There's a cancer in this subculture of gangs. Either you treat the cancer or it'll eat you alive.'

So these are bleak tales that confront the abyss of violence and drugs in the barrio. But their utopian themes are muted; hope is traced back to the figure of the mother, the girlfriend, the loyal grandparents, the proud old men of the barrio. And these men and women appear helpless in the face of this senseless violence. Such is the message of the didactic text.

Notes

1. *Zoot Suit* (1981). Released by Universal Pictures. Director: Luis Valdez; Screenplay: Luis Valdez, based on the play of the same name; Cinematography: David Myers; Cast: Daniel Valdez (Henry Reyna), Edward James Olmos (El Pachuco), Charles Aidman (George), Tyne Daly (Alice), John Anderson (Judge), Able Franco (Enrique), Mike Gomez (Joey), Alma Rose Martinez (Lupe), Rose Portillo (Della). For reviews, see Aufderheide, 1982/3; Sterritt, 1982; Thomas, 1981; Winsten, 1982; Keneas, 1982; Rickey, 1982; Broeske, 1982.

2. *Colors* (1988). Released by Orion. Director: Dennis Hopper; Screenplay: Michael Schiffer, based on a story by Schiffer and Richard Dilello; Cinematography: Haskell Wexler; Cast: Robert

Duvall (Bob Hodges), Sean Pean (Danny McGavin/Pacman), Maria Conchita Alonso (Louisa Gomez), Randy Brooks (Ron Delaney), Grand Bush (Larry Sylvester), Don Cheadle (Rocket), Gerardo Mejia (Bird), Glenn Plummer (High Top), Rudy Ramos (Melindez), Trinidad Silva (Frog), Damon Wayans (T-Bone). For reviews, see Fiorillo, 1988; Benson, 1988; Jenkins, 1988; Denby, 1988; Ebert, 1988; Gelmis, 1988; Ansen, 1988; Corliss, 1988; Hoberman, 1988; Rollyson, 1989; Kael, 1988.

3. *American Me* (1992). Released by Universal Pictures. Director: Edward James Olmos; Screenplay: Floyd Mutrux and Desmond Nakano, based on a story by Mutrux; Cinematrography: Reynaldo Villalobos; Cast: Edward James Olmos (Santana), William Forsythe (J. D.), Pepe Serna (Mundo), Danny De La Paz (Puppet), Evelina Fernandez (Julie), Cary Hiroyuki Tagawa (El Japo), Daniel Villarreal (Little Puppet), Sal Lopez (Pedro), Daniel A. Haro (Huero), Vira Montes (Esperanza), Domingo Ambriz (Pie Face), Vic Trevino (Cheetah), Tom Bower (Dornan), Panchito Gomez (Santana as an adolescent), Steve Wilcox (J. D. as an adolescent), Richard Coca (Mundo as an adolescent). For reviews and critical readings see Turan, 1992; Denby, 1992c; Farolino, 1992; Anderson, 1992b; Kroll and Wright, 1992; Brown, 1992b; also Keller, 1994, pp. 210–211; Newman, 1996; and Fregoso, 1993, pp. 122–134.

4. *Bound by Honor* (1993). Released by Hollywood Pictures. Director: Taylor Hackford; Screenplay: Jimmy Santiago Baca, Jeremy Iacone, and Floyd Mutrux, based on a story by Ross Thomas; Cinematography: Gabriel Berstain; Cast: Damian Chapa (Miklo), Jesse Borrego (Cruz), Benjamin Bratt (Paco), Enrique Castillo (Montana), Victor Rivers (Magic Mike), Delroy Lindo (Bonafide), Tom Towles (Red Ryder), Lanny Flaherty (Big Al), Billy Bob Thorton (Lightning), Noah Verduzco (Juanito). For reviews and critical commentary, see Tepper, 1994; Turan, 1993; Bernard, 1993; Medved, 1993; Mathews, 1993; Blackburn, 1993; Morales, 1993; Keller, 1994, pp. 162, 210; Fregoso, 1993, p. 123. The film was released as a video with the title *Blood In Blood Out*.

5. A style of dress, a flashy type of man's suit with padded shoulders, fitted waist, knee-length coat, and trousers narrow at the ankles, introduced in the 1940s; zoot-suiter – one who wears a zoot suit; also associated with the so-called lower class, pachuco, or zoot suit style of dress, imported from El Paso into Los Angeles (Gonzales, 1993, p. 159). Zooters 'wore their hair long, full and well greased' (Turner and Surace, 1956, p. 16).

6. See Chapter 3, note 5, for the discussion of the two female hood movies, *Mi Vida Loca* (1994) and *Set It Off* (1996). These films represent significant departures from the male hood genre. The prison, Godfather, drug-dealing, drive-by, cocaine narrative is absent, as are the themes of violent sexuality, homophobia, and conflict with neighboring gang formations, including the Aryan Brotherhood.

7. As indicated in Chapter 1, these films were produced during the so-called 'Decade of the Hispanic,' so named by the Coors Corporation.

8. According to Fregoso (1993, p. 123) *American Me* takes its title from Griffith (1948). The original script for the film, written by Floyd Mutrux in 1974, was based on real people and events, ' and was inspired by a Chicano gang leader named Cheyenne who was killed in prison in 1972' (Theodore, 1993, p. 36; Fregoso, 1993, p. 123). The figure of Montana is also the inspiration for *Bound by Honor* (Fregoso, 1993, p. 123).

9. Turner and Surace's (1956) account of this event makes no mention of the Sleepy Lagoon murder case.

10. See garcia (1999) on the importance of dances and dance halls as cinematic referents for Chicano youth culture. In *Mi Familia, Mi Vida Loca, Zoot Suit* and *La Bamba* the dance hall is presented as a public site where Chicanos and Chicanas negotiate their 'gender, generational, and ethnic identities' (p. 317).

11. The film was criticized for its staginess (Sterritt, 1982), sketchy narrative (Keneas, 1982), diluted historicism, objectification of women, its presentation of Chicanos and Chicanas as passive agents of history, and its 'privileging of "white saviors"' (Fregoso, 1993, p. 24).

12. In the 1960s, as noted in Chapter 1, there was a cycle of urban Hispanic gang films, which included *West Side Story* (1961). This cycle is repeated in the 1990s, in part because, as Davis (1990) observes, 'Hollywood is eager to mine Los Angeles barrios and ghettos for every last lurid image of self-destruction and community holocaust' (p. 87; also quoted in Fregoso, 1993, pp. 124–125).

13. *Warriors* is a story about a Coney Island gang that runs a 'murderous gauntlet of rival gangs to get home from the Bronx' (Gelmis, 1988). When released, life seemed to mirror art, for gangs came to the theatres, property was damaged, there were brawls, and 'at least three killings' (Gelmis, 1988).

14. It is useful to contrast the prison scenes in the two films. *Zoot Suit* presents prison cells as open, airy spaces, as sets for dialogue and song. In *American Me* the prison is a harsh, cold, gray metallic place. Chico State Prison, the site of the filming, had to be repainted to give it the proper feel because it looked too good to be a prison (Fregoso, 1993, p. 130).

15. Hackford's previous films include *La Bamba, White Nights, An Officer and a Gentleman, Everybody's All-American.*

16. The Mafia genre will not go away, as evidenced by such recent TV series as *Falcone* and *The Sopranos* as well as Martin Scorsese's *GoodFellas* and *Casino*, Barry Levinson's *Bugsy*, and the Mafia comedies, which include Jonathan Demme's *Married to the Mob*, Harold Ramis's *Analyze This*, and James Caan playing the head of a Mafia family in *Mickey Blue Eyes* (see Weinraub, 2000).

17. Of course Kay, Michael's wife, will have none of this. In each of the films she calls Michael a killer and a thief. Jameson (1990, p. 34) suggests that the Mafia material in the first film connects the figure of the aging patriarch to the pursuit of legitimate business investments. By the end of the second film Michael has become a legitimate businessman. The second film merges American business with American imperialism and the Cuban Revolution. The third film forges a link with Rome and the new international economy. The series is about this tension between family and the family's business. Michael repeatedly shuts Kay out of the business. The last shot of the first film dramatically underscores this exclusion. Kay is at the end of the hallway, looking into Michael's inner chambers. The door is slowly closed, and she is left in the darkness.

18. Boyd (1997) argues that the *Godfather* films 'are a brilliant example of a Marxist-influenced revisionist history, functioning as an astute treatise on ethnicity, assimilation and the relevance of political economy to the understanding of twentieth-century American history' (p. 85).

19. These films were read by some as a 'glorification of the parasitic, hustling milieu of the black urban underworld' (Guerrero, 1993a, p. 96). For commentary on John Singleton's remake of *Shaft* starring Samuel L. Jackson, see Mitchell (2000).

20. Recall Nino's death in *New Jack City*; see also *King of New York* (1990), and *Sugar Hill* (1994).

7

Spike's Place

> It [*Clockers*] will be the final movie of its sort [hood]. ... It was our intention to be the final nail in the coffin. ... It's dead! It's over! Move on! I loved *Boyz N the Hood* and *Menace II Society*, but ... the genre is at its end now. (Spike Lee quoted in Weinraub, 1995, p. B1)
>
> It [*Clockers*] is the 'hood' movie to end all hood movies. (Taubin, 1995b)
>
> You are sellin' your own people death. (Tyrone's mother to Strike in *Clockers*)
>
> And this ain't no TV movie violence bullshit neither. This stuff out here is real. Real guns kill you dead. (Strike to Tyrone in *Clockers*)

Spike Lee's *Clockers* (1995)[1] ends the black filmmaker cycle of ghetto-action-drug-hood movies. Somehow this seems fitting. Lee's 1989 *Do the Right Thing* launched a generation of young black filmmakers.[2] Singleton, the Hughes brothers, and others would use the apparatuses of cinematic realism, and the resources of black youth culture and the hip hop movement, to tell stories about young black men in the hood. These were coming-of-age, didactic, social problems-based films about black male angst. They located racism, gangs, drugs, and racial violence in the urban wastelands of Reagan and Bush's post-industrial America (Watkins, 1998, p. 170).[3]

Building on the criticisms of hooks (1990, 1996), Wallace (1992), Baraka (1993), Lubiano (1997), Watkins (1998), Reid (1993, p. 108), Gray (1995, p. 52), Guerrero (1993a, pp. 140–151), Kellner (1997, pp. 76–77), Giroux (1996, p. 40), Bambara (1996, pp. 193–198), Boyd (1997, pp. 25–26); Gilroy (2000), Tate (1992), and others, I will argue that Lee's films do not offer a site of radical cinematic racial resistance.[4] Rather, his movies (like Singleton's) embody a black postnationalist essentialism (Wallace, 1992, p. 125). This essentialism is compatible with the politics of a conservative black middle class.

Baraka contends that Lee is the quintessential buppie. His texts are caricatures of 'the black revolutionary politics and art of the 1960s' (Baraka, 1993, p. 147). According to Ellis (1989), Tate, (1992), and Boyd (1997, p. 25), Lee's 'New Black Aesthetic' is clearly inherited from the Black Arts Movement of the sixties. Boyd (1997, p. 25) suggests that this new aesthetic 'shamelessly borrows' from these earlier, more radical political formations.

I will develop these arguments, through a discussion of *She's Gotta Have It* (1986), *School Daze* (1988), *Do the Right Thing* (1989), *Mo' Better Blues* (1990), *Jungle Fever* (1991), *Malcolm X* (1992), and *Get On the Bus* (1996), giving primary attention to *Do the Right Thing* and *Clockers*. I begin by examining Lee's broader cinematic project. I then locate *Do The Right Thing, Clockers*, and the hood movies within that context.

Lee's Cinematic Realism

As realistic cinematic texts, Lee asserts that his films 'Tell it like it is. ... They force America to come to grips with the problems of racism' (Lubiano, 1997, p. 101). Lee's films make race visible. He sees himself as a voice for the real, a voice that effects the realities of racism. Cinematic realism is the bedrock of his project. He establishes reality through a narrative camera that transparently invokes an authoritative sense of immediacy and authenticity (Lubiano, 1997, p. 104). Lee's realism thus discloses the truth about racism's realities. He invites his viewers to 'accept what is offered as a slice of life because the narrative contains elements of "fact"' (Lubiano, 1997, p. 105).

In this way Lee use the apparatuses of cinematic realism to make the lives of African Americans visible to white America. His films are littered with shots of graffiti painted on walls. The graffiti on Sal's pizzeria in *Do the Right Thing* states, 'Tawana told the Truth' (Lubiano, 1997, p. 105). Realism's claims to truth thus become self-evident, but whose truth is being told?

Of course realism is itself a cinematic production. When Lee says he is 'Telling it like it is' he is telling it like it is according to a cinematic and narrative logic that is deeply ideological, and embedded in the so-called 'New Black Aesthetic.' On this aesthetic, hooks (1994) observes that Lee (and Allen and Albert Hughes) refuses to 'see that while there may be aspects of fictional reality portrayed in a film that are familiar, the film is not documentary ... it is a fiction' (p. 150). Further, the purpose of the Black Aesthetic is to do 'more than tell it like it is – it's to imagine what is possible' (hooks, 1994, p. 237).

There is very little black consciousness or political activism in Lee's movies. His films restate, in elegant cinematic form, the 'place of our present' (Baraka, 1993, p. 153). His is a socio-comedic, or allegorical, realism (Baker, Jr, 1993, p. 167). It refuses the mission that defined the Black Arts Movement in the 1960s, namely the project that used art as a form of cultural and political resistance.

Lubiano (1997, p. 98) contends that it may not be possible for a radical race consciousness film to earn money within the politics of Hollywood.[5] However, as Boyd (1997) observes, Lee and the filmmakers in the current era have successfully traded on the commodity status of a new, less radical, more middle class Blackness. 'This has allowed them to infiltrate mainstream white institutions while still providing some sense of an African American aesthetic' (pp. 25–26). In this way, paradoxically, these films have 'contributed to ... the end of what Stuart Hall calls the essential black subject' (Gray, 1995, p. 52).

The claim for being radical lies at the level of Lee's cinematic politics. His highly individualized style foregrounds his presence in the text. (He acts in nearly every one of his films.) His films are filled with multiple narrative lines and plots. His stories are open-ended (Watkins, 1998, pp. 161–162). Visually, he uses jump-cuts, tilted camera angles, fluid crane shots, and extreme close-ups. Actors speak directly to the audience (Reid, 1993, p. 103). While his stories are reworked for a white and black middle-class audience, they are grounded in black cultural imagery, codes, and idioms (Reid, 1993, p. 104; Baker, Jr, 1993, pp. 170–171). His musical scores use contemporary black jazz artists (Terence Blanchard,

Bill Lee, Branford Marsalis Quartet). Quotations from Zora Neale Hurston open *She's Gotta Have It*. The mural in Nola's loft refers to 'Malcolm X, Bob Marley, the liberation struggle in South Africa, and recent racial killings of black New Yorkers' (Reid, 1993, p. 97).

Lee's films self-consciously foreground a racial politics that attempts to force white America to recognize the problems of race (Lubiano, 1997, p. 101). At the same time, Lee has been at the forefront in bringing more blacks into the American film industry. His typically all-black films create a hermetic space, or worlds of blackness that 'seem entirely removed from the dominant White culture' (Baker, 1993, p. 156). In these spaces he examines the subordinate status of African Americans within the worlds of dominant white capitalism (Watkins, 1998, p. 139; Shohat, 1991, p. 240).

In his fifteeen feature films, to date[6] Lee explores the ideological conflicts between light- and dark-skinned African Americans, as well as between middle- and working-class blacks, black hip hop culture, black urban poverty, and drug addiction. He consistently examines the tensions, hierarchies, and ambiguities that operate in black culture, repeatedly returning to the multiple ways in which gendered blackness is socially constructed and given meaning (Watkins, 1998, p. 146).

In making his version of the black world visible, Lee explores a handful of themes. Always interpreted from the black, male, heterosexual perspective, these themes include: black sexuality, the sexually active, independent black woman, interracial sexual relations (*She's Gotta Have It, Jungle Fever*); identity politics and the fraternity–sorority system on an all-black college campus (*School Daze*); race politics, interracial group conflict, black middle-class family life (*Do The Right Thing, Jungle Fever, Crooklyn*); the world of African-American jazz (*Mo' Better Blues*); black male politics (*School Daze, Get On the Bus*); sports and the black athlete (*He Got Game*); Jewish, Italian, and black community relationships (*Do the Right Thing, Mo' Better Blues, Summer of Sam*); black history (*Malcolm X, Four Little Girls*); gangs, the hood, drug addiction, and inner-city violence (*Clockers*).

From this film cycle, the following themes are apparent. Lee is opposed to miscegenation, is anti-gay, endorses a compulsory heterosexual identity politics, regards blackness not as a political category, but as a signifier of cultural identity, and does not imagine a new multicultural America based on a new black militancy (Marble, 1992, p. 302). Nonetheless, it is also clear that Lee regards himself as a major cinematic spokesperson for black America.[7]

But Lee's Afrocentric aesthetic is not the radical or militant aesthetic of the Black Arts Movement of the 1960s and 1970s (Baraka, 1993). His is a conservative aesthetic that appears radical. Culturally, Lee's films reproduce a neo-nationalistic, essentializing masculinist gender and identity politics. Such moves undermine his claim to be a politically radical or progressive filmmaker (Lubiano, 1997, p. 108). Lee's films reproduce long-standing black stereotypes. The problems of race are reduced to liberal solutions, solutions that are remarkably conservative; namely more jobs, hard work, no drugs, no guns, and less prejudice (hooks, 1989, pp. 177–178). No black power movement here; blacks just need to stay in their place, and aspire to the goals of the black middle class. This is a neo-nationalism about race, not class or gender.

Sex and Class in Spike's Place

Bambara (1996, p. 193) observes that when the images of women in Lee's films are 'programmed together, a disturbing picture emerges.' Lee's gender politics are compulsively patriarchal, heterosexual, homophobic, and misogynist. Posters of naked women are nailed to the wall in the barbershop in the short film, *Joe's Bed-Stuy Barbershop*. These same posters reappear in *Mo' Better Blues*. In *School Daze* (*SD*), a male character speaks of 'pussy,' and another says 'Meow.' Nola is raped in *She's Gotta Have It* (*SGHI*), as is Jane in *SD*.

Lee (1988) says of these forced-sex scenes: 'It's a sexual act that transforms things.... In *She's Gotta Have It*, is Jamie's rape of Nola, and in *School Daze* it's ... Dap finding out that Julian [Jane's lover] coerced Jane into going to bed with Half Pint' (p. 113; also quoted in Reid, 1993, p. 95). The use of rape as a narrative device for moving the story forward can only be judged as misogynist.[8] If this is how it is in black male sexual culture, then Lee's challenge is to not reproduce the rape narrative. Rather his challenge is to imagine how it might be different; how a new, non-violent, loving sexual politics might be lived into existence.

Homophobia is invoked with the phrase 'Puerto Rican cocksuckers' in *Do the Right Thing* (*DRT*), the 'fairy' and Ritchie characters in *Summer of Sam*, the declaration by Errol, the killer in the last stages of AIDS in *Clockers*, 'I ain't no homo-sexual!,' and the negative treatment of Opal, Nola's lesbian friend in *SGHI*. Real men, in *SD*, are not virgins, and not fags; being sexual is a 'dick-thing.' In *DRT* and *SGHI* women are presented as the constant subjects of the male erotic gaze. While men may have multiple lovers, women cannot. Thus Nola, the woman with three lovers (Jamie, Mars, Greer) in *SGHI*, is called a freak by the men in her life. But Mars qualifies the use of this term: 'All men want freaks in bed, we just don't want 'em for a wife.'

Nola arouses masochistic and insatiable male sexual fantasies. She is the sexual other who cannot be contained or controlled, and 'fifteen bogus men offer their sex to her' (Reid, 1993, p. 98). She is defined solely through her sexuality, which is rooted in her body, but defined in male, heterosexual terms. She is dependent on men for her sexual definitions of self (Reid, 1993, p. 97). She is not a sexually independent black female protagonist (Reid, 1993, p. 98).

SGHI is a depressing, denigrating portrait of black women (hooks, 1996, p. 235). We share Nola's despair when, at the end of the rape scene, Jamie asks, 'Whose pussy is this?' and she answers, 'It's yours.'

Lee demonizes uncontrolled female sexuality. Sexually independent women are presented as threats to the black male heterosexual identity (Wallace, 1992, p. 129). Thus Flipper reacts angrily in *Jungle Fever* when Vivian, Gator's crack addict girl-friend, states 'I'll suck your dick for $5.' He turns to his young daughter, 'Don't you ever do anything like that!' (He later calls Vivian a whore.) Lee equates oral sex with prostitution, gay sexuality, and AIDS. More broadly, however, oral sex is connected to a 'vast range of illicit sexual practices and psychosexual developments beyond the pale of compulsory heterosexuality' (Wallace, 1992, p. 129). This includes such 'perverse passions as interracial sex [*Jungle Fever*] and drug addiction' (Wallace, 1992, p. 129).

Lee, according to hooks (1994, pp. 158–159), exploits the culture's voyeuristic obsession with interracial sex. Interracial romances are treated in some detail in *Jungle Fever* and *Malcolm X*, but Lee appears 'Unwilling and possibly unable to imagine that any bond between a white woman and a black man could be based on ties other than pathological ones' (p. 159). Lee seems unable to have much 'sympathy for, or insight into ... women' (Kassabian, 1991, p. 259). Every black female in *DRT*, for example, 'whether she be mother, daughter, or sister, is constructed at some point as a sex object' (hooks, 1989, p. 182; also quoted in Reid, 1993, p. 105). Jones (1993) is even harsher: 'the Black women in Lee's [films] ... embody traditional "female" concerns, monogamy and physical appearance ... in stark contrast to the *real* issues faced by the men in [his] films' (p. 254, italics in original).

And so it is for *School Daze*, which also, as noted above, has its rape scene. In this film, as he does in *Jungle Fever*, Lee uses dark and light skin color as a method of coding race and sexuality. He reproduces the stereotype that connects uncontrolled (or wild) female sexuality with darker skin, and controlled, civilized sexuality with whiteness (Wallace, 1992, p. 130; Lubiano, 1997, p. 116). In *SD* the Jigaboos are black women with Afro hairstyles. The Jigaboos are in conflict with the Wannabees, light-complexioned black women who have straight hair. 'The Wannabees wanna be White, and Jigaboos wanna be "wannabees" ... don't nobody wanna be Black' (Baraka, 1993, p. 148).

A complex identity and gender politics is played out within this color aesthetic. The Militant is militant because he hates light-skinned persons. The women establish their sexual identities through what they wear, their eye color, their make-up, and whether or not they straighten their hair (Lubiano, 1997, p. 116). The film ends on a curious and superficially radical note, calling for everyone to 'Wake Up.' But the charge seems aimed more for the audience than to the *Animal House* characters who live in this black college world (Baraka, 1993, p. 148).

The film's homophobia blends into its negative treatment of women. It reproduces, at this level, Robert Park's assertion that 'the Negro is the lady of the races' (1950b, p. 280; quoted in Lubiano, 1997, p. 116). Yet, as Lubiano observes (1997, p. 116), Lee shows black men that they can counter this feminist/gay impression by being 'real' men, by being straight, black, and powerfully sexual.[9]

Mo' Better Blues adds anti-Semitism to the mix of negative stereotypes that Lee presents in his films. The brothers Moe and Josh who own the club where Bleek plays 'parade the worst stereotypes of "New York Jews." They are cheap, money-grubbing, brash, loud and offensive' (Kassabian, 1991, p. 259). Kassabian (1991) observes that 'Their characterization ... is beneath the dignity of further comment' (p. 259).[10]

Baraka (1993) suggests that the 'essential centers of Spike's films are always in contradiction to the metaphor of his announced themes' (p. 152). So *School Daze* is about blackness and skin color and identity politics, not about black colleges and the value of higher education in the black community. And *She's Gotta Have It* is about black men and their sexual identities. Just as *Jungle Fever* is about the inability of the black or white family to accept its own pathologies, including drug addiction and violence.

Thus Lee's films skim the surface of the problems they take up, seldom registering new understandings or criticisms of race, gender, and oppression in the black community today. The structures of racism, gender, sexuality, and class conflict in the end are left unanalyzed (Baraka, 1993, p. 153).

Do the Right Thing

Little new can be written about *DRT*, which is Lee's third feature film (see hooks, 1990, pp. 173–184; Baraka, 1993, pp. 148–149; Baker, Jr, 1993, pp. 168–175; Watkins, 1998, pp. 157–169; as well as Reid, 1997a, 1993, pp. 100–108; Denzin, 1991a, pp. 125–136; Bogle, 1994, pp. 318–323; Guerrero, 1993a, pp. 148–155; Kellner, 1997).[11] In *DRT* Mars (he of two earlier lives, one with Michael Jordan,[12] the other in *SGHI*) becomes Mookie. The college student is now a messenger and delivery man for the white bourgeoisie. The militant is 'bugged out' and the black scholar is named Smiley. He mumbles and stutters. He 'is a spastic who sells pictures of Malcolm and Dr King' (Baraka, 1993, p. 149). As hooks (1990) observes, 'it is bitterly ironic that the two black leaders whose images are sold in the community were highly educated, articulate critical thinkers, yet the person who attempts to keep their memory alive … is inarticulate' (p. 179). Paradoxically, the mainstream political character is Da Mayor, a disillusioned alcoholic. His advice to Mookie is 'Do the Right Thing.' It is never clear what this is.

The film was inspired by the Howard Beach killings in Queens in December 1986. Michael Griffith, an African American, was fatally beaten by 'Italian-American youths armed with baseball bats when he was leaving a pizzeria in the predominantly white Howard Beach section of Queens' (Pouzoulet, 1997, pp. 37–38; also Kellner, 1997, pp. 103–104). But nothing in the film refers directly to this episode.[13]

It is the hottest day of the year.[14] It is closing time at Sal's. Radio Raheem (Bill Nunn) walks in with his boombox blasting 'Fight the Power.' He demands that Sal put up the posters of Malcolm and Martin on the pizzeria's Wall of Fame (which only contains photos of famous Italian Americans, including Sinatra, Stallone, and De Niro). Sal (Danny Aiello) tells him to 'turn off the jungle music now!' He picks up a baseball bat and smashes the radio. Mookie tells him to stop. Raheem and Sal fight. A crowd appears. The police come. Radio Raheem is killed by the police. A race riot starts. Mookie throws a garbarge can into Sal's front window. The crowd rushes in. Smiley drops a match. Fire breaks out. Sal's pizzeria burns down.

For the militant blacks in the film, Sal's Pizzeria symbolizes the oppressive presence of white capitalism in the ghetto. Sal's refusal to place the photos of Malcolm and Martin on the walls of his establishment represents this oppression. In a symbolic ending, Smiley places the photos of Malcolm and Martin on the Wall of Fame. Thus is maintained the essential tension of the film: violence (Malcolm) versus non-violence (Martin). Ironically, these two forms of black revolutionary struggle are reduced to the location of two photographs on a wall.

159

But surely, as hooks (1989, p. 176) notes, black liberation goes beyond the question of a picture on a wall, beyond the issue of representation.

Public Enemy's rap song urges the viewer to 'Fight the Power,' but how this struggle should be carried out is never clarified (Kellner, 1997, p. 77). Mookie throws a garbage can through Sal's window, and this is the act that triggers the final violence in the film. But the next day he is paid over-time by Sal. For fighting the power, Mookie gets his job back with double pay ($500). Sal has insurance money to cover the costs of rebuilding his pizzeria. Nothing has changed.

Lee seems to suggest that Mookie has done the right thing. After all he is paid off. In this gesture Lee weakly implies that a 'violently aggressive Black energy of revolt can lead to Black economic empowerment' (Baker, 1993, p. 173). In contrast Radio Raheem challenged the members of the community to boycott the pizzeria because Sal would not post the pictures of African Americans on his Wall of Fame. The murder of Raheem suggests that Lee does not endorse the use of this classic form of protest connected to Martin Luther King. Indeed the film trivializes these forms of black struggle (Guerrero, 1993a, p. 149).

This trivialization is further accented by comparing Buggin Out and Raheem with Mookie, who is 'the film's calculating middleman, positioned between Sal and the community' (Guerrero, 1993a, p. 149). Lee reduces the film's conflict to a dispute between personalities, to personal and group bigotry, not to the larger structures of institutional racism. The futility of political action is connected to mob action, and a fleeting episode of discontent that produces Raheem's death and the torching of Sal's place (Guerrero, 1993a, p. 154). White racist patriarchal capitalism easily absorbs hits like this.

Raheem's murder trivializes the civil rights and black liberation movement. In turn, Mookie can scarcely be regarded as a leader of the non-violent masses. Baraka (1993, p. 149) observes that Mookie enters the struggle late, and appears uncommitted and alienated from the other members of the black community. For Baraka, this late entrance into the battle 'elaborates Spike's class stand with excruciating clarity! ... [His] is some kind of petit bourgeois "leadership"' (p. 149).[15]

By showing a young black male instigating violence, Lee reinforces the arguments of the New Right. Young black males are threats to law and order in America. In perpetuating this stereotype, Lee suppresses the racism of Vito and Pino, Sal's sons. By letting their hatred of blacks stand, Lee legitimates their racism. But ostensibly they do the right thing by not entering into the violence. And in the end, as the police murder a young black man, nobody comes forward to help. At the same time, the film reinforces the idea that the '"lunatic" violence erupting in "segregated" black communities finally hurts black people more than anyone else' (hooks, 1990, p. 175).

The film's messages are contradictory. Lee tells the viewer to 'Fight the Power' and 'Do The Right Thing' (Kellner, 1997, p. 77). But what is the right thing? Right for whom? Non-violence appears to be a questionable tool for social change. However, it is not clear that violence offers a viable alternative. Kellner (1997) suggests that 'one could even read the film as questioning social violence, by demonstrating that it ultimately hurts the people in the neighborhoods in which it explodes' (p. 77). In interviews Lee (1989) aligned himself with

Malcolm. He stated, 'The character I play ... is from the Malcolm X school of thought: "An eye for an eye." Fuck the turn-the-other-check shit. If we keep up that madness we'll all be dead' (p. 34; also quoted in Kellner, 1997, p. 104).

Despite its contradictions, the film,

> Better than any other film of the period ... touched on a great deal of the discontent and unexplained anger that was so much a part of urban life during the Reagan eighties. The movie says ... that race relations in America remain abysmal; that racism and ethnic tensions underlie the façade of American life. (Bogle, 1994, p. 322)

It is this façade that the hood movies of the nineties exploited. And of course, in a strange perversion of Malcolm's principles, the 'eye for an eye' school of thought would be taken to a new level in the hood films. Now young black men with automatic weapons in their hands, and driven by a warped code of violence, could establish their self-identity by murdering a member of an opposing street gang. At one level this is the legacy of *DRT*.

And this is sadly ironic, for as hooks (1990) observes, Lee understands that art is political, that film can be a medium 'to chart new political agendas without aesthetic compromise ... art can serve as a force shaping and transforming the political climate' (p. 184).

Thus Lee says to his white viewers, 'Listen, if white America has to squirm for two hours, if they're really uncomfortable watching this film, that's just too fucking bad. Because that's the way it is all the time for black people' (Lee, quoted in hooks, 1990, p. 173). But many blacks also find the film hard to watch (hooks, 1990, p. 182). This is so for many reasons, including: the use of racial stereotypes to represent black males (Sweet Dick Willie, ML, Coconut Sid); the focus on racism as prejudice; the sexist treatment of women; 'the causal treatment of a symbolic incest scene' (hooks, 1990, p. 182);[16] the fetishistic display of designer clothing and ethno-fashions (hooks, 1989, p. 177); and the treatment of black males as victims.

Clockers: Men with Guns and Drugs

There is a benign, ironic, playground-like simplicity to *DRT*. The film has no guns, drugs (except alcohol), homeboys, or drive-bys. There is no violent rap, only Public Enemy saying 'Fight the Enemy.' The enemy is white capitalist society, not the Mafia, or gang-bangers who belong to the Crips, or the Bloods. There are no prisons, no black (or brown) Godfathers, and there is little of the disturbing inter-ethnic hatred that characterizes *America History X*. Lee's violence takes the form of hate speech, epitomized when black, white, Korean, Puerto Rican, and Hispanic men hurl racial insults at one another. The burning of Sal's is an afterthought, an accident. The playful innocence of *DRT* is not present in *Clockers*, which Ebert (1998d, p. 155) calls a murder mystery.

Clockers is not a typical hood movie.[17] It does not have the brooding existential themes that mark *Boyz N the Hood, Menace II Society, Colors, Bound By Honor*, or *American Me*. This is a story about drug dealers, called clockers, because they work around the clock (Rollyson, 1996, p. 90). It is not about a drug addict (although they are present), or a young man in the hood who is being told to stay away from the violent hip hop street and drug culture. It is not a coming-of-age film, *per se*.

However, the first shots in the film's montage title sequence tell the viewer that this is a story with hood themes. The camera 'travels across a succession of grisly police photos of murder scenes – black male bodies torn apart by bullets' (Taubin, 1995b, 1995c). These bodies are 'sprawled awkwardly on the pavement, their blood staining the concrete, they seem to have been halted in mid-flight, astonished by the fact of their sudden death' (Ebert, 1998d, p. 154). This credit sequence segues into a scene with four black teenagers (clockers) rapping about rap and rap performers on the benches in front of the projects. The all too aliveness of these young men stands in stark contrast to the credit sequence's 'corpses which are so graphically dead' (Bradley, 1995, p. 29).

This scene quickly turns into a police shakedown. A squad car shrieks to a halt. Police officers accost the young men ('What are ya carrying?'; 'Where's the vials man?'; 'Open your fuckin' mouth man, lift up your tongue'; 'Take off your fuckin' pants, or whatever you call 'em'; 'Spread your butt cheeks man, spread 'em, lets go'; 'Pull up your pants bitch'). A mother watches this scene from a fourth-floor apartment window. The police car drives off, and the young men are left with their pants down around their knees. Welcome to Strike's world.

This is primarily a story about two people, Rocco Klein (Harvey Keitel), a street-weary cop, and Strike (Ronnie Dunham), the key clocker. Strike deals drugs, but he does not take them. Strike has his own crew of dealers who live in Brooklyn. Strike works for Rodney, the neighborhood drug czar. The benches are where Strike and his crew meet. Still a teenager, Strike is trapped in a world he wants no part of, the world of crime, drugs, dealing, and violence. His situation is symbolized by his bleeding ulcer.

Ebert (1998d) is right. This is a murder mystery, and it is told in four acts. In Act One the viewer is taken into Strike's world. In Act Two a murder occurs. In Act Three, the hunt for the murderer unfolds. Rocco believes that Strike did it. The narrative lurches forward, through a series of confrontational scenes between the hunter (Rocco) and the hunted (Strike). In Act Four, a second murder occurs, the murderers are revealed, and the story ends with Strike leaving town.

Act One: 'I Love Trains'

Strike knows his life is out of control, but he does not know how to change it. Lee's camera, with 'its erratic rhythms and circular patterns' (Taubin, 1995b), brilliantly catches the confining claustrophobic tensions in Strike's world. Everything he encounters seems to increase his sense of being confined, like a bug under a bell jar. Incessant rap music pounds against his ears. He is constantly hassled by the police, other dealers, and users. Twice he is symbolically raped: once by the police, once by Rodney. He is battered by a protective mother, stomped by a black housing cop. Everywhere he turns people seem to be watching him. He seeks escape inside his apartment, where his Lionel electric trains run around and around on a single track (Taubin, 1995b). Strike is in love with trains. ('I don't like sports. I like trains.') He has videos of trains, recordings that tell their names and histories. He dreams of a world beyond the projects. His trains will take him away from that world; they 'represent an open track out of clocking into freedom' (Ebert, 1998d, p. 155; also Rollyson, 1996, p. 91).

Rodney mentors Strike, and Strike mentors 12-year-old Tyrone. Tyrone's mother is mad at Strike for corrupting her son ('You all nothing but good for nothin' death dealin' scum'). André the Giant is a cop who warns Strike:

> I been lookin' out for you since you was a little boy. You mess with that little boy Tyrone, I gonna mess you up so much, you wish I killed you ... you don't have to live like this. There's more than just those projects out there. Don't you wanta go somewhere you never been before? I mean you love trains, but you've only ridden the subway.

Strike's mother rejects him and his life style. In contrast she has only praise for her other son, Victor, a driven man, who holds down two jobs, is happily married, and is the father of two young children.

Act Two: The Murder

Rodney tells Strike that he can advance his career by killing Darryl Adams, a dishonest drug dealer ('Nigger stealin' from me') who is also the night manager at Ahab's, a fast-food restaurant and market. Rodney tells Strike:

> You're like my son. I had a dream last night. I'm standin' in the desert with all my kids. They're laid out like they're my army. God came up and pointed to you and said, 'This one's going to be your soul and staff.' God said that. Strike, you really want off the benches, you deal with Darryl for me.

Strike stands outside Ahab's with a gun, but is unable to approach Darryl. He runs into Victor in a bar and tells him he needs a man murdered. Victor is drunk, angry, and depressed, but tells Strike he has a friend who can take care of Darryl. Strike walks away and confronts Darryl. In the next scene Strike is part of a crowd, looking at the corpse.

The police take control of the situation. (Spike Lee is present as a by-stander, dressed as a utility repair man.)

> Cop: Welcome to the show that never ends ... we got a black male, dead man, neighborhood says there was four shots fired, shooter does a Carl Lewis.

The police roll the body over. Darryl's head, oozing blood, sticks to the concrete street.

> Cop: Live by the gun, die by the gun.
> Rocco: Kid had brains, bing, bing, bing, ricochet rabbit. ... Another stain on the sidewalk.

Act Three: The Hunt

In the next scene Victor confesses to the shooting, telling Rocco it was in self-defense. 'This guy flexed on me, just jumped out of nowhere. I shot him.' Rocco doesn't believe Victor.

> Rocco: Where'd you carry the gun? Were you there [Ahab's] before, with your kids?
> Victor: My two kids, I barely see my two kids. I'm always working. When I come home I'm exhausted. Have you ever come home so tired, you hated the sound of your own kids cryin'? Your own flesh and blood. My wife says, so quit a job. You got two. ... I'm tryin' man. I'm really tryin'. I'm tryin' to move us out of the projects.
> Rocco: Victor, 'If you did pull the trigger, there has to be a reasonable answer, other than what you've told me here. Why would Darryl, the night manager of Ahab's, try to rob you in his own parkin' lot? I think there had to be somethin' personal.
> Victor: It was self-defense.

Rocco beliefs Strike is the murderer, and that Victor is covering for him. He tells his partner Mazilli, 'This confession sounds like horseshit.' Mazilli disagrees, 'Why would Victor willingly go to prison to protect his brother? He got religion, comes in, makes a confession.... Give it up! We got the shooter.' But Rocco will not let it go. He confronts Strike, 'I'm not happy about this. Your brother fessed up ... what do you think happened? Did you know Darryl Adams? ... You clockin? How long you been clockin'?'

Rocco's men harrass Strike. They stop him on the street, and force him up against a wall, arms outstretched: 'Strike my man, this is a new day.... Law and order, a new budget. Crack down on drugs and crime, niggers and spics.'

Strike seeks solace with his trains. He shows Tyrone his train set, which is laid out in one large room in his apartment:

> Look, Lionel trains, they was built in the early 1900s. They ran on dry cell batteries. World War Two the motherfuckers started gettin' electricity. They made new ones. [*The train passes a sign with a large gun in the corner that reads 'No More Packing.'*]

Like a good mentor, Strike next shows Tyrone how to cut and separate cocaine:

> *Strike:* If I ever see or hear about you messing with this stuff man.... I'll put a cap in your ass. [*He gets a gun from beneath his bed mattress and points it at Tyrone.*] And this ain't no TV movie violence bullshit neither. This stuff out here is real. Real guns kill you dead.... I keeps this for all those ill niggers out there, like Errol. That brother's crazy.... If he ever creep up on me I gonna get his ass, and you better be prepared to do the same.... Listen, any flash shit you want in the world, this how you get it, pumping this white shit right here, hustlin' and don't forget that shit neither. You smart, answer me this, boss buys him a key for $22,000 dollars cuts it up into thirty-five $10 bottles, boss takes 60 percent, $17,000 dollars profit, leavin' up $7,000, 50 percent of which is mine. How much for me?'
>
> *Tyrone:* 3500.
>
> *Strike:* My man, keep hittin' them books. If I ever catch you playin' hookie, I put a cap in your ass.

Braced again by Rocco, Strike collapses from his bleeding ulcer and is hospitalized. Rodney picks him up as he leaves the hospital:

> What, you and homicide fuck buddies now? ... We got another big order comin' in. God created anything better than crack cocaine, he kept that shit for himself. I mean that shit is like truth serum, it will truly expose who you are ... I don't never want to hear about you usin' that shit.

(The screen moves back and forth between shots of youth and adults buying and smoking crack cocaine, and shots of Strike with his train set, staring out of the window.)

Rocco's men increase their surveillance of the drug scene in Strike's neighborhood. Five white yuppie youths in a silver Mercedes Benz, with Connecticut plates, are placing their order outside Ahab's. They are confronted by a white policeman:

> What's up boys? Hey, nice car you got. Whatcha come down from Connecticut to buy some hamburgers and malts? Buy anything else today? You like soul food? You like to wear lipstick? You like skirts? You ever suck a black man's dick? Big, sixteen inch tall baby? Cause if I toss this car and I find any drugs I got twelve baboons in a cage gonna be callin' you boys Mary all night long. Whose got the drugs? Give 'em up now.

Rocco picks up Strike and drives him to the precinct station. In an exercise in hate speech, they hurl the following words back and forth at one another:

> *Rocco:* I know you did it! You're a coldblooded, evil, junkyard nigger. ... You're nothin' but a cold fuckin' fart.
>
> *Strike:* You don't know nothin' about me. You're nothin' but a racist ass, nigger-hatin' cop.

Rocco: I read you like a Marvel fuckin' comic book. I been inside your fuckin' pea-sized brain twenty fuckin' years. You don't play me. I play you.

Rodney watches this scene. He gives Strike a ride away from the station. In the front seat of his car he forces a gun into Strike's mouth:

If I ever hear about you talkin' to that homocide one more time, that Rocco mother-fucker ... if I hear my name come up at all, I'll know it was you and I'm gonna kill you. Do you understand me? Now get your motherfuckin' ass out of my car.

Act Four: Leaving Town

As Rocco and Mazilli are picking up Rodney on a warrant, Strike is preparing to leave town. Rocco tells Rodney that Strike served him up. In a note to his landlord, Strike writes, 'Dear Mr Herman Brown, I had to leave suddenly. If my little brother swings by, he can have my train set.' While packing, he discovers that his gun is missing. He stops and gives Victor's wife $5000 for bail. She tells him he needs to talk to his mother. Rocco stops Strike and tells him, 'Rodney makes bail tomorrow. He believes you turned him in. Do me a favor and tell me what really happened.'

The clockers turn against Strike, 'You fuckin' snitch. You ratted on Rodney!' Rodney calls Errol from jail, 'Strike put me here. You know what you gotta do.' Strike visits his mother, who is sleeping. He softly kisses her and leaves.

Errol comes after Strike with a gun. Tyrone sees Errol before Strike does. Tyrone pulls out the gun he has borrowed from Strike (shades of Caine and Anthony from *Menace II Society*) and kills Errol.

André begs Rocco to let Tyrone go. Rocco speaks to Tyrone:

You did wrong, you know that. You were scared. You get straight A's. You're smart. Don't they call you white boy. All you wanta do is do the right thing. So you get a gun to protect yourself and your mother. So there you are ridin' your bike, but you got the gun, it's for protection. All of a sudden there's Errol, the stone killer standin' right in front of you ... you see him reaching for a gun, stuck in his waist, you know he is gonna get you. You never fired that gun before. You're scared. There's no time to think, his finger is on the trigger. Boom boom, The gun just appeared in your hand. That's what happened and if I ask you what happened, when I turn the tape recorder on, you're gonna tell me that's what happened. Now where did you find the gun?

Tyrone: In the bushes near my building ... I, I, I borrowed it by accident from Strike. I was tryin' to give it back to him, but he doesn't talk to me anymore.

In front of a crowd, which includes Strike's mother, true to his promise, André kicks and stomps Strike for messing with Tyrone:

André: You ruined that boy's life, you fuckin' parasite! It's motherfuckers like you that mugged Rosa Parks.

Strike: Who's Rosa Parks?

André: You stupid, ignorant motherfucker. You're done with these streets, done with this project, done with New York. If I ever see you again I'll kill you.

Rodney comes after Strike, who runs back to the police station, where Rocco blames him for what Tyrone did: 'He did it for you. He was protecting you. Now he's a 12-year-old murderer.... You tell me how Rodney pressured you into cappin' Darryl Adams. Tell me the truth' (On the split screen there is a shot of Darryl firing a gun at Victor.) Strike's mother enters the room:

If you don't get your hands off my son, you better. Victor called me from the bar [*shot of Victor on the phone, 'Look, I'm sick and tired, somebody's gotta pay'*]. He came back in the house an hour later, crying, 'I shot somebody … it was like somebody else was pullin' the trigger' [*shot of Victor shooting Darryl*]. That's what happened. What is going to happen to my son?

Strike: [*To mother*] Did you get the money from Sharon [Victor's wife]?

Mother: [*Throwing the money in his face*] My son Victor said it was self-defense. Believe him!

Strike's world is collapsing. Sledge-hammer in hand, Rodney shatters all the glass in Strike's car. (In big letters, Mazilli writes 'YOU IS DEAD' on the side of the car.)

Rocco: So where you wanta live Ronnie?

Strike: I don't know. You tell me.

Rocco: We's going to the Port Authority Bus Terminal.

Strike: Take me to Penn Station.… Look, Rocco, before I get out man just answer me this one question. Why were you so gung ho about all this shit man? Most cops, brothers killin' other brothers, no big thing. What made you care about me, Victor, Darryl Adams, Tyrone?

Rocco: If I ever see you again, I'll book you on charges of criminal solicitation, and conspiracy to commit murder. I'll let André beat you down again. I'll pick up Rodney on the same charges and I'll make sure you two share the same cell. Same fuckin' bed. Do you understand me clearly?

Strike: Ya, I understand you clearly. I just wanta say thank you. You know for gettin' me out of town [*a beeper goes off*]. That ain't mine man. I stopped doin' that.

As Strike exits the car, a black man in a suit, white shirt, and bow tie comes near Rocco's car, shouting, 'Get your copy of *Final Call*.' He holds the newspaper up to the car window. The headlines read, 'Justice in Black and White.'

The camera turns to Victor leaving the police station, where he is met and embraced by his wife, mother, and sons. The screen fills with a shot of a dead black man on the benches, blood running from his head, a gun in his hand.

Mazilli: Another stain on the sidewalk.

Cop 1: They should blow these projects to Timbukto.

Cop 2: Why bother, they kill each other anyway, one of those self-cleaning ovens.

Mazilli walks across the street, past Spike Lee, as the utility repair man. Lee is drinking a quart of beer ('That kid looks like he got shot up').

In a final sequence Tyrone is playing with Strike's train set, talking to his mother. He is repeating Strike's story about the history of trains: 'When trains ran on batteries, you know, and after World War II, right, when people started gettin' electricity in their houses they made these.'

Lee segues from the electric train set to a real train, showing Strike gazing out of a train window as it crosses a high plains Western desert landscape, passing a sign that reads 'NO MORE Packing.' A piano softly plays in the background as the train glides over its tracks. The afternoon sun fills the coach with amber light. And Strike's face, cupped between his hands, shares the screen with the white glow of the sunset reflected through the train window.

Reading the Film: The Critics' Response

According to the *New York Times* (2000), 30,000 Americans die annually by gunfire, including 4000 children and teenagers. There are more than 190 million firearms in civilian hands, about 65 million are handguns. Lee wants the guns to go.

In Lee's world 'there are no positive choices for black men born into the underclass' (Taubin, 1995c; also Giroux, 1996, p. 44). This is his didactic message. There is no escape. Young black men must stop killing one another. Black on black crime must stop. The young men in this world are practicing genocide on themselves, and cheap guns are the cause. Drugs, *per se*, are not the issue. The clockers don't use drugs. Drugs are a way of life, a way to make money, though death is a cost of doing business (Ebert, 1998d, p. 155).

The film's colorful, garish exterior street scenes and dark, gritty interiors have the 'texture of oversaturated 16mm Kodachrome' (Taubin, 1995c). These high color intensities give the film an expressive, jarring surrealistic visual intimacy. It is as if its colors are too vivid. They are at once desolate and hallucinatory. This is Lee's intention, to place the viewer inside Strike's visual world, to let us get inside his skin, make us feel the agony of his experience.

The critics were generally favorable, praising Lee's bold, naturalistic narrative for its brooding, unsettling quality (Turan, 1995a; Sterritt, 1995; Bradley, 1995, p. 29). Sterritt (1995) argued that Lee was finally taking up problems that can no longer be ignored, namely the destructive world of crack-cocaine and its effects on African-American neighborhoods and families. Pawelczak (1995) observed that Lee's film is the visual equivalent of rap, that it has rap's flamboyance and rawness, the buzz of street slang, and hyperactive visuals, although the streets are clean, 'the urban ubiquity of drug litter is absent ... there are no vials, no needles' (Bradley, 1995, p. 32).

According to Bradley (1995, p. 32) this absence weakens the film's impact, reinforcing the impression that Lee's social vision has tinges of what Paul Gilroy (quoted in Bradley, 1995, p. 32) calls, 'brownstone pastorale.' Lee is angry because black youth culture has no historical memory. Strike asks 'Who's Rosa Parks?' At the same time, the larger socio-historical context is missing in the film, including the connections to the Mafia (Pawelczak, 1995). (This theme was not present in Price's original novel, which focused primarily on the world of those at the bottom of the drug hierarchy.) Lee was also praised for showing how the cynical, dark world of the racist cops psychologically collides with the world of young black children growing up in the ghetto (Turan, 1995a).

It is hard to identify with any of Lee's characters. I feel distance from Strike, perhaps even pity, as he gazes out of the train window. I worry about Tyrone, who is now deep into Strike's fantasy world of trains. In the end I am drawn to Strike's mother, who pleads Victor's case. I rejoice as Victor is reunited with his wife, mother, and sons outside the Halls of Correction. With Rocco I feel only pity, but, curiously, I share Rodney's anger at Strike as he destroys Strike's car.

Lee's representations of white racism are not attractive. He presents the white police as unfeeling men who have little, if any, respect for black youth and their place in the black community. A murder is just another blood-stain on the sidewalk. The projects are self-cleaning ovens – shades of Nazi racism. Black men in jail engage in homosexual rape and they love young white boys.

Lee vividly captures Strike's world, and its scenes of harassment and inter-rogation, the racist slurs, profanity, 'the streams of vituperation and tirade' (Denby, 1995). At this level Lee sets himself against a black culture that has become too accepting of violence, guns, and dead young men lying in the street. He is relentless in the delivery of the message, 'No More Packing – no more guns' (Denby, 1995), but this works against the narrative. Lee wants it both ways. He wants to send a moral message while maintaining emotional distance from his subject matter (Turan, 1995a). And the moral message is dubious. Rocco tells Strike to get out of town. Ebert (1985d) asks, 'Is that the answer? That the infection of drugs and guns is so deep that the only sane action is to get out of town?' (p. 155).

The Oliver Stone-like moralizing is off-putting (Mathews, 1995b). In the end the polemicist trips up the dramatist when he tries to tie up all the loose ends in this weak murder-mystery (Ansen, 1995; Taubin, 1995b). 'It's an opera without a tragic ending' (Schickel, 1995). When the mystery is taken away, this wants to be, as Taubin (1995b) argues, the 'Hood movie to end all hood movies.' It may not be that, but it effectively captures the prison-house of racism that circulates every day in the hoods and barrios of black and brown America.

Conclusions

In the end no one can dispute the fact that Lee's cinematic apparatus works. He is a gifted filmmaker, with an eye for nuance, the vernacular, the everyday, black and white popular culture, and the multiple spaces that make up the black public sphere.[18] Most troubling, as argued above, are his politics. Lee merges the new black aesthetic with a non-hegemonic black neo-nationalism. This is not a nationalism based on radical political practice, or a call for cultural resistance. Through the skillful cinematic use of black idiom, popular music, and fashion, Lee's film evokes a vernacular neo-nationalism. This has the effect of creating a feeling of momentary empowerment, an empowerment that affirms black experience in the present (hooks, 1990, p. 178). But this is a non-critical nationalism. Lee never directly engages the world of his characters; they function as one-dimensional archetypes (hooks, 1990, pp. 178–179). Indeed, as Baraka (1993, 153) argues, his men and women lack both agency and the will, or desire, to resist (also hooks, 1989, p. 179).

Watkins (1998, p. 135) disputes these criticisms, arguing that Lee's cultural productions[19] invoke race pride ('Stay black!'), while successfully blending popular culture resistance and identity politics. According to Watkins, Lee appropriates 'resources from the dominant culture industry to establish a base … from which to launch commodities … that vigorously enunciate what Cornel West characterizes as the "new cultural politics of difference"' (p. 135). For West (1990), this politics of difference is a strategy that turns the cultural worker into a critical organic catalyst. This is a 'person who stays attuned to the best of what the mainstream has to offer … yet maintains a grounding in affirmative and enabling subcultures of criticism' (p. 33). West calls for prophetic critics and artists of color to be 'exemplars of what it means to be intellectual freedom fighters' (p. 33). These are cultural workers who are simultaneously located within the mainstream, while being 'clearly aligned with groups who vow to keep alive potent traditions of critique and resistance' (p. 33).

Watkins contends that Lee is such a worker, noting that he has openly criticized the racial politics of Hollywood, while demanding that black filmmakers have greater creative control of their films. Watkins further asserts that Lee's representational strategies and 'directorial signature ... [show how] ... black American filmmaking can be deployed to engage, it not occasionally oppose, competing discourses about race and the culture wars that drive the social and political struggles of the period' (p. 136).

Is this enough? One wonders. Kellner (1997) observes that Lee's politics of identity ... works primarily to indict racism and to promote the interests of black identity and pride, channeled largely through cultural style' (p. 100). Still, Kellner notes that Lee's films do attack 'at least some of the many forms of sex, race gender and class oppression. While they might not ultimately provide models of a "counterhegemonic cinema" ... they provide some engaging and provocative cinematic interventions that are far superior to the crass genre spectacles of the Hollywood cinema' (p. 100).

Is this enough? Baker (1993) compares Lee to the grandfather in Ralph Ellison's novel *Invisible Man*. The grandfather talks about the 'Black man living with his "head in the lion's mouth" and acting as a "spy in the enemy's camp" in order to make a successful way out of "noway" in America' (p. 174). In some senses, Lee is like Ellison's grandfather, only he is getting '"paid in full" for reporting decisively from the inside on the straight skinny of racism and domestic colonialism in these United States' (p. 174). But in his way, and one wishes his reports were more militant, and more decisive.

Notes

1. *Clockers* (1995). Universal Pictures release of a 40 Acres and a Mule Filmworks Production. Producer: Martin Scorsese, Spike Lee, and Jon Kilik; Director: Spike Lee; Screenplay: Richard Price and Spike Lee, based on the novel by Richard Price. Director of Photography: Malik Hassan Sayeed; Cast: Harvey Keitel (Rocco Klein); John Turturro (Larry Mazilli); Deroy Lindo (Rodney); Mekhi Phifer (Strike); Isaiah Washington (Victor); Keith David (André the Giant); Pee Wee Love (Tyrone); Regina Taylor (Iris Jeeter); Tom Byrd (Errol Barnes). For reviews see Ansen (1995), Brown (1995), Denby (1995), Mathews (1995b), Medved (1995), Pawelczak (1995), Schickel (1995), Sterritt (1995), Taubin (1995b, 1995c), Turan (1995a); also Pouzoulet (1997), Reid (1997a, p. 8). For critical assessments of Lee's project more generally, see the essays in Reid, 1997b, especially Kellner, 1997, and Pouzoulet, 1997; also Reid, 1993, pp.104–108; Lubiano, 1997; Baraka, 1993; Baker, 1993; Boyd, 1997, pp. 24–30; hooks, 1996, pp. 165–66; 1994, pp. 155–164; 1992, pp. 126–27; 1990, pp. 173–184; Watkins, 1998, pp. 107–168.

2. Watkins (1998) asserts that Lee's *She's Gotta Have It* (1998) 'established the precedent for the reemergence of black cinema as a viable commercial product' (p. 108).

3. Of course other hood movies would appear after 1995, including: *Set It Off* (1996), *Dangerous Minds* (1996), *Hoodlum* (1997); even Lee's *He Got Game* (1998) would take up the ghetto-centered narrative once more. Paris Barclay's *Don't Be a Menace to South Central While Drinking Your Juice in the Hood* (1996) is a spoof of this film cycle. I disagree with Watkins (1998, p. 170), who contends that the ghetto-action film cycle is not necessarily associated with Lee.

4. Watkins (1998, p. 135), disagrees, asserting that Lee embodies what Cornel West (1990) calls the new cultural politics of difference and resistance. Reid (1997a) suggests that Lee's black nationalism resembles the type of white populist heroes found in Frank Capra films. 'Lee's populism ... features a black individual caught in the claws of white industry and institutions ... and patriarchal

conventions' (p. 15). Kellner (1997) ironically reads Lee's aesthetics within a radical Brechtian model, but finds that Lee's black cultural identity politics do not contain a politics of resistance or black liberation.

5. Still, Lee openly criticizes the Hollywood establishment and its treatment of black filmmakers. In turn, his films have generally been denied Oscar nominations (Katz, 1998, p. 811).

6. *She's Gotta Have It* (1986), *School Daze* (1988), *Do the Right Thing* (1989), *Mo'Better Blues* (1990), *Jungle Fever* (1991), *Malcolm X* (1992), *Crooklyn* (1994), *Clockers* (1995), *Get On the Bus* (1996), *Girl 6* (1996), *Four Little Girls* (1997), *He Got Game* (1998), *Summer of Sam* (1999), *Bamboozled* (2000), *Original Kings of Comedy* (2000).

7. Lee vigorously campaigned to be the director of *Malcolm X*, for example. Guerrero (1993a, pp. 198–201) reviews the controversy surrounding this project.

8. Lee justifies these representations thusly: 'I know that black men do a lot of things that are fucked up and I've tried to show some of the things that we do' (Lee, quoted in hooks, 1996, p. 232).

9. In *Get On the Bus* But Lee returns to the issue of gay sexuality. Flip (André Braugher), the aspiring actor, constantly mocks, taunts, and ridicules the two gay men on the bus, as he brags about the number of women he has seduced.

10. But see Baraka, 1993, pp. 151–152.

11. Danny Aiello won an Oscar nomination for Best Supporting Actor, and Spike was nominated for Best Original Screenplay (Bogle, 1994, p. 323).

12. Lee made a series of Nike ads with Michael Jordan, in which he played a character named Mars Blackmon (Watkins, 1998, p. 134). Like Jordan, Lee had to confront charges concerning Nike's labor practices and the fact that its ads encouraged working-class black youth to 'covet high-priced shoes' (Watkins, 1998, p. 265).

13. Lee (1989) indicates that he was making an allusion to the Howard Beach incident in the film 'by using a pizza parlor. The white kids … could be the sons of the owner of the pizzeria' (pp. 24–25).

14. Lee (1989) describes his use of the notion of the hottest day,

While I was in the grocery store, I heard a radio broadcast that two Black youth had been beaten up by a gang of white youths in Bensonhurst…. Just the other day some Black kids fired up a white cab driver in Harlem. New York City is tense with racial hatred. Can you imagine if these incidents had taken place in the summer, on the hottest day of the year? (pp. 32–33).

15. Or, as in *Summer of Sam* (1999), he functions as a television journalist, reporting from the sidelines.

16. Here hooks is referring to the scene near the beginning of the film when the camera focuses on Mookie (Lee) lying in bed with Jade (his sister in the film, and his sister in real life, Jolie Lee), and Mookie's touching Jade's body in a way that has an erotic dimension (hooks, 1990, p. 182).

17. Richard Price wrote the script, which was based on his novel of the same name. Originally Martin Scorsese and Robert De Niro were scheduled to make the film. They dropped the project, to make *Casino*. Lee then came in as director, and Harvey Keitel took the part written for De Niro (Rollyson, 1996, p. 92). Lee rewrote Price's script. Denby (1995) suggests that the film seems to combine two different time periods in New York City, 'the late-eighties peak of the crack madness … and the Giuliani era of greater police vigilance, with its nonstop surveillance of drug dealers' (p. 72).

18. For example *Bamboozled* (2000) uses the format of a contemporary minstrel TV show to turn blackface into a national craze.

19. These productions include, of course, Lee's film production company, 40 Acres and a Mule, his retail store, Spike Lee Joint, his music recording company, and his music video productions. These are all located in the Fort Greene section near Brooklyn Heights, which is where Lee was born, and still lives (see Pouzoulet, 1997, p. 33; Watkins, 1998, p. 134). In December 1996 Lee announced a collaboration with the Madison Agenue advertising agency DDB Needham, which handles accounts for McDonald's and Budweiser. This led to the formation of Spike/DDB, with Lee the 51 percent majority shareholder, president, and creative director. Anheuser-Busch, the owners of Budweiser, sponsored a promotion tour and advance bookings for Lee's 1996 film *Get On the Bus* (Gilroy, 2000, pp. 242–243). Multiculturalism and blackness have become big international business. Lee leads 'a new contingent of cultural brokers: a hip vanguard in the business of difference' (Gilroy, 2000, p. 242).

Part Four: a new racial aesthetic

8

Screening Race

> Presently in America a war is being fought. Forget about guns, planes and bombs, the weapons from now on will be the newspapers, magazines, TV shows, radio, and FILM. The right has gotten BOLD ... any piece of art that doesn't hold the party line is subject to attack. It's war in the battleground of culture. (Lee, 1992, p. xiii; also quoted by Watkins, 1998, p. 137)

> A marginalized group needs to be wary of the seductive power of realism, of accepting all that a realistic representation implies. (Lubiano, 1997, p. 106)

> Aesthetics then is more than a philosophy or theory of art and beauty; it is a way of inhabiting space ... a way of looking and becoming.... I find compelling a racial aesthetic that seeks to uncover and restore links between art and revolutionary politics. (hooks, 1990, pp. 104, 111)

A single problem, moving in several directions at the same time, has guided this study. I have sought to understand Hollywood's cinema of racial violence, a cinema represented in more than twenty films released between 1987 and 1998. Produced by mainstream Anglo, African-American, and Latino/a filmmakers, this cinema located racial violence in the black and brown public sphere. Spike Lee is right. At one level, America's war on race occurred in the spaces and the battlegrounds created by these films. It was and remains a war fought on the battlefields of cultural representation.

The crack-cocaine wars, the War on Drugs, and the 'Just say No to Drugs' campaign of the Reagan years coincided with the appearance of a new war zone in the national popular imagination – the black and brown hood. In the spaces of this war zone, dark-skinned youth in gangs engaged in drive-bys as a new form of entertainment. Rap music and hip hop culture became signifiers of a new and violent racial order. In the minds of many, rap music meant racial violence. And this violence was spreading everywhere, threatening white America. Joel Schumacher's 1995 film *Falling Down*, starring Michael Douglas, spoke for many male white Americans. They were not going to take this violence falling down. They were going to fight back. The hood movies represented another version of this battle, another way of fighting back.

So it remains to situate this study within its historical moment, to return to the beginning and take up again the task of offering an interpretive framework for the understanding of the cinema of racial violence. Critical race theory and a feminist cultural studies framework have informed my analysis. I have examined the ways in which these films framed a particular version of the violent, gendered cinematic racial order. This cinema of racial violence was shaped by a politics of representation that valued whiteness and a new conservative cultural racism.

My discussion in previous chapters has focused on the following interconnected issues: Anglo filmmakers and their stories of race and the white man's burden; women, gendered violence in the hood, and the feminine challenge to the violent assimilation narrative; comedy, sex, race, and homoeroticism in the biracial cop-buddy film; the hyperghetto and America's post-industrial wasteland; gangs and brown prison Godfathers; the prison as a violent, interracial sexual social order; the Mafia myth; clockers and homophobia in Spike's place.

In this conclusion I come back to the filmmakers and their uses of the realistic cinematic apparatus. I offer preliminary observations on the possibilities of a critical ethnic cinema, a cinema that honors racial and cultural difference. I begin with a brief aside on the hood movies, turning then to the aesthetic arguments of the Black Arts Movement of the 1960s and 1970s. I next examine the didactic realistic cinema of the new black aesthetic. I compare and contrast these two aesthetics in the hopes of fashioning a counter-hegemonic cinematic aesthetic for the twenty-first century. I write against the backdrop of the Black Arts Movement of the 1960s and 1970s. I want their dream to live again.[1] I end with observations on critical race theory, a new aesthetic of color, and a radical cinema of racial difference.

Race in the Hood

The hood race films came in two forms: action-comedy interracial, cop-buddy series (*Lethal Weapon, Die Hard*); and films that emphasized didactic, social realist, social problems messages. These were utopian tales, shaped by a dialectic of fear and hope. There were some women's stories, but primarily these were coming-of-age, all-male narratives, dealing with violence on the streets and in prison. A uniform conservative moral message was conveyed. Young men must have strong role models. They must respect their elders, go to school, get good educations and become responsible members of the black or brown middle class. These films do not take up critical race, Marxist, feminist, or post-colonial theories of racism, empowerment, and liberation. They articulate a neo-nationalistic, essentializing, homophobic, masculinist gender and identity politics. (Spike Lee's films epitomize these tendencies.)

The New Right blamed persons of color for the problems that were located in the ghetto. The repressive efforts of the Right were anchored in the crack-cocaine wars that extended from the mid-1980s to the mid-1990s. The hood films narrate the cocaine wars. These wars were accompanied by increased police surveillance in the ghetto. This new police state contributed to a sense that the ghetto had once again become a violent nation, or a crumbling internal colony within the great American cities of Los Angeles and New York. Black, brown, and Italian Mafias took control of an underground drug economy. Racial gangs on the street and in prison recruited youth of color for this project. Soon young men were shooting one another in drive-bys and gang wars. The police kept white America safe from the crazed violence that was operating in the ghetto.

These race stories are not progressive or subversive films. Indeed, they created deep generational, gender, and class divisions within the black and brown middle classes. Women called the films misogynist. The black and brown middle class objected to the guns, drugs, and gang warfare. Black activists from the sixties said they were reactionary (Baraka, 1993, p. 153).

Sadly, as films about race and racism, they do not attack the essential underlying ideologies and material conditions that perpetuate racial oppression in America today. This is the case even for the films made by black and brown filmmakers. These filmmakers seem unwilling and unable to attack the ideology in which they and their films are so firmly embedded. They do not rupture the veneer of this larger racial apparatus. It is as if they are trapped by the very violence they want to criticize. Hence these are not politically subversive texts (see Comolli and Narboni, 1976, p. 27; Denzin, 1995a, p. 192). They do not advance the project of the earlier Chicana/o and Black Arts cultural movements.

The Black Arts Movement

Participants in the Black Arts Movement of the 1970s waged a cultural war against centuries of segregation in the United States (William J. Harris, 1998, p. 1344). This battle was ignited by the civil rights movement, the women's movement, the chicano movement, and the anti-war movement. It drew upon ideologies central to the national liberation struggles in Africa, Asia, and Latin America, including Maoism in Asia, Castroism in Cuba, Che Guevarism in Latin America, and Fanonism in Africa and Algeria (William J. Harris, 1998, p. 1344; Masilela, 1993, pp. 107–108; Noriega, 1992b, p. 141; Diawara, 1993a, pp. 3–11). Artists, poets, scholars, playwrights, filmmakers, and performers of color, including Angela Davis, Jayne Cortez, Sonia Sanchez, Etheridge Knight, Lucille Clifton, Don L. Lee, Ishmael Reed, Amiri Baraka, Henry Dumas, Daniel and Luis Valdez, Gregory Naven and Edward James Olmos, called for a radical re-ordering of the Western cultural aesthetic.

They rejected the white Eurocentric Enlightenment model that called politicized art 'propaganda.' They sought an art that was unique to their cultural experiences. Gayle (1997) argued, 'few ... would disagree with the idea that unique experiences produce unique cultural artifacts, and that art is a product of such cultural experiences' (p. 1876).

There was a conscious attempt to 'forge an unbreakable link between artistic production and revolutionary politics' (hooks, 1990, p. 106). This connection between art and politics was everywhere present on the cultural landscape. Thus Mulvey and Wollen (1989) show how revolutionary art in Mexico in an earlier period (1920s) also connected art and politics. Painter Frida Kahlo and photographer Tina Modotti, for example, used their art to construct a mythic national past that would offer a revolutionary agenda for the Mexican nation (see Mulvey and Wollen, 1989, p. 83; also quoted by hooks, 1990, p. 107).[2]

Similarly, artists within the Black Arts Movement crafted their version of an artistic and political aesthetic that advanced the cause of a radical, separatist black politics (William J. Harris, 1998, p. 1344; Neal, 1998; Fuller, 1968, 1997; Gayle, 1971/1997). These artists sought empowerment through art. They rewrote history to include spaces for the black power (and Chicano) movements, the black church, links to folklore and the oral tradition, and the African and Latin diaspora. They used various regimes of realism to present stories and images about black and brown communities under siege. Soundtracks echoed themes from the civil rights movement.

The original Black Arts Movement eschewed protest art because such art based its arguments on an appeal to white morality and a white Eurocentric artistic aesthetic. Etheridge Knight, quoted by Neal (1998, p. 1450), defines protest art thusly, contending that any black person

> who masters the techniques of his [or her] particular art form, who adheres to a white aesthetic, and who directs his [or her] work toward a white audience is, in one sense, protesting. And implicit in the act of protest is the belief that a change will be forthcoming once the masters are aware of the protester's 'grievance' (the very word connotes begging, supplications to the gods). Only when that belief has faded and protestings end, will Black art begin.... Unless the Black artist establishes a 'Black aesthetic' he [or she] will have no future at all.

Thus the black artist gives up on the project of speaking to a white audience (Gayle, 1997, p. 1875). The need to create a unique black aesthetic, to create new artistic forms and new values, is very clear.

Gayle (1997, p. 1875) frames this demand in terms of W. E. Du Bois's concept of the veil. In an often-quoted passage, Du Bois (1903) argued,

> The Negro is ... born with a veil, and gifted with a second sight in this American world – a world which yields him no true self-consciousness, but only lets him see himself through the revelation of the other world. It is a particular sensation, this double-consciousness, this sense of always looking at one's self through the eyes of others, or measuring one's soul by the tape of a world that looks on in amused contempt and pity. One ever feels his twoness – an American, a Negro, two souls, two thoughts ... two warring ideals in one dark body. (p. 3)

A black aesthetic would cut through this veil, and give black people a new mirror to look into, a mirror that did not hang behind a white veil. This mirror speaks to and from the souls of black folk.

This mirror, this aesthetic, is an ethics of representation that expresses the truth of racial injustice as lived by the oppressed. In this world ethics, epistemology, and aesthetics will 'interact positively and be consistent with the demands of a more spiritual world' (Neal, 1998, p. 1451). On this point Neal was clear, 'the Black Arts Movement is an ethical movement' (Neal, 1998, p. 1451). This aesthetic creates new standards of beauty. Black is beautiful. Blacks have style, flair, their speech exhibits distinctive rhythms. This aesthetic rejects white standards of beauty, including those connected to white or light skin and straight hair (Fuller, 1997, p. 1813).

Gayle (1997) elaborates:

> The question for the black critic today is not how beautiful is a melody, a play, a poem, or a novel, but how much more beautiful has the poem, melody, play, or novel made the life of a single black [person]? How far has the work gone in transforming an American Negro into an African-American or black man? This Black Aesthetic, then, as conceived by this writer, is a corrective – a means of helping black people out of the polluted mainstream of Americanism. (p. 1876)

Gayle contended that black art required new standards and new tools of evaluation (p. 1876). According to Karenga (1997), there were three criteria for black art: it must be functional, collective, and committed. Functionally, this art would support and 'respond positively to the reality of a revolution' (p. 1973). It would not be art for art's sake; rather, it would be art for our sake, art for 'Sammy the shoeshine boy, T. C. the truck driver and K. P. the unwilling soldier' (p. 1974). Karenga is clear: 'we do not need pictures of oranges in a bowl, or trees standing innocently in the midst of a wasteland ... or fat white women smiling lewdly.... If we must paint oranges or trees, let our guerrillas be eating those oranges for strength and using those trees for cover' (p. 1974; see also Gayle, 1971, p. xxiii).

Collectively, black art comes from people, and must be returned to the people, 'in a form more beautiful and colorful than it was in real life ... art is everyday life given more form and color' (Karenga, 1997, p. 1974). Such art is democratic; it celebrates diversity, personal and collective freedom, and speaks to the everyday people and their concerns in the world. It is not elitist.

After Fanon, these filmmakers and artists conceptualized the ghetto as an internal racial colony (Diawara, 1993a, p. 9; Fuller, 1997, p. 1813). This colony, like a cancer, was buried deep in the belly of the larger white racist society. The short-lived blaxploitation film movement of the 1970s embodied many of these values (Diawara, 1993a, p. 9). As Diawara (1993a, p. 9) observes, Van Peebles' Sweetback can be read as a hero of decolonization. Sweetback represents all of the black outlaws who came before him: Stagolee, Bigger Thomas, Chester Himes' criminals, Ellison's invisible man, Malcolm X – the archetype of the black man running from the law.

As argued in previous chapters, the Black Arts Movement resurfaces in the 1990s with a new generation of filmmakers, and is called 'the new black aesthetic' (Boyd, 1997, p. 25). The films analyzed in this study embody that aesthetic, which some have also called the 'new black realism' (Massood, 1996, p. 88; Diawara, 1993a, p. 23). This regime must bear witness to its own cinema of racial violence.

A Cinema of Racial Violence

The New Right under Reagan, Bush, and Gingrich, reversed the economic, educational, and political entitlements of the civil rights movement of the 1960s. These efforts had disastrous effects on life in America's inner cities. The politicans of the New Right made race visible in new ways. They succeeded in coding violence with race, with black youth, with gangs, drive-bys, rap music and hip hop culture.

The hood movies offered one set of responses to this so-called 'national moral crisis.' This was a historical project. This group of filmmakers was responding to a particular set of economic, cultural, and political conditions. Thus was produced a complex politics of representation. The filmmakers were criticized for making violent films about the violence they said was in the hood. Directors from Edward James Olmos, to Spike Lee, John Singleton, and the Hughes brothers argued that they were only telling it like it was; that the violence they represented was there because of what the Right had done. It was a stand-off.

Using the apparatuses of cinematic realism, these films erased the notion of a unified or essential racial subject. Still, they created their own notion of the racial subject, the young black or brown man in the hood with a gun. These social problems-based films brought the violence of the hood directly in front of the viewer. These didactic texts called for an end to the genocide in the hood. 'NO MORE PACKING' screams Spike Lee, and the Hughes brothers and Olmos have close-ups of little children holding guns.

The conservative political consequences of this new cinematic realism were made clear in California after the race riots in Los Angeles in 1992. On national television Pete Wilson, the (Republican) governor of the state, suggested that

> Everyone in America should see the movie *Boyz N the Hood*. In that movie, a strong father makes the difference for his teenaged son ... [who is] about to rush ... out and try to avenge his best friend who has just been gunned down in a mindless, senseless gang war.... Now ... that movie says we need a strong father and welfare is no suitable replacement for that (Reeves and Campbell, 1994, pp. 246–247).

A Mimetic Realism

Filmmakers using the new black aesthetic brought the 'real' world of the hood in front of the viewer. Lubiano (1997, pp. 104–112), drawing on Mercer (1988), argues that their realist methods relied on the operation of four cinematic techniques: transparency, immediacy, authority, and authenticity. The hood filmmakers acted as if their cameras were neutral recording devices, presenting the hood as it really was, telling the truth through their slices of life imagery. Thus the films claimed a truth that was transparent – visible – in reality. This was not a personal cinema, it was objective and authoritative. The filmmakers used documentary-like footage (the opening scenes in *Menace*) and shots of political posters (*Boyz*) to lend historical authenticity to their texts.

Their invisible cameras offered detailed close-up images that filled the screen. This was an authentic realism that was everywhere, but nowhere more visible then in the blood-soaked stains that spilled across sidewalks after drive-bys. The use of vernacular speech, rap music, and hip hop fashion further authenticated the visual text and the spoken narrative, giving them an even greater aura of realism. This social-problems-based cinematic realism demanded that viewers react in horror to senseless youthful genocidal violence.

The black filmmakers of the 1990s were committed to a mimetic conception of representation (Mercer, 1988, p. 53). They assumed that an objective reality was out there, that it existed, and that it could be captured cinematically. Thus they sought to present the referential realities of race using a grammar of visual or mimetic realism. Paradoxically, they sought to do this using the same codes, methods, techniques, and conservative story lines as mainstream Hollywood, whose racist cinematic apparatuses they openly resisted.

Lubiano (1997) contends that a realism used thusly, and uncritically, 'as a mode for African American art implies that our lives can be captured by the representation of enough documentary evidence, or by insistence on another truth' (p. 105). When the graffiti in *Do the Right Thing* reads 'Tawana told the Truth', there is an assertion that her story was true and real, actual and concrete, that it was a story of a real rape (Lubiano, 1997, p. 105).

There are several problems with such assertions. First, whose truth is operating? Must Tawana be telling the truth before we can accept the 'larger truth about sexual abuse of African American women by Euro-American men? Is this "truth" compared to the "truth" of their abuse by African American men? Compared to what other African American women say? Compared to what Alice Walker ... says about African American men?' (Lubiano, 1997, p. 105).

In staking out its claims to truth, this version of cinematic realism also creates the conditions for its own deconstruction, and this is so on the following grounds. First, telling it like it is assumes that you can in fact tell it like it is; that there is but one telling. But this is not the case, for conservatives tell it differently than radical black feminists, for example.

Second, adherence to the regimes of white racial realism belies an acceptance of one version of what the real is, and one version of how the real is made visible. As argued in Chapter 1, the apparatuses of mainstream realism lead to the production of films that have the authenticity of modernist naturalistic ethnographies. These texts purport to present lived reality. In so doing, they perform particular gendered versions of race, they reinscribe familiar cultural stereotypes. They reproduce white stereotypes of dark-skinned persons. These constructions and representations of 'blackness' or 'brownness' enter public discourse, and are accepted as real (Lubiano, 1997, p. 107).

Third, this realist apparatus creates an implicit demand for members of racial minorities to set the record straight, to make public stereotypes and misunderstandings conform to the truth of the real facts. There is a risk in setting the record straight; namely whose record is being corrected, with what methods and with what representations? By agreeing that the record should be set straight, one gives an authority to the existing representations. By using the selfsame methods that created the racist representations in the first place, one enters a battle over which record is truthful, accurate, or correct. Lubiano (1997) notes that the post-Harlem Renaissance 'black aesthetic critics ... built a political and intellectual movement around an assertion of a countertruth against the distortions of cultural racism' (p. 106). This has not been the case for users of the new black aesthetic.

Fourth, the reproduction of the sounds and sights of African-American (and Hispanic) vernacular culture is problematic. There is a danger in 'repeating the masculinism and heterosexism of vernacular culture' (Lubiano, 1997, p. 196).

Further, there is no guarantee that a text will be counter-hegemonic just because it represents, romanticizes, or criticizes the vernacular (see Lubiano, 1997, p. 119, note 19).

Indeed, fifth, the use of the vernacular as a method for establishing authenticity can reproduce a problematic version of essentialism; the belief that certain characteristics are 'inherently part of the core being of a group' (Lubiano, 1997, p. 109). These kinds of representations may contribute to a naïve and stereotypical notion of the unified racial subject. Thus hip, cool, jiving black males have a 'predilection for playing craps, drinking, using or selling drugs, or raping white women, or being a jungle savage … or being on welfare – the list goes on and on' (Lubiano, 1997, p. 111). The relationship between authenticity and essentialism must always be made problematic.[3]

Sixth, in making a claim for presenting it as it is, the realistic filmmaker also makes a counterclaim: reality is this way, and not this way. In its silence about alternative representations, the film asserts its own hegemonic power over its situated version of the real. Thus, for example, many of the hood films take up the topic of AIDS, and black men dying of this disease. Yet no hood filmmaker presents a positive view of gay men and the gay black community. Nor do these filmmakers take up the nurturing responses to AIDS victims by the black church and the black family. As a consequence, only black homophobia is presented.

Realism and the Didactic Protest Film

This form of racial realism was used by the black (and brown) filmmakers of the 1990s for didactic or moral purposes. Singleton, Olmos, the Hughes brothers, and Lee were sending moral messages to white as well as black and brown America. Lee (as quoted earlier) said he wanted to 'Force America to come to grips with the problem of racism' (quoted in Lubiano, 1997, p. 101). Within the framework of the older black aesthetic these were protest films (Neal, 1998, p. 1450). They used the narrative and cinematic techniques of mainstream Hollywood cinema. They were protesting conditions in the ghetto and sending their message to white America. They spoke in terms of a white and black middle-class morality. These were wake-up calls to the larger culture to understand the problems in the black and brown community. And, in many cases, they blamed members of the racial community for these problems.

The new filmmakers embraced a protest art, an art that had been rejected by the members of the original Black Arts Movement. They articulated a white aesthetic that was filtered through the formulations of the original Black Arts Movement. But while the films of the 1970s attempted to establish a counter-aesthetic, the films of the 1990s embodied a white social problems aesthetic. In this regard they were what Neal called 'protest art.'

As protest art they enacted an essentializing social problems ideology (see Mills, 1963, p. 527). This ideology emphasized identity politics, and the values of home and community. These films focused on the democratic values of American society, irrespective of race, including the myths of success, and the values of family, home, romantic love, education, and hard work. They centered their visual imagery on the problems of community disorganization. These problems were caused by pathological, dope-using, gun-carrying unadjusted individuals: the young black or brown male in a gang. It is an understatement to say that they did not present violence, drugs, or gangs in a positive light.

These films borrowed the format of the Victorian melodrama, with narratives organized around the poles of good and evil. Heroes and heroines were confronted with evils, temptations, obstacles, and conflict which they overcame, through luck, the help of family, friends, lovers, or police. They were rewarded, if they were lucky, by the love of a good man or good woman, and a safe place in respectable black or brown middle-class society.

In the hood movies a societal condition (violence, gangs, and drugs in the hood) coincides with a personal problem (absent fathers), a character defect (attraction to violence), and a violent act (killing someone). These conditions function, in turn, as dramatic devices that allow the filmmaker to tell a story with a moral message. This message includes commentary on the individual, his or her problem, and the larger society that contains, creates, and reacts to the problem. Didacticism is the distinguishing feature of these films; they attempt to teach and inform an audience about a problem – drugs, violence, and gangs in the hood – and its solution, or lack thereof (Roffman and Purdy, 1981, p. viii; Denzin, 1991b, p. 13).

A circular logic organizes these didactic texts. Racial violence, murder, and father absence are the central social problems in the hood. These problems create social disorganization and pathology. These pathologies are happening because of a deterioration in key values connected to family, hard work, and personal responsibility. Because of this deterioration, and because of these pathologies, the hood is a pathological community. It experiences its pathology and disorganization through the signifiers connected to the pathology: rap, hip hop, and the drug-dealing culture. The pathological members of the community are maladjusted. These violent drug-dealing youth have not been successfully socialized into the Christian values of the local moral community.

The answer to the problem of social disorganization is clear. And here the hood films, as protest art, side with white society. The police must help the community get rid of the dope and drug dealers. Greater state intervention by the police is necessary if order is to be restored. Fathers must come home to their children, and grandchildren must listen to their grandparents.

As argued above, in their anti-violence these films do not take up the larger political and economic situations that produced the so-called 'disorganization' in the first place. Documentary footage from the 1965 Los Angeles race riots and close-ups of posters showing Ronald Reagan smiling are not sufficiently political. Thus, at this level, the hood films failed to realize their own political agenda. They only repeated an age-old social disorganization, social problems story; that is, 'We have a problem here, come help us' (see Mills, 1963, p. 542). And in so doing they confirmed the prophecy that protest art in the racial arena is doomed to fail if it only speaks from a white political and moral aesthetic.

179

An Aesthetic of Color and Critical Race Theory

Back to the present. Baker (1997), commenting on the legacies of the Black Arts Movement, observed that the

> creative and critical dreams of new black artistic forms were endorsed by emergent literatures and critical traditions around the world. In the United States alone, Native American, Chicano, and Chicana, and gay and lesbian writers, critics and scholars acknowledged ... their enormous debt to the strategies, authors and works of the Black Arts movement ... the Black Aesthetic ... continues to enrich artistic traditions, and critical debate that will enliven the twenty-first century. (p. 1806)

Here I attempt to chart one version of that legacy.[4] A feminist, Chicana/o, and black performance-based aesthetic uses cinema, art, photography, music, dance, poetry, painting, theatre, performance texts, autobiography, narrative, story-telling, poetic, and dramatic language to create a critical counter-hegemonic race consciousness, thereby extending the post-civil rights Chicana/o and Black Arts cultural movements into this century. These practices serve to implement critical race theory (hooks, 1990, p. 105; Smith, 1993, p. xxvi; 1994, xxii; Gonzalez, 1998; Joyce, 1987; Davis, 1998, p. 155; Collins, 1991, 1998; Ladson-Billings, 2000; Parker, 1998; Parker et al., 1998; Scheurich, 1997, pp. 144–158; Anzaldua, 1987; Trinh, 1992). Critical race theory 'seeks to decloak the seemingly race-neutral, and color-blind ways ... of constructing and administering race-based appraisals ... of the law, administrative policy, electoral politics ... political discourse [and education] in the USA' (Parker et al., 1998, p. 5). It attempts 'to chart radical and subversive directions for dialogues about race and strategies for resistance' (hooks, 1990, p. 177).

Thus is hooks' call for a counter-hegemonic cinema of race, and Collins' (1991, 1998) dream of an Afrocentric feminist agenda for the 1990s, advanced into the next decade. Artists, filmmakers, activists, theorists, and practionners enact a standpoint epistemology that sees the world and resistances to it from the point of view of oppressed persons of color, especially women. Representative sociopoetic and interpretive works in this tradition include those of Shange (1977), Joyce (1987), Neal (1988), Jordan (1998), Baraka (1998), Jones (1998), as well as the more recent arguments of hooks (1990, 1996), Smith (1993, 1994), Davis (1998), Anzaldua (1987), Noriega (1996), Trinh (1992), and others. This aesthetic is also informed by successive waves of the Asian and Native American, women's, gay, lesbian, and bisexual movements, who 'use their art as a weapon for political activism' (William J. Harris, 1998, p. 1384; also Nero, 1998, p. 1973).

Ethics and an Anti-Aesthetic

With hooks (1990, p. 110), who borrows from Foster (1983), I seek a discourse on aesthetics that is not trapped by the modernist agenda.[5] This agenda locates aesthetics outside of, or apart from, history. Thus Foster (1983) calls for an anti-aesthetic, or postmodern aesthetic, that is 'cross-disciplinary in nature, that is sensitive to cultural forms in a politic (e.g. feminist art), or rooted in a vernacular – that is, to forms that deny the idea of a privileged aesthetic realm' (p. xv). This anti-aesthetic is subversive and utopian. It creates a space for the filmmaking and artistic representational practices of previously marginalized groups. It empowers members of such groups to break with naturalism and realism as the standard ways of representing reality. It suggests that there are multiple artistic audiences for such work. It contends that there are multiple aesthetic measures of a work's value. It values transgressive and oppositional representations.

This is a political and ethical aesthetic. It erases the modernist distinction between epistemology, ontology, aesthetics, and ethics. In a feminist, communitarian sense, this aesthetic contends that ways of knowing (epistemology) are always moral and ethical. They always involve conceptions of who the human being is (ontology), including how matters of difference, oppression, and injustice are socially organized. The ways in which these relationships are represented involve interpretive practices that answer to a political and epistemological aesthetic, what is good, true, and beautiful.

For the anti-aesthetic, all aesthetics and standards of judgment are based on particular moral standpoints. There is no objective, morally neutral standpoint. Hence, an Afrocentric feminist aesthetic (and epistemology) stresses the importance of truth, knowledge, and beauty. Such claims are based on a concept of storytelling, and a notion of wisdom that is experiential and shared. Storytellers, including filmmakers, take what they tell from experience, passing along the truths of this experience to others. In the telling, this experience becomes an experience for those watching and listening to the story being told (Benjamin, 1968, p. 87; McMurtry, 1999, p. 14). Truth lies in these stories and their morals.

Wisdom so conceived is derived from local, lived experience, and expresses lore, folktale, and myth. This is a dialogical epistemology and aesthetic. It enacts an ethic of care and an ethic of personal and communal responsibility (Collins, 1991, p. 214). Politically, this aesthetic imagines how a truly democratic society might look, including one free of race prejudice and oppression (Feagin, 2000, pp. 270–271). This aesthetic values beauty and artistry, movement, rhythm, color, and texture in everyday life. It celebrates difference and the sounds of many different voices. It expresses an ethic of love, fellowship, and mutual empowerment.

This ethic presumes a moral community that is ontologically prior to the person. This community has shared moral values, including the concepts of care, shared governance, neighborliness, love, kindness, and the moral good (Christians, 2000, pp. 144–149). This ethic embodies a sacred existential epistemology that locates persons in a non-competitive, non-hierarchical relationship to the larger moral universe. It declares that all persons deserve dignity and a sacred status in the world. It stresses the value of human life, truth telling, and non-violence (Christians, 2000, p. 147).

This ethical aesthetic is dialogical and enabling. In generating social criticism, it also engenders resistance. It empowers persons to action (Christians, 2000, p. 147). It helps them imagine how things could be different in the everyday world. It imagines new forms of human transformation and emancipation. It enacts these transformations through dialogue. If necessary, it sanctions non-violent forms of civil disobediance (Christians, 2000, p. 148). This aesthetic imagines and locates the downtrodden and the oppressed in the construction of new and liberating cultural formations. It opposes a culture of silence. It resists political programs that are led by those currently in power. It offers new forms of representation that create the space for new forms of critical race consciousness. It shows the oppressed how to find a voice in the spaces of oppression.

Thus theorists and filmmakers alike critically enage and interrogate the anti-civil rights agendas of the New Right (see Jordan, 1998). But this is not a protest or integrationist initiative aimed solely at informing a white audience of racial injustice. It dismisses these narrow agendas. In so doing it rejects classical Eurocentric and post-positivist standards for evaluating literary, artistic, and research work.

The New Counter-Hegemonic Anti-Aesthetic

To summarize, the new counter-hegemonic anti-aesthetic is shaped by the following understandings:

- No topic is taboo, including sexuality, sexual abuse, death, and violence.
- Texts are sought that speak to women and children of color; to persons who suffer from violence, rape, racial and sexist injustice.
- Ethics, aesthetics, political praxis, and epistemology are joined; every act of representation, artistic or research, is a political and ethical statement (see Neal, 1998, p. 1451). There is no separate aesthetic or epistemological realm regulated by transcendent ideals, although an ethics of care should always be paramount.
- Claims to truth and knowledge are assessed in terms of multiple criteria, including asking if a text:
  (a) interrogates existing cultural, sexist, and racial stereotypes, especially those connected to family, femininity, masculinity, marriage, and intimacy (Neal, 1998, p. 1457);
  (b) gives primacy to memory and its connections to concrete lived experience;
  (c) uses dialogue and an ethics of personal responsibility; values beauty, spirituality, and a love of others;
  (d) implements an emancipatory agenda committed to equality, freedom, and social justice and participatory democratic practices;
  (e) emphasizes community, collective action, solidarity, and group empowerment (Denzin, 1997, p. 65; Pizarro, 1988, pp. 63–65; hooks, 1990, p. 111).
- It presumes an artist, filmmaker, and social researcher who is part of, and a spokesperson for a local moral community, a community with its own symbolism, mythology, and storytelling traditions.
- It asks that the writer-artist draw upon vernacular, folk and popular culture forms of representation, including: proverbs, work songs, spirituals, sermons, prayers, poems, choreopoems (Shange, 1977), folktales, blues (Davis, 1998), jazz, rap, film, paintings, theatre, movies, photographs, performance art,

murals, and *corridos* (see Hill, 1998; Pizarro, 1988, p. 65; Fregoso, 1993; Noriega, 1996).

- It seeks artists-researchers-writers who produce works that speak to and represent the needs of the community (drug addiction, teenage pregnancy, murder, gang warfare, AIDS, dropping out of school).
- It understands that no single representation or work can speak to the collective needs of the community. Rather, local communities are often divided along racial, ethnic, gender, residential, age, and class lines.

Thus are sought emancipatory, utopian cinematic texts grounded in the distinctive styles, rhythms, idioms, and personal identities of local folk and vernacular culture. These films record the history of injustices experienced by the members of an oppressed group. They show how members of a local group have struggled to find places of dignity and respect in a violent, racist, and sexist civil society.

These films are sites of resistance. They are places where meanings, politics, and identities are negotiated. They transform and challenge all forms of cultural representation, white, black, Chicano, Asian, Native American, gay, or straight.

In her poem 'Power', black lesbian poet Audre Lorde talks about taking action in the world. She writes (1998, p. 1627):

The difference between poetry and rhetoric
is being
ready to kill
yourself
instead of your children.

In lines such as these, critical race theory is connected to a heightened race consciousness. This critical race consciousness, in turn, is translated into cinematic texts.

Aesthetics and Cinematic Practices

As argued in Chapter 1, within the contemporary black and Chicana/o film communities, there are a specific set of film practices associated with this counter-hegemonic anti-aesthetic project.[6] These practices inform and shape the narrative and visual content of these experimental texts. They include:

- experiments with narrative forms, including jazz, blues, folk ballads, and *corridos* that honor long-standing African-American and Chicano discourse tradiions (Noriega, 1992b, pp. 152–153; Fregoso, 1993, pp. 70–76);
- the use of improvisation, *mise-en-scène*, and montage to fill the screen with multi-racial images, and to manipulate and deconstruct bicultural visual and linguistic codes;
- the use of personal testimonials, life stories, folktales, cultural myth, voice-overs, and off-screen narration to provide overall narrative unity to a text (Noriega, 1992b, pp. 156–159).
- a celebration of key elements in African-American and Chicano culture, especially the themes of resistance, maintenance, affirmation, and neo-indigenism,

183

or *mestizaje* (Noriega, 1992b, p. 150), thereby challenging assimilation and melting-pot narratives;

- production of texts that deconstruct machismo, the masculine identity, and the celebration of works that give the black woman and Chicana subject an active part in the text, while criticizing such timeworn stereotypes as the virgin, whore, supportive wife, or home-girl (Fregoso, 1993, pp. 29, 93–94);
- a rejection of essentializing approaches to identity; an emphasis on a processual, gendered performance view of self, and the location of identity within, not outside, systems of cultural and media representation.
- a refusal to accept the official race-relations narrative of the culture, which privileges the ideology of assimilation, while contending that black and Hispanic youth pose grave threats for white society (Fregoso, 1993, p. 29).

Many of these cinematic practices are displayed in films made in the 1990s by directors of color, including Bill Duke's *Rage in Harlem* (1991), Charles Burnett's *To Sleep With Anger* (1990), Mira Nair's *Mississippi Masala* (1992), Spike Lee's *Crooklyn* (1994), John Singleton's *Higher Learning* (1995) and *Rosewood* (1997), Gregory Nava's *Mi Familia* (1995), and Ang Lee's *Eat Drink Man Woman* (1994).

These films articulate an aesthetic of production that celebrates ethnic culture, while interrogating racial and gender stereotypes. They challenge assimiliation narratives. They emphasize community, family, and family solidarity. They experiment with narrative and visual form, use personal testimonials, voice-overs, and off-screen narration. They refuse the didactic social problems form of discourse; indeed, they refuse to locate pathology in the ethnic community. They do not invoke the state as the agency of salvation for the blighted, violent, drug-using minority community. They do not connect the signifiers of race with rap music, hip hop culture, and youth violence. They work from within ethnic culture to present a cinema of pride and cultural resistance. Thus these films stand in bold contrast to the hood films of the 1990s.

Implementing the Anti-Aesthetic

In Chapter 1 I outlined a series of structural commonalities that have shaped Hollywood's cinematic racial order. These commonalities included: nineteenth- and twentieth-century racist ideologies; a racist popular culture; a racist performance vocabulary; gender-specific cinematic racial stereotypes; a segregated society; a racist studio production system; the appearance of theatres in racial ghettos; minority actors, actresses, directors, and an expanding minority film audience; the civil rights and women's movements of the 1960s and 1970s; a tradition of producing realistic social problems films.

Today, few of these factors have changed. The various civil rights movements are fighting for their lives. Once more there is a Republican administration in the White House and another generation of conservatives attempt to undo the gains of the last quarter-century. Cinematic and everyday racism is still present. The Hollywood studio system only promotes a narrow range of race-based films:

those that will entertain within an action, cop-buddy, or comedy format. So while the minority audience gets larger and Magic Johnson Theatres are now open in Harlem, these multiplexes can only show the films Hollywood makes. And while Spike Lee's recent film *Bamboozled* (2000) may mock the minstrel tradition of blackface, the film speaks to a larger truth about the culture's unwillingness to face up to its own racist past.

Valerie Smith (1997) observes that African Americans still live with the legacies of D. W. Griffith's *The Birth of a Nation*, the film that many claim is the 'inaugural moment of African American cinema' (p. 1). It's all here: realistic cinema, a cinema that would tell the truth about America's post-Civil War racial history. Everything is present: the prejudices, the stereotypes, the use of parallel editing, cuts back and forth between action sequences, close-ups of actors in blackface. The images of blacks found in this film have been reproduced 'throughout the history of U.S. cinema' (Valerie Smith, 1997, p. 1). Smith is clear. These images are racist, and they 'threaten the lives of "real" black people' (p. 1).

The new aesthetic of racial difference begins by challenging these representations. It searches for alternative representations that are neither racist or sexist. Paraphrasing Valerie Smith (1997, p. 1), this black (and ethnic) cinema can be read as a search for new and different representations of black and brown subjects. It is understood that there is no longer any single representation that can be coded as more or less authentic. This search moves in two directions at the same time: the production of positive images that will replace negative representations; and the desire to criticize, and re-code, negative images.

The first impulse can be seen in the films by Burnett, Duke, and Nair noted above, as well as Kasi Lemmons' *Eve's Bayou* (1997) and Maya Angelou's *Down in the Delta* (1998), contemporary films about black women and their families. Carl Franklin's *Devil in a Blue Dress* and Julia Dash's *Daughters of the Dust* can also be included in this category. In contrast, Bill Duke's *A Rage in Harlem*, like Lee's *Bamboozled*, deconstructs previous racist stereotypes about black community life in America, turning the negative into a series of jokes.

However, it is no longer sufficient to offer examples of good and bad films, including inventories of negative images. It is time to move away from the search for an essentialist (and good) black or brown subject, time to refuse cultural and biological essentialisms (Hall, 1996b, p. 472).[7]

Two Case Studies

Consider Zeinabu irene Davis's 1999 film *Compensation*, which was entered in the 2000 Sundance Film Festival. This is a black-and-white silent film, set in Chicago in two time periods: the turn of the twentieth-century and the present day. It tells the story of two deaf African-American women (Malindy, Malaika) and their respective relationships with two hearing African-American men (Arthur and Nico). The film uses a simple Joplinesque piano as its musical soundtrack.

Davis dedicates the film to Paul Laurence Dunbar, 'America's Negro Poet Laureate' (1872–1906).[8] The film opens with a series of photographs, dated

Chicago, early 1900s. These are seldom-seen slices of African-American history. They are images of turn-of-the-twentieth-century middle-class blacks comfortably at home in an urban black public sphere. The screen informs the viewer: 'Colored population of Chicago doubles – 1900–1910.' On screen the streets fill with shots of middle-class blacks in expensive suits and dresses. The next storyboard informs the viewer: 'W. E. B. Du Bois publishes *Souls of Black Folks*, 1903.' The next storyboards state: '*The Chicago Defender* begins publication, 1905' and 'Scott Joplin's classic Negro opera "Treemonisha" published, 1911.'

Davis cleverly uses the methods of silent film to tell a story about the two deaf women. Both women write their messages on chalkboards, just as a silent film uses a printed text to convey storyline. The film uses a cinematic language and a form of montage that brings the rhythms of deaf and hearing African-American culture dramatically and vividly alive. Indeed, Davis's use of the hearing/deaf dichotomy can be read as a metaphor for black and white relationships. Each woman repeatedly questions her ability to have a relationship with a hearing man. Malaika's sister tells her 'Deaf and hearing relationships don't work…. Hearing people just don't understand our struggles for civil rights.'

The film moves back and forth between the stories of the two couples, and the two time periods. In pairing the two deaf women with hearing men, Davis privileges language and literacy. Arthur cannot read, while Nico is a librarian, a man of books. Both couples fall in love, and each relationship confronts the epidemics of its time period: tuberculosis for Arthur,[9] who works in the meat plants in the stockyards, and being HIV-positive for Malaika.

After its opening photo-montage, the film turns to its story of 'Malindy Brown, a woman of much talent and ample learning.'[10] Malindy attends the Kendall School of the Deaf, 1893. 'The school segregates in 1906, and colored children are expelled.' Dressed in a long white, flowing dress, Malindy is sitting on the sand on the beach, under an umbrella, eating an apple. Her black face is framed by the ribbon on her white sunhat. Malindy meets Tildy Evans, a black 12-year-old migrant. They run through the sand to the edge of the water. 'Trust and respect blossom…. Malindy teaches Tildy the fundamentals of learning.' Malindy writes on her chalkboard, 'My Moma says you smarter than white people … you could be another Booker T. Washington if you was not deaf and dumb.' Tildy writes back, 'I'm not dumb.' The sound of the waves are heard in the background.

Malindy and Tildy meet Arthur Jones, a 'lonely migrant of meager means' who comes walking along the beach carrying a walking stick and a mandolin. He asks Malindy if she wants some fish? She writes, 'I do not speak like you.' He replies, 'I can't read Miss.' She signs that she wants him to play his mandolin. In the next scene Malindy is shown writing a letter protesting segregation at the Kendall School of the Deaf. She informs her reader that she is now in business for herself as a successful seamstress.

The film shifts to the present, 'Chi-Town – Chicago – present day,' with a shot of the Chicago skyline and its skyscrapers. Malaika Brown, printer and aspiring graphic artist, is dancing on the beach. Nico Jones, children's librarian and godchild of Ogan, jogs by and waves. Malaika ignores him. She writes in the sand, 'I don't go out with hearing people.' Nico attends sign language classes and learns to sign ASL. He and Malaika begin courting. Nico immerses himself in Malaika's world, which includes the world of deaf dancers. Malaika refuses to consummate their relationship.

Malaika sends Nico a letter, telling him she is HIV-positive, and this is why she has not allowed them to consummate their relationship. Nico longs to see her, but they do not answer each other's telephone calls. Nico prays. In a moving sequence an off-screen female softly voice sings an African spiritual. Davis's camera graces the sillhouttes of African art displayed on the walls in Nico's apartment. In a sequence of scenes (which may be fantasy) Nico and Malaika appear together on the beach. He plays drums for her and she dances in front of him. They stand together on the waterfront. He places his arm over her shoulder as they gaze at geese flying across the water.

Davis shifts the story back to Arthur and Malindy. Arthur has stopped seeing Malindy. He sends her a letter which reads:

> I have contracted tuberculosis and I have to be kept apart so my condition will not affect others ... I would have liked to have been your hearing voice in the world.... My life shall end before ... I learn to read well enough to read the book of Dunbar poems that you once gave me.

Arthur delivers a message to Malindy as she sits on the beach: 'I send you the poem "Compensation" which reminds me so much of my dear mother back in Mississippi.' This poem is then read to Arthur by his minister,

> Because I had loved so deeply
> Because I had loved so long,
> God in His great compassion
> Gave me the gift of song.
> Because I have loved so deeply
> And sung with such faltering breath,
> The Master in infinite mercy
> Offers the boon of Death.

As the minster finishes reading these lines, Arthur dies.

The camera moves to Malindy, still on the beach, gazing at the water. The screen fills with shots of the sun dancing off the water. These shots dissolve into dazzling prisms of light. Then the camera returns to the beach, to a small altar-like arrangement, candles burning, cotton plants growing in the sand, small buds along their stems. Suddenly a cotton bud opens into a beautiful white cotton flower. Like an elegant white rose, its presence fills the screen. The screen dissolves into a reverse triangular drawing labeled 'AYIZAN, Healer & Protector.'

Compensation is a powerful film. It is boldly experimental. Illness and death are presented as forces that persons cannot control. The death of a loved one is blunted by the gift of love itself. That gift compensates for life's losses. In showing this, Davis's film brings great dignity and respect to the situations of African-American women and men. At the same time her film honors African-American culture and history.

This is not a protest film. It is not angry. It is quietly spiritual and empowering as it presents these women and their silent voices. Like the films of Charles Burnett and Julie Dash, it lifts Du Bois's veil. It anchors its story firmly and proudly within the everyday worlds of African Americans and their lives.

In the language of the Black Arts Movement, this is film art that is functional, collective, and committed. This film is for deaf and hearing black women. It is democratic; it celebrates diversity and personal freedom. It shows Chicago's racial ghettos as internal colonies, cut off from white society. This version of the black aesthetic stands in stark contrast to the hood movies analyzed in earlier chapters of this book.

Now Carl Franklin's overlooked 1995 film *Devil in a Blue Dress*. This film is based on the novel by Walter Mosley (1990) of the same name. The opening credit sequence is framed with vivid nighttime colors of black, purple, blue, and red. A blues singer croons, 'I got a West Side baby. She lives way cross town.' Stylized cut-out images of African-American men and women in evening dress dance across the screen. Orange and yellow light streams from upstairs windows above a corner bar. Couples embrace and dance below a street light. Women in tight dresses cross their legs and smile at men. Men gossip with one another and lean against expensive limousines. The blues singer continues, 'She sets my soul on fire.' The back of a naked woman appears in the upstairs window. 'Ya, I got a West Side baby. She lives clear cross town. And when I'm with my baby, I don't want a soul around. Now Monday mornin' early, someone knocked at my door. I know it wasn't my baby, cause she never knocked before.'

The camera pulls back, revealing the larger street scene, which is filled with black city night-life. This scene segues into the summer of 1948. Real cars honk and come down the street. The blues singer continues singing. We cut to an upstairs bar. Denzel Washington as Easy Rawlins begins to narrate, 'It was summer 1948 and I needed money.' Thus does the film begin, a story of racism, violence, and oppression in post-World War II Los Angeles.

Franklin's film, like Davis's, illuminates and honors seldom-seen slices of African-American community life. Mosley's Easy Rawlins mysteries celebrate black art, religion, and music. Mosley tells stories about the struggles of black Americans attempting to create their own cultural, political, and economic spaces in mid-twentieth-century Southern California. Franklin's film brings Mosley's world alive, a Raymond Chandler city of corruption, betrayal, double-crosses, *femmes fatales*, race prejudice, and macho men beating up one another. Like *Compensation*, this is film art that is functional, collective, and committed. It gives a black man the power of the white private eye. It shows how black immigrants from the South created their own moral community in urban Los Angeles, a community of care, love, and mutual empowerment.

Franklin and Mosley turn a gentle eye on the eccentrics and odd persons who inhabit this space. They fold the music of jazz and blues into the night-life. They expose the economic underside of racial discrimination. Importantly, they tell a story with profound human implications; that is, the lived side of mid-twentieth-century racism for middle-class blacks.

These two films embody a version of a new aesthetic of color, an aesthetic that reconnects to the Black Arts Movement of the 1970s. They quietly present their version of a critical cinema of racial difference. They avoid violence. They celebrate cultural differences. They honor the art, rituals, myths, and religions of black culture. They ask how cinema can help create critical race consciousness. This is a black aesthetic that works for the twenty-first century.

In Conclusion

Popular culture, Stuart Hall (1996b) reminds us, is mythic, a theatre of desires, a space of popular fantasies. 'It is where we go to discover who we are' (p. 474). And in answering this existential question, we find that our conceptions of self and other are grounded always in misplaced notions of racial difference, of whiteness and privilege. We must always be on guard concerning what we learn about ourselves.

In his review of *Bamboozled*, Jeff MacGregor (2000) describes what he has learned about blacks in America by watching film and television:

> Black people are frightening. Black people are criminals. Black people are violent. Black people are athletic. Black people are successful members of the professional class. Black people are drug addicts. Black people are great entertainers. Black people are loving members of big families. Black people are musical. Black people are funny. Black people are loud. Black people are angry. Black people are churchgoers. Black people are always in trouble. Black people are frightening.

> This is what television has taught me about race in my own country. I am a 42-year-old American male and I am white and this is what I have learned from a lifetime of situation comedies and one-hour cop dramas and commercials and those earnest documentaries.

And what can we say of white people? It is not enough to turn the tables, to ask of all persons of color what they have learned from a lifetime of watching whites on television and on the movie screen.

But even more is at issue. Ralph Ellison, Richard Wright, and James Baldwin framed the questions a half-century ago, and Walter Mosley, Angela Davis, bell hooks, and June Jordan re-phrase them today. How can we use art, cinema and literature to communicate across our barriers of race and religion, class, color and region? How can we share in our common humanity, while valuing our differences? How can the interests of democracy and art converge? How can we use our literature, cinema, and critical social science to advance the goals of this democratic society? (Ellison, 1952). 'How can we overcome the structures of racism that are so deeply engrained in the marrow of this democracy?' (Feagin, 2000, p. 270).

The cultural spaces of racial difference, Hall (1996b, p. 474) tells us, are profoundly dialogic, always tangled up in complex, interconnecting ways. Someday those who wore blackface out of choice will find that those who are really black or brown have painted their faces white. And now the white masks are black, and the black and brown masks are multi-colored – a million off-white hues, mahogany, golden, dusky, tan and muddy brown, black, and satin. And in this colorful carnival-like space, a space that Bakhtin (1968) would take delight in, a new cinematic racial order is born. This is a racial order that truly honors racial difference. In its celebrations of difference, it unmasks and frees everyone. Here at the end, stealing a line from Ralph Ellison and Louis Armstrong, persons of color will no longer have to ask, 'What Did I Do to be so Black and Blue?' (Ellison, 1952, p. 8).

Thus from the violence of the hood movies of the 1990s, a new cinematic culture of non-violence is imagined. In this new space we begin to undo a hundred years of racism and violence and injury, a hundred years of a racist cinematic order. Farewell D. W. Griffith.

Notes

1. I am mindful of the criticisms of the movement, which came in four forms. There were those, like Ralph Ellison (see Clark, 1988, for a review), who opposed the concept of a black engaged art, contending that art should be above and beyond the world of everyday experience (see Ellison, 1964, p. 120; also McPherson, 2000, p. 127). Describing his goal in *Invisible Man* (1952), Ellison said: 'I was trying to avoid another novel of racial protest' (p. xviii). Further, the black artist has no obligation to engage directly in liberation struggles (Baker, 1997, p. 1804). Second, critics argued that the movement failed because art cannot produce social change; it is no substitute for political, economic, or social action (Clark, 1980, p. 91). Third, some argued that the Black Arts Movement subordinated art to politics and imposed the narrow aesthetic paradigms of realism and naturalism on its followers (hooks, 1990, p. 108). Fourth, many leveled charges of black racism, anti-semitism, homophobia, misogynism, and essentialism against the movement (see Clark, 1980, pp. 98–99; Cade, 1970; Wallace, 1990; Christian, 1997, pp. 2014–2016; Baker, 1997, pp. 1804–1806; hooks, 1990, pp. 106–111). Baker (1997, pp. 1804–1896) Christians (1997, pp. 2011–2020), William Harris (1998, pp. 1694–1698), and hooks (1989, pp. 103–113) show how black feminist artists in the last two decades have extended the movement and its aesthetics into the present. Novelists, essayists, dramatists, playwrights, and poets, including Jordan, Lorde, Morrison, Walker, Shange, Naylor, Smith, hooks, and Dove, interrogate the sexist and homophobic themes contained in the works of the first generation in the movement. These women examine spirituality, gender, sexuality, motherhood, family relations, family violence, incest (see below), and multiple forms of blackness while experimenting with new textual forms, including: children's literature, performance texts, non-linear narrative, jazz improvisation, African and black Caribbean language, cosmologies and mythologies, oral story-telling traditions, call/response formats, quilting metaphors, talking-back texts, and texts that self-consciously signify (Gates, 1988).

2. Here they show parallels between the Mexican Renaissance (Rivera), and Soviet art, Berlin Dadaism, and French Surrealism (and Cubism) in the same period.

3. Hall (1996b, p. 472), after Spivak (1990), addresses the notion of strategic essentialism, indicating that in certain historical moments a form of strategic essentialism has been necessary. But this may no longer be the case. Indeed, strategic essentialism can essentialize, naturalize, and dehistoricize differences in problematic ways (Hall, 1996b, p. 472; see also Lott, 1997, p. 93).

4. The following section draws from Denzin, 2000, pp. 909–914.

5. Extending Dewey (1934), this agenda views aesthetics as that branch of philosophy dealing with the politics of the aesthetic experience, including concepts of beauty and standards of value in judging artistic expressions. It builds on Benjamin's (1968, p. 243) call for a political, revolutionary aesthetic that supports democracy (Kellner, 1989, p. 124) and avoids the turn to state-sponsored war and fascism (Benjamin, 1968, p. 243; also Gilroy, 2000, p. 231).

6. The implementation of the 1968 New Communicators Program (see Chapter 1, note 40) at the University of Southern California and the University of California at Los Angeles produced first- and second-generation minority filmmakers called by some the 'black and brown Los Angeles Schools' (see Diawara, 1993a; Masilea, 1993; Noriega, 1992b, p. 142; 1996, pp. 7–8; Fregoso, 1993, pp. 31, 129). Funding for this project was cut back under the Reagan administration in the 1980s. According to Masilela (1993, p. 107), there were two distinct waves or groups of filmmakers. The first wave included Gerima and Burnett, and the second group, Dash and Woodberry. The post-civil rights filmmakers implemented their version of critical race theory, especially the arguments of Fanon.

7. It is perhaps also time to move away from revisionist stories about the civil rights movement told from the white point of view. Films that do this include *Mississippi Burning* (1988), *A Time to Kill* (1996), *The Chamber* (1996), *Ghosts of Mississippi* (1996). I would also include Banderas's *Crazy in Alabama* (1999) in this category, but not Singleton's *Rosewood* (1997).

8. 'Compensation' is the title of a Dunbar poem (p. 187) (see Barksdale and Kinnamon, 1972b, p. 361). Dunbar was known for his dialect poetry which celebrated the contributions of blacks in the Civil War and in the building of America (see Trudier Harris, 1998, p. 602; Barkesdale and Kinamon, 1972a, pp. 357–358).

9. Dunbar also died of tuberculosis.

10. Davis may have taken this name from a poem by Dunbar, 'When Malindy Sings' (see Barksdale and Kinnamon, 1972b, pp. 357–358).

Appendix: Filmography

Incomplete Listing of African-American Films: 1967–2000[1]

Year/Film	African-American actor/actress	African-American director
1967		
Guess Who's Coming to Dinner	S. Poitier	
Hurry Sundown	R. Hooks, D. Carroll	
In the Heat of the Night	S. Poitier	
1968		
Black Jesus*	W. Strode	
Black Like Me	R. St Jacques	
Dark of the Sun	J. Brown	
Green Berets	R. St Jacques	
If He Hollers. Let Him Go	R. St Jacques	
100 Rifles	J. Brown	
Salt and Pepper	S. Davis, Jr	
1969		
Learning Tree	K. Johnson, E. Evans	G. Parks
Lost Man	S. Poitier	
Putney-Swope	A. Johnson	R. Downey
The Reivers	R. Crosse	
Riot	J. Brown	
Uptight, Slaves	R. St Jacques, R. Dee	J. Dassin
1970		
Cotton Comes to Harlem	G. Cambridge, R. St Jacques	O. Davis
The Great White Hope	J. Earl Jones	
The Landlord	P. Bailey, L. Gossete	
The Liberation of L. B. Jones	R. L. Browne, Y. Kotto	
They Call Me Mister Tibbs!	S. Poitier	
Watermelon Man	G. Cambridge, E. Parsons	Melvin Van Peebles
1971		
Shaft*	R. Roundtree	G. Parks
Sweet Sweetback's Baadasssss Song*[2]	Melvin Van Peebles, J. Amos, R. Hughes	Melvin Van Peebles
1972		
The Big Bird Cage	P. Grier	
Black Gunn*	J. Brown	
Blacula*	W. Marshall	
Buck and the Preacher	S. Poitier, H. Belafonte, R. Dee	S. Poitier
Come Back, Charleston Blue	G. Cambridge	M. Warren
Cool Breeze*		
Final Comedown*	R. St Jacques	
Georgia, Georgia	D. Sands	

Year/Film	African-American actor/actress	African-American director
1972 *(continued)*		
Lady Sings the Blues	D. Ross, R. Pryor, B. Williams	
Legend of Nigger Charlie	F. Williamson, T. O'Neil	
The Man*	J. E. Jones	
Melinda*	R. Cash	H. Robertson
Shaft's Big Score!*	R. Roundtree	G. Parks
Slaughter*	J. Brown	
Soul Soldier	R. Johnson	
Sounder	P. Winfield, K. Hooks, C. Tyson	
Superfly*	R. O'Neal	G. Parks, Jr
1973		
Black Caesar*	F. Williamson	
Book of Numbers*	R. St Jacques	R. St Jacques
Charlie One-Eye*	R. Roundtree	
Cleopatra Jones*	T. Dobson	
Coffy	P. Grier	
Detroit 9000*	H. Rhodes	
Five on the Black Hand Side	G. Turman	O. Williams
Gordon's War*	P. Winfield	O. Davis
Live and Let Die	G. Henry, Y. Kotto, G. Holder	
The Mack*	M. Julien	
Scream, Blacula, Scream*	W. Marshall, P. Grier	
Shaft in Africa*	R. Roundtree	
The Slams*	J. Brown	
Slaughter's Big-Rip-Off*	J. Brown	
The Soul of Nigger Charlie	F. Williamson	
The Spook Who Sat by the Door	L. Cook	I. Dixon
Superfly T. N. T.*	R. O'Neal	R. O'Neal
Trick Baby*		
Trouble Man*	R. Hooks, P. Kelly	
1974		
Amazing Grace	M. Mabley, R. Cash	S. Lathan
Black Godfather*	P. Grier	
Blazing Saddles	C. Little	
Claudine	R. Cash, J. E. Jones	
Foxy Brown*	P. Grier	
Klansman	O. J. Simpson	
Super Cops		G. Parks
The Take*		
The Towering Inferno	O. J. Simpson	
Uptown Saturday Night	H. Belafonte, B. Cosby, S. Poitier	S. Poitier
Willie Dynamite	D. Sands	G. Moses
1975		
Bush Mama		H. Gerima
Cleopatra Jones and the Casino of Gold*	T. Dobson	
Cooley High	G. Turman	M. Schultz
Dolemite*	R. Moore	D. Martin
Friday Foster*	P. Grier	

Year/Film	African-American actor/actress	African-American director
1975 *(continued)*		
Let's Do It Again	H. Belafonte, B. Cosby, S. Poitier	S. Poitier
Mahogany	D. Ross	B. Gordy
Mandingo	K. Norton	
1976		
The Bingo Long Traveling ALL-Stars and Motor Kings	S. Paige, B. Williams, R. Pryor	
Car Wash	R. Pryor, I. Dixon	M. Schultz
Deadly Hero	J. E. Jones	
*The Human Tornado**	R. Moore	C. Roquemore
Leadbelly		G. Parks
River Nigger	J. E. Jones, C. Tyson	
Rocky	C. Weathers	
Silver Streak	R. Pryor	
Sparkle	D. Harewood, I. Cara	
Which Way is Up?	R. Pryor	M. Schultz
1977		
Greased Lightning	R. Pryor	M. Schultz
The Greatest	M. Ali	
Killer of Sheep		C. Burnett
*Monkey Hustle**	R. Moore	
Passing Through		
Piece of the Action	B. Cosby, S. Poitier, J. E. Jones L. Clark	S. Poitier
Roots (TV)	J. Amos, M. Angelov	
1978		
Blue Collar	R. Pryor, Y. Kotto	
California Suite	R. Pryor, B. Cosby	
*Petey Wheatstraw**	R. Moore	C. Roquemore
Remember my Name	A. Woodard	
The Wiz	D. Ross, R. Pryor, L. Horne	
1979		
Richard Pryor Live in Concert	R. Pryor	
Rocky II	C. Weathers	
1980[3]		
American Gigolo	B. Duke	
The Blues Brothers	C. Calloway, R. Charles, J. Brown A. Franklin	
Brubaker	Y. Kotto, M. Freeman	
The Empire Strikes Back	B. D. Williams	
Fort Apache: The Bronx	P. Grier	
In God We Trust	R. Pryor	
The Shining	S. Crothers	
Stir Crazy	R. Pryor	
Wholly Moses	R. Pryor	
1981		
Bustin' Loose	R. Pryor	
Carbon Copy	D. Washington	
History of the World, Part I	G. Hines	
Quest for Fire	R. Chong	

Year/Film	African-American actor/actress	African-American director
1981 *(continued)*		
Ragtime	H. Rollins, Jr, S. Jackson	
Wolfen	G. Hines	
1982		
Conan the Barbarian	J. E. Jones	
Fast Times at Ridgemont High	F. Whitaker	
48 Hours	E. Murphy	
Harry and Son	M. Freeman	
Losing Ground		K. Collins
Nighthawks	B. D. Williams	
An Officer and a Gentleman	L. Gossett, Jr	
Richard Pryor Live on the Sunset Strip	R. Pryor	
Rocky III	Mr T.	
Some Kind of Hero	R. Pryor	
The Toy	R. Pryor	
Wild Style	Fab Five Freddy	
1983		
Cross Creek	A. Woodard	
Deal of the Century	G. Hines	
Flashdance	J. Beals	
Illusions		J. Dash
Jaws 3-D	L. Gossett, Jr	
Return of the Jedi	B. D. Williams	
Richard Pryor Here and Now	R. Pryor	
Streets of Fire	R. Townsend	
Sugar Cane Alley		E. Palcy
Superman 3	R. Pryor	
Trading Places	E. Murphy	
1984		
Beat Street	R. Chong, J. Beals	S. Lathan
Best Defense	E. Murphy	
Beverly Hills Cop	E. Murphy	
Bless Their Little Hearts		B. Woodberry
Brother from Another Planet	J. Morton	
City Heat	R. Roundtree	
Conan the Destroyer	G. Jones	
Cotton Club	G. and M. Hines, L. McKee, Mario Van Peebles, L. Fishburne	
Hair Piece		A. Chenzira
My Brother's Wedding		C. Burnett
Places of the Heart	D. Glover	
Purple Rain	Prince, C. Williams III	
Revenge of the Nerds	L. Scott	
A Soldier's Story	A. Caesar, H. Rollins, Jr, D. Washington	
1985		
American Flyers	R. Chong, R. Townsend	
Brewster's Millions	R. Pryor	

Year/Film	African-American actor/actress	African-American director
1985 *(continued)*		
The Bride	J. Beals	
City Limits	J. E. Jones	
The Color Purple	D. Glover, W. Goldberg, O. Winfrey, A. Caesar, R. Chong, L. Fishburne	
Commando	R. Chong	
Fear City	B. D. Williams	
Krush Grove		M. Schultz
Last Dragon		M. Schultz
Mad Max Beyond the Thunderdome	T. Turner	
Quicksilver	L. Fishburne	
Rappin'	Mario Van Peebles	
Silverado	D. Glover	
Soul Man	R. Chong	
A View to a Kill	G. Jones	
White Nights	G. Hines	
Witness	D. Glover	
1986		
The Color of Money	F. Whitaker	
Crossroads	J. Seneca	
Delivery Boys	Mario Van Peebles	
Golden Child	E. Murphy	
Heartbreak Ridge	Mario Van Peebles	
Iron Eagle	L. Gossett, Jr	
Jo Jo Dancer, Your Life is Calling	G. Hines	
Jumpin' Jack Flash	W. Goldberg	
Mona Lisa	K. Tyson	
Platoon	F. Whitaker	
Power	D. Washington	
Ratboy	R. Townsend	
Round Midnight	D. Gordon	
Running Scared	G. Hines	
Serpent and the Rainbow	P. Winfield, Z. Mokae, K. Tyson	
She's Gotta Have It	T. C. Jones, S. Lee, R. Dowell	S. Lee
Soul Man	J. E. Jones, R. Chong	
Streets of Gold	W. Snipes	
Under the Cherry Moon	Prince	
Vamp	G. Jones	
Wildcats	W. Snipes	
1987		
Angel Heart	L. Bonet	
Beverly Hills Cop II	E. Murphy	
Burglar	W. Goldberg	
Critical Condition	R. Pryor	
Cry Freedom	D. Washington	
Deadly Illusion	B. D. Williams	
Eddie Murphy Raw	E. Murphy, S. Jackson	
Fatal Beauty	W. Goldberg	
Gardens of Stone	J. E. Jones	
Good Morning Viet Nam	F. Whitaker	

Year/Film	African-American actor/actress	African-American director
1987 *(continued)*		
Hollywood Shuffle	R. Townsend	R. Townsend
Leonard, Part 6	B. Cosby	
Lethal Weapon	D. Glover	
Matewan	J. E. Jones	
The Principle	L. Gossett, Jr	
Siesta	G. Jones	
Sign O' the Times	Prince	
Street Smart	M. Freeman	
1988		
Action Jackson	C. Weathers	
Bat 21	D. Glover	
Bird	F. Whitaker	
Clara's Heart	W. Goldberg	
Clean and Sober	M. Freeman	
Coming to America	E. Murphy, A. Hall, J. E. Jones, S. Jackson	
Die Hard	R. VelJohnson	
For Queen and Country	D. Washington	
Hairspray	R. Brown, C. Prince	
I'm Gonna Git You Sucka		K. I. Wayans
Little Nikita	S. Poitier	
Looking for Langston		I. Julien
Midnight Run	Y. Kotto	
Mississippi Burning	D. McCrary	
Moving	R. Pryor	
Off Limits	G. Hines	
Red Heat	L. Fishburne	
School Daze	L. Fishburne, J. Seneca, S. Jackson, O. Davis, T. Campbell	S. Lee
Scrooged	A. Woodard	
Shoot to Kill	S. Poitier	
The Telephone	W. Goldberg	
1989		
Casualties of War	V. Rhames	
*Do the Right Thing***	O. Davis, R. Dee, S. Jackson	S. Lee
Driving Miss Daisy	M. Freeman	
A Dry White Season	Z. Mokaee, W. Ntshona	E. Palcy
Field of Dreams	J. E. Jones	
Glory	D. Washington, M. Freeman	
Harlem Nights	E. Murphy, R. Foxx, D. Reese, A. Hall	E. Murphy
Lean on Me	M. Freeman	
Lethal Weapon 2	D. Glover	
Major League	W. Snipes	
Mighty Quinn	D. Washington	
Miss Firecracker	A. Woodard	
Sea of Love	S. Jackson	
Sidewalk Stories	C. Lane	C. Lane
Tap	G. Hines, S. Davis, Jr	

Year/Film	African-American actor/actress	African-American director
1990		
Another 48 Hours	E. Murphy	
Bird on the Wire	B. Duke	
Bonfire of the Vanities	M. Freeman	
Car Wash	B. Duke	
Daughters of the Dust		J. Dash
Def by Temptation		J. Bond III
Die Hard 2	R. VelJohnson, J. Amos, A. Evans	
Downtown	F. Whitaker	
Ghost	W. Goldberg	
GoodFellas	S. Jackson	
Graffiti Bridge	Prince	
Heart Condition	D. Washington	
Homer and Eddie	W. Goldberg	
House Party	C. Reid, C. Martin	R. Hudlin
Hunt for Red October	J. E. Jones	
King of New York	L. Fishburne, W. Snipes	
Long Walk Home	W. Goldberg	
Mo' Better Blues	D. Washington, S. Jackson, W. Snipes	S. Lee
RoboCop	W. Pugh	
To Sleep With Anger	D. Glover, P. Butler, M. Alice	C. Burnett
1991		
Another You	R. Pryor	
*Boyz N the Hood***	A. Bassett, L. Fishburne	J. Singleton
Cadence	L. Fishburne	
Chameleon Street	W. Harris	W. Harris
City of Hope	A. Bassett	
Class Action	L. Fishburne	
Five Heartbeats	M. Wright, D. Carroll	R. Townsend
Flight of the Intruder	D. Glover	
Fried Green Tomatoes	C. Tyson, S. Shaw	
Grand Canyon	D. Glover	
Hangin' with the Homeboys		J. Vasquez
Jungle Fever	W. Snipes, O.Davis, R. See, S. Jackson	S. Lee
Last Boy Scout	D. Wayans	
Livin' Large		M. Schultz
Mister Johnson	M. Ezioshi	
*New Jack City***	Ice-T, V. Williams, T. C. Johns, W. Snipes	Mario Van Peebles
One False Move		C. Franklin
Pure Luck	D. Glover	
A Rage in Harlem	D. Glover, F. Whitaker, R. Givens	B. Duke
Regarding Henry	B. Nunn	
Richochet	D. Washington	
Robin Hood, Prince of Thieves	M. Freeman	
Soapdish	W. Goldberg	
*Straight Out of Brooklyn***		M. Rich

Year/Film	African-American actor/actress	African-American director
1991 *(continued)*		
Strictly Business	J. Phillips	K. Hooks
True Identity		C. Lane
1992		
The Bodyguard	W. Houston	
Boomerang	E. Murphy	
Crying Game	F. Whitaker	
Deep Cover	L. Fishburne	B. Duke
Diggstown	L. Gossett, Jr	
Distinguished Gentleman	E. Murphy	
Gladiator	C. Gooding, Jr	
Grand Cnyon	A. Woodard, D. Glover	
The Hand that Rocks the Cradle	E. Hudson	
*Juice***	T. Shakur, S. Jackson	E. Dickerson
Lethal Weapon 3	D. Glover	
Love Field	D. Haysbert	
Malcolm X	D. Washington, A. Basset, S. Lee	
Mississippi Masala	D. Washington, J. Sennica, M. Nair	
Mo' Money	D. Wayans	
Passenger 57	W. Snipes	K. Hooks
Passion Fish	A. Woodard, A. Bassett	
Patriot Games	S. Jackson, J. E. Jones	
The Player	W. Goldberg	
The Power of One	M. Freeman	
Predator II	D. Glover	K. Hooks
Rich in Love	A. Woodard	
Rising Sun	W. Snipes	
Sarafina	W. Goldberg	
Sister Act	W. Goldberg	
Sneakers	S. Poitier, J. E. Jones	
South Central	G. Plummer, B. Minns	
Unforgiven	M. Freeman	
White Men Can't Jump	W. Snipes	
White Sands	S. Jackson	
Wisecracks	W. Goldberg	
1993		
Amos and Andrew	S. Jackson	
Boiling Point	W. Snipes	
Bopha!	D. Glover, A. Woodard	M. Freeman
CB4	C. Rock	T. Davis
Cool Runnings	D. E. Doug	J. Taub
Cop and a Half	R. Dee	
Demolition Man	W. Snipes	
The Fear of a Black Hat		R. Cundieff
A Few Good Men	W. Bodison	
Fugitive	L. S. Caldwell	
Heart and Soul	A. Woodard	
Jurassic Park	S. Jackson	
*Just Another Girl on the I R T***	A. Johnson	L. Harris
Made in America	W. Goldberg	

Year/Film	African-American actor/actress	African-American director
1993 *(continued)*		
*Menace II Society***	S. Jackson, T. Turner	A. and A. Hughes
Much Ado About Nothing	D. Washington	
National Lampoon's Loaded Weapon 1	W. Goldberg, S. Jackson	
The Pelican Brief	D. Washington	
Philadelphia	D. Washington	
*Poetic Justice***	J. Jackson, T. Ferrell, T. Shakur	J. Singleton
Posse	Mario Van Peebles, W. Strode	Mario Van Peebles
Sandlot	J. E. Jones	
Saint of Fort Washington	D. Glover	
Searching for Bobby Fischer	L. Fishburne	
Sister Act 2	W. Goldberg	
Six Degrees of Separation	W. Smith	
Swing Kids		T. Carter
What's Love Got to Do With It?	A. Bassett, L. Fishburne	
Who's the Man?	Q. Latifah	
1994		
Above the Rim	T. Shakur	
Ace Ventura: Pet Detective	T. Loc	
Alma's Rainbow	J. Copeland	A. Chenzira
Angels in the Outfield	D. Glover	
Beverly Hills Cop III	E. Murphy	
Blown Away	F. Whitaker	
Blue Chips	A. Woodard, S. O'Neal	
Clear and Present Danger	J. E. Jones	
Crooklyn	A. Woodard, D. Lindo	S. Lee
Corina, Corina	W. Goldberg	
Forrest Gump	M. Williamson	
Fresh	S. Nelson	
Jason's Lyric	A. Payne	
Lightning Jack	C. Gooding, Jr	
Maverick	D. Glover	
Pulp Fiction	S. Jackson	
The Shawshank Redemption	M. Freeman	
Sister Act 2	W. Goldberg	
Sugar Hill	W. Snipes	
Surviving the Game	Ice-T	E. Dickerson
1995		
Boys on the Side	W. Goldberg	
*Clockers***	D. Lindo, I. Washington	S. Lee
Crimson Tide	D. Washington	
Cry, the Beloved Country	J. E. Jones	
Dead Presidents	L. Tate, C. Tucker	A. and A. Hughes
Devil in a Blue Dress	D. Washington	C. Franklin
Die Hard With a Vengeance	S. Jackson	
Friday	Ice Cube, N. Long	F. Gary Gray
Get Shorty	D. Lindo	
Glass Shield		C. Burnett
Higher Learning	L. Fishburne, Ice Cube	J. Singleton
Losing Isaiah	S. Jackson	

Year/Film	African-American actor/actress	African-American director
1995 *(continued)*		
How to Make an American Quilt	M. Angelou, A. Woodard	
Kiss of Death	S. Jackson	
Moonlight and Valentino	W. Goldberg	
Operation Dumbo Drop	D. Glover	
Othello	L. Fishburne	
Outbreak	M. Freeman	
Panther	C. Rock, A. Bassett	Mario van Peebles
Se7ven	M. Freeman	
Tales from the Hood	C. Williams III	R. Cundieff
To Wong Foo, Thanks for Everything, Julie Newmar	W. Snipes	
Vampire in Brooklyn	E. Murphy	
Virtuosity	D. Washington	
Waiting to Exhale	W. Houston, A. Bassett	F. Whitaker
The Walking Dead	A. Payne	
White Man's Burden	H. Belafonte	
1996		
The Associate	W. Goldberg	
Basquiat	J. Wright	
Bulletproof	D. Wayans	E. Dickerson
Chain Reaction	M. Freeman	
The Chamber	B. Jackson	
Courage Under Fire	D. Washington	
Dangerous Minds		
Eddie	W. Goldberg	
A Family Thing	J. E. Jones	
Feeling Minnesota	D. Lindo	
Fled	L. Fishburne	
Ghosts of Mississippi	W. Goldberg	
Get on the Bus	O. Davis	S. Lee
Girl 6	T. Randle	S. Lee
The Glimmer Man	K. I. Wayans	
Great White Hype	S. Jackson	
Independence Day	W. Smith	
Mission: Impossible	V. Rhames	
Moll Flanders	M. Freeman	
Nutty Professor	E. Murphy	
Phat Beach		
Preacher's Wife	D. Washington, W. Houston	
Ransom	D. Lindo	
Theodore Rex	W. Goldberg	
Once Upon a Time When We Were Colored	A. Freeman	
Don't Be A Menace to South Central While Drinking Your Juice in the Hood		P. Barclay
Set It Off	Q. Latifah, J. Pinkett, V. Fox	F. Gary Gray
Space Jam	M. Jordan	
Spirit Lost	R. Taylor	N. Barnette
A Time to Kill	S. Jackson	

Year/Film	African-American actor/actress	African-American director
1997		
Amistad	M. Freeman, D. Hounsou	
The Apostle	J. Beasley, M. Braxton	
Beverly Hills Ninja	C. Rock	
Boogie Nights	D. Cheadle	
Booty Call	J. Foxx, V. Fox	
Con Air	V. Rhames	
Contact	A. Bassett	
Cop Land	M. Yoba	
Dangerous Ground	Ice Cube, V. Rhames	
Double Team	D. Rodman	
Eve's Bayou	J. Smollett, M. Good, S. Jackson	K. Lemmons
Gattaca	B. Underwood	
Gone Fishin'	D. Glover	
Good Burger	K. Thompson	
Gridlock'd	T. Shakur	
Hoodlum	L. Fishburne, V. Williams B. Duke	
Jackie Brown	P. Grier, S. Jackson	
Junior's Groove	L. Whitfield	
Kiss the Girls	M. Freeman	
Love Jones	L. Tate	
Mad City	A. Busia, Bingwa	
Mean Guns	Ice-T	
Men in Black	W. Smith	
Metro	E. Murphy	
Money Talks	C. Tucker	
Murder at 1600	W. Snipes	
Nothing to Lose	M. Lawrence	
One Eight Seven	S. Jackson	
Park Day	M. Calhoun, H. Harper	
Rosewood	D. Cheadle	J. Singleton
Soul Food	V. William, V. Fox	
Sprung	T. Campbell	R. Cundieff
Steel	S. O'Neal	
Volcano	D. Cheadle	
1998		
Ambushed	C. Vance	E. Dickerson
American History X	A. Brooks	
Armageddon	M. C. Duncan	
Belly	Nas, DMX, Method Man	H. Williams
Beloved	O. Winfrey, D. Glover, T. Newton	
The Big Hit	B. Woodbine	
Blade	W. Snipes	
Blind Faith	C. Dutton, C. Vance	E. Dickerson
Blues Brothers 2000	J. Morton, B. B. King	
Body Count	V. Rhames, F. Whitaker	
Bulworth	H. Berry	
City of Angels	A. Braugher	
Deep Impact	M. Freeman	
Deep Rising	D. Hounsou	
Doctor Dolittle	E. Murphy	

Year/Film	African-American actor/actress	African-American director
1998 *(continued)*		
Down in the Delta	A. Woodard, W. Snipes	M. Angelou
Enemy of the State	W. Smith	
The Faculty	U. Raymond	
Fallen	D. Washington	
Hard Rain	M. Freeman	
He Got Game	D. Washington	S. Lee
Holy Man	E. Murphy	
How Stella Got Her Groove Back	A. Bassett, W. Goldberg, R. King	K. R. Sullivan
I Got the Hook Up	Master P	M. Martin
I Still Know What You Did Last Summer	Brandy, M. Phifer	
Lethal Weapon 4	D. Glover	
Living Out Loud	Q. Latifah	
The Negotiator	S. Jackson	F. Gary Gray
One True Thing		C. Franklin
Out of Sight	V. Rhames	
The Players Club	L. Raye	Ice Cube
Primary Colors	A. Lester	
The Red Violin	S. Jackson	
Ride	M. DeSousa, Snoop Dogg	M. Shelton
Rush Hour	C. Tucker	
Shadrach	J. F. Sawyer	
The Siege	D. Washington	
Sphere	S. Jackson	
U.S. Marshals	W. Snipes	
The Waterboy	L. Gilliard	
What Dreams May Come	C. Gooding	
Why Do Fools Fall In Love	H. Berry, V. Fox. L. Tate	
Woo	J. Pinkett	
1999		
Any Given Sunday	J. Foxx	
Arlington Road	R. Gossett	
The Best Man	T. Diggs, N. Long	M. Lee
Black and White	Method Man, Power, Raekwon	
Blue Streak	M. Lawrence, D. Chappelle	
The Bone Collector	D. Washington	
Bowfinger	E. Murphy	
The Breaks	L. Bentley, L. Divine	
Bringing Out the Dead	V. Rhames	
Chill Factor	C. Gooding	
The Cider House Rules	D. Lindo, E. Badou	
Cookie's Fortune	C. Dutton	
Crazy in Alabama	J. Beasley	
Deep Blue Sea	S. Jackson, LL Cool J	
Deep End of the Ocean	W. Goldberg	
Deep Impact	M. Freeman, B. Underwood	
Deuce Bigalow: Male Gigolo	E. Griffin	
Foolish	E. Griffin, Master P	
Galaxy Quest	D. Mitchell	
The General's Daughter	C. Williams III	

Year/Film	African-American actor/actress	African-American director
1999 *(continued)*		
Ghost Dog	F. Whitaker	
Girl, Interrupted	W. Goldberg	
Go	T. Diggs	
The Green Mile	M. Duncan	
Hot Boyz	Silkk	Master P
The Hurricane	D. Washington	
Instinct	C. Gooding	
In Too Deep	O. Epps, N. Long	
Liberty Heights	R. Johnson	
Life	E. Murphy, M. Lawrence	
Light It Up	U. Raymond, V. Williams	
Love Stinks	T. Banks, B. Bellamy	
The Matrix	L. Fishburne	
Mod Squad	O. Epps	
Mumford	A. Woodard	
Murder of Crows	C. Gooding	
Music of the Heart	A. Bassett	
New Blood	S. Wayans	
The Prodigy	J. Earl	
Raw Nerve	Mario Van Peebles	
South Park: Bigger, Longer, Uncut	I. Hayes	
Star Wars: Episode I – The Phantom Menace	S. Jackson	
Summer of Sam		S. Lee
Thicker than Water	Ice Cube	R. Cummings
Three Kings	Ice Cube	
Titus	H. J. Lennix	
Trippin'	D. Richmond, M. Campbell	D. Hubbard
True Crime	I. Washington, L. G. Hamilton	
200 Cigarettes	D. Chappelle	
Urban Menace	Snoop Dogg, Ice-T	
Varsity Blues	E. Swinton	
Whispers	A. Bassett	
Wild Wild West	W. Smith	
Wings Against the Wind	A. Bassett, D. Cheadle	E. Palcy
The Wishing Tree	A. Woodard	
The Wood	T. Diggs, O. Epps	
The Wrecking Crew	Ice-T, Snoop Dogg	
2000		
Bamboozled	S. Glover, D. Wayans	S. Lee
Big Momma's House	M. Lawrence	
Boesman and Lena	A. Bassett	
Dogma	C. Rock, S. Hayek	
Gladiator	D. Hounsou	
A House Divided	L. G. Hamilton	
Kings of Comedy		S. Lee
Love and Basketball	S. Lathan, O. Epps, A. Woodard	G. Prince
Love's Labour's Lost	A. Lester	
Mission: Impossible II	T. Newton	
Mission to Mars	D. Cheadle	

Year/Film	African-American actor/actress	African-American director
2000 *(continued)*		
Next Friday	Ice Cube, T. Jones	
Nutty Professor II: The Klumps	E. Murphy	
The Patriot	S. Huey	
The Perfect Storm	A. Payne	
Reindeer Games	C. Williams III	
Romeo Must Die	D. Lindo, DMX, Aaliyah	
Rules of Engagement	S. Jackson, B. Underwood	
Scary Movie	R. Hall, M. Wayans	K. Wayans
Scream 3	D. Richmond	
Shaft	S. Jackson, R. Roundtree	J. Singleton
Supernova	A. Bassett	
Texas Rangers	U. Raymond	
What's Cookin'	A. Woodard	
The Whole Nine Yards	M. Duncan	

Incomplete Listing of Hispanic, Chicana, and Chicano Films: 1961–2000[4]

Year/Film	Hispanic/Chicana/o actor/actress	Hispanic/Chicana/o director
1961		
El Cid		
The Guns of Navarone	A. Quinn	
West Side Story	R. Moreno	
The Young Savages	P. Seurat	
1963		
Kings of the Sun		
1964		
The Night of the Iguana		
1965		
The Pawnbroker	J. Sanchez, J. Hernandez	
1966		
The Money Trap	R. Montalban	
The Wild Angels		
1969		
Marlowe	R. Moreno	
100 Rifles	R. Welch	
1971		
Bananas	C. Montalban	
1972		
Man of La Mancha		
1973		
Badge 373		
1976		
Assault on Precinct Thirteen		

Year/Film	Hispanic/Chicana/o actor/actress	Hispanic/Chicana/o director
1978		
Up in Smoke	C. Marin	
1979		
Boardwalk		
Boulevard Nights	D. De la Paz	
Walk Proud		
The Warriors		
1980		
Cheech and Chong's Next Movie	C. Marin	
The Exterminator		
1981		
Cheech and Chong's Nice Dreams	C.Marin	
Zoot Suit	E. Olmos	L. Valdez
1982		
Blade Runner	E. Olmos	
The Border	E. Carillo, M. Viescas	
Missing		
Things Are Tough All Over	C. Marin	
Wild Style	Crazy Legs	
1983		
Bad Boys	E. Morales	
Erendira	C. Ohana	R. Guerra
Still Smokin'	C. Marin	
1984		
The Ballad of Gregorio Cortez	E. Olmos	
The Corsican Brothers	C. Marin	
Repo Man	E. Estevez	
1985		
The Breakfast Club	E. Estevez	
Kiss of the Spider Woman	R. Julia	H. Babenco
The Offical Story	N. Aleandro	
Saving Grace	E. Olmos	
Stand Alone		
St Elmo's Fire	E. Estevez	
1986		
The Mission		
Three Amigos!	A. Arau	
Platoon		
1987		
Born in East L.A.	C. Marin	
Extreme Prejudice	M. Alonso	
La Bamba	E. Morales, L. Phillips	L. Valdez
The Principal	E. Morales	
Stakeout	E. Estevez	
The Untouchables	A. Garcia	
1988		
Colors	M. Alonso, R. Ramos, T. Silva	
The Milagro Beanfield War	R. Blades	
Moon over Parador	R. Julia	

Year/Film	Hispanic/Chicana/o actor/actress	Hispanic/Chicana/o director
1988 *(continued)*		
Night Before	T. Silva	
Stand and Deliver	E. Olmos, L. Phillips	R. Menendez
Two to Tango		H. Olvera
Women on the Verge of a Nervous Breakdown	C. Maura, A. Banderas	P. Almodovar
1989		
Casualties of War	J. Leguizamo	
Cousins	N. Aleandro	
Do the Right Thing	R. Perez	
Old Gringo	J. Smits	L. Puenzo
1990		
A Show of Force	E. Estrada, A. Garcia, L. Phillips	
Havana	R. Julia	
Men at Work	E. Estevez	
Vital Signs	N. Aleandro	
1991		
The Addams Family	R. Julia	
Hangin' with the Homeboys	J. Leguizamo	J. Vasquez
Kiss me a Killer		M. de Leon
McBain	M. C. Alonso	
1992		
American Me	E. Olmos	E. Olmos
Belle Epoque	P. Cruz	F. Trueba
El Mariachi		R. Rodriguez
Jamon Jamon	P. Cruz	J. Luna
Like Water for Chocolate	L. Cavazos	A. Arau
The Mambo Kings	A. Assante, A. Banderas	
White Men Can't Jump	R. Perez	
1993		
Addams Family Values	R. Julia	
Bound by Honor (Blood In, Blood Out)	J. Borrego, D. Chapa	
Carlito's Way	J. Leguizamo	
Fearless	R. Perez	
Money For Nothing		R. Menendez
Philadelphia	A. Banderas	
1994		
Color of Night	R. Blades	
I Like It Like That	L. Valez, J. Seda	D. Martin
It Could Happen to You	R. Perez	
A Million to Juan	P. Rodriguez	P. Rodriguez
Mi Vida Loca	A. Aviles, S. Lopez, J. Vargas	
1995		
Desperado	A. Banderas	R. Rodriguez
My Family/Mi Familia	J. Smits, E. Olmos	G. Nava
Mirage	E. Olmos	
The Perez Family	T. Alvarado, C. Cruz	
Money Train	J. Lopez	

Year/Film	Hispanic/Chicana/o actor/actress	Hispanic/Chicana/o director
1995 *(continued)*		
To Wong Foo, Thanks for Everything Julie Newmar	J. Leguizamo	
1996		
Courage Under Fire	L. D. Phillips	
Evita	A. Banderas	
The Fan	J. Leguizamo	
From Dusk Til Dawn	C. Marin, S. Hayek	R. Rodriguez
Romeo + Juliet	J. Leguizamo	
Tin Cup	C. Marin	
1997		
Anaconda	J. Lopez Ferrara	
Boogie Nights	L. Guzmán	
Fools Rush In	S. Hayek	
Hoodlum	A. Garcia	
The Pest	J. Leguizamo	
Scorpion Spring	R. Blades, A. Aviles	
Selena	J. Lopez, E. Olmos	G. Nava
Star Maps	D. Spain, E. Figueroa	M. Arteta
U Turn	J. Lopez	
Who the Hell Is Juliette?	Y. Ortega	C. Marcovich
1998		
Antz (animated)	J. Lopez	
The Big Hit	A. Sabato	
Body Count	J. Leguizamo	
Desperate Measures	A. Garcia	
The Faculty		R. Rodriguez
La Cucaracha	A. Patino	J. Perez
The Mask of Zorro	A. Banderas	
Out of Sight	J. Lopez, L. Guzman	
Paulie	C. Marin	
Snake Eyes	L. Guzman	
Sparkler	F. Prinze, Jr	
The Velocity of Gary	S. Hayek, Y. Diaz	
Why Do Fools Fall in Love?		G. Nava
The Wonderful Ice Cream Suit	E. Olmos, E. Morales	
1999		
The 13th Warrior	A. Banderas	
All About My Mother	P. Cruz	P. Almodovar
Best Laid Plans	A. Nivola	
The Bone Collector	L. Guzmán	
Buena Vista Social Club		
Cradle Will Rock	R. Blades	
Crazy in Alabama		A. Banderas
Dance with the Devil	R. Perez	A. de la Iglesia
Dogma	S. Hayek	
Joe the King	J. Leguizamo	
The Limey	L. Guzmán	
Magnolia	L. Guzmán	
Mambo Café	Thalia	R. Gonzalez
Play It to the Bone	A. Banderas	

Year/Film	Hispanic/Chicana/o actor/actress	Hispanic/Chicana/o director
1999 *(continued)*		
Secret Life of Girls	M. Delfino	
She's All That	F. Prinze, Jr	
Summer of Sam	J. Leguizamo, J. Esposito	
Wild Wild West	S. Hayek	
2000		
All the Pretty Horses	R. Blades, P. Cruz	
Bless the Child	J. Smits	
Boys and Girls	F. Prinze, Jr	
The Cell	J. Lopez	
Chain of Fools	S. Hayek	
Down to You	F. Prinze, Jr	
Knockout	M. Alonso	
What's Cookin'	M. Ruehl, M. Carman	

Incomplete Listing of Asian and Asian-American Films: 1961–2000

Year/Film	Asian and Asian-American actor/actress	Asian and Asian-American director
1962		
Experiment in Terror		
The Horizontal Lieutenant	M. Umeki	
Lonely Are the Brave		
A Majority of One		
The Manchurian Candidate		
Merrill's Marauders		
My Geisha	Y. Tani	
Satan Never Sleeps		
War Hunt		
1963		
China Clipper		
Confessions of an Opium Eater	L. Ho, R. Loo, J. Kim	
Cry of Battle		
Diamond Head		
55 Days at Peking		
Flight from Ashiya		
A Girl Named Tamiko	M. Umeki	
The Main Attraction		
PT-109		
Shock Corridor		
The Ugly American	E. Okada	
Who's Been Sleeping in My Bed?		
1964		
Fate Is the Hunter		
Honeymoon Hotel		
McHale's Navy		
Man in the Middle		
The Seven Faces of Dr Lao		
The 7th Dawn		

Year/Film	Asian and Asian-American actor/actress	Asian and Asian-American director
1964 *(continued)*		
The Troublemaker		
Woman in the Dunes	K. Kishida, E. Okada	H. Teshigahara
A Yank in Vietnam		
1965		
Genghis Khan		
In Harm's Way		
None but the Brave		
Once a Thief		
Once Before I Die		
The Return of Mr Moto		
1966		
An American Dream		
Arrivederci, Baby!		
The Art of Love		
Lt Robinson Crusoe, U.S.N.	N. Kwan	
Paradise, Hawaiian Style	I. Tsu	
The Sand Pebbles		
The Silencers		
Walk, Don't Run	M. Taka	
1967		
Ambush		
Beach Red		
A Countess from Hong Kong		
First to Fight		
Red Line 7000	G. Takei	
Thoroughly Modern Millie	N. Morita, J. Soo	
To Kill a Dragon		
1968		
Black Lizard	A. Miwa, I. Kimura	
The Destructors		
The Green Berets	G. Takei, J. Soo	
Nobody's Perfect		
The Private Navy of Sgt O'Farrell		
The Shoes of the Fisherman		
1969		
Alice's Restaurant	T. Chen	
The Chairman		
The Great Bank Robbery		
Hell in the Pacific		
M*A*S*H		
True Grit		
The Wrecking Crew	N. Kwan	
1970		
The Hawaiians	T. Chen, K. Luke, Mako	
Husbands		
Kashmiri Run		
The Losers		
The McMasters	N. Kwan	

Year/Film	Asian and Asian-American actor/actress	Asian and Asian-American director
1970 *(continued)*		
There was a Crooked Man		
Tora! Tora! Tora!	T. Masuda, K. Fukasuku	
Skullduggery	P. Suzuki	
1971		
Dreams of Glass		
Little Big Man		
McCabe and Mrs Miller		
One More Train to Rob	F. Nuyen	
Which Way to the Front		
1972		
The Big Game		
The Carey Treatment		
The Hunting Party		
Welcome to the Club		
1973		
Battle for the Planet of the Apes		
Charley Varrick		
Enter the Dragon	B. Lee	
Lost Horizon		
That Man Bolt	J. Ging, M. Mayama	
1974		
Chinatown	J. Hong	
The Island at the Top of the World	Mako	
The Man with the Golden Gun	C. Lee, R. Loo	
1975		
Airport 1975		
Mame		
One of Our Dinosaurs Is Missing		
S*P*Y*S		
The Terminal Man		
The Trial of Billy Jack		
The Yakuza	K. Keiko, K. Takakura	
1976–1981[5]		
1982		
Chan Is Missing	W. Moy, M. Hayashi	W. Wang
Gandhi		
Reassemblage		Trinh T. Minh-ha
The Year of Living Dangerously		
1983		
The Hatchet Man		
1984		
Adventures of Buckaroo Banzai	R. Ito	
Gremlins	K. Luke	
The Karate Kid	N. Morita, E. Shue	
The Killing Fields	Haing Ngor	
Merry Christmas, Mr Lawrence	R. Sajanitim, Tajesgu	N. Oshima
A Passage to India	V. Banerjee	

Year/Film	Asian and Asian-American actor/actress	Asian and Asian-American director
1985		
Dim Sum	L. Chew, K. Chew, V. Wong	W. Wang
Mishima	K. Ogata, M. Shlonoya	
My Beautiful Laundrette	S. Jaffrey, R. Seth, G. Warnecke	
Rambo: First Blood Part II	G.K. Cheuny	
Year of the Dragon	J. Lone	
1986		
A Great Wall	P. Wang	P. Wang
Gung Ho	S. Yamamura, S. Shimono	
The Karate Kid Part II	N. Morita, D. Kamekona	
Platoon		
Ran	T. Nakadai, A. Terao	A. Kurosawa
Running Brave		
Tokyo-Ga		
1987		
Empire of the Sun	B. Kwouk, M. Ibu	
The Funeral	N. Miyamoto, T. Yamazaki	J. Itami
Last Emperor	J. Lone, J. Chen, V. Wang	
Tampopo	T. Yamazaki, N. Miyamoto	J. Itami
A Taxing Woman	N. Miyamoto, R. Mikuni	J. Itami
1988		
Rambo II	M. de Jonge, D. Shoua	
Salaam Bombay!	S. Syed, S. Qurrassi	M. Nair
A Taxing Woman's Return	N. Miyamoto, R. Mikuni	J. Itami
Tetsuo: Iron Man (animated)	T. Taguchi	S. Tsukamoto
Tokyo Pop	T. Deyama	F. Kuzui
1989		
Black Rain	K. Takakura, Y. Matsuda	S. Imamura
Casualties of War	T. Le	
Eat a Bowl of Tea	V. Wong, R. Wong	W. Wang
Mystery Train	M. Nagase, Y. Kudoh	
True Believer	Y. Okumoto	
1990		
Alice	D. Cheng, K. Luke	
Come See the Paradise	T. Tomita, S. Shimono	
Dreams		A. Kurosawa
The Freshman	B. D. Wong	
Ju Dou	G. Li, L. Bao-tain	Z. Yimou
1991		
Rhapsody in August	S. Murase, H. Igawa	A. Kurosawa
1992		
City of Joy	O. Puri, S. Azmi	
Mississippi Masala		M. Nair
Mr Baseball	K. Takakura, A. Takanashi	
My Samurai	Mako	
Supercop	J. Chan	
1993		
Bhaji on the Beach		G. Chadha
Combination Platter	J. Lau, L. Chan	T. Chan
Farewell My Concubine	L. Cheung, G. Li, L. Qi	C. Kaigne

Year/Film	Asian and Asian-American actor/actress	Asian and Asian-American director
1993 *(continued)*		
Hard Target		J. Woo
Heaven and Earth	H. Thi Le, J. Chen	
The Joy Luck Club		W. Wang
M. Butterfly		
Rising Sun	C-H. Tagawa, Mako	
The Story of Qiu Ju	G. Li, L. L. Sheng	Z. Yimou
Supercop 2	M. Yeoh	
The Wedding Banquet	W. Chao, M. Chin	A. Lee
1994		
Chungking Express	T. Leung	W. Kar-Wai
The Crow	B. Lee	
Double Happiness	S. Oh	M. Shum
Eat Drink Man Woman	S. Lung, C. -L.Wu	A. Lee
Golden Gate	J. Chen, T. Ma	
The Jungle Book	J. Lee	
Little Buddha	Y. Ruocheng	
The Painted Desert		M. Harada
The Scent of Green Papaya	T. Nu Yen-khe	T. A. Hung
True Lies	T. Carrere	
1995		
The Hunted	J. Lone, J. Chen	
Johnny Mnemonic	T. Kitano	
Maborosi	M. Esumi	H. Kore-eda
Mortal Kombat	R. Shou	
The Perez Family		M. Nair
Picture Bride	Y. Kudoh, A. Takayama, K. Hatta	
Sense and Sensibility		A. Lee
Smoke		W. Wang
1996		
Broken Arrow		J. Woo
High School High	T. Carrere	
Jackie Chan's First Strike	J. Chan	
Kama Sutra: A Tale of Love	S. Choudhury	M. Nair
The Pillow Book	K. Ogata, Y. Oida	
Precious Find	J. Chen	
Rumble in the Bronx	J. Chan	S. Tong
Shall We Dance?	K. Yakusho, T. Kusakari	M. Suo
1997		
Beverly Hills Ninja	R. Shou	
Chinese Box		W. Wang
Face/Off	J. Chou	J. Woo
Fireworks	T. Kitano	T. Kitano
Happy Together	T. Leung, L. Cheung	W. Kar-Wai
Heist	J. Chen	
The Ice Storm		A. Lee
Kull the Conqueror	T. Carrere	
Kundun	T. Tsarong	
Mortal Kombat: Annihilation	R. Shou	
Mr Nice Guy	J. Chan	S. Hung

Year/Film	Asian and Asian-American actor/actress	Asian and Asian-American director
1997 *(continued)*		
Red Corner	B. Ling	
Seven Years in Tibet	B. D. Wong	
Tomorrow Never Dies	M. Yeoh	
1998		
The Big Hit		K. Wong
Forever Fever	A. Pang, M. Tan	G. Goei
Lethal Weapon 4	J. Li	
My Son the Fanatic	O. Puri	
Mulan (animated)		
The Red Violin	S. Chang	
The Replacement Killers	C. Yun-Fat	
Rounders	P. Yoshida	
Rush Hour	J. Chan	
What Dreams May Come	R. Chao	
Who Am I?	J. Chan	
Wild Side	J. Chen	
Xiu Xiu	Lu Lu	J. Chen
1999		
Anna and the King	C. Yun-Fat	
Anywhere But Here		W. Wang
East is East	O. Puri	
The Emperor and the Assassin	L. Gong	K. Chen
Gorgeous	J. Chan	
I'll Remember April	N. Morita, Y. Tokuhiro	
Molly	L. Liu	
Moonlight Express	M. Yeoh, L. Cheung	
Payback	L. Liu	
Play It to the Bone	L. Liu	
Ride with the Devil		A. Lee
Snow Falling on Cedars	Y. Kudoh	
2000		
Charlie's Angels	L. Liu	
Crouching Tiger, Hidden Dragon	C. Yun-Fat, M. Yeoh	A. Lee
In the Mood for Love	T. Leung	W. Kar-Wai
Mission: Impossible II		J. Woo
Romeo Must Die	J. Li, R. Wong	
Shanghai Noon	J. Chan, L. Liu	
Twin Warriors	J. Li	
What's Cookin'	J. Chen	G. Chadha

Notes

1. I thank Sylvia Allegretto, Shawn Miklaucic, Michael Elavsky, Jack Bratich, and Mark Nimkoff for their assistance in the construction of this filmography. Sources: Bogle (1994), Guerrero (1993), Massood (1996), Diawara (1993a), Reid (1993), and The Internet Movie Database, *http://us.imdb. com/*. This list stops on 20 August 2000.

2. * = Defined as a blaxploitation film (see Guerrero, 1993, pp. 69–112).

   ** = Defined as 'hood' movie (see Massood, 1996).

3. Bogle (1994) calls the 1980s the Era of Tan, 'a time when films did all they could to make audiences forget the blackness of a black star ... most black performers found themselves playing supporting roles' (p. 268). Hence, there are fewer African-American films *per se* for this decade when compared to the 1970s. Those listed here include films where African-Americans had major supporting, but not necesarily leading, roles.

4. Sources: Fregoso (1993), Keller (1994).

5. For these years, a comprehensive list of Asian-American films is not available. A search to gather such a list was attempted without success. Film review annuals, such as *Film Review Annual*, *New York Times Film Review*, *Magill's Cinema Annual*, and *Filmfacts*, are all without subject indexes and/or did not include information for these years.

Bibliography

Ablemann, Nancy, and John Lie. 1995. *Blue Dreams: Korean Americans and the Los Angeles Riots.* Cambridge, Mass.: Harvard University Press.

Adorno, T. W., Else Frenkel-Brunswick, Daniel J. Levinson, and R. Nevitt Sanford. 1950. *The Authoritarian Personality.* New York: Harper and Row.

Aguilar-San Juan, Karin. 1994. 'Introduction: Linking the Issues: From Identity to Activism,' pp. 1–20 in Karin Aguilar-San Juan (ed.), *The State of Asian America: Activism and Resistance in the 1990s.* Boston: South End Press.

Allinson, Ewan. 1994. 'It's A Black Thing: Hearing How Whites Can't,' *Cultural Studies*, 8: 438–456.

Altman, Rick. 1987. *The American Film Musical.* Bloomington: Indiana University Press.

Altman, Rick. 1986. 'A Semantic/Syntactic Approach to Film Genre,' pp. 26–40 in Barry Keith Grant (ed.), *Film Genre Reader.* Austin: University of Texas Press. (Originally published in *Cinema Journal*, 23, no. 3, Spring 1984: 6–18.)

Anderson, Benedict. 1992. *Imagined Communities.* London: Verso.

Anderson, Elijah. 1999. *Code of the Street.* New York: W. W. Norton.

Anderson, Elijah. 1990. *Streetwise.* Chicago: University of Chicago Press.

Anderson, Elijah. 1978. *A Place on the Corner.* Chicago: University of Chicago Press.

Anderson, John. 1993. 'Review of *Menace II Society*,' *Newsday*, 26 May, Part II: 63.

Anderson, John. 1992a. 'Review of *Lethal Weapon III*,' *Newsday*, 15 May, Part II: 67.

Anderson, John. 1992b. 'Review of *American Me*,' *Newsday*, 13 March, Part II: 74.

Anderson, Lisa M. 1997. *Mammies No More: The Changing Image of Black Women on Stage and Screen.* New York: Rowman & Littlefield.

Andrews, David L. 1996. 'The Fact(s) of Michael Jordan's Blackness: An Excavation in Four Parts,' *Sociology of Sport Journal*, 13: 125–158.

Ansen, David. 1995. 'Review of *Clockers*,' *Newsweek*, 25 September: 92.

Ansen, David. 1993. 'Review of *Passion Fish*,' *Newsweek*, 11 January: 52.

Ansen, David. 1991a. 'Review of *Grand Canyon*,' *Newsweek*, 30 December: 47.

Ansen, David. 1991b. 'Review of *A Rage in Harlem*,' *Newsweek*, 13 May: 71.

Ansen, David. 1988. 'Review of *Colors*,' *Newsweek*, 18 April: 73.

Anzaldua, Gloria. 1987. *Borderlands/La Frontera.* San Francisco: Aunt Lute.

Appadurai, Arjun. 1996. *Modernity at Large: Cultural Dimensions of Globalization.* Minneapolis: University of Minnesota Press.

Appadurai, Arjun. 1993. 'Patriotism and Its Future,' *Public Culture*, 5: 411–429.

Aufderheide, Pat. 1982/3. 'Review of *Zoot Suit*,' *Film Quarterly*, Winter: 44.

Auster, Albert, and Leonard Quart. 1988. *How the War Was Remembered: Hollywood and Vietnam.* New York: Praeger.

Austin, Regina. 1995. 'Sapphire Bound!' pp. 426–437 in Kimberle Crenshaw, Neil Gotanda, Gary Peller, and Kendall Thomas (eds), *Critical Race Theory: The Key Writings that Formed the Movement.* New York: New Press.

Baker, Houston A., Jr. 1997. 'The Black Arts Movement,' pp. 1791–1806 in Henry Louis Gates, Jr, and Nellie Y. McKay (eds), *The Norton Anthology of African American Literature.* New York: W. W. Norton & Company.

Baker, Houston A., Jr. 1995. 'Critical Memory and the Black Public Sphere,' pp. 5–38 in The Black Public Sphere Collective (ed.), *The Black Public Sphere: A Public Culture Book.* Chicago: University of Chicago Press.

Baker, Houston A., Jr. 1993. 'Spike Lee and the Commerce of Culture,' pp. 154–176 in Mantha Diawara (ed.), *Black American Cinema.* New York: Routledge.

Bakhtin, Mikhail. 1968. *Rabelais and His World.* Cambridge, Mass.: MIT Press.

Baldwin, James. 1962. *Another Country.* New York: Dial Press.

Balingit, JoAnn. 1992a. 'Review of *Grand Canyon*,' pp. 158–161 in Frank N. Magill (ed.), *Magill's Cinema Annual: 1992: A Survey of the Films of 1991*. Englewood Cliffs, NJ: Salem Press.

Balingit, JoAnn. 1992b. 'Review of *Boyz N the Hood*,' pp. 55–59 in Frank N. Magill (ed.), *Magill's Cinema Annual: 1992: A Survey of the Films of 1991*. Englewood Cliffs, NJ: Salem Press.

Bambara, Toni Cade. 1996. *Deep Sightings & Rescue Missions*. Edited and with a Preface by Toni Morrison. New York: Vintage.

Baraka, Amiri. 1998. 'Black Art,' pp. 1501–1502 in Patricia Liggins Hill (ed.), *Call & Response: The Riverside Anthology of the African American Tradition*. Boston: Houghton Mifflin. (Originally published in 1969.)

Baraka, Amiri. 1997. *The Autobiography of LeRoi Jones*. Chicago: Lawrence Hill Books.

Baraka, Amiri. 1993. 'Spike Lee at the Movies,' pp. 145–153 in Mantha Diawara (ed.), *Black American Cinema*. New York: Routledge.

Barksdale, Richard, and Keneth Kinnamon. 1972a. 'Reconstruction and Reaction: 1865–1915: Paul Dunbar,' pp. 349–352 in Richard Barksdale and Keneth Kinnamon (eds), *Black Writers of America: A Comprehensive Anthology*. Englewood Cliffs, NJ: Prentice-Hall.

Barksdale, Richard, and Keneth Kinnamon (eds). 1972b. *Black Writers of America: A Comprehensive Anthology*. Englewood Cliffs, NJ: Prentice-Hall.

Barthes, Roland. 1972. *Mythologies*. New York: Hill and Wang.

Basinger, Jeanine. 1986. *The World War II Combat Film: Anatomy of a Genre*. New York: Columbia University Press.

Bataille, Gretchen, and Charles L. P. Silet. 1985. *Images of American Indians on Film: An Annotated Bibliography*. New York: Garland.

Benjamin, Playthell. 1991. 'Review of *New Jack City*,' *Village Voice*, 19 March: 49.

Benjamin, Walter. 1968. *Illuminations*. Edited with an Introduction by Hannah Arendt. New York: Harcourt, Brace & World, Inc.

Benson, Sheila. 1988. 'Review of *Colors*,' *Los Angeles Times*, 15 April, *Calendar*: 1.

Berg, Charles Ramirez. 1992. '*Bordertown*: The Assimilation Narrative and the Chicano Social Problem Film,' pp. 29–46 in Chon A. Noriega (ed.), *Chicanos and Film: Representation and Resistance*. Minneapolis: University of Minnesota Press.

Bernard, Jami. 1993. 'Review of *Bound By Honor*,' *New York Post*, 30 April: 27.

Bernard, Jami. 1991a. 'Review of *Grand Canyon*,' *New York Post*, 24 December: 21.

Bernard, Jami. 1991b. 'Review of *A Rage in Harlem*,' *New York Post*, 3 May: 38.

Bernard, Jami. 1991c. 'Review of *New Jack City*,' *New York Post*, 8 March: 45.

Billison, Anne. 1992. 'Review of *Grand Canyon*,' *New Statesman & Society*, 24 April: 1.

Blackburn, Olly. 1993. 'Review of *Bound By Honor*,' *Sight and Sound*, October: 39.

Blauner, Robert. 1972. *Racial Oppression in America*. New York: Harper and Row.

Blumer, Herbert. 1965. 'The Future of the Color Line,' pp. 322–336 in John McKinney and Edgar T. Thompson (eds), *The South in Continuity and Change*. Durham, NC: Duke University Press.

Blumer, Herbert. 1958. 'Race Prejudice as a Sense of Group Position,' *Pacific Sociological Review*, 1: 3–21.

Bobo, Jacqueline. 1992. 'The Politics of Interpretation: Black Critics, Filmmakers, Audiences,' pp. 65–74 in Gina Dent (ed.), *Black Popular Culture: A Project by Michele Wallace*. Seattle: Bay Press.

Bogle, Donald. 1994. *Toms, Coons, Mulattoes, Mammies, and Bucks: An Interpretive History of Blacks in American Films*. 3rd edn. New York: Continuum.

Bordwell, David. 1996. 'Contemporary Film Studies and the Vicissitudes of Grand Theory,' pp. 3–36 in David Bordwell and Noel Carroll (eds), *Post-Theory: Reconstructing Film Studies*. Madison: University of Wisconsin Press.

Bourgois, Phillipe. 1997. 'In Search of Horatio Alger: Culture and Ideology in the Crack Economy,' pp. 57–76 in Craig Reinarman and Harry G. Levine (eds), *Crack In America: Demon Drugs and Social Justice*. Berkeley: University of California Press.

Boyd, Todd. 1997. *Am I Black Enough For You? Popular Culture From the 'Hood' and Beyond*. Bloomington: Indiana University Press.

Bradley, David. 1995. 'Spike Lee's Inferno, The Drug Underworld,' *New Times*, Arts & Leisure: 29, 32.

Broeske, Pat H. 1982. 'Review of *Zoot Suit*,' pp. 389–392 in Frank N. Magill (ed.), *Magill's Cinema Annual: 1982: A Survey of the Films of 1981*. Englewood Cliffs, NJ: Salem Press.

Brown, Georgia. 1995. 'Review of *Clockers*,' *Village Voice*, 19 September: 71.

Brown, Georgia. 1993. 'Review of *Menace II Society*,' *Village Voice*, 1 June: 52.

Brown, Georgia. 1992a. 'Review of *Passion Fish*,' *Village Voice*, 8 December: 61.

Brown, Georgia. 1992b. 'Review of *American Me*,' *Village Voice*, 17 March: 56.

Brown, Georgia. 1991a. 'Review of *Grand Canyon*,' *Village Voice*, 31 December: 52.

Brown, Georgia. 1991b. 'Review of *A Rage in Harlem*,' *Village Voice*, 7 May: 55.

Brown, Jeffrey A. 1996. 'Gender and the Action Heroine: Hardbodies and the Point of No Return,' *Cinema Journal*, 35: 52–71.

Browne, Nick. 1989. 'Orientalism as an Ideological Form: American Film Theory in the Silent Period,' *Wide Angle*, 11, no. 4 (October): 23–31.

Buehrer, Beverley Bare. 1996. 'Review of *Dangerous Minds*,' pp. 123–124 in Beth A. Fhaner and Christopher P. Scanlon (eds), *Magill's Cinema Annual: 1996: A Survey of the Films of 1995*. Detroit: Gale.

Butler, Samuel. 1903. *The Way of All Flesh*. London: Jonathan Cape.

Cade, Toni (ed.). 1970. *The Black Woman*. New York: Random House.

Canby, Vincent. 1992. 'Review of *Lethal Weapon III*,' *New York Times*, 15 May: C16.

Chan, Kenneth. 1998. 'The Construction of Black Male Identity in Black Action Films of the Nineties,' *Cinema Journal*, 37: 35–48.

Chow, Rey. 1995. *Primitive Passions: Visuality, Sexuality, Ethnography and Contemporary Chinese Cinema*. New York: Columbia University Press.

Chow, Rey. 1993. *Writing Diaspora: Tactics of Intervention in Contemporary Cultural Studies*. Bloomington: Indiana University Press.

Christian, Barbara T. 1997. 'Literature Since 1970,' pp. 2011–2020 in Henry Louis Gates, Jr and Nellie Y. McKay (eds), *The Norton Anthology of African American Literature*. New York: W. W. Norton & Company.

Christians, Clifford. 2000. 'Ethics and Politics in Qualitative Research,' pp. 133–155 in Norman K. Denzin and Yvonna S. Lincoln (eds), *Handbook of Qualitative Research*, 2nd edn. Thousand Oaks, Calif: Sage.

Clark, Mike. 1992. 'Street-Smart Wit Helps "White Men" Jump: Review of *White Men Can't Jump*,' *USA Today*, 27 March: 1D.

Clough, Patricia Ticineto. 1994. *Feminist Thought: Desire, Power and Academic Discourse*. Cambridge, Mass.: Blackwell.

Clough, Patricia Ticineto. 1992. *The End(s) of Ethnography: From Realism to Social Criticism*. Newbury Park, Calif: Sage.

Coleman, Travor W. 1993. '"Wiggers": White Teens Identify with Black Hip-Hopper,' *Detroit Free Press*, 25 April: 1A, 6A.

Collins, Patricia Hill. 1998. *Fighting Words: Black Women and the Search for Justice*. Minneapolis: University of Minnesota Press.

Collins, Patricia Hill. 1991. *Black Feminist Thought*. New York: Routledge.

Combs, Richard. 1990. 'Review of *Black Rain*,' *Monthly Film Bulletin*, 1 January: 8.

Comolli, Jean-Luc, and Jean Narboni. 1976. 'Cinema/Ideology/Criticism,' pp. 22–30 in Bill Nichols (ed.), *Movies and Methods: An Anthology, Vol. One*. Berkeley: University of California Press. (Originally published in *Screen*, 12, no. 1 (Spring 1971): 27–36.)

Cook, David A. 1981. *A History of Narrative Film*. New York: W. W. Norton.

Corliss, Richard. 1993. 'Review of *Passion Fish*,' *Time*, 25 January: 69.

Corliss, Richard. 1988. 'Review of *Colors*,' *Time*, 18 April: 82.

Cortés, Carlos E. 1992. 'Who is Maria? What is Juan? Dilemmas of Analyzing the Chicano Image in U. S. Feature Films,' pp. 74–93 in Chon A. Noriega (ed.), *Chicanos and Film: Representation and Resistance*. Minneapolis: University of Minnesota Press.

Cormack, Richard G. 1993. 'Review of *"Passion Fish*,"' pp. 288–291 in Frank N. Magill (ed.), *Magill's Cinema Annual: 1993: A Survey of the Films of 1992*. Englewood Cliffs, NJ: Salem Press.

Cormack, Richard G. 1992. 'Review of "*A Rage in Harlem*,"' pp. 307–310 in Frank N. Magill (ed.), *Magill's Cinema Annual: 1992: A Survey of the Films of 1991*. Englewood Cliffs, NJ: Salem Press.

Crenshaw, Kimberle, Neil Gotanda, Gary Peller, and Kendall Thomas. 1995. 'Introduction,' pp. xii–xxxii in Kimberle Crenshaw, Neil Gotanda, Gary Peller, and Kendall Thomas (eds.), *Critical Race Theory: The Key Writings that Formed the Movement*. New York: New Press.

Cripps, Thomas. 1979. *Black Film as Genre*. Bloomington: Indiana University Press.

Dash, Leon. 1996. *Rosa Lee: A Mother and Her Family in Urban America*. New York: Basic Books.

Dash, Leon, and Susan Sheehan. 1998. '21st and Vietnam: The Making of Teen Killers,' *The Washington Post*, 29 November: A1, A20–A22.

Davis, Allison, and John Dollard, 1940. *Children of Bondage*. Washington, DC: American Council on Education.

Davis, Angela Y. 1998. *Blues Legacies and Black Feminism: Gertude 'Ma' Rainey, Bessie Smith, and Billie Holiday*. New York: Pantheon Books.

Davis, Mike. 1990. *City of Quartz*. London: Verso.

Delalis, George. 1994. 'Review of *Menace II Society*,' pp. 228–231 in Frank N. Magill (ed.), *Magill's Cinema Annual: 1994: A Survey of the Films of 1993*. Englewood Cliffs, NJ: Salem Press.

Denby, David. 1995. 'Review of *Clockers*,' *New York*, 18 September: 72.

Denby, David. 1993a. 'Review of *Passion Fish*,' *New York*, 15 February: 60.

Denby, David. 1993b. 'Review of *Menace II Society*,' *New York*, 31 May: 54.

Denby, David. 1992a. 'Review of *Grand Canyon*,' *New York*, 13 January: 46.

Denby, David. 1992b. 'Review of *Lethal Weapon III*,' *New York*, 1 June: 56.

Denby, David. 1992c. 'Review of *American Me*,' *New York*, 23 March: 60.

Denby, David. 1991. 'Review of *Boyz N the Hood*,' *New York*, 29 July: 49.

Denby, David. 1988. 'Review of *Colors*,' *New York*, 18 April: 100.

Dent, Gina (ed.). 1992. *Black Popular Culture: A Project by Michele Wallace*. Seattle: Bay Press.

Denzin, Norman K. 2000. 'The Practices and Politics of Interpretation,' pp. 897–922 in Norman K. Denzin and Yvonna S. Lincoln (eds), *Handbook of Qualitative Research*, 2nd edn. Thousand Oaks, Calif: Sage.

Denzin, Norman K. 1997. *Interpretive Ethnography: Ethnographic Practices for the 21st Century*. Thousand Oaks, Calif: Sage.

Denzin, Norman K. 1995a. *The Cinematic Society: The Voyeur's Gaze*. London: Sage.

Denzin, Norman K. 1995b. '*White Men Can't Dunk*? Race, Gender and the Postmodern Emotional Self,' *Social Perspectives on Emotion*, 3: 33–54.

Denzin, Norman K. 1993. 'Rain Man In Las Vegas: Where is the Action for the Postmodern Self?' *Symbolic Interaction*, 16: 65–77.

Denzin, Norman K. 1992. *Symbolic Interactionism and Cultural Studies*. Cambridge, Mass: Blackwell.

Denzin, Norman K. 1991a. *Images of Postmodern Society: Social Theory and Contemporary Cinema*. London: Sage.

Denzin, Norman K. 1991b. *Hollywood Shot by Shot: Alcoholism in American Cinema*. New York: Aldine de Gruyter.

Desser, David. 1991. '"Charlie Don't Surf": Race and Culture in the Vietnam War Films,' pp. 81–102 in Michael Anderegg (ed.), *Inventing Vietnam: The War in Film and Television*. Philadelphia: Temple University Press.

Dewey, John. 1934. *Art as Experience*. New York G. P. Putnam's.

Diawara, Mantha. 1993a. 'Black American Cinema: The New Realism,' pp. 3–25 in Mantha Diawara (ed.), *Black American Cinema*. New York: Routledge.

Diawara, Mantha. 1993b. 'Noir by Noirs: Toward a New Realism in Black Cinema,' *African American Review*, 27, no. 4: 525–538.

Dieckmann, Katherine. 1987. 'Review of *Lethal Weapon*,' *Village Voice*, 10 March: 60.

Dimitriadis, Greg. 1996. 'Hip Hop: From Live Performance to Mediated Narrative,' *Popular Music*, 15, no. 2: 179–194.

Doane, Mary Ann. 1987. *The Desire to Desire: The Woman's Film of the 1940s*. Bloomington: Indiana University Press.

Drake, St Clair, and Horace R. Cayton. 1945. *Black Metropolis*. New York: Harcourt, Brace.

Du Bois, W. E. B. 1978. *On Sociology and the Black Community*. Edited with an Introduction by Dan S. Green and Edwin D. Driver. Chicago: University of Chicago Press.

Du Bois, W. E. B. 1920. *Darkwater: Voices from Within the Veil*. New York: Schocken.

Du Bois, W. E. B. 1903. *The Souls of Black Folk: Essays and Sketches*. New York: Fawcett. (Reprinted 1989, New York: Bantam.)

Dyson, Michael Eric. 1996. *Between Good and Bad Gangsta Rap: Bearing Witness to Black Culture*. New York: Oxford University Press.

Ebert, Roger. 1998a. 'Review of *Lethal Weapon*,' pp. 456–457 in *Roger Ebert's Video Companion*, 1998 edn. Kansas City: Andrews and McMeel.

Ebert, Roger. 1998b. 'Review of *Lethal Weapon 2*,' p. 457 in *Roger Ebert's Video Companion*, 1998 edn. Kansas City: Andrews and McMeel.

Ebert, Roger. 1998c. 'Review of *Lethal Weapon 3*,' pp. 457–458 in *Roger Ebert's Video Companion*, 1998 edn. Kansas City: Andrews and McMeel.

Ebert, Roger. 1998d. 'Review of *Clockers*,' pp. 154–155 in *Roger Ebert's Video Companion*, 1998 edn. Kansas City: Andrews and McMeel.

Ebert, Roger. 1994a. 'Review of *Boyz N the Hood*,' pp. 93–94 in *Roger Ebert's Video Companion*, 1994 edn. Kansas City: Andrews and McMeel.

Ebert, Roger. 1994b. 'Review of *Grand Canyon*,' pp. 282–283 in *Roger Ebert's Video Companion*, 1994 edn. Kansas City: Andrews and McMeel.

Ebert, Roger. 1994c. 'Review of *A Rage in Harlem*,' pp. 579–580 in *Roger Ebert's Video Companion*, 1994 edn. Kansas City: Andrews and McMeel.

Ebert, Roger. 1994d. 'Review of *White Men Can't Jump*,' pp. 792–793 in *Roger Ebert's Video Companion*, 1994 edn. Kansas City: Andrews and McMeel.

Ebert, Roger. 1994e. 'Review of *Passion Fish*,' pp. 539–540 in *Roger Ebert's Video Companion*, 1994 edn. Kansas City: Andrews and McMeel.

Ebert, Roger. 1992. '"White Men" Hustles Laughs in Jump Beyond Basketball: Review of *White Men Can't Jump*,' *Chicago Sun Times*, 28 March: 18.

Ebert, Roger. 1988. 'Review of *Colors*,' *New York Post*, 18 April: 21.

Ebert, Roger. 1987. 'Review of *Lethal Weapon*,' *New York Post*, 6 March: 24.

Edelstein, David. 1989. 'Review of *Lethal Weapon II*,' *New York Post*, 7 August: 43.

Edwards, Keith. 1992. 'Review of *Lethal Weapon III*,' *Films in Review*, August: 269.

Egan, Timothy. 1999. 'Crack's Legacy: Soldiers of the Drug War Remain on Duty,' *New York Times*, 1 March: A1, A16.

Ellis, Trey. 1993. *Home Repairs*. New York: Simon and Schuster.

Ellis, Trey. 1989. 'The New Black Aesthetic,' *Before Columbus Review*, 15 May: 4, 23.

Ellison, Ralph. 1996a. *Flying Home*. Edited and with an Introduction by John F. Callahan. New York: Random House.

Ellison, Ralph. 1996b. 'Mintons,' pp. 545–554 in Robert Gottlieb (ed.), *Reading Jazz: A Gathering of Autobiography, Reportage, and Criticism from 1919 to Now*. New York: Pantheon Books. (Originally published in *Esquire*, 1959.)

Ellison, Ralph. 1986. *Going to the Territory*. New York: Random House.

Ellison, Ralph. 1964. *Shadow and Act*. New York: Random House.

Ellison, Ralph. 1952. *Invisible Man*. New York: Random House.

Fanon, Frantz. 1986. *Black Skin, White Masks*. London: Pluto.

Farolino, Audrey. 1992. 'Review of *American Me*,' *New York Post*, 13 March: 34.

Feagin, Joe. R. 2000. *Racist America*. New York: Routledge.

Feagin, Joe R., and Hernan Vera. 1995. *White Racism*. New York: Routledge.

Feng, Peter. 1996. 'Being Chinese American, Becoming Asian American: Chan Is Missing,' *Cinema Journal*, 35: 88–118.

Fernando, S. H., Jr. 1994. *The New Beats: Exploring the Music, Culture, and Attitudes of Hip Hop*. New York: Doubleday.

Fiedler, Leslie. 1988. 'The Montana Face,' pp. 744–752 in William Kittredge and Annick Smith (eds), *The Last Best Place: A Montana Anthology*. Seattle: University of Washington Press. (Originally published 1949.)

Fielder, Leslie. 1971a. 'Montana: or the End of Jean-Jacques Rousseau,' pp. 133–141 in *The Collected Essays of Leslie Fiedler, Vol. I*. New York: Stein and Day. (Originally published in the *Partisan Review* as 'Montana', December, 1949.)

Fiedler, Leslie. 1971b. 'Montana: P.S.,' pp. 331–336 in *The Collected Essays of Leslie Fiedler, Vol. II*. New York: Stein and Day.

Fiedler, Leslie. 1971c. 'Montana: P.P.S.,' pp. 337–342 in *The Collected Essays of Leslie Fiedler, Vol. II*. New York: Stein and Day.

Fiedler, Leslie. 1966. *Love and Death in the American Novel* (rev. edition). New York: Stein and Day.

Fine, Michelle. 1997. 'Witnessing Whiteness,' pp. 57–65 in Michelle Fine, Lois Weis, Linda C. Powell, and L. Mun Wong (eds), *Off White: Readings on Race, Power and Society*. New York: Routledge.

Fine, Michelle, Linda C. Powell, Lois Weis, and L. Mun Wong. 1997. 'Preface,' pp. vii–xii in Michelle Fine, Linda C. Powell, Lois Weis, and L. Mun Wong (eds), *Off White: Readings on Race, Power, and Society*. New York: Routledge.

Fiorillo, C. M. 1989. 'Review of *Lethal Weapon II*,' *Films in Review*, October: 483.

Fiorillo, C. M. 1988. 'Review of *Colors*,' *Films in Review*, August–September: 414.

Fiorillo, C. M. 1987. 'Review of *Lethal Weapon*,' *Films in Review*, May: 299.

Flamm, Matthew. 1992. 'Review of *Lethal Weapon III*,' *Films in Review*, May: 25.

Foster, Hal. 1988. 'Wild Signs,' pp. 251–268 in Andrew Ross (ed.), *Universal Abandon? The Politics of Postmodernism*. Minneapolis: University of Minnesota Press.

Foster, Hal. 1983. 'Postmodernism: A Preface,' pp. ix–xvi in Hal Foster (ed.), *The Anti-Aesthetic: Essays on Postmodern Culture*. Port Townsend, Wash.: Bay Press.

Foucault, Michel. 1978. *The History of Sexuality, An Introduction, Volume 1*. New York: Vintage Books.

Francke, Lizzie. 1996. 'Review of *Dangerous Mind*,' *Sight and Sound*, January: 37.

Frazier, E. Franklin. 1968. 'Human, All Too Human: The Negro's Vested Interest in Segregation,' pp. 283–291 in G. Franklin Edwards (ed.), *E. Franklin Frazier on Race Relations*. Chicago: University of Chicago Press.

Frazier, E. Franklin. 1957. *Black Bourgeoisie*. Glencoe, Ill.: Free Press.

Fregoso, Rosa Linda. 1993. *The Bronze Screen: Chicana and Chicano Film Culture*. Minneapolis: University of Minnesota Press.

Friedman, Lester D. (ed.). 1991a. *Unspeakable Images: Ethnicity and the American Cinema*. Urbana: University of Illinois Press.

Friedman, Lester D. (ed.). 1991b. 'Celluloid Palimpsests: An Overview of Ethnicity and the American Film,' pp. 11–35 in Lester D. Friedman (ed.), *Unspeakable Images: Ethnicity and the American Cinema*. Urbana: University of Illinois Press.

Friedwald, Will. 1990. *Jazz Singing: America's Great Voices from Bessie Smith to Bebop and Beyond*. New York: Charles Scribner's Sons.

Fuller, Hoyt. 1997. 'Towards a Black Aesthetic,' pp. 1810–1816 in Henry Louis Gates, Jr and Nellie Y. McKay (eds), *The Norton Anthology of African American Literature*. New York: W. W. Norton & Company. (Originally published in *The Critic*, 1968 by Thomas More Association.)

Fung, Richard. 1994. 'Seeing Yellow: Asian Identities in Film and Video,' pp. 161–172 in Karin Aguilar-San Juan (ed.), *The State of Asian America: Activism and Resistance in the 1990s*. Boston: South End Press.

Gabrenya, Frank. 1992. 'Slam-Dunk! "White Men" Hoops Scores With Humor, Action: Review of *White Men Can't Jump*,' *Columbus Dispatch*, 27 March: 16.

Gaines, Donna. 1991. *Teenage Wasteland: Suburbia's Dead End Kids*. New York: Pantheon.

Gaines, Jane. 1997. 'The Scar of Shame: Skin Color and Caste in Black Silent Melodrama,' pp. 61–82 in Valerie Smith (ed.), *Representing Blackness: Issues in Film and Video*. New Brunswick, NJ: Rutgers University Press.

Gans, Herbert. 1979. 'Symbolic Ethnicity: The Future of Ethnic Groups and Cultures in America,' *Ethnic and Racial Studies*, 2: 1–20.

garcia, matt. 1999. 'The "Chicano" Dance Hall,' pp. 317–342 in Cameron McCarthy, Glenn Hudak, Shawn Miklaucic, and Paula Saukko (eds), *Sound Identites*. New York: Peter Lang.

Garvey, Marcus. 1969. *Philosophy and Opinions of Marcus Garvey* (Vols 1–2), Edited by Amy Jacques Garvey. New York: Atheneum.

221

Gates, Henry Louis, Jr. 1998. 'The White Negro,' *The New Yorker*, 11 May: 62–65.

Gates, Henry Louis, Jr. 1988. *The Signifying Monkey: A Theory of African-American Literary Criticism*. New York: Oxford University Press.

Gayle, Addison, Jr. 1997. 'The Black Aesthetic,' pp. 1870–1877 in Henry Louis Gates, Jr. and Nellie Y. McKay (eds), *The Norton Anthology of African American Literature*. New York: W. W. Norton & Company. (Originally published in 1971.)

Gayle, Addison, Jr. 1971. 'Introduction,' pp. xv–xxiv in Addison Gayle, Jr (ed.), *The Black Aesthetic*. New York: Doubleday.

Gelmis, Joseph. 1988. 'Review of *Colors*,' *Newsday*, 15 April, Part III: 3.

Gelmis, Joseph. 1987. 'Review of *Lethal Weapon*,' *Newsday*, 6 March, Part III: 5.

George, Nelson. 1998. *Hip Hop America*. New York: Viking.

Giddens, Gary. 1998. *Visions of Jazz: The First Century*. New York: Oxford University Press.

Gilroy, Paul. 2000. *Against Race*. Cambridge, Mass.: Harvard University Press.

Gilroy, Paul. 1995. '"After the Love Has Gone": Bio-politics and Etho-poetics in the Black Public Sphere,' pp. 53–80 in The Black Public Sphere Collective (ed.), *The Black Public Sphere: A Public Culture Book*. Chicago: University of Chicago Press.

Gilroy, Paul. 1992. 'It's a Family Affair,' pp. 303–316 in Gina Dent (ed.), *Black Popular Culture*. Seattle: Bay Press.

Giroux, Henry. 2000. *Impure Acts*. New York: Routledge.

Giroux, Henry A. 1997. 'White Squall: Resistance and the Pedagogy of Whiteness,' *Cultural Studies*, 11: 376–389.

Giroux, Henry A. 1996. *Fugitive Cultures, Race, Violence & Youth*. New York: Routledge.

Giroux, Henry A. 1994. *Disturbing Pleasures*. New York: Routledge, 1994.

Giroux, Henry. 1992. *Border Crossings: Cultural Workers and the Politics of Education*. New York: Routledge.

Goffman, Erving. 1967. 'Where the Action Is,' pp. 149–270 in Erving Goffman, *Interaction Ritual*. New York: Anchor.

Goldman, Ilene S. 1996. 'Crossing Borders: Ramon Menendez's *Stand and Deliver* (1987),' pp. 81–94 in Chon A. Noriega and Ana M. López (eds), *The Ethnic Eye: Latino Media Arts*. Minneapolis: University of Minnesota Press.

Gonzales, Phillip B. 1993. 'Historical Poverty, Restructuring Effects, and Integrative Ties: Mexican-American Neighborhoods in a Peripheral Sunbelt Economy,' pp. 149–171 in Joan Moore and Raquel Pinderhughes (eds), *In the Barrios: Latinos and the Underclass Debate*. New York: Russell Sage Foundation.

Gonzalez, Francisca E. 1998. 'Formations of Mexicananess: *Trenzas de Identidades Multiples* Growing up Mexicana: Braids of Multiple Identities,' *International Journal of Qualitative Studies in Education*, 11: 81–102.

Grant, Edmond. 1992. 'Review of *Boyz N the Hood*,' *Films in Review*, February: 53.

Gray, Herman. 1995. *Watching Race: Television and the Struggle for 'Blackness'*. Minneapolis: University of Minnesota Press.

Gray, Herman. 1993. 'African-American Political Desire and, the Seductions of Contemporary Cultural Politics,' *Cultural Studies*, 7: 364–373.

Green, Roberta F. 1993. 'Review of *Juice*,' pp. 191–194 in Frank N. Magill (ed.), *Magill's Cinema Annual: 1993: A Survey of the Films of 1992*. Englewood Cliffs, NJ: Salem Press.

Griffith, Beatrice Winston. 1948. *American Me*. Boston: Houghton Mifflin.

Guerrero, Ed. 1993a. *Framing Blackness: The African American Image in Film*. Philadelphia: Temple University Press.

Guerrero, Ed. 1993b. 'The Black Image in Protective Custody: Hollywood's Biracial Buddy films of the Eighties,' pp. 237–246 in Mantha Diawara (ed.), *Black American Cinema*. New York: Routledge.

Hadley-Garcia, George. 1990. *Hispanic Hollywood: The Latins in Motion Pictures*. New York: Citadel Press.

Hall, Stuart. 1996a. 'New Ethnicities,' pp. 441–449 in David Morley and Kuan-Hsing Chen (eds), *Stuart Hall: Critical Dialogues in Cultural Studies*. London: Routledge.

Hall, Stuart. 1996b. 'What Is This "Black" in Black Popular Culture?' pp. 465–475 in David Morley and Kuan-Hsing Chen (eds), *Stuart Hall: Critical Dialogues in Cultural Studies*. London: Routledge.

Hall, Stuart. 1996c. 'Gramsci's Relevance for the Study of Race and Ethnicity,' pp. 411–440 in David Morley and Kuan-Hsing Chen (eds), *Stuart Hall: Critical Dialogues in Cultural Studies*, London: Routledge.

Hall, Stuart. 1989. 'Cultural Identity and Cinematic Representation,' *Framework*, 36: 68–81.

Hall, Stuart. 1981. 'The Whites of Their Eyes: Racist Ideologies and the Media,' pp. 36–37 in George Bridges and Rosalind Brunt (eds), *Silver Linings*. London: Lawrence & Wishart.

Hamond, John. 1991. 'Lester Young,' pp. 25–31 in Lewis Porter (ed.), *A Lester Young Reader*. Washington, DC: Smithsonian Institution Press.

Hampton, Lionel, 1996. 'Lionel Hampton,' pp. 122–130 in Robert Gottlieb (ed.), *Reading Jazz: A Gathering of Autobiography, Reportage, and Criticism from 1919 to Now*. New York: Pantheon Books.

Haraway, Donna J. 1997. *Modest_Witness@Second_Millennium.FemaleMan_Meets_OncoMouse*. New York: Routledge.

Harrington, Walt. 1992. *Crossings: A White Man's Journey Into Black America*. New York: HarperCollins.

Harris, Trudier. 1998. '"No More Shall They in Bondage Toll": African American History and Culture, 1865–1915: Paul Laurence Dunbar,' pp. 600–604 in Patricia Liggins Hill, Bernard W. Bell, Trudier Harris, William J. Harris, R. Baxter Miller, Sondra A. O'Neale, with Horace A. Porter (eds), *Call & Response: The Riverside Anthology of the African American Literary Tradition*. New York: Houghton Mifflin.

Harris, William J. 1998. '"Cross Roads Blues": African American History and Culture, 1960 to the Present,' pp. 1343–1385 in Patricia Liggins Hill, Bernard W. Bell, Trudier Harris, William J. Harris, R. Baxter Miller, Sondra A. O'Neale, with Horace A. Porter (eds), *Call & Response: The Riverside Anthology of the African American Literary Tradition*. New York: Houghton Mifflin.

Haywood, Anthony Gar. 1987. *Fear of the Dark*. New York: Berkley Prime Crime.

Haywood, Anthony Gar. 1988. *You Can Die Trying*. New York: Berkley Prime Crime.

Haywood, Anthony Gar. 1993. *Not Long for This World*. New York: Berkeley Prime Crime.

Healey, Joseph F. 1995. *Race, Ethnicity, Gender and Class*. Thousand Oaks, Calif: Pine Forge Press.

Hebdige, Dick. 1984. *Subculture: The Meaning of Style*. London: Routledge.

Higashi, Sumiko. 1991. 'Ethnicity, Class and Gender in Film: DeMille's *The Cheat*,' pp. 112–139 in Lester D. Friedman (ed.), *Unspeakable Images: Ethnicity and the American Cinema*. Urbana: University of Illinois Press.

Hill, Patricia Liggins, Bernard W. Bell, Trudier Harris, William J. Harris, R. Baxter Miller, Sondra A. O'Neale, with Horace A. Porter (eds), 1998. *Call & Response: The Riverside Anthology of the African American Literary Tradition*. New York: Houghton Mifflin.

Himes, Chester. 1998. *Yesterday Will Make You Cry*. Introduction by Melvin Van Peebles. New York: W.W. Norton.

Himes, Chester. 1977. *My Life of Absurdity: The Autobiography of Chester Himes, Volume II*. New York: Doubleday.

Himes, Chester. 1972. *The Quality of Hurt: The Autobiography of Chester Himes, Volume I*. New York: Doubleday.

Himes, Chester. 1965. *Cotton Comes to Harlem*. New York: Allison & Busby.

Himes, Chester. 1960. *All Shot Up*. New York: Allison & Busby.

Himes, Chester. 1959. *The Crazy Kill*. New York: Allison & Busby.

Himes, Chester. 1957. *A Rage in Harlem*. New York: Vintage.

Himes, Chester. 1945. *If He Hollers Let Him Go*. New York: Doubleday & Co., Inc.

Hirschberg, Lynn. 1998. 'Warren Beatty Is Trying to Say Something,' *New York Times Magazine*, 10 May: 20–38.

Hoberman, J. 1991. 'Review of *Boyz N the Hood*,' *Village Voice*, 16 July: 58.

Hoberman, J. 1988. 'Review of *Colors*,' *Village Voice*, 19 April: 62.

hooks, bell. 1996. *Reel to Real: Race, Sex and Class at the Movies*. New York: Routledge.

hooks, bell. 1994. *Outlaw Culture: Resisting Representations*. New York: Routledge.

hooks, bell. 1992. *Black Looks: Race and Representation*. Boston: South End Press.

hooks, bell. 1990. *Yearning: Race, Gender, and Cultural Politics*. Boston: South End Press.

Horowitz, Ruth. 1983. *Honor and the American Dream: Culture and Identity in a Chicano Community*. New Brunswick, NJ: Rutgers University Press.

Jameson, Fredric. 1992. *The Geopolitical Aesthetic: Cinema and Space in the World System*. Bloomington: Indiana University Press.

Jameson, Fredric. 1991. *Postmodernism, or, The Cultural Logic of Late Capitalism*. Durham, NC: Duke University Press.

Jameson, Fredric. 1990. *Signatures of the Visible*. New York: Routledge.

Jankowski, Martin Sanchez. 1991. *Islands in the Street: Gangs and American Urban Society*. Berkeley: University of California Press.

Jenkins, Steve. 1988. 'Review of *Colors*,' *Monthy Film Bulletin*, November: 326.

Johnson, Charles. 1941. *Growing Up in the Black Belt: Negro Youth in the Rural South*. Washington, DC: American Council on Education.

Johnson, LouAnne. 1992. *My Posse Don't Do Homework* (retitled as *Dangerous Minds*). New York: St Martin's Press.

Jones, Jacquie. 1993. 'The Construction of Black Sexuality,' pp. 247–256 in Mantha Diawara (ed.), *Black American Cinema*. New York: Routledge.

Jones, LeRoi. 1998. *Home: Social Essays With a New Preface by the Author*. Hopewell, NJ: The Ecco Press.

Jordan, June. 1998. *Affirmative Acts*. New York: Doubleday.

Joyce, Joyce Ann. 1987. 'The Black Canon: Reconstructing Black American Literary Criticism,' *New Literary History*, 18, no. 2: 335–344.

Karenga, Maulana. 1997. 'Black Art: Mute Matter Given Force and Function,' pp. 1973–1977 in Henry Louis Gates, Jr. and Nellie Y. McKay (eds), *The Norton Anthology of African American Literature*. New York: W. W. Norton & Company. (Originally published in W. King and E. Anthony (eds), *Black Poets and Prophets*. New York: Mentor Press, 1972.

Kassabian Anahid. 1991. 'Review of *Mo' Better Blues*,' pp. 158–261 in Frank N. Magill (ed.), *Magill's Cinema Annual: 1990: A Survey of the Films of 1989*. Englewood Cliffs, NJ: Salem Press.

Katz, Ephraim. 1998. *The Film Encyclopedia*, 3rd edn, rev. by Fred Klein and Ronald Dean Nolen. New York: HarperPerennial.

Katz, Jesse. 1996. 'Special Report, Part I: Tracking the Genesis of the Crack Trade,' *Los Angeles Times*, 20 October: 22.

Kehr, David. 1992. '"White Men" Scores, With Style and Warmth: Review of *White Men Can't Jump*,' *Chicago Tribune*, 27 March: 20.

Keller, Gary D. 1994. *Hispanics and United States Film: An Overview and Handbook*. Tempe, Ariz.: Bilingual Review/Press.

Kellner, Douglas. 1997. 'Aesthetics, Ethics and Politics in the Films of Spike Lee,' pp. 73–106 in Mark A. Reid (ed.), *Spike Lee's Do the Right Thing*. New York: Cambridge University Press.

Kellner, Douglas. 1989. *Critical Theory, Marxism and Modernity*. Baltimore, MD: Johns Hopkins University Press.

Kemp, Philip. 1993. 'Review of *Passion Fish*,' *Sight and Sound*, September: 51.

Kemp, Philip. 1992. 'Review of *Grand Canyon*,' *Sight and Sound*, May: 50.

Keneas, Alex. 1982. 'Review of *Zoot Suit*,' *Newsday*, 22 January, Part II: 7.

Kennedy, Lisa. 1992. 'The Body in Question,' pp. 106–111 in Gina Dent (ed.), *Black Popular Culture*. Seattle: Bay Press.

Kermode, Mark. 1992. 'Review of *Lethal Weapon III*,' *Sight and Sound*, August: 57.

Kilborn, Peter T. 1999. 'Bias Worsens for Minorities Buying Homes,' *New York Times*, 16 September: A15.

King, Neal. 1999. *Heroes in Hard Times: Cop Action Movies in the US*. Philadelphia: Temple University Press.

Kroll, Jack. 1992. 'Review of *Lethal Weapon III*,' *Newsweek*, 25 May: 91.

Kroll, Jack, and Lyndia Wright. 1992. 'Review of *American Me*,' *Newsweek*, 30 March: 66.

Labov, William. 1972. 'Rules for Ritual Insults,' pp. 120–169 in David Sudnow (ed.), *Studies in Social Interaction*, New York: Free Press.

Ladson-Billings, Gloria. 2000. 'Racialized Discourses and Ethnic Epistemologies,' pp. 257–278 in Norman K. Denzin and Yvonna S. Lincoln (eds), *Handbook of Qualitative Research*, 2nd edn. Thousand Oaks, Calif: Sage.

Lee, Benjamin. 1997. *Talking Heads: Language, Metalanguage, and the Semiotics of Subjectivity.* Durham, NC: Duke University Press.

Lee, Spike. 1992. *By Any Means Necessary: The Trials and Tribulations of the Making of Malcolm X ... Including the Screenplay.* New York: Hyperion.

Lee, Spike. 1988. *Uplift the Race: The Construction of School Daze.* New York: Simon and Schuster.

Lee, Spike. 1989. *Do the Right Thing: A Spike Lee Joint.* New York: Fireside Press.

Leland, John, and Alison Samuels. 1997. 'The New Generation Gap.' *Newsweek*, 17 March: 52–57, 59–60.

Levy, Joe. 1992. 'Review of *Lethal Weapon III*,' *Village Voice*, 26 May: 70.

Lewis, Leon. 1990. 'Review of *Lethal Weapon, II*,' pp. 217–220 in Frank N. Magill (ed.), *Magill's Cinema Annual: 1990: A Survey of the Films of 1989.* Englewood Cliffs, NJ: Salem Press.

Lipsitz, George. 1994. 'We Know What Time It Is: Race, Class and Youth Culture in the Nineties,' pp. 17–28 in Andrew Ross and Tricia Rose (eds), *Microphone Fiends: Youth Music and Youth Culture.* New York: Routledge.

List, Christine. 1992. 'Self-Directed Stereotyping in the Films of Cheech Marin,' pp. 183–194 in Chon A. Noriega (ed.), *Chicanos and Film: Representation and Resistance.* Minneapolis: University of Minnesota Press.

Locke, Alain. 1968. 'The New Negro,' pp. 3–18 in Alain Locke (ed.), *The New Negro: An Interpretation.* New York: Johnson Reprint Corporation. (Originally published 1925, New York: Albert & Charles Boni, Inc.)

López, Ana M. 1991. 'Are All Latins from Manhattan? Hollywood, Ethnography, and Cultural Colonialism,' pp. 404–424 in Lester D. Friedman (ed.), *Unspeakable Images: Ethnicity and the American Cinema.* Urbana: University of Illinois Press.

Lott, Tommy L. 1997. 'A No-Theory of Contemporary Black Cinema,' pp. 83–96 in Valerie Smith (ed.), *Representing Blackness: Issues in Film and Video.* New Brunswick, NJ: Rutgers University Press.

Lubiano, Wahneema. 1997. 'But Compared to What? Reading Realism, Representation, and Essentialism in *School Daze*, *Do the Right Thing*, and the Spike Lee Discourse,' pp. 97–122 in Valerie Smith (ed.), *Representing Blackness: Issues in Film and Video.* New Brunswick, NJ: Rutgers University Press.

Lyman, Stanford, M. 1998. 'Gunnar Myrdal's *An American Dilemma* After a Half Century: Critics and Anticritics,' *International Journal of Politics, Culture and Society*, 12: 327–389.

Lyman, Stanford M. 1990a. 'Race, Sex, and Servitude: Images of Blacks in American Cinema,' *International Journal of Politics, Culture and Society*, 4: 49–77.

Lyman, Stanford M. 1990b. 'The Race Relations Cycle of Robert E. Park,' pp. 128–135 in Stanford M. Lyman, *Civilization: Contents, Discontents, Malcontents and Other Essays in Social Theory.* Fayetteville: University of Arkansas Press.

Lyman, Stanford M. 1990c. 'Interactionism and the Study of Race Relations at the Macrosociological Level: The Contribution of Herbert Blumer,' pp. 136–148 in Stanford M. Lyman, *Civilization: Contents, Discontents, Malcontents and Other Essays in Social Theory.* Fayetteville: University of Arkansas Press.

Lyman, Stanford M. 1990d. 'The Significance of Asians in American Society,' pp. 149–159 in Stanford M. Lyman, *Civilization: Contents, Discontents, Malcontents and Other Essays in Social Theory.* Fayetteville: University of Arkansas Press.

Lyman, Stanford M. 1977. *The Asian in North America.* Santa Barbara, Calif.: ABC-Clio, Inc.

Lyman, Stanford M. 1972. *The Black American in Sociological Thought.* New York: Putnam's Sons.

Lyman, Stanford M. 1970. *The Asian in the West.* Reno: Social Science & Humanities Publications, no. 4, Western Studies Center, University of Nevada.

McCarthy, Cameron, Alicia Rodriguez, Shuaib Meacham, Stephen David, Carrie Wilson-Brown, Heriberto Godina, K. E. Supryia, and Ed Buendia. 1996. 'Race, Suburban Resentment and the Representation of the Inner City in Contemporary Film and Television,' *Cultural Studies*, 1: 121–140.

McCarthy, Cameron. 1998. *The Uses of Culture.* New York: Routledge.

McGrady, Mike. 1989a. 'Review of *Black Rain*,' *Newsday*, 22 September, Part III: 3.

McGrady, Mike. 1989b. 'Review of *Lethal Weapon II*,' *Newsday*, 7 July, Part III: 3.

MacGregor, Jeff. 2000. 'TV, the Movies Abused (and Abusive) Stepchild: Review of Spike Lee's *Bamboozled*,' *New York Times*, Sunday, 8 October: Arts and Leisure, A-ll, 34.

McKee, James B. 1993. *Sociology and the Race Problem*. Urbana: University of Illinois Press.

McMurtry, Larry. 1999. *Walter Benjamin at the Dairy Queen*. New York: Simon & Schuster.

McPherson, James Alan. 2000. *A Region Not Home*. New York: Simon & Schuster.

McRobbie, Angela. 1994. 'Review of *Menace II Society*,' *Sight and Sound*, January: 50.

Malinxe. 1997. 'CIA Director John Deutch Experiences Watts Firsthand,' *Rap Pages*, February: 27–28.

Marble, Manning. 1992 'Race, Identity, and Political Culture,' pp. 292–303 in Gina Dent (ed.), *Black Popular Culture: A Project by Michele Wallace*. Seattle: Bay Press.

Marchetti, Gina. 1993. *Romance and the 'Yellow Peril': Race, Sex, and Discursive Strategies in Hollywood Fiction*. Berkeley: University of California Press.

Marchetti, Gina. 1991. 'Ethnicity, the Cinema, and Cultural Studies,' pp. 277–309 in Lester D. Friedman (ed.), *Unspeakable Images: Ethnicity and the American Cinema*. Urbana: University of Illinois Press.

Margolis, Harriet. 1999. 'Stereotypical Strategies: Black Film Aesthetics, Spectator Positioning, and Self-Directed Stereotypes in *Hollywood Shuffle* and *I'm Gonna Git You Sucka*,' *Cinema Journal*, 38: 50–66.

Masilela, Ntongela. 1993. 'The Los Angeles School of Black Filmmakers,' pp. 107–117 in Mantha Diawara (ed.), *Black American Cinema*. New York: Routledge.

Maslin, Janet. 1995. 'Review of *Dangerous Minds*,' *New York Times*, 11 August: C3:1.

Massood, Paula J. 1996. 'Mapping the Hood: The Genealogy of City Space in *Boyz N the Hood* and *Menace II Society*,' *Cinema Journal*, 35: 85–97.

Massood, Paula J. 1993. 'Review of "*Menace II Society*,"' *Cineaste*, 20: 44.

Mast, Gerald. 1976. *A Short History of the Movies*, 2nd edn. Indianapolis: Bobbs-Merrill.

Mathews, Jack. 1995a. 'Review of *Dangerous Minds*,' *Newsday*, 11 August, Part II: 82.

Mathews, Jack. 1995b. 'Review of *Clockers*,' *Newsday*, 13 September, Part II: 82.

Mathews, Jack. 1993. 'Review of *Bound By Honor*,' *Newsday*, 30 April, Part II: 71.

Mathews, Jack. 1991a. 'Review of *Grand Canyon*,' *Newsday*, 24 December, Part II: 46.

Mathews, Jack. 1991b. 'Review of *A Rage in Harlem*,' *Newsday*, 3 May, Part II: 82.

Mathews, Jack. 1991c. 'Review of *Boyz N The Hood*,' *Newsday*, 12 July, Part II: 60.

Medved, Michael. 1995. 'Review of *Dangerous Minds*,' *New York Post*, 11 August: 43.

Medved, Michael. 1993. 'Review of *Bound By Honor*,' *New York Post*, 30 April: 29.

Mercer, Kobena. 1988. 'Diaspora Culture and the Dialogic Imagination: The Aesthetics of Black Independent Film in Britain,' pp. 50–61 in Mbye B. Cham and Claire Andrade-Watkins (eds), *BlackFrames: Critical Perspectives on Black Independent Cinema*. Cambridge, Mass: MIT Press.

Mills, C. Wright. 1963. *Power, Politics and People: The Collected Essays of C. Wright Mills*. Edited with an Introduction by Irving Louis Horowitz. New York: Ballantine.

Mitchell, Elvis. 2000. 'How "Shaft" Defined a Self-destructive Genre,' Sunday *New York Times*, Arts & Leisure, 30 April: 28–29.

Moore, Joan, and James Diego Vigil. 1993. 'Barrios in Transition,' pp. 27–49 in Joan Moore and Raquel Pinderhughes (eds), *In The Barrios: Latinos and the Underclass Debate*. New York: Russell Sage Foundation.

Morales, ed. 1993. 'Review of *Bound By Honor*,' *Village Voice*, 11 May: 62

Morley, David, and Kuan-Hsing Chen (eds). 1996. *Stuart Hall: Critical Dialogues in Cultural Studies*. London: Routledge.

Mosley, Walter. 1994. *The Little Yellow Dog*. New York: Pocket Books.

Mosley, Walter. 1993. *Black Betty*. New York: Pocket Books.

Mosley, Walter. 1992. *White Butterly*. New York: Pocket Books.

Mosley, Walter. 1991. *A Red Death*. New York: Pocket Books.

Mosley, Walter. 1990. *Devil in a Blue Dress*. New York: Pocket Books.

Moynihan, Daniel. 1965. *The Negro Family: The Case for National Action*. Washington, DC: US Department of Labor.

Mulvey, Laura, and Peter Wollen. 1989. 'Freda Kahlo and Tina Modotti,' pp. 81–110 in Laura Mulvey (ed.), *Visual and Other Pleasures*. Bloomington: Indiana University Press.

Musser, Charles. 1991. 'Ethnicity, Role-playing, and American Film Comedy: From *Chinese Laundry Scene* to *Whoopee* (1984–1930),' pp. 82–111 in Lester D. Friedman (ed.), *Unspeakable Images: Ethnicity and the American Cinema*. Urbana: University of Illinois Press.

Myrdal, Gunnar. 1944. *An American Dilemma: The Negro Problem and Modern Democracy*. New York: Harper.

Nagel, Joanne. 1996. *American Indian Ethnic Renewal: Red Power and the Resurgence of Identity and Culture*. New York: Oxford University Press.

Neal, Larry. 1998. 'The Black Arts Movement,' pp. 1448–1450 in Patricia Liggins Hill, Bernard W. Bell, Trudier Harri's, William J. Harris, R. Baxter Miller, Sondra A. O'Neale, with Horace A. Porter (eds), *Call & Response: The Riverside Anthology of the African American Literary Tradition*. Boston: Houghton Mifflin. (Originally published in *Visions of A Liberated Future*. New York: Thunder's Mouth Press, 1988.)

Negron-Muntaner, Frances. 1996. 'Drama Queens: Latino Gay and Lesbian Independent Film/Video,' pp. 59–78 in Chon A. Noriega and Ana M. López (eds), *The Ethnic Eye: Latino Media Arts*. Minneapolis: University of Minnesota Press.

Nelson, Havelock, and Michael A. Gonzales. 1991. *Bring the Noise: A Guide to Rap Music and Hip-Hop Culture*. New York: Harmony Books.

Nero, Charles L. 1998. 'Toward a Black Gay Aesthetic: Signifying in Contemporary Black Gay Literature,' pp. 1973–1987 in Patricia Liggins Hill, Bernard W. Bell, Trudier Harris, William J. Harris, R. Baxter Miller, Sondra A. O'Neale, with Horace A. Porter (eds), *Call & Response: The Riverside Anthology of the African American Literary Tradition*. New York: Houghton Mifflin.

Newman, Kathleen. 1996. 'Reterritorialization in Recent Chicano Cinema: Edward James Olmos *American Me* (1992),' pp. 95–106 in Chon A. Noriega (ed.), *Chicanos and Film: Representation and Resistance*. Minneapolis: University of Minnesota Press.

Newman, Kathleen. 1992. 'Latino Sacrifice in the Discourse of Citizenship: Acting Against the "Mainstream," 1985–1988,' pp. 59–73 in Chon A. Noriega (ed.), *Chicanos and Film: Representation and Resistance*. Minneapolis: University of Minnesota Press.

Newman, Kim. 1991. 'Review of *New Jack City*,' *Sight and Sound*, September: 41.

Newman, Kim. 1989. 'Review of *Lethal Weapon II*,' *Monthly Film Bulletin*, October: 305.

New York Times. 2000. 'Editorial: The Scourge of Guns,' 5 September: A30.

Noriega, Chon A. 1996. 'Imagined Borders: Locating Chicano Cinema in America/America,' pp. 3–21 in Chon A. Noriega and Ana M. López (eds), *The Ethnic Eye: Latino Media Arts*. Minneapolis: University of Minnesota Press.

Noriega, Chon A. 1992a. 'Introduction,' pp. xi–xxvi in Chon A. Noriega (ed.), *Chicanos and Film: Representation and Resistance*. Minneapolis: University of Minnesota Press.

Noriega, Chon A. 1992b. 'Between a Weapon and a Formula: Chicano Cinema and Its Contexts,' pp. 141–167 in Chon A. Noriega (ed.), *Chicanos and Film: Representation and Resistance*. Minneapolis: University of Minnesota Press.

Noriega, Chon A. 1988. 'Review of *Lethal Weapon*,' pp. 210–213 in Fragil N. Magill (ed.), *Magill's Cinema Annual: 1992: A Survey of the Films of 1981*. Englewood Cliffs, NJ: Salem Press.

Noriega, Chon A. and Ana M. López. 1996. 'Introduction,' pp. ix–xxii in Chon A. Noriega and Ana M. López (eds), *The Ethnic Eye: Latino Media Arts*. Minneapolis: University of Minnesota Press.

Page, Helen E. 1997. '"Black Male" Imagery and the Media Containment of African American Men,' *American Anthropologist*, 99: 99–111.

Park, Kyeyoung. 1996. 'Use and Abuse of Race and Culture: Black–Korean Tension in America,' *American Anthropologist*, 98: 492–499.

Park, Robert Ezra. 1950a. 'Our Racial Frontier on the Pacific,' pp. 136–151 in Robert Ezra Park, *Race and Culture*. Glencoe, Ill.: Free Press. (Originally Published in *Graphic*, 9, 1926: 192–196.)

Park, Robert Ezra. 1950b. 'Education in its relation to the Conflict and Fusion of Cultures,' pp. 261–283 in Robert Park, *Race and Culture*. Glencoe, Ill.: Free Press. pp. 261–283. (Originally published in *American Sociological Review*, 13, 1918: 38–63.)

Parker, Laurence. 1998. 'Race Is ... Race Ain't: An Exploration of the Utility of Critical Race Theory in Qualitative Research in Education,' *Qualitative Studies in Education*, 11: 43–55.

Parker, Laurence, Donna Deyhle, Sofia Villenas, and Kristin Crosland Nebeker. 1998. 'Guest Editor's Introduction: Critical Race Theory, and Qualitative Studies in Education,' *Qualitative Studies in Education*, 11: 5–6.

Pawelczak, Andy. 1995. 'Review of *Clockers*,' *Films in Review*, 11 December: 100.

Pelecanos, George. 1991. 'Review of *New Jack City*,' *Cineaste*, 18, no. 3: 49.

Perkins, William Eric. 1996. 'Youth's Global Village: An Epilogue,' pp. 258–274 in William Eric Perkins (ed.), *Droppin' Science: Critical Essays on Rap Music and Hip Hop Culture*. Philadelphia: Temple University Press.

Pinderhughes, Howard. 1997. *Race in the Hood*. Minneapolis: University of Minnesota Press.

Pizarro, Marc. 1998. '"Chicana/o Power": Epistemology and Methodology for Social Justice and Empowerment in Chicana/o Communities,' *Qualitative Studies in Education*, 11: 57–79.

Porter, Lewis. 1991. 'Preface,' pp. ix–xiii in Lewis Porter (ed.), *A Lester Young Reader*. Washington, DC: Smithsonian Institution Press.

Portes, Alejandro, and Robert Manning. 1986. 'The Immigrant Enclave: Theory and Empirical Examples,' pp. 47–68 in Susan Olzak and Joanne Nagel (eds), *Competitive Ethnic Relations*. New York: Academic Press.

Pouzoulet, Catherine. 1997. 'The Cinema of Spike Lee: Images of a Mosaic City,' pp. 31–49 in Mark A. Reid (ed.), *Spike Lee's Do the Right Thing*. Cambridge: Cambridge University Press.

Price, Richard. 1992. *Clockers*. Boston: Houghton Mifflin.

Pride, Richard A. 1995. *The Confession of Dorothy Danner: Telling a Life*. Nashville: Vanderbilt University Press.

Purdum, Todd, S. 1997. 'Exposé on Crack Was Flawed, Paper Says,' *New York Times*, 13 May: A1, A10.

Radhakrishnan, R. 1994. 'Is the Ethnic "Authentic" in the Diaspora?' pp. 219–234 in Karin Aguilar-San Juan (ed.), *The State of Asian America: Activism and Resistance in the 1990s*. Boston: South End Press.

Radway, Janice. 1988. 'Reception Study: Ethnography and the Problems of Dispersed Audiences and Nomadic Subjects,' *Cultural Studies*, 3: 359–376.

Rainer, Peter. 1993. 'Review of *Menace II Society*,' *Los Angeles Times*, 26 May, Calendar: 1.

Rainer, Peter. 1992. 'Review of *Lethal Weapon III*,' *Los Angeles Times*, 15 May, Calendar: 1.

Randall, Dudley (ed.). 1984. *Homage to Hoyt Fuller*. Detroit: Broadside Press. Reeves, Jimmie L., and Richard Campbell. 1994. *Cracked Coverage: Television News, the Anti-Cocaine Crusade, and the Reagan Legacy*. Durham, NC: Duke University Press.

Reid, Mark A. 1997a. 'Introduction,' pp. 1–15 in Mark A. Reid (ed.), *Spike Lee's Do the Right Thing*. Cambridge: Cambridge University Press.

Reid, Mark A. (ed.). 1997b. *Spike Lee's Do the Right Thing*. Cambridge: Cambridge University Press.

Reid, Mark A. 1997c. *PostNegritude Visual and Literary Culture*. Albany: SUNY Press.

Reid, Mark A. 1993. *Redefining Black Film*. Berkeley: University of California Press.

Reinarman, Craig, and Harry G. Levine. 1997. 'The Crack Attack: Politics and Media in the Crack Scare,' pp. 18–51 in Craig Reinarman and Harry G. Levine (eds), *Crack in America: Demon Drugs and Social Justice*. Berkeley: University of California Press.

Richard, Alfred Charles, Jr. 1992. *The Hispanic Image on the Silver Screen: An Interpretive Filmography from Silents into Sound, 1898–1935*. Westport, Conn.: Greenwood Press.

Rickey, Carrie. 1982. 'Review of *Zoot Suit*,' *Village Voice*, 27 January:46.

Ríos-Bustamante, Antonio. 1992. 'Latino Participation in the Hollywood Film Industry, 1911–1945,' pp. 18–28 in Chon A. Noriega (ed.), *Chicanos and Film: Representation and Resistance*. Minneapolis: University of Minnesota Press.

Ro, Ronin. 1996. *Gangsta: Merchandizing the Rhymes of Violence*. New York: St Martin's Press.

Roffman, Peter, and Jim Purdy. 1981. *The Hollywood Social Problems Film*. Bloomington: Indiana University Press.

Rogin, Michael. 1996. *Blackface, White Noise: Jewish Immigrants in the Hollywood Melting Pot*. Berkeley: University of California Press.

Rogin, Michael. 1986. '"The Sword Became a Flashing Vision": D. W. Griffith's "The Birth of a Nation,"' *Representations*, Winter: 150–195.

Rollyson, Carl. 1996. 'Review of *Clockers*,' pp. 90–92 in Beth A. Falmer and Christopher P. Scanlon (eds), *Magill's Cinema Annual: 1996: A Survey of the Films of 1995*. Detroit: Gale Research.

Rollyson, Carl. 1989. 'Review of *Colors*,' pp. 88–90 in Franch N. Magill (ed.), *Magill's Cinema Annual: 1992: A Survey of the Films of 1991*. Englewood Cliffs, NJ: Salem Press.

Romney, Jonathan. 1991. 'Review of *A Rage in Harlem*,' *Sight and Sound*, September: 46.

Rose, Arnold. 1964. *The Negro in America*. New York: Harper Torchbook.

Rose, Tricia. 1994. *Black Noise: Rap Music and Black Culture in Contemporary America*. Hanover, NH: Wesleyan University Press.

Rozen, Leah. 1992. 'Review of *White Men Can't Jump*,' *People*, 13 April: 61.

Ryan, Michael, and Douglas Kellner. 1988. *Camera Politica*. Bloomington: Indiana University Press.

Sallis, James. 1994. *Black Hornet*. New York: Carroll & Graf Publishers, Inc.

Sallis, James. 1993. *Moth*. New York: Carroll & Graf Publishers, Inc.

Sallis, James. 1992. *The Long-Legged Fly*. New York: Carroll & Graf Publishers, Inc.

Sallis, James. 2000. *Chester Himes: A Life*. New York: Walker & Co.

Sanchez-Jankowski, Martin. 1991. *Islands in the Streets*. Berkeley: University of California Press.

Sanders, William B. 1994. *Gangbangs and Drive-bys: Grounded Culture and Juvenile Gang Violence*. New York: Aldine de Gruyter.

Sarris, Andrew. 1968. *The American Cinema: Directors and Directions: 1929–1968*. New York: Dutton.

Sartre, Jean-Paul. 1943. *Being and Nothingness*. New York. Philosophical Library.

Scheurich, James J. 1997. *Research Methods in the Postmodern*. London: Falmer Press.

Schickel, Richard. 1995. 'Review of *Clockers*,' *Time*, 18 September: 108.

Schickel, Richard. 1987. 'Review of *Lethal Weapon*,' *Time*, 23 March: 86.

Scott, Bobby, 1996. 'The House in the Dark,' pp. 450–467 in Robert Gottlieb (ed.), *Reading Jazz: A Gathering of Autobiography, Reportage, and Criticism from 1919 to Now*. New York: Pantheon Books.

Shah, Sonia. 1994. 'Roses, Rites, and Racism: Interview with Sophea Mouth,' pp. 119–124 in Karin Aguilar-San Juan (ed.), *The State of Asian America: Activism and Resistance in the 1990s*. Boston: South End Press.

Shange, Ntozake. 1977. *For Colored Girls Who Have Considered Suicide When the Rainbow Is Enuf*. New York: Simon and Schuster.

Shohat, Elia. 1991. 'Ethnicity-in-Relations: Toward a Multicultural Reading of American Cinema,' pp. 215–250 in Lester D. Friedman (ed.), *Unspeakable Images: Ethnicity and the American Cinema*. Urbana: University of Illinois Press.

Siskel, Gene. 1992. '"White Men Can't Jump" Is a Full-Court Pleasure: Review of *White Men Can't Jump*,' *Chicago Tribune*, 27 March: 13.

Smith, Anna Deavere. 1994. *Twilight: Los Angeles, 1992*. New York: Anchor Books.

Smith, Anna Deavere. 1993. *Fires in the Mirror*. New York: Anchor Books.

Smith, Dinitia. 1997. 'The Indian in Literature Is Catching Up,' *New York Times*, 21 April: B1, B4.

Smith, Valerie. 1997. 'Introduction,' pp. 1–12 in Valerie Smith (ed.), *Representing Blackness: Issues in Film and Video*. New Brunswick, NJ: Rutgers University Press.

Spear, Allan H. 1968. 'Introduction,' pp. v–xxii in Alain Locke (ed.), *The New Negro: An Interpretation*. New York: Johnson Reprint Corporation (Originally published 1925, Albert & Charles Boni, Inc.)

Spivak, Gayatri. 1990. 'In a Word: Interview,' with Ellen Rooney. *Differences* 1, no. 2: 124–155.

Stam, Robert. 1991. 'Bakhtin, Polyphony and Ethnic/Racial Representation,' pp. 251–276 in Lester D. Friedman (ed.), *Unspeakable Images: Ethnicity and the American Cinema*. Urbana: University of Illinois Press.

Stam, Robert. 1989. *Subversive Pleasures: Bakhtin, Cultural Criticism and Film*. Baltimore, Md: Johns Hopkins, University Press.

Stanfield, John H., III. 1994. 'Ethnic Modeling in Qualitative Research,' pp. 175–188 in Norman K. Denzin and Yvonna S. Lincoln (eds), *Handbook of Qualitative Research*. Thousand Oaks, Calif: Sage.

Staples, Brent. 1996. 'Dying to be Black: The Suburban Romance with Urban Violence,' *New York Times*, 9 December: A–10.

Sterritt, David. 1992. 'Review of *Grand Canyon*,' *Christian Science Monitor*, 3 January: 12.

Sterritt, David. 1991a. 'Review of *New Jack City*,' *Christian Science Monitor*, 22 March: 13.

Sterritt, David. 1991b. 'Review of *Boyz N the Hood*,' *Christian Science Monitor*, 22 July: 11.

Sterritt, David. 1995. 'Review of *Clockers*,' *Christian Science Monitor*, 13 September: 13.

Sterritt, David. 1982. 'Review of *Zoot Suit*,' *Christian Science Monitor*, 21 January: 18.

Tasker, Yvonne. 1998. *Working Girls: Gender and Sexuality in Popular Cinema*. London: Routledge.

Tasker, Yvonne. 1993. *Spectacular Bodies: Gender, Genre, and the Action Cinema*. London: Routledge.

Tate, Greg. 1992. *Flyboy in the Buttermilk*. New York: Fireside Press.

Taubin, Amy. 1995a. 'Review of *Dangerous Minds*.' *Village Voice*, 22 August: 52.

Taubin, Amy. 1995b. 'Review of *Clockers*,' *Sight and Sound*. October: 45.

Taubin, Amy. 1995c. 'Review of Clockers,' *Village Voice*, 19 September: 71.

Tepper, Kirby. 1994. 'Review of *Bound By Honor*,' pp. 49–52 in Frank N. Magill (ed.), *Magill's Cinema Annual: 1994: A Survey of the Films of 1993*. Englewood Cliffs, NJ: Salem Press.

Theodore, Terry. 1993. 'Review of *American Me*,' pp. 35–39 in Frank N. Magill (ed.), *Magill's Cinema Annual: 1993: A Survey of the Films of 1992*. Englewood Cliffs, NJ: Salem Press.

Thomas, Kevin. 1981. 'Review of *Zoot Suit*,' *Los Angeles Times*, 30 September: Calendar: 1.

Toop, David. 1984. *Rap Attack: African Jive to New York Hip Hop*. Boston: South End Press.

Trinh, T. Minh-ha. 1992. *Framer Framed*. New York: Routledge.

Trinh, T. Minh-ha. 1991. *When the Moon Waxes Red: Representation, Gender and Cultural Politics*. New York: Routledge.

Trinh, T. Minh-ha. 1989. *Woman, Native, Other: Writing Postcoloniality and Feminism*. Bloomington: Indiana University Press.

Tucker, Kenneth H., Jr. 1993. 'Aesthetics, Play and Cultural Memory: Giddens and Habermas on the Postmodern Challenge,' *Sociological Theory*, 11: 194–211.

Turan, Kenneth. 1995a. 'Review of *Clockers*,' *Los Angeles Times*, 13 September, Calendar: 1.

Turan, Kenneth. 1995b. 'Review of *Dangerous Minds*,' *Los Angeles Times*, 11 August, Calendar: 1.

Turan, Kenneth. 1993. 'Review of *Bound by Honor*,' *Los Angeles Times*, 30 April, Calendar: 1.

Turan, Kenneth. 1992. 'Review of *American Me*,' *Los Angeles Times*, 13 March, Calendar: 1.

Turan, Kenneth. 1991a. 'Review of *Grand Canyon*,' *Los Angeles Times*, 25 December, Calendar: 1.

Turan, Kenneth. 1991b. 'Review of *A Rage in Harlem*,' *Los Angeles Times*, 3 May, Calendar: 1.

Turner, Ralph H., and Samuel J. Surace. 1956. '"Zoot-Suiters and Mexicans": Symbols in Crowd Behavior,' *American Journal of Sociology*, 62: 14–20.

Valdivia, Angharad N. 1996. 'Rosie Goes to Hollywood: The Politics of Representation,' *Review of Education/Pedagogy/Cultural Studies*, 18: 129–141.

Van der Meer, Tony. 1984. 'Introduction,' pp. 4–6 in David Toop, *Rap Attack: African Jive to New York Hip Hop*. Boston: South End Press.

Van Leer, David. 1997. 'Visible Silence: Spectatorship in Black and Gay Lesbian Film,' pp. 157–182 in Valerie Smith (ed.), *Representing Blackness: Issues in Film and Video*. New Brunswick, NJ: Rutgers University Press.

Van Peebles, Melvin. 1998. 'Introduction: His Wonders to Perform,' pp. 11–21 in Chester Himes, *Yesterday Will Make You Cry*. New York: W. W. Norton.

Wagner, Venise. 1996. 'Crossover: So How Come So Many White Suburban Youths Want to be Black? A Special Report,' *San Francisco Examiner Magazine*, 10 November: 8–10, 24, 26.

Wallace, Michele. 1993. 'Race, Gender, and Psychoanalysis in Forties Film: Lost Boundaries, Home of the Brave, and the Quiet One,' pp. 257–271 in Mantha Diawara (ed.), *Black American Cinema*. New York: Routledge.

Wallace, Michele. 1992. '*Boyz N the Hood* and *Jungle Fever*,' pp. 123–131 in Gina Dent (ed.), *Black Popular Culture: A Project by Michele Wallace*. Seattle: Bay Press.

Wallace, Michele. 1990. *Black Macho and the Myth of the Superwoman, with a New Introduction*. London: Verso.

Watkins, S. Craig. 1998. *Representing: Hip Hop Culture and the Production of Black Cinema*. Chicago: University of Chicago Press.

Weinraub, Bernard. 2000. 'CBS Wonders How "Falcone" Went Wrong,' *New York Times*, 10 April: B3.

Weinraub, Bernard. 1995. 'Black Film Makers Are Looking Beyond Ghetto Violence,' *New York Times*, 11 September: B1, B4.

Weinraub, Bernard. 1998. '"Beloved" Tests Racial Themes at Box Office,' *New York Times*. 13 October: B-1, B-8.

Weinraub, Bernard, 1997. '"A Film Director Collects Honors, not Millions,' *New York Times*, 30 January: B-1, B-8.

Welsh, James M. 1993. 'Review of *Lethal Weapon III*,' pp. 211–213 in Frank N. Magill (ed.), *Magill's Cinema Annual: 1993: A Survey of the Films of 1992*, Englewood Cliffs, NJ: Salem Press.

Welsh, James M. 1992. 'Review of *New Jack City*,' pp. 260–262 in Frank N. Magill (ed.), *Magill's Cinema Annual: 1992: A Survey of the Films of 1991*. Englewood Cliffs, NJ: Salem Press.

West, Cornel. 1999. *The Cornel West Reader*. New York: Basic Books.

West, Cornel. 1994. *Race Matters*. New York: Vintage.

West, Cornel. 1990. 'The New Cultural Politics of Difference,' pp. 3–32 in Russell Ferguson, Martha Gever, Trinh T. Minh-ha, and Cornel West (eds), *Out There: Marginalism and Contemporary Culture*. Cambridge, Mass.: MIT Press.

West, Cornel. 1988. 'Interview with Cornel West' by Anders Stephanson, pp. 269–286 in Andrew Ross (ed.), *Universal Abandon? The Politics of Postmodernism*, Minneapolis: University of Minnesota Press.

Williams, John A. 1989. 'Foreword,' pp. 1–3 in Chester Himes, *The Third Generation*, New York: Thundermouth Press.

Wilmington, Michael. 1992a. 'Review of *Passion Fish*,' *Los Angeles Times*, 9 December, Calendar: 3.

Wilmington, Michael. 1992b. 'Review of *New Jack City*,' *Los Angeles Times*, 8 March, Calendar: 14.

Wilmington, Michael. 1989. 'Review of *Lethal Weapon II*,' *Los Angeles Times*, 7 July, Calendar: 1.

Wilmington, Michael. 1987. 'Review of *Lethal Weapon*,' *Los Angeles Times*, 6 March, Calendar: 4.

Winsten, Archer. 1982. 'Review of *Zoot Suit*,' *New York Post*, 22 January: 43.

Wong, Eugene Franklin. 1978. *On Visual Media Racism: Asians in the Motion Pictures*. New York: Arno Press.

Woods, Robin. 1986. *Hollywood From Vietnam to Reagan*. New York: Columbia University Press.

Wootton, Adrian. 1987. 'Review of *Lethal Weapon*,' *Monthly Film Bulletin*, August: 243.

Wright, Will. 1975. *Sixguns & Society: A Structural History of the Western*. Berkeley: University of California Press.

Yanow, Scott. 1996. 'Lester Young,' pp. 995–998 in Michael Erlewine, Vladimir Bogdanov, Chris Woodstra, and Scott Yanow (eds), *All Music Guide to Jazz*, 2nd edn. San Francisco: Miller Freeman Books.

Index

Index

Index

Pulp Fiction 113
Purple Heart 36
Putney Swope 27

race, screening of 171–90
race relations
  assimilationist model 2, 6, 8, 17, 20, 28,
    38, 39, 60, 86, 129–30
  cinematic racial order and American
    theories of 18t
  Park's four-stage theory 6
  two sided agenda 1–2
  understanding of through mass
    media 2–3
  white missionary model 75–7
race riots 2, 27, 39
  Los Angeles 6, 54, 114, 176
racial difference
  new politics of 5–9
  social science and cinema of 38–40
racial order, cinematic *see* cinematic
  racial order
racist ideologies
  nineteenth/twentieth century 21, 22
Raft, George 121
Rage in Harlem, A 10, 18t, 64, 65,
  77–82, 83, 99, 121, 184, 185
Raintree County 27
Raisin in the Sun 27
Rambo series 37
rap 3, 4, 10, 21, 48, 114–15, 119, 171
rape
  in barrio films 135
  in Lee's films 157
Reagan, Ronald 2, 4, 5, 7, 114, 129,
  130, 171, 175
realism
  and the didactic protest film 178–9
  see also cinematic realism
Red River 18t
Redman and the Child, The 30
Reed, Ishmael 173
Regarding Harry 52
Reol 24
Republicans 5, 10, 184
Reservoir Dogs 113
resistance cinema 39–40
Return of the Dragon 37
Rhapsody in August 37
Rich 8, 86
Right Cross 30
Rio Conchos 27
Rising Sun 8, 37
Road to Rio 30
Rocky 28

Romancing the Stone 31
Roosevelt administration 26, 30
Rosewood 184

St. Louis Blues 27
Sallis, James 78
Salt of the Earth 31
Salvador 31
Sanchez, Sonia 173
Sands of Iwo Jima, The 36
Scarface 121, 150
Scarlet West, The 18t
School Daze 28, 156, 157, 158
Searchers, The 30
self
  race and the 53–4
separatist movements 39
Set It Off 10
Shadows 27
Shaft 4, 18t, 28, 112, 151
Shakur, Tupac 115
Shelton, Ron 8, 55
She's Gotta Have It 28, 156, 157, 158
Show Boat 27
silent cinema 21, 22, 29–30
Silver Streak 28
Simpson, O.J. 6, 28
Singleton, John 8, 86, 111, 112–13, 114, 115,
  118, 119, 120, 128, 130, 154, 176, 178
Sleepy Lagoon murder case 136, 137
Smith, Valerie 112, 185
Snipes, Wesley 55, 121
Snoop Doggy Dogg 115
social consciousness films 26, 30
social science
  and the cinema of racial
    difference 38–40
social science utopian discourse 2
Soldier's Story 24
Song of the Gringo 18t
Sounder 28
Spaghetti Western 31
Squaw Man, The 18t, 30
Stand Alone 31
Stand and Deliver 32, 72
star system 21–2
stereotypes 4–5, 9, 20, 22–3, 24, 25, 29,
  99, 177
Sterritt, David 167
Stir Crazy 28
Straight Out of Brooklyn 114
Strictly Business 99
Summer of Sam 156, 157
Superfly 28, 112, 151
Sutton, Charles S. 125

About the Author

Norman K. Denzin is Distinguished Professor of Communications, College of Communications Scholar, and Research Professor of Communications, Sociology, Cinema Studies, and Humanities at the University of Illinois, Urbana-Champaign. He is the author of numerous books, including *Interpretive Ethnography, The Cinematic Society, Images of Postmodern Society, The Research Act, Interpretive Interactionism, Hollywood Shot by Shot, The Recovering Alcoholic* and *The Alcoholic Self*, which won the Charles Cooley Award from the Society for the Study of Symbolic Interaction in 1988. In 1997 he was awarded the George Herbert Award from the Study of Symbolic Interaction. He is past editor of *The Sociological Quarterly*, editor of *Cultural Studies–Critical Methodologies*, co-editor of *The Handbook of Qualitative Research*, 2nd edn. and *Qualitative Inquiry*, and series editor of *Cultural Studies: A Research Annual* and *Studies in Symbolic Interaction*.

Printed in the United States
71832LV00002B/154-228